THE FOUNDATION
AND CONSTRUCTION OF ETHICS

International Library of Philosophy and Scientific Method

EDITOR: TED HONDERICH

A Catalogue of books already published in the
International Library of Philosophy and Scientific Method
will be found at the end of this volume

FRANZ BRENTANO

The Foundation
and Construction of Ethics

COMPILED FROM HIS LECTURES ON
PRACTICAL PHILOSOPHY BY
FRANZISKA MAYER-HILLEBRAND

*English Edition edited
and translated by
Elizabeth Hughes Schneewind*

New York
HUMANITIES PRESS

Originally published in 1952
by A. Franke, Bern, as
Grundlegung und Aufbau der Ethik

First published in English in the United States of America 1973
by Humanities Press Inc.
450 Park Avenue South
New York, N.Y. 10016

This translation in English
© *Elizabeth Hughes Schneewind 1973*

ISBN 0–391–00254–6

Printed in Great Britain

Contents

v

CONTENTS

Preface to the English Edition

Franz Brentano's *Grundlegung und Aufbau der Ethik* was published in 1952 by A. Franke in Bern. The book is based upon the notes which Brentano used for his lectures on practical philosophy at the University of Vienna from 1876 to 1894. The preparation of the book, which was begun by Professor Alfred Kastil, was completed after Kastil's death by Professor Franziska Mayer-Hillebrand. This, the first English translation of the work, is one of a series of translations supported by the Franz Brentano Foundation under the general editorship of Professor Roderick M. Chisholm of Brown University. As of this writing, three other works have appeared in the series, all published by Routledge & Kegan Paul. They are *The True and the Evident* (trans. Chisholm, Politzer and Fischer; 1966), *The Origin of Our Knowledge of Right and Wrong* (trans. Chisholm and Schneewind; 1969), and *Psychology from an Empirical Standpoint* (trans. Rancurello, Terrell, and McAlister; 1972).

The present book is strictly a translation of the 1952 German edition. Professor Mayer-Hillebrand's Foreword to that edition is included at the end. The numbered footnotes that appear throughout the text are hers; those with asterisks are mine.

Brentano used many quotations, frequently without giving an exact textual reference. Except where otherwise indicated, the translations are mine. If published translations exist, I have referred the reader to the translation, also. All references to Kant indicate volumes and pages in the Akademie-Ausgabe. Brentano frequently quotes from English philosophers. Whenever I could locate the source of these quotations, I reinstated the original English text. However, I have indicated where, and how, his German translation varied materially from the original, as this may have affected his interpretation.

Brentano's literary style is, for the most part, quite straightforward. Such comments on technical terminology as I deemed necessary are included in footnotes in the text.

I would like to thank Dr Linda L. McAlister for her numerous helpful suggestions and criticisms and Prof. Chisholm for his comments and his invaluable assistance in bringing this translation into being.

ELIZABETH HUGHES SCHNEEWIND

Pittsburgh, Pennsylvania

Introduction

1. *Theoretical and practical disciplines*

No one who has ever read Sophocles' *Antigone* can forget the heavenly chorus of the elderly Thebans in praise of the power of mankind: 'There are many mighty things, and none is mightier than man.' The poet describes man overcoming the boundaries of the sea and defying the hurricane; conquering with the plough the inexhaustible forces of the earth and obliging it to offer up its yearly tribute; catching the fishes of the sea and the birds of the air in his nets; pursuing victoriously the wild animals, in the depths of the forests and on the peaks of the mountains; and subjecting the horse and the mighty ox to the yoke. Then the poet turns his gaze to higher things. He depicts man, inventing language and dispatching his thoughts and wishes into the breasts of others in the form of words; founding states and giving laws; defying the powers of the heavenly bodies by safeguarding himself against frost and rain and by overcoming serious illnesses. He may work as a blessing or as a curse for everything lying within his vast sphere of influence, depending upon whether he chooses good or evil as his goal.

What is the foundation of man's power, which no other creature in our experience can measure up to? It lies solely in *knowledge*. There are many other beings living who are swifter and physically stronger, who have better natural weapons for attack and defence, and who have more acute senses and a greater wealth of instincts, but man's knowledge serves him as a substitute for all these gifts and makes him the master. He has not always been so mighty, for science has a history. It has developed slowly from feeble germs; the power of man has expanded in proportion to their growth. Bacon of Verulam points out how within recent times the invention of the compass and the printing press has revolutionized cultural life. He is the source of that oft-quoted saying, 'Knowledge is power.' Somewhat earlier, the invention of gun-powder had made possible weapons which completely revolutionized the art of war, and later, the inventions utilizing the forces of steam, heat, electricity, and chemicals made man the lord of nature to an extent that exceeds Bacon's highest expectations.

'Knowledge is power': is this true of *all* knowledge? The answer is, yes. None is without some practical influence, be it direct or indirect. A typical example is one used by Condorcet in his *Sketch for an Historical Picture of the Progress of the Human Mind.** The investigations of conic sections begun in ancient times by Archimedes and Apollonius were at first of purely theoretical, mathematical interest. Centuries later Kepler made their work applicable to astronomy, but again only because of a theoretical interest. Yet as a result the investigations became of practical use, inasmuch as the progress made in astronomy did a great deal to forward navigation. The seaman who avoids a shipwreck by observing with precision the geographical latitude and longitude owes the fact that he is alive to theories which originated solely from a yearning for knowledge twenty centuries earlier.

Hence we may say that *all* knowledge is power. But how then does it happen that only certain scientific disciplines are designated as practical, while others are called theoretical? The theoretical disciplines include, e.g., physics, chemistry, biology, psychology; the practical, e.g., architecture, strategy, politics, medicine.

In order to make the difference clear, let us consider what the two groups have in common. Each is a unified collection of facts which belong together. They are not truths which are arbitrarily heaped together, but rather classes of truths.

Every class is constructed for some purpose, but not all for the same purpose. In the theoretical sciences classes are constructed solely with the interests of knowledge in mind. These are best served when internally related truths—Aristotle's ἐπιστήμη—are combined into a single science. The more closely connected truths are placed closer together so that we can get a picture of their natural relations. In this manner research is most likely to thrive. It requires a division of labour, and this follows according to the

* Trans. June Barraclough (London: Weidenfeld & Nicolson, 1955).

difference in talents. For people vary greatly in their gifts. One is better at observation, another at abstraction and deduction. One has a greater gift for psychical research, another for research into external nature. One man is unable to solve the simplest geometric problems because he has no intuitive sense of space, yet is excellent at making psychological observations and analyses; another seems incapable of making even the most elementary distinctions within the sphere of the phenomena of consciousness but proves himself quite superior in biology or astronomy. These differences between capabilities and the need for divisions of labour determine the boundaries when it is a question of pure theory, i.e. where knowledge is its own end.

It is quite different with the so-called practical disciplines, or arts (τέχνη)—the designation given them by Aristotle. The guiding principle with respect to these is the grouping together and ordering of truths in relation to a goal which lies outside the realm of knowledge. Here human endeavour pursues other goals, and their attainment often requires a motley variety of kinds of knowledge which have very little intrinsic relation to one another. One example already mentioned is architecture, which culls the knowledge which serves its ends from the most varied fields of inquiry: mechanics, acoustics, optics, chemistry, aesthetics, sociology, etc. Another example is medicine, where knowledge from anatomy, physiology, botany, chemistry, climatology, etc., is plainly indispensable.

Consideration of the goal of a practical discipline differentiates it from the others, just as it determines its unity. Each has a unique goal: pharmaceutics concerns health; ship-building, ships; military strategy, victory; housekeeping, comfort. In many cases the aim of one art is subordinate to that of another; that is, it is a means to it. Consider, e.g., the relation between the art of saddle-making and the art of riding, or between the art of the man who makes weapons and the art of the man who fences. In both these instances the latter is the primary art, the former the secondary. The former gives heed to demands of the latter and teaches us which means are required to fulfil them, but they do not tell us whether the demands themselves are appropriate. Thus the former arts are subordinate to the latter in just the way their ends are subordinate to those of the latter.

However, an art or practical discipline which governs another

3

may be subordinate to yet a third. For example, consider the series, gesticulation, rhetoric, politics, or the series, saddle-making, riding, strategy, politics.

But these series cannot go on *ad infinitum*. Every endeavour has a goal which is not desired simply for the sake of yet another thing; otherwise, desire would be empty and have no object. Metaphysics handles the question of whether the series of causes goes on indefinitely or must end with a first cause. Aristotle held that the latter is evidently the case, although not everyone recognizes the fact. But that there cannot be an infinite series of ends he thought to be evident to all.

2. *The concept and the value of ethics*

And just as there must be an ultimate end, there must be one practical discipline which is not subordinate to any other, viz. one which instructs us about the highest end and the choice of means conducive to it. This discipline is usually called ethics, or moral philosophy.

It is obviously the highest of all practical disciplines, being related to them as architecture is related to the crafts of unskilled labourers. Its teachings are of the greatest importance for life. He who recognizes the goal at which he ought to aim is like the marksman who sees his target; he has a far better chance of striking it than someone who just shoots at random.

Those who have expressed doubts as to whether the progress and increase of human knowledge is a blessing have neglected to think about this science. No one disputes that greater knowledge means greater power; but does this power work for the salvation of man? Rousseau answered this question in the negative and condemned the so-called progress of civilization. There is a kernel of truth contained in this condemnation: science can be truly beneficial only when men possess a sufficient quantity of ethical knowledge. So far we have too little, and it has not been sufficiently disseminated. The entire progress of technology can end in disaster if it is not under the guidance and control of the highest practical discipline, ethics.

Ethical knowledge is important for all men, but it is of particular interest to lawyers—provided that they care for more than the mere letter of the law. Jurisprudence, too, belongs to the practical disciplines. And the decisions of politicians should also be guided by ethical knowledge. The laws of the state are prescriptions for action, and, according to all the greatest thinkers, they should be determined in accordance with the very same goals which the individual is to pursue as his ultimate aims. That is why Aristotle relates the investigation of the highest good very closely to politics, so closely, indeed, that he regards it as a branch of politics. He points out that the primary practical disciplines are all subordinate to politics, e.g., military strategy, oratory, economics. Jeremy Bentham—to name but one of the most eminent among modern thinkers—also thought that ethics and legislation have a common goal; while he considered them two separate disciplines, he thought they were to be distinguished only according to the extent of their jurisdiction. 'All actions, whether public or private, fall under the jurisdiction of morals. It is a guide which leads the individual, as it were, by the hand through all the details of his life, all his relations with his fellows. Legislation cannot do this; and, if it could, it ought not to exercise a continual interference and dictation over the conduct of men. . . . In a word, legislation has the same centre with morals, but it has not the same circumference.'[1]

3. The name, 'Practical Philosophy'

In accordance with a usage which has become quite familiar to us since Herbart's day, this most sublime of all practical disciplines is also known as practical philosophy. What is the import of this designation? Is it that ethics is the practical discipline which belongs to philosophy, just as agriculture and medicine belong to the natural sciences? This is true of ethics, but not only of ethics. To be sure, ethics bears the same sort of internal relation to the theoretical branches of philosophy, especially psychology, as do agriculture and medicine to organic chemistry and physiology. But there are other practical disciplines with the same status with-

[1] From *Traité de la Législation Civile et Pénale*, trans. and ed. from Bentham's *Introduction to the Principles of Morals and Legislation* by Etienne Dumont (Brussels, 1840), p. 124.

[Brentano gave his own German translation. I have quoted from the English translation by R. Hildreth, entitled *Theory of Legislation* (London: Trübner, 1864), p. 60.]

in philosophy, e.g., aesthetics and logic. Each has the task of serving a particular ideal, a unique spiritual perfection. There are three such ideals, which correspond to the three basic types of psychical activity: presentation, judgment, and interest. The perfection peculiar to presenting is beauty; that to judging, truth; that to being interested (loving and hating), ethical goodness. Hence this relation cannot constitute the distinctive and sufficient reason why ethics, in particular, is called practical philosophy.

The name philosophy came into being as a term expressing modesty at a time when the Greek Sophists had brought the old name, Sophia, into ill-repute through the misuse they made of it in passing themselves off as teachers of wisdom. (Similarly, misuse in our own time has made it almost necessary to abolish the name philosophy.) In contrast to the superficial observer, the wise man is he who presses onward to the very last principles, the influence of which extends over a vast area—indeed, throughout the universe. Hence Aristotle chose to give the name 'wisdom' to metaphysics, rather than to any other theoretical discipline, because it concerns itself with the ultimate foundation of things and the question whether they are indebted for their being to a creative understanding which follows an orderly plan embracing the entire universe. The position of metaphysics within the theoretical realm is analogous to that of ethics within the practical realm. Just as the former is the knowledge of the ultimate principles of being and truth, the latter is the knowledge of the principles of action. Thus ethics, too, has been described as wisdom, but as *practical* wisdom: it is practical philosophy.

4. *The task of ethics*

We would now have an adequate explanation of the *term* ethics— if we already had a material definition of the *concept*. For a mere verbal definition never gives a clear perception of the nature and character of a discipline. To gain such a perception, we must examine the multiplicity of tasks which a discipline comprises. We receive only the vaguest notion of the character of mathematics when we are told that it is the science which teaches us how to measure.

In order to awaken still further interest in ethics—*ignoti nulla cupido*—I shall enumerate some of its most important tasks. This

6

will have the additional advantage of displaying the divisions into which I intend to divide the subject-matter.

(*a*) First of all, it is clear that ethics deals with those ends which are worthy of being pursued for their own sake. If it turns out that there are several such ends, conflicts may occur. In this case ethics will have to determine their relative worth, or at least offer certain methods for making comparisons.

(*b*) Ethics has the further task of determining the most important means of attaining these ends; that is, the rules for action.

(*c*) But will not such rules perhaps be completely useless, if the knowledge of them is not sufficient to influence our actions? This possibility makes it necessary to investigate the question of freedom; however this investigation may turn out, it most certainly will exclude any such doubt.

(*d*) But even if the rules are not useless, the knowledge of them will not have the same degree of influence in every case. Some recognize what is right and act in a way contradictory to their knowledge. Mere knowledge is not enough. Knowledge is power, but not taken in itself. Other dispositions and preconditions are required. What use is architecture without building materials or the art of military strategy without soldiers? What use is the art of writing or painting if the hand is crippled? What is true of such cases in general is also true of ethical knowledge. Even in cases where we have ethical knowledge it is often difficult to act in accordance with it. Deeply rooted inclinations and powerful emotions can drive us to act in the contrary manner. Ethical insight is consequently of a greatly varying degree of usefulness, depending upon the nature of the other ethical dispositions. In the *Nicomachean Ethics*, Aristotle goes so far as to designate a large number of people as being unsuited to study ethics because their imperfect ethical dispositions would prevent them from profiting from such studies. Indeed, he makes a remark which should be downright discouraging to many people, if it is to be believed. He sets no store by the young, for he thinks they are swayed too greatly by emotions and are ruled by passion. It does not help, he adds, for a person to be old in years if he still has the character of an immature youth. For the defect is not youth as such, but the dependence upon passion in one's endeavours. I now think—and fortunately this is also substantiated by experience—that sometimes just the reverse may be the case. Highly developed ethical powers may appear in the early years; even a young person may attain the self-control proper to a man.

Ethics must take full account of these differences in ethical dispositions. It is a practical discipline, and its doctrines aim at winning power. But this is easier with those possessing a virtuous disposition than with those of a vicious and imperfect moral disposition. As a consequence, ethics has a twofold task.

First, to investigate what constitutes beneficial and detrimental dispositions—how they are developed, maintained, and strengthened and how they weaken and disappear.

Second, to establish how it is possible to act rightly in spite of the imperfection of one's ethical dispositions. We see how parents who have a true sense of their duty give their children moral guidance and steer them away from temptations which they are probably not yet strong enough to resist, etc. We notice that the state forbids certain things, not because they are to be censured as such but because they are liable to bring about disorder, and sets up preventive laws. No well-ordered state can do without such laws, provided they do not go too far and restrict freedom of movement in an unpleasant and unnecessary way. The individual guides himself in the same way. Everyone has ethical imperfections. Ethical guidance is of the greatest importance, and he who does not know or who fails to regard the rules offered will fall far short of the mark that he recognizes as the right one.

Another very important object of ethics is social relations, which are founded upon virtue. The union which they bring about strengthens the individual and leads him to accomplishments of which a person living in isolation is incapable. Friendships constitute one such social bond—or at any rate those friendships which are truly worthy of the name. The ethics of ancient times had a predilection for friendship. All the Socratic schools did studies of it; Aristotle devoted two entire books of the *Nicomachean Ethics* to this virtue. Epicurus also investigated the matter thoroughly. Marriage and the family constitute a different social bond, though related in essential respects to friendship. The state is yet another. We have already noted the close connection between politics and ethics. Once ethics is fully developed in every respect it can absorb the entire philosophy of law and the state. The religious community, or church, is also to be included in the branch of ethics which treats of social relations. At this point further questions

8

arise. For instance, is the formation of religious communities a good thing, either as such or under certain circumstances? In what relation should such a community stand to the state: should they be independent of one another? Are the highest aims of mankind best served when the spiritual and the secular powers are joined, or when they are separate? And so forth.

Thus we are presented with a rich abundance of problems. It is my hope that, by enumerating them, even in such a general form, I have communicated some feeling for what ethics is about.

(e) There is one important investigation which I have failed to mention; yet it is to be placed at the apex. Above all, we must form some judgment about the starting-point of investigations into morality, about the foundations of moral insight. There is much confusion about this matter; nowhere in the field of ethics is there such a great divergence of opinion as there is with respect to the principles of ethical knowledge.

It would certainly be desirable, also, to present the ethical views of the most significant thinkers in a brief historical survey. There is great dissension among them, and thus it is not only interesting but also quite necessary to become familiar with the various attempts at a solution. At this point, however, we can only investigate the most important directions which such attempts have taken, letting, in each case, one system stand for a host of similar ones.

Just one more remark about the distinctive character of the 'normative sciences', to which ethics is generally thought to belong.[2] If we compare a physics textbook with a handbook of architecture, hygiene, or even logic, we notice immediately that the latter do not merely teach us how people actually build, and what rules to follow in order to remain healthy or in order to draw correct conclusions; they also teach us how we ought to build, how we ought to organize our lives and our clothing, and how we ought to carry out proofs and draw conclusions. To be sure, in these cases 'law' is also used in the sense in which we speak of laws in physics—as a summary of individual facts—but even these laws are subordinate to an *ought*. Since, in common parlance, the term, 'law', is sometimes used in one of these senses

---

[2] This portion has been completed in accordance with Franz Hillebrand's lectures on ethics, which are based upon Brentano's work.

9

and sometimes used in the other, the expression, 'norm', has been introduced for this second sort of law and the expression, 'normative sciences', for those sciences which consist of such norms. In this way the ambiguity is avoided.

But how does a science come to be setting up norms? Where do certain disciplines get the right to voice propositions of the form, 'It should be so,' instead of, 'It is so'? Certainly there is no one there who actually issues commands; expressions such as, 'Logic commands . . .,' are obviously to be taken in a figurative sense. The reason is that the norms which these sciences contain present the conditions under which a certain goal that we have chosen for ourselves can be attained. Take logic, for example: if you wish to form correct judgments and avoid errors, you must draw conclusions in such and such a way.

It is also possible to avoid the imperative and replace it with the hypothetical form, for it means nothing more than: if you want a given thing, you must act in such and such a way. The imperative in, e.g., logic, is taken for granted, since the aim, to do what is correct—in this case, to draw the proper conclusions—is taken for granted.

Accordingly a normative science is ultimately characterized by the fact that all the cognitions that comprise it serve one single end. This end is the thread which binds together things that are in other respects utterly different from one another.

PART ONE

THE PRINCIPLES OF ETHICAL KNOWLEDGE

Preliminary Remarks Concerning
the Difficulties of this Part

The questions with which we are now to concern ourselves are difficult, but we can neither avoid them nor postpone work on them. If we did, we would have to take the most important propositions on faith, which would not lead to or help us to gain knowledge. Our task is to establish ethics as a science.

It should be a sufficient comfort to note that difficulties frequently have their attractions. If we are successful, the enjoyment of the contrast is a splendid reward; we compare our former state of ignorance with the clarity we have gained and feel ourselves repaid.

But in order to reach this state, we must proceed methodically and with care, preparing the way step by step. For nothing could be more wrong-headed than to gloss quickly over a difficult point so as to be through with it as quickly as possible. Working this way we no more make progress than does the uncomprehending reader who merely turns the pages in a book which is scientifically laid out.

I

The Extent to which Principles of Knowledge can be an Object of Investigation and Controversy

---

5. There are such things as immediate insights

In a science it is not possible to prove every opinion which we set forth. For every proof rests upon certain presuppositions; if we prove these, it is upon the basis of still further presuppositions. But this process cannot go on forever. We cannot avoid this infinite regress by arguing in a circle, for then we simply explain the term in question by means of the same term, but in a disguised form. (However, some proofs of this kind are utterly undisguised. Molière parodies them in *The Imaginary Invalid*: 'Mihi a docto doctore domandatur causam et rationem, quare opium facit dormire. A quoi respondeo: Quia est in eo virtus dormitiva,* cujus est natura sensus stupifire'.†)

Hence we must start with unproven principles, with immediate assumptions. This point is the basis for the attacks of the ancient sceptics: the first principles are arbitrary and therefore all proofs untenable. Even Pascal (1625–62) was troubled by it. He said it would be best if we could define every word and prove every proposition, and thought it unfortunate that we cannot. But his regret was quite unjustified. A simple comparison of the process of defining with the process of setting up a proof would have set him straight. When someone asks us the meaning of a word unfamiliar to him, we do not always have at our disposal a word

* Brentano has 'soporifica'.
† Brentano has 'assoupire'.

14

that has the same meaning but is easier to understand, i.e. a definition, but sometimes we do not need one because we can get him to understand the meaning by showing him things which are designated by the name in question. Similarly, we lose nothing by basing proofs upon propositions which cannot be proven. Of course, they may not be just any arbitrary assumptions; if they were, everything based upon them would be groundless. They must be immediately guaranteed, i.e. they must be insights which exclude all possibility of error.

Propositions of this kind are the only true principles of knowledge. They are of two varieties. One kind are perceptions of individual facts, the rest are general laws of the type that are comprehended on the basis, not of a knowledge of every individual instance to which they apply but of the concepts they contain.

An example of the first kind is my recognizing that I am now seeing or thinking. I may be wrong in believing what I see: I may be dreaming. And what I think may be mistaken. But I am directly certain *that* I am seeing or *that* I am thinking.

Examples of the latter are my judging that two things are more than one, or that something red is as such not green, or that no triangle can have four sides, or that a whole cannot exist without its parts.

Such immediately certain judgments, then, must underlie all proofs as their principles.

6. Controversies about the principles of knowledge

1. It might be thought that there could be no arguments concerning the principles of knowledge; because they are immediately certain, it would seem that they must be available to all, without difficulty. They are the starting-points of investigation: is it not paradoxical that they are, at the same time, the object of an investigation and of differences of opinion? How can we enter into such a controversy, except on the basis of these principles themselves? Yet there are disputes about them, of two kinds.

(*a*) There are controversies about which propositions we should begin with in order to reach conclusions about various particular problems.

(*b*) There are controversies about whether the propositions used as starting-points are really immediately certain.

2 (ad *a*). That arguments of the first kind should arise is not difficult to understand. Consider any simple mathematical theorem, e.g. the one about the sum of the angles of a triangle. There are innumerable mathematical principles; the question is, which ones will be useful for our proof?

A person may have such severe doubts in this case that he does not even know in which of the two classes of principles he ought to search: among the perceptions or among the axioms, i.e. the propositions which are immediately evident from the concepts. This question arises, for instance, in connection with the general law of causality and the law of inertia.

3 (ad *b*). It is more difficult to comprehend why there should be arguments of the second kind. At first glance it seems simply unthinkable that there could be any doubt about immediately evident truths and that, if there is, there could be any value to evident judgments.

We shall discuss each problem separately, in accordance with the Cartesian principle of dividing a complex question into its elementary parts in order to conquer individually each difficulty it contains. 'Divide and conquer' applies to research, too.

Thus we ask first how it can happen that differences of opinion arise concerning what is immediately evident. Again, two cases must be distinguished.

(*a*) It frequently occurs that someone takes something to be immediately certain when it is not. Psychology has explained how this is possible by showing us that our judgment often follows habitual inclinations. There are even natural instincts that play a part in judgments, e.g. the impulse to accept everything we perceive through the senses. We believe blindly in all that we see, hear, touch, etc.; that is, we accept colours, sound, hard and soft, etc., as being real. Indeed, this belief is a constituent of the very acts of perception. Other impulsive judgments are the result of habit. We expect similar things under similar circumstances and are surprised if our expectations are ever contradicted by experience. Certainly, we must correct our judgment in such a case, but if anyone had told us ahead of time that our firm conviction was an error, or even that it was not immediately certain, we would have passionately denied it. Columbus experienced such opposition when his plans came into collision with the axiom that there could be no antipodes; he met, as it were with an impenetrable wall. Because such instinctive or habitual judgments can be subjectively thoroughly convincing, we may confuse them with evident judgments, for the two have this characteristic in common.

(β) The reverse may be the case also. Someone may deny a proposition while another asserts, correctly, that he is perfectly certain of it, i.e. that his judgment affirming it is immediately evident. Once again, there are two cases to be distinguished, the one easier, the other more difficult to explain.

The simpler concerns the perception of individual facts. I perceive something which someone else does not perceive. Indeed, if we take the word perception in its strict sense, this is always the case. Perception in this sense includes only internal perception, which is evident. No one can share with me my internal perceptions, and hence it can easily come to pass that someone will contradict me with regard to them.

The more difficult case is the one concerning the acceptance of a universal law which is evident from the concepts, i.e. an immediately acknowledged *a priori* truth. How is dissension possible here? Such truths become evident from the concepts, of which both of the dissenting parties are in possession; thus it would seem that the necessary conditions for the appearance of the evident judgment are present in both. Whence the argument? Some have actually rejected out of hand the possibility of such cases. One person, they say, cannot lack the discernment which another possesses, or be convinced of the very opposite. He may express the opposite conviction in mere words, but he cannot think it. Even Aristotle was of this view. Nevertheless it is not unthinkable for principles of this sort to be disputed. For the fact that a proposition is of the kind the truth of which can be grasped immediately from the concepts does not mean that everyone possesses the concepts, i.e. is able to think them, and also does not mean that the proposition must in fact become evident to everyone who contemplates the concepts. We frequently think about concepts without forming a judgment about them, just as we can think about a set of premises and yet fail to draw the conclusion which follows from them; for instance, when we are inattentive. I might, say, imagine two groups of things, one of which consists of six things, the other of two halves with three things each, and

17

yet fail to form any judgment about the two groups being the same size.

In this case, we form no judgment because our attention is turned elsewhere; in some others, we are prevented by exhaustion. And there are other factors that can prevent the evident judgment from being formed, for instance, a spurious argument. The judgment is frequently suspended; sometimes, indeed, the contradictory judgment takes its place. Nevertheless, the proposition remains one which *can* be discerned directly from the concepts. The man who judges with discernment cannot err. Nor, of course, will an error be made by the man who accepts his judgment out of blind trust.

As an example of a case in which judgment has been suppressed by specious argument, we may note that some have erred even about the law of contradiction. If any law is immediately evident, it is this one, and yet even it has been questioned, both in modern times and in antiquity. We might hold that it can only have been denied verbally and not seriously contradicted in thought. This does quite often happen. But is it always so? What happens when the denial of this axiom becomes elevated to the fundamental principle of a whole school of philosophy? For this has occurred: consider Hegel. Most likely this is an instance in which people have been taken in and blinded by specious arguments such as the following.

The circumference of a circle contains as many points as the circle has radii, for every radius ends in a point and there can be no point in the circumference which is not the end of a radius. Now a circle which has a diameter just half that of a larger circle is half as big. But a concentric circle with half the diameter has just as many radii as the larger circle in which it is contained. Therefore the smaller circumference apparently contains no fewer points than the one which is twice as big.

Zeno of Elea (*c.* 520 B.C.) posed another such aporia, wishing to show by means of it that there can be no motion. Where does the flying arrow come from? From the bow of the archer. Where does it finally end up? At the target. Between the two there lies a space of indeterminate length which it has travelled in a determinate amount of time. In half that time it travelled half the distance, and so on. But how does that happen? When does it actually move? Not in the past, for it is gone; not in the future, for it has not yet come to be. Then it must be in the present. But the present is only a single point, and the arrow cannot travel any distance within a point. Now people will say, 'But the circle with twice the diameter certainly is twice as big; motion certainly does take place.' And having been overwhelmed by these paradoxes, they admit that there can be such things as contradictions. Only after they have forgotten these spurious arguments are they able, once again, to discern the truth of the law of contradiction. Attending once more without prejudice to the meaning of the words, they recognize that something cannot be both true and false at the same time.

Like inattentiveness, exhaustion, and self-contradictory, spurious arguments, habit can also prevent the discerning judgment from being formed. We have frequently had the experience of holding quite tenaciously and without justification to something which turned out to be false, declaring it to be immediately evident; afterwards we feel suspicion even where it is not called for.

7. Is the possibility of doubt injurious to the value of evidence?

We now understand how there can be doubts and disputes about what is immediately evident, but our very awareness of this fact may have led to still further doubts. In allowing this possibility, are we not in effect admitting that even immediately evident judgments are not a trustworthy foundation for the sciences? In other words, does evidence with respect to judgments not lose all value because of this possibility?

Answer: why should it? Perhaps because a person who forms a judgment with discernment has to admit the possibility that someone else may make the opposite judgment with discernment? If this were true, matters would be in a sorry state indeed; all the difference between truth and falsehood would be wiped out. But there can be no question of this. If I discern something, I also discern that no one can *discern* the opposite. He who judges the opposite to be the case can only be judging blindly.

Or is evidence supposed to be worthless because blind judgments are sometimes confused with evident judgments? This does happen, but does not obliterate the distinction between the two:

19

quite the opposite, for without the distinction there could be no such confusion. In order to understand what 'an evident judgment' means, we must already have experienced evident judgments and distinguished them from blind ones. Thus, whoever entertains such an idea merely demonstrates that he is not clear about what it means to judge with discernment. In fact, faulty judgments are frequently formed on this subject. Some people seem to think that the evidence of a judgment is a mark by which its truth can be recognized. If so, we would always have to establish first whether the judgment in question bore this mark, and doing so would itself entail a judgment. In order to recognize *this* judgment as true we would have to know that it bore the mark of evidence, and in order to know this we would need to form another evident judgment, and so on *ad infinitum*. This view, which was seen to be wrong as far back as Aristotle, betrays itself frequently in those interpretations of evident judgments which claim that knowing something and perceiving that one knows it are two different acts.

No, that is not the way things are. The discerning judgment is itself the knowledge of its own truth, not the measure of it. It needs no such measure. Rather, it is the measure of the truth of other judgments which cannot be denied without contradicting those which are evident.[3]

8. *Review of this chapter*

Let us take a glance back at what has been said. It is not possible, but also not necessary, to prove all judgments. There are immediately discernable judgments, be they evident perceptions or *a priori* general laws, which can be discerned directly from the concepts. Such judgments cannot be false, but blind, subjectively convincing judgments which are in fact erroneous may sometimes be taken to be evident.

[3] Sect. 7 takes into account analyses that Brentano made later and was added to the text by Kastil. Cf. *The True and the Evident* (trans. Chisholm, Politzer and Fischer, London: Routledge & Kegan Paul, 1966) particularly the section 'Reflections on the Theory of the Evident' and 'On the Evident' and also Kastil, 'Ontologischer und gnoseologischer Wahrheitsbegriff' in *Zur Philosophie der Gegenwart* (Brentano-Gesellschaft, Prag, 1934).

Without evident judgments there would be no science, but only heaps of rules sanctioned by habit. The fact that we may ask if a given judgment is evident does not prevent us from judging with discernment or from building sciences upon the absolutely trustworthy foundation of evident judgments.

II

The Dispute about the Principles of Ethical Knowledge

9. Autonomous and heteronomous systems of ethics: ethical relativism; three examples of attacks on proposed principles

Many sciences are ridden with disputes concerning their principles. Not even mathematics is free of them, but nowhere do they rage so fiercely as in the field of ethics. Indeed, the confusion and the differences of opinion are so great that many people believe there is no natural basis of ethics in reason. What is right and what wrong, what is morally good and what morally bad is determined solely by positive prescriptions (including those which are set forth in public opinion). Aristotle tells us that such controversy and confusion was already prevalent in his time; today, after more than two thousand years, the situation is still just as he described it then. The same conclusion is still drawn from the confusion, even by those not otherwise inclined to scepticism.

Let us take a closer look at this chaos, the sight of which has made so many give up all hope. Which matters are under dispute? All of them, alas—more points are called into question than anyone would think possible.

Autonomous systems of ethics are to be distinguished from heteronomous.[4] In a heteronomous system of ethics, decisions about what is good and bad stem from an authority; that is, the criterion of what is moral lies in positive legislation. But if our own personal insight is called upon as the decisive authority, rather than a positive law, we have an autonomous system. It is a

[4] This remark has been expanded in accordance with Franz Hillebrand's lectures on ethics.

logical consequence of a heteronomous conception of ethics that there is no universally binding moral law, but at most arbitrary regulations. The sceptics say that nothing is true, the subjectivists or relativists that everything is true, but only for the man who is making the judgment. The latter appeal primarily to the differences in conceptions of morality prevalent at various times and among different peoples. Thus we are faced with two decisions of paramount importance:

1. Are there any universally valid principles concerning our moral behaviour, or are the principles we accept arbitrarily established?

2. Assuming that there are some principles, which ones can justifiably be made the foundation of ethics? Actually, absolute scepticism has no place in a chapter about moral principles, for it recognizes no ultimate principles at all. But as Aristotle showed, this doctrine is self-refuting, for he who can know nothing with certainty is also unable to know that he cannot know anything. But ethical relativism plays a more important role, which we shall refer to again and again.

To begin with we shall concern ourselves with the second question.

Since the greatest minds have occupied themselves with ethical investigations for so many centuries, it is not surprising that a number of principles have already been suggested. But (1) in some instances, opponents contend that they are not immediately evident; (2) in others, they deny that they really lead to ethical consequences; (3) in still others, they make both these objections.

If their accusations are correct, then the advocates of these various principles have failed to establish a scientific foundation for ethics, and the view of the relativists would appear to be justified. Right now we shall look more closely into the groups of principles and clarify them by means of examples.

10. *Illustration of the first sort of case (Clarke)*[5]

Samuel Clarke (1675-1729), a younger contemporary of John Locke who became particularly significant for German philosophy

---

[5] It was his work which stimulated Brentano to give special attention to the English moral philosophers, as can be seen from the marginal notes in his copy of Alexander Bain's *Mental and Moral Science* (London, 1868).

through his interesting correspondence with Leibniz, claimed to have established that ethics, like mathematics, is concerned with relations. Numbers involve a particular kind of relation, viz. relations of size. But there are other kinds; all things, acts, and persons involve specific relations, among them the relations of fitness and unfitness of application of different things one to another. They are analogous to geometrical congruence and incongruence: 'All wilful wickedness and perversion of right is the very same insolence and absurdity in moral matters as it would be in natural things for a man to pretend to alter the certain proportions of numbers, to take away the demonstrable relations and properties of mathematical figures, to make light darkness and darkness light, or to call sweet bitter and bitter sweet.'* The very will of God is directed by these relations, and ours *ought* to be. Given the concepts of certain things, reason recognizes these ethical relations as eternal, universally valid, and absolutely immutable truths. In particular, certain duties to God are to be discerned in this way. We owe him honour, love, and adoration because of his attributes. The characteristic of fitness, or congruence, appears almost more clearly in these acts than when we lay one geometrical figure upon another which is congruent to it. It is the same with certain duties towards our fellow men, especially justness and fairness. We ought to treat our neighbours as we wish them to treat ourselves. All things of the same nature bear to any other thing the same relation of fitness or unfitness, as the case may be. Injustice in actions is the same as contradictions in theories; one is as contrary to reason as is the other. That is why it is impossible for a man not to be as ashamed when he is convicted of an injustice as when he is taken in by a contradiction. It is a proposition about fitness that gives rise to the duty of gratitude for favours received. It is obviously unfitting when good is repaid with evil.[6]

Many people shared Clarke's view, but others contested it, saying they were unable to discover any such relation of congru-

* Clarke, 'Discourse Upon Natural Religion', Boyle Lectures (1705), reprinted in *British Moralists*, ed. Selby-Bigge, vol. 2, para. 491.

[6] Samuel Clarke, 'Demonstration of the Being and Attributes of God' (1705), and 'A Discourse concerning the Unchangeable Obligation of Natural Religion' (1708). Cf. O. Kraus, *Die Werttheorien* (R. M. Rohrer, Brünn, 1937), p. 75 ff.

ence or even to imagine what sort of a relation it was supposed to be. In fact, if we examine the analogy with the congruent geo-metrical figures, it appears that a kind of similarity is meant; but how can the duty to love and adore God rest upon such a re-lation? Is there any similarity between the divine attributes and the act of adoration?

Our duties towards our neighbour are supposed also to rest upon such relations of similarity, and here it seems somewhat more appropriate to speak of likeness, although there is certainly not a perfect or universal likeness. Actually, though, people vary greatly from one another, so that unlike treatment may lay a greater claim to being called congruent than like treatment. But is this congruence more than a mere metaphor? Why should it be less congruent to repay good with evil than to repay evil with good?

11. *Illustration of the second type of case (the utilitarians)*

I shall take as my illustration the school of the utilitarians.[7] This is the name given themselves by those moral philosophers who teach that the goodness or badness of an act depends upon whether it furthers or is injurious to the happiness of all beings who think and have emotions. The law which they hold to be valid without exception and from which they derive all special precepts is that one ought to aim at the happiness of everyone as the highest goal. This proposition is recognized in some form in almost every ethical system, although not always as immediately evident. Even the utilitarians do not usually claim that it is immediately evident; rather, they seek to give an empirical proof of it based upon the fact that everyone desires his own happiness—even ascetics, who seek their pleasure in self-torment. But how is the law they set up supposed to follow from this empirical fact?

Many attempts have been made at a deduction.

(*a*) On the basis of the dependence of the individual's happiness upon the happiness of all.

Criticism: There are many cases in which there is no such

---

[7] John Locke (1632–1707) is to be considered the founder of the utilitarian school; cf. his *Essay Concerning Human Understanding*. Its most eminent advocates include David Hume (1711–76), Jeremy Bentham (1748–1832), and J. S. Mill (1806–73).

dependence, where, on the contrary, these two interests are opposed. Think of constancy in the face of martyrdom, or of the bravery of a soldier—indeed, of any self-sacrifice, even on to death. The histories of Regulus, Leonidas, Giordano Bruno, and the Christian martyrs demonstrate that this reputedly universal law does not have unconditional validity; indeed, it lacks validity in the cases of precisely those actions that we usually admire most.

(*b*) Another attempt: 'Each person ought to aim at his own happiness; therefore everyone taken together ought to aim at the happiness of all.'

Criticism: If each person places his own happiness above all else, then there is no one who considers the happiness of all above all else. Their argument is a mere paralogism in which 'all' is handled in the same way as 'each' or 'one'.

(*c*) A third attempt at a proof rests upon the principle that people eventually come to have a liking and a desire for frequently used means without regard to the end they were originally employed to attain; for instance, we often start out by making ourselves useful and agreeable to someone simply in return for favours he has offered us, but end up by serving him with no thought of our own interest. This development is in accordance with nature; such behaviour is by nature correct for mankind.

Criticism: 1. What is the meaning of 'in accordance with nature' in this context? Does it mean 'in accordance with laws of nature'? Everything is natural in this sense, sickness as well as health, error as well as knowledge, wicked as well as virtuous behaviour.

2. Also, this principle is not universally operative. Many people begin as egoists and remain so. Thus [assuming that we ought to follow what is 'natural'] the behaviour of those who lose sight of their own interest would be no more deserving of approval than is the behaviour of these egoists.

3. If it is countered that egoists do turn into altruists more often than not, we must ask, first, why what is usual should be right, or better than what is not. If it is, why is inferior conduct referred to as 'vulgar' or 'ordinary', while deeds of especial value are called 'extraordinary?' And in the second place, it is highly questionable whether this is in fact what usually happens.

4. The process appealed to here is a consequence of the limit-

ations of our consciousness, which prevents us from keeping several things in view at the same time, or at least makes it difficult to do so. Thus it is that, in concentrating on the means generally used, we forget the end. However, it is common not only for altruism to develop out of motives initially egotistical but also for a miser to develop a blind and foolish passion for money. He completely forgets the aim and acquires a senseless desire for the means, just as if they were the end.

If the utilitarians say that we censure avarice and praise the love of our neighbour because the former is injurious to the general good while the latter assists it, they are quite right. But the reply is irrelevant, for the supreme utilitarian principle is not to be presupposed but to be grounded upon the psychological fact in question. This answer leads to a vicious circle.

5. Another point to be made is that we encounter again and again in utilitarianism the previously remarked confusion between a law in the sense of a law of nature and a law in the sense of a precept or rule of right conduct. What is in accord with psychological laws may fail to agree with the laws of logic, for example. It is a law of psychology that we generally trust external perception, yet this trust is irrational and involves an error.

If a utilitarian retorts that when he speaks of what is in accordance with nature he is not referring to everything which happens according to laws of nature but rather to what accords with a natural precept, then he is guilty of *petitio principii*. The accordance of the principle with nature in the latter sense is precisely what is to be proved.

(*d*) A fourth attempt appeals to the fact that the great majority of people always approve of conduct which accords with the utilitarian principle. However:

(α) Does this not debase the concept 'moral' and strip it of its value? That the majority approves of something does not make it worthy of approval.

(β) The majority is not to be relied upon. Individuals often sacrifice their future happiness to the present moment. Think how often acts that promote the interests of the ruling party, the party superior in numbers, are unjust.

(γ) What the majority approves can often be judged better from their deeds than from their words; the latter may sound altruistic, while the former are egotistical.

(e) An attempt has been made by Fechner to base the principle upon God and his retributive justice. However:

(α) This changes the motive.

(β) How do we know that this is what God wills? In order to judge whether God can really have willed a certain law, we must already know what is good, ethically right conduct.

(γ) If an appeal is made to divine revelation, the question of whether God's word is worthy of belief remains open, even if we can be quite certain that it *is* God's word. And this question can itself be answered only on the basis of ethical knowledge.

12. *Illustration of the third kind of case (Wollaston)*

Wollaston was a contemporary of Clarke, although somewhat older (1659–1724). He declared the proposition that one ought not to lie to be an evident principle and believed he could derive all other ethical precepts from it. For, in his view, we can lie not only in word but also in deed; a deed which contradicts one or more true propositions is necessarily bad. And every instance of wickedness, be it omission or commission, contains the denial of some truth, e.g. the violation of a contract denies that the contract was made. This is a contradiction not in words but by means of deeds. The robbing of a traveller constitutes a denial that what was taken from him is his.

An act is good if failure to perform it would be bad in the sense just explained or if the act opposite to it is bad.

An act is indifferent if neither the performance of it nor the failure to perform it contradicts any truth.

Wollaston believed that his theory harmonized most beautifully with the facts. He thought it made comprehensible how human morality progresses; its progress depends upon the advances of science. And he supposed that it would by no means obliterate the difference between misdeeds and moral errors. The latter occur when the agent believes the false proposition asserted by his deed to be true. In such cases the act is bad, but the agent is not to be blamed.[8]

First, let us consider the evidence of the principle. According

[8] William Wollaston, 'The Religion of Nature Delineated' (London, 1722). [Reprinted in *British Moralists*, ed. Selby-Bigge (Oxford, 1897), vol. II.] Cf. O. Kraus, *Die Werttheorien*, p. 76 ff.

to Wollaston, the proposition that one ought not to lie is supposed to be immediately discernable from the concepts it contains.
If so, it would have to be valid without exception. But many
important men teach the opposite inasmuch as they recognize
cases in which it is justifiable to say what is not true. Plato makes
use of the following example. Suppose a madman leaves his knife
with me and demands to have it back at a time when all the
indications are that he will commit a murder with it. Is it immoral to deny that I have the knife with me? There may be occasions when it is only by lying that a man is able to keep a secret
which has been entrusted to him and which would cause great
harm if divulged. Is lying even then not permissible? There have
been very noble and rigorously moral people who could find nothing immoral in such lies.

How about the derivation? These instances certainly do not
support the thesis that the principle is evident from the beginning;
but even assuming it were evident, it would still not be an adequate basis for morality. Part of lying is the intent to deceive. If
someone pronounces an untruth in such a way that it could
deceive no one, his utterance is not a lie and the reproaches which
apply to a liar do not touch him; think, for instance, of an ironic
speech of praise or the words of an actor upon the stage. But
then how can every bad act be a lie, as Wollaston claims? If by
means of his behaviour a man says, 'I shall not keep the contract,'
he surely cannot believe that his refusal makes anyone else question
the existence of the contract. Thus he has no intent to deceive.
When reminded of a promise he had made, Napoleon said, 'I'm
not about to make myself a slave to my own words!' Conscious
of the importance of the right which had been tramped underfoot,
he disdained all deception. His behaviour was shamelessly insolent,
but he did not lie.

Moreover, even if the intent to deceive were not part of lying,
but only the conscious deviation from the truth, Wollaston's
theory would still fail. How are we to understand the statement
that someone is denying a truth by his behaviour? Wollaston
would explain it by saying that he acts as he ought to only if there
were no such truth. Very well, then: in order to recognize that a
truth is denied by an action, we must know how we ought and
how we ought not to act in the relevant situation. In other words,
we must know what is good and what is bad in the instance

given. But if we must already know this in order to make any application of Wollaston's principle, then this principle is utterly useless. It presupposes the knowledge it is supposed to give us.

To summarize what we have said against Wollaston's theory: it lacks self-evidence. But even if it were evident, it would not be a suitable basis for ethics. For there are many bad actions which contain no intent to deceive and which therefore cannot be called lies. But if all that is meant by a lie is a conscious deviation from the truth, what is the meaning of 'lying by means of an act?' Here lying could only mean the perverseness of an act, i.e. acting as one ought not to. Then, certainly, Wollaston's proposition is beyond attack: 'Act as you ought to act.' But it has also become a barren tautology.

We were right in posing Wollaston's principle as an example of the third group of principles; both its evidence and its usefulness are to be contested. Let us present Kant's attempt at formulating a principle as a further example of this kind.

13. A further illustration of the third kind of case (Kant)

1. Kant (1724–1804) is the third of the famous German philosophers. Before him, Leibniz (1646–1716) and Christian Wolff (1679–1754) were the only ones to attain real fame. The latter is not now much revered, although he used to dominate German universities and had influence outside Germany as well. Kant, who at first was in complete accord with his teachings, considered him the second greatest German philosopher after Leibniz. Today, however, his own fame outshines theirs by far. Even during his lifetime his philosophy gave impetus to a powerful movement. It was with reference to him that Schiller coined the epigram:

When kings are abuilding, the haulers are busy—just as a single rich man provides nourishment for many beggars.

Schiller was an enthusiastic admirer of his, and attempts have been made to trace Kant's influence in his dramas. Goethe, on the other hand, was by nature an adamant opponent. Tobacco and Kant's philosophy came close to annihilating his friendship with Schiller just as it was beginning. If he occasionally admits the truth of a Kantian proposition, it is because he bows to the view then predominant among professional philosophers with a modesty quite comprehensible in someone who does not consider himself one of their number. But whenever he begins to speculate himself, he displays an entirely different spirit. Goethe is an unshakeable empiricist; the only philosophy he considers possible is the sort of empirical philosophy that Kant attacks and that has not a single point in common with Kantian philosophy. Herder, whose repulsion was equal to that felt by Goethe, but whose manner was far less reserved, engaged in passionate polemics against Kant and consequently incurred invectives against himself. On the other hand, Kant's followers were so filled with enthusiasm that one of them, Reinhold (1758–1823), dared to prophesy that within a hundred years Kant would be as revered as Christ. Now that did not come to pass, yet many do hold Kant to be the Aristotle of modern philosophy, or even to be the greatest philosopher who ever lived. Even after the collapse of the German systems of idealism Kant's esteem remained unshaken; indeed, it was precisely the natural scientists who loved to confess themselves his followers and proclaim his fame, while they could do nothing but shake their heads with scorn and disdain at the idealists. Today, of course, a transformation is taking place. The majority of scientists repudiate Kant, but we would very likely be right in hazarding a guess that they have not read him. Even the philosophers are no longer unanimously in agreement with him, and it looks as though his opponents are growing in number. But whatever the future may decide about the true value of his philosophy, his intellectual gifts and historical position make him an outstanding thinker.

2. We are concerned here solely with his attempt to lay a firm foundation for ethics, i.e. with his doctrine of the categorical imperative. How does the situation look? Kant wants to supply us with a formal principle which we can use as a criterion for whether any given rule of action is not merely hypothetical and applicable to special circumstances but absolutely universally and categorically valid. A hypothetical imperative tells us how to behave, what to do or to abstain from doing, when we have set ourselves a particular goal, but a categorical imperative commands absolutely. It is not a conditional but an absolute 'You ought'. And because it imposes a universal obligation, such a rule must contain an *a priori* element, and this in turn cannot lie, in Kant's view, in the contents of the precept, for the contents of any idea are necessarily taken from experience. Rather, it must belong to the form of the

31

proposition. Thus the problem is to formulate a proposition which is free of all content and which, as a purely formal law, can serve us as a criterion of whether a maxim is a valid categorical command. Kant refers to objective basic principles with these characteristics as maxims; the one he sets up for the ethical sphere he calls a 'categorical imperative'. He formulates it in several different ways in various places in his works. The *Foundations of Morals* (*Grundlegung zur Metaphysik der Sitten*) contains two formulations:

'Act as though the maxim of your action were by your will to become a universal law of nature,' and

'Act in accordance with a maxim which you could at the same time will to become a universal law.'*

But in the *Critique of Pure Reason* the categorical imperative runs:

'Act so that the maxim of your will could hold at any time [simultaneously] as the principle of a universal legislation.'†

Kant shows by means of an example how he envisages administering this formal criterion in order to deduce the absolutely obligatory nature of a rule. The question he considers is whether a man may keep for himself goods entrusted to him without any sort of receipt. Anyone with healthy moral sentiments says no, and Kant seeks to justify this answer by showing how, in the light of the categorical imperative, it is obligatory to return the goods. If the maxim were to declare it permissible to keep the goods in such cases, it could not hold as the principle of a universal legislation. For if it were elevated to a universal law it would lead to a contradiction and nullify itself: if it were a universal principle that anyone could keep goods with which he had been entrusted, no one would entrust anybody with anything. It would be impossible to apply the principle; therefore it could not be carried out; therefore it would nullify itself.

Only that course of behaviour can be considered moral which is pursued purely out of respect for this formal moral law, purely from consciousness of our duty (which according to Kant is the

* Sect. II, vol. IV, p. 421 in the Akademie edition. All further references will be to this edition.

† Part 1, Book I, chap. 1, ¶ 7, p. 31. Brentano omits the bracketed word. Translation of both these works are to be found in *Critique of Practical Reason and other Writings in Moral Philosophy* (trans. Beck, University of Chicago Press, 1949).

same thing as respect for the categorical imperative). What is done from other motives, and most particularly what is done for the sake of pleasure, can never count as moral. 'Duty! Thou sublime and great name which contains nothing which pleases and ingratiates itself, but demands submission and sets up a law that successfully demands to be respected, even if not always followed, and before which all inclinations fall silent, even if they are secretly working against it. What is thy worthy origin, and where are we to find the root of thy noble descent, which proudly casts out any relation to inclination? To stem from this root is the immutable condition of that one value which men are able to give themselves.'* So runs the great question, and the answer to it is: It lies in reason, the faculty which elevates mankind above the sensual world. Truly a rigorous morality, which declares war squarely against all natural impulses! But this very strictness and boldness enticed enthusiastic followers: not only wooden executers of duty, but even such a man as Friedrich Schiller! Kant himself finds cause for the greatest admiration precisely in this universal validity which is free of any admixture of emotion. At the end of the *Critique of Practical Reason* he says, 'Two things fill the mind with ever fresh and increasing admiration and awe, the oftener and more steadily they are reflected on: the starry heavens above me and the moral law within me.' (161).

3. Needless to say, we must not allow ourselves to be so dazzled by all this rhetoric that we are prevented from testing out whether this famous categorical imperative is to be counted as a genuine principle of reason.

To lay our cards on the table right away: the results of this test will be just as negative as they were with Wollaston. For Kant's principle, too, lacks not only evidence but also relevance, i.e. no ethical consequences can be deduced from it. Even philosophers who in other respects have a very high opinion of Kant— for instance Mansel, who next to Hamilton is the most significant representative of the so-called intuitive school—hold his categorical imperative to be a philosophical fiction. No one who has not already fallen under the spell will admit to finding such a principle within himself, and if it were really a fact of pure reason

* Kant, *Critique of Practical Reason*, V, 861. Brentano omits some clauses and gives the quote not quite perfectly; I have translated it as he gives it.

Kant would certainly not have had to discover it; he would only have had to give the correct explanation of its true nature and its origin.

But if there is nevertheless someone or other who believes that it is directly evident, it is simply an ordinary case of feeling an impulse to assent on the basis of a habit or previous bias. And it turns out, by the way, that most of the people who profess belief in the categorical imperative imagine something quite different from what Kant had in mind.

4. But Kant's categorical imperative is not only a fiction; it is also of no use in ethics. No ethical law can be deduced from it, and the deduction which Kant himself attempted 'failed grotesquely', as John Stuart Mill has noted.

(*a*) Above all, it is erroneous to suppose that a law which is not applicable to anything is thereby nullified. This is true neither of laws of nature nor of laws in the sense of norms.

It never happens that a body moves forward in a straight line absolutely undisturbed, but it is nevertheless a law of nature that a moving body, if it remains undisturbed, must move forward in a straight line with a uniform velocity *in infinitum*. Likewise, it is true that the sum of the angles of a billion-sided figure equals two billion minus 4 R, even if there exists no such polygon.

And the same is true of laws in the second sense. A penal law which obligates the judge to mete out a certain punishment for a given offence is not rendered null because, for fear of the punishment, no one commits such an offence; on the contrary, it is under these circumstances that it shows itself truly effective. Likewise with the moral law, as is shown by the following example. Consider the question whether a man is obligated to keep his word to a robber who has attacked him and freed him only upon being promised ransom. Inasmuch as it conflicts with the categorical imperative, Kant would reject the maxim, 'I am not bound to keep my word in such a case.' For if this maxim were followed, no robber would ever again make such an agreement. But this law would be as effective here as the sort of penal law already discussed; it would not be nullified, and would even be most happily effective if it had the consequence of preventing all further attempts at extortion.

(*b*) It is also erroneous to suppose that the law would be without application if, when elevated to a universal law, it was rendered null to a certain extent. Kant believes that, under the circumstances he cites, the result would be that no one would entrust anything to anyone without a receipt. He overlooks a number of relevant considerations. For people could still entrust things to others in the belief that they will get them back. He to whom they had been entrusted would not, it is true, return them because he felt an obligation to do so, but other motives might be effective; if the goods were stolen, for instance, the receiver might return them because he felt it dangerous to keep them any longer. Think how often promises and agreements are effective among men who feel themselves bound neither by the law nor by their consciences. (An agreement to a joint theft, assassination, etc.)

If, then, Kant's law is taken to be a precept or norm, the consequences he draws are false. But even if it is conceived in the other of the two ways, as a law of nature, i.e. as a universal and necessary fact, the results are untenable. The lender might be unaware of the law of nature which declares that no one will return what is entrusted to him without a receipt, for there certainly are many laws of nature that we do not know. Or even if he does know it, he may fail to think of it in this case. Many circumstances could give rise to this. For instance, he might have found that promises are usually kept and expect out of habit that it will be so in this case, too. Or someone may entice the object away from him by flattery; or he may be gullible and have faith because people would rather believe than not; and so forth.

Furthermore, what about the cases in which a receipt is issued or some other sort of circumstantial proof exists but is lost? In this instance Kant's deduction could not be made, and yet the retaining of the entrusted goods is no less immoral. Perhaps, with his sharp wits, he could dream up an argument in this case, too, but it would have to be of quite a different order. And the very fact that it would have to be so contrived indicates how unnatural Kant's explanation is, for all moral cases of essentially the same kind demand essentially the same foundation.

(c) How badly Kant's argument fails is also revealed by the fact that the most absurd and immoral rules can be deduced in a precisely analogous fashion. For example: Is it permissible to comply with someone who wishes to bribe me? Answer: Yes, for if the opposite maxim were elevated to a universal law of nature no one would try to bribe anyone; consequently the law would be without application and would render itself null.

(*d*) Another telling point against the categorical imperative in Kant's sense was made by F. E. Beneke (1798–1854). The question is how we are supposed to construe the generality required, for it is well known that there are various degrees of generality. By leaving away more and more of the determining conditions, we rise to higher and higher stages of generality. Kant has left us with no directions as to how far we are to go in the process of generalizing when we construct our maxims—a most disturbing omission, for we reach contradictory results, depending upon the stage at which we halt. For example, suppose a friend entrusts me with a secret. Circumstances then arise in which I can prevent a great evil from befalling my friend by breaking silence, a virtue that is usually so highly extolled. May I reveal the secret? Let us seek counsel from the categorical imperative. We can lay down the maxim, 'One ought to reveal a secret entrusted to one if by doing so one will keep from misfortune the person who entrusted it to one.' But we can also construct the more general maxim, 'One ought to reveal a secret entrusted to one'. Opposing results follow from these maxims. According to the first, the revelation is permissible, for if it becomes the ruling maxim people will not stop entrusting each other with promises. Therefore, according to Kant, it could be made a universal law. But the second could not, for it would have the opposite consequence, i.e. I would be required to keep silence, even if it led to the ruin of my friend.

5. Thus, in order to work with the categorical imperative we need a standard for the degree of generalization to be permitted. But then we must call in another principle, and the categorical imperative surrenders its position as the highest principle. And Kant really does get reduced to this in his attempts to justify it. He demonstrates that the universal application of a maxim could under certain circumstances be harmful to all, including myself; if we wished to elevate such a maxim to a universal law we would fall into a contradiction with ourselves, for no one can desire his own unhappiness. Now that sounds altogether different! For I do not come into contradiction with myself absolutely, but only if I will what is best in general, including my own happiness. Thus the categorical imperative is preceded by the following train of thought. Each man's happiness is dear to him, but everyone

recognizes that he can have it only in harmony with the whole; hence he deems the happiness of all to be the highest good. Happiness, which according to Kant is the opposite of what is moral, suddenly appears as the highest standard, and the categorical imperative has become merely hypothetical. Here Kant falls away completely from his own tenets.

14. *Completion of the picture of confusion*

I believe these illustrations are sufficient to show how the principles set up by the most revered moral philosophers come up against doubts and contradictions and how in some cases the evidence claimed for them has been denied, in others their effectiveness has been contested, and in yet others, including the most famous, attacks have been made on both their claims to evidence and to efficacy. 'Are we to base ethics on such principles as these?' is the question we still ask today. And the doubt does not concern simply the individual principle, but also the matter of which category it belongs to. Is it *a priori* or *a posteriori*, an axiom or a perception? Kant and Clarke hold it to be *a priori*, while the utilitarians are empiricists.

But it is possible to conceive much greater uncertainty and dissension than this. We have mentioned nothing which does not occur in other sciences, even in mathematics, although there the weight of opinion leans heavily to one side. But in ethics the doubt is far more extensive. The dispute concerns not only whether this or that particular principle is the one to be recognized and whether these principles are axioms or perceptions, but also whether they are cognitions or feelings. Many thinkers, some of them very famous, hold that in ethics the principles are established not by our cognitive faculties but by our emotions.

We have outlined, in its main features, the picture of confusion. Of course, we can only gain a complete image of it by scrutinizing all the details, but at this point it will be easy for the imagination to paint in the remainder of the colourful maze.

Of all the differences we have mentioned the last is the most profound. We must try to become clear about it above all else.

III

Are the Principles of Ethics Cognitions or Feelings?

---

15. *Arguments for the two sides*

A. *Arguments to show they are cognitions*

1. Even in ancient times voices could be heard in favour of feelings. Indeed, if Hume is to be believed, they were the majority, but he was of this persuasion himself and his judgment may well have been influenced by his predilection for it. In any case it is a fact that Epicurus and his followers viewed feelings of pleasure and pain as the standard for decisions about what is good and bad.

In recent times many thinkers have spoken in favour of the faculty of emotion: Locke's influential disciple, Lord Shaftesbury (1670–1713); also the founder of political economy, Adam Smith (1723–90); and as mentioned already, the sceptic David Hume (1711–76). J. F. Herbart (1776–1841) and his widespread following belong here in some sense, too, as does H. Lotze (1817–80) in the opposite respect. He says in his *Mikrokosmos* that the basic principles of ethics are always given sanction in quite a different way from the truths of knowledge. They are expressions of a faculty of emotion sensitive to values.[9]

Now, is this not a very paradoxical doctrine? At first glance, there appears to be much that speaks against it.

(*a*) Indeed, we might well ask if it is not quite absurd. What are the first, immediate assumptions of a science if not those cog-

---

[9] Cf., in *Die Werttheorien*, Oskar Kraus' remarks about Lord Shaftesbury (p. 77), Adam Smith (p. 104), David Hume (p. 103), and H. Lotze (p. 157ff.).

nitions upon which all others rest, the premises of all the conclusions that are drawn in the science? These premises are, of course, as much judgments as the conclusions themselves, and if the latter are to be certain the norm must also be sure judgments, or cognitions. How, then, can anyone possibly doubt the absurdity of the doctrine that the first premises of ethics are not cognitions, but feelings?

(*b*) We have stated that ethics is dominated by a dispute about principles, that there are differences of opinion about what is to count as good and what as bad. But we can dispute only about what is either true or false, not about matters of feeling: 'De gustibus non est disputandum.'

(*c*) We assume that what we deem to be morally good or bad is so for every rational being, even for God; for it is only on this assumption that the belief in a divine justice that rewards the good and punishes the bad makes sense. But in that case the foundations of morality must be determined by reason, and it is for precisely this reason that, like all correct judgments about true and false, they must be the same for all intelligent creatures. It would be quite different if these foundations were laid by the emotions, for then they would depend entirely upon the particular structure of the human species. Under these circumstances, it would be just as possible for other rational beings to have an ethic contrary to ours as it is impossible for them to have a different sort of logic, for one kind of animal enjoys eating what another spurns as disgusting. The English moral philosopher Richard Price (1723–91) attacks Francis Hutcheson (1694–1747), an advocate of the view that morality rests on feelings, in the following terms: 'According to this doctrine, the Creator could just as well have attached the same feelings to the opposite actions.'* This he considers sufficient grounds for rejecting the view.

In attacking Hume, Kant, too, emphasizes the universal validity

---

* I have translated the quote as given by Brentano, as I cannot locate any statement of precisely this form in Price. In any case, the criticism is to be found: 'Our perception of right, or moral good, . . . and of wrong, or moral evil . . . are (according to Hutcheson) particular modifications of our minds, . . . which the contrary actions might have occasioned, had the Author of nature so pleased . . .'—Price, *A Review of the Principal Questions in Morals* (1758), in *British Moralists*, ed. Selby-Bigge, vol. II, sect. 585.

of the moral law: it is universally valid, therefore it comes by way of reason. In point of fact, he says, the idea that one species might hold to be virtuous what another considers vicious is untenable; even less viable is the idea that God's moral taste is opposed to that of rational creatures. Just think how surprised we would be at the Last Judgment, with everything topsy-turvy!

B. *Arguments to show that the principles of ethics are feelings*

Viewed in this manner, everything seems to militate against the sentimental theory:* the theory that ethics rests on feelings. But we would be overly hasty if we were to make our decision now, for the advocates of this view have had no chance yet to speak up and present their reasons, which are of a kind that might well win over some people who had just been convinced of the opposite. Let us give the stage to the acutest among their number.

David Hume treated the question in three places, beginning with his first and most thorough work, *A Treatise on Human Nature*. To be sure, this book, because it contained such a painstaking investigation and demanded so much effort on the part of the reader, was not well received. Without fretting about it, Hume quite sensibly set about putting his thoughts into a simpler and more comprehensible form. Thus it was that the *Essays and Treatises on Several Subjects* came into being. Because of their more elegant style and more popular composition, from which the subtler arguments are frequently omitted, to be replaced by analogies, these essays found many readers and caused Hume to rise rapidly to fame. In the last of the four books,† entitled *An Enquiry Concerning the Principles of Morals*, the first paragraph runs as follows.‡

---

* I shall use this somewhat old-fashioned term, formerly used in reference to the theories of Hume, Hutcheson, etc., to translate Brentano's term, *Gefühlstheorie*. This seems preferable to any phrase containing the word 'emotion' or any of its forms because emotive theories, common in recent times, are quite different.

† Some earlier editions of the *Essays and Treatises* appeared in four volumes. However, this division does not pertain to the present editions of Hume's works.

‡ Brentano gives a German translation of this passage, which is to be found in sect. I of *An Enquiry Concerning the Principles of Morals*, ed.

'There has been a controversy started of late, much better worth examination, concerning the general foundation of Morals: whether they be derived from Reason, or from Sentiment; whether we attain the knowledge of them by a chain of argument and induction, or by an immediate feeling . . .; whether, like all sound [assumptions pertaining to]* truth and falsehood, they should be the same to every rational intelligent being; or whether, like the [taste for]† beauty and deformity, they be founded entirely on the particular fabric and constitution of the human species.

'The ancient philosophers, though they often affirm, that virtue is nothing but [agreement with]‡ reason, yet, in general, seem to consider morals as deriving their existence from taste and sentiment. On the other hand, our modern enquirers, though they also talk much of the beauty of virtue, and deformity of vice, yet have commonly endeavoured to account for these distinctions by metaphysical reasonings, and by deductions from the most abstract principles of the understanding. Such confusion reigned in these subjects, that an opposition of the greatest consequence could prevail between one system and another, and even in the parts of almost each individual system; and yet nobody, till very lately, was ever sensible of it. The elegant Lord Shaftesbury . . . first gave occasion to remark this distinction. . . . [Such confusion reigned formerly, that this opposition between the systems (and within some of them) was not noticed, until, recently, Lord Shaftesbury drew attention to it.]'

Immediately afterwards Hume presents the arguments on both sides, ending up with a compromise.§

'These arguments on each side . . . are so plausible, that I am apt to suspect . . . that *reason* and *sentiment* concur in almost all moral determinations and conclusions. The final sentence . . . which pronounces characters and actions amiable or odious, praiseworthy or blameable; that which stamps on them the mark of . . . approbation or censure; that which renders morality an active

---

Selby-Bigge (Oxford University Press, 1902), pp. 170–1. I have reinstated the original English; but where the German seemed inaccurate I have put a translation of it in square brackets, giving Hume's phrase in a footnote, unless no corresponding phrase appears at all.

* '. . . judgments of . . .'   ‡ '. . . conformity to . . .'
† '. . . perception of . . .'   § Op. cit., pp. 172–3.

principle [determining our actions] and [makes virtue a source of happiness for us, and vice a source of misery]:*... I say, that this final sentence depends on some internal sense or feeling, which nature has made universal in the whole species. For what else can have an influence of this nature? [It is impossible for the understanding to predetermine, of itself, what will arouse our love and hate; the truths of the understanding, if they arouse neither desire nor aversion, can only effect the cool consent of the understanding and cannot have any influence on our behaviour. Only that which touches our heart by the nobility of its beauty can speak to our feelings. However, in order that the feeling may speak out, the path must often be smoothed by much reasoning; distinctions must be made, conclusions drawn, remote comparisons carried out, and complicated relations investigated. Thus the influence of the understanding is preparatory; it has the task of placing the object about which the feelings are to make a decision in its proper light, which essentially determines the correctness of that decision. We go through a similar process with some varieties of beauty. In order to sense beauty, we often must prepare ourselves by lengthy and tedious reasonings. It is much the same with morality. Hence it is that there are disputes about good and bad and that legal cases not only treat the facts but also include lengthy proofs and deductions of reason concerning guilt and innocence, just as though the matter at hand were a proposition of geometry or a physical theory.]'†

* '... constitutes virtue our happiness and vice our misery ...'

† Here the deviations are so numerous that I have translated the entire passage. Hume reads, 'But in order to pave the way for such a sentiment, and give a proper discernment of its object, it is often necessary, we find, that much reasoning should precede, that nice distinctions be made, just conclusions drawn, distant comparisons formed, complicated relations examined, and general facts fixed and ascertained. Some species of beauty, especially the natural kinds, on their first appearance, command our affection and approbation; and where they fail of this effect, it is impossible for any reasoning to redress their influence, or adapt them better to our taste and sentiment. But in many orders of beauty, particularly those of the finer arts, it is requisite to employ much reasoning, in order to feel the proper sentiment; and a false relish may frequently be corrected by argument and reflection. There are just grounds to conclude, that moral beauty partakes much of

Hume declares himself content with this compromise for the time being, but in the long run he was not able to appease his scholarly conscience with a simple manoeuvre for skirting around the decision about such an important question of principles. Thus he returns to the problem in the appendix and, upon the basis of a number of arguments no less thoroughgoing than those which appear in the *Treatise*, but more clearly formulated, places himself squarely on the side of the sentimental theme. Let us analyse his case.

1. It is easy, he says,* for a false hypothesis to present an appearance of correctness, as long as it remains quite general, employs expressions without defining them, and makes use of analogies instead of examples. As long as everything is floating freely in a vacuum, the opponent's blows can find no mark. This is particularly to be seen in that philosophy which attributes to reason, alone, without the assistance of sentiment, the determination of all moral distinctions. It is impossible to give this hypothesis even one intelligible meaning in so much as a single instance, no matter how impressive a figure it may cut so long as it struts about making general declamations and distinctions. Let us examine, for instance, the crime of ingratitude, which occurs where we note, on the one hand, a known and acknowledged goodwill together with the rendering of good service and, on the other, ill will or indifference coupled with ill services or neglect. If we analyse all these circumstances and investigate, with our reason alone, what constitutes the disservice or the reprehensibility, we will never reach a solution. What is judged by reason must be either an actual occurrence or characteristic, or a relation. Now which of these can it be in this case, which concerns the crime involved in ingratitude?

A. If any man wishes to claim that what we call a crime is a fact, let him point to this fact. When does it exist? What is it? By means of which sense or which capacity is it perceived? It dwells in the spirit of the person who is ungrateful; hence this person must

---

this latter species, and demands the assistance of our intellectual faculties, in order to give it a suitable influence on the human mind.'

* The material summarized in the remainder of this section is to be found in Appendix I of the *Enquiry*, pp. 285–94 in Selby-Bigge.

perceive it, or have a consciousness of it. But in the soul of this person we find only ill will or indifference. We cannot say that these are crimes under all circumstances, but only when they are directed towards persons who have previously shown us goodwill and rendered us good services. Thus we may conclude that the crime of ingratitude is not a particular isolated fact but arises from a complex of circumstances which, upon being presented to an observer, arouse in him a feeling of disapprobation as a result of the particular structure and cultivation of his spirit.

B. Someone might say this presentation of the matter is incorrect.

What is referred to as a crime does not consist in a particular fact which our faculty of knowledge assures us is real but in certain moral relations that the understanding discovers in the same way as the truths of geometry and algebra. This is what many of Hume's contemporaries said. But what sort of relations are they supposed to be?

First: the attempt to establish such a relation between the two persons.

In the case presented above I can see the goodwill and kind offices of the one person and the ill will and abuse of the other. These two positions are contrary; does the crime consist in this relation?

But suppose that someone has shown me ill will and done me injury, whereas I treated him indifferently or even with benevolence and courtesy. Here again the relation is one of contrariety, yet my behaviour is not displeasing; indeed, under certain circumstances it may be quite laudable. Twist and turn this matter as you will, morality simply cannot be founded upon a relation. It always has to appeal to the feelings.

Second: the attempt to establish such a relation between the various aspects of the criminal's condition.

If we say that $2 + 3 = 10:2$, the relation involved is perfectly comprehensible. I understand that if ten is divided into two equal parts, each of these parts contains just as many units as $2 + 3$. But when it comes to comparing this relation of equality with the equality of various parts which are to be distinguished in the soul of the ungrateful person, I must confess that I am unable to follow. What sort of units are these supposed to be, and what is the relation that is to result in immorality? We have only to stop expressing ourselves in vague and general terms and to examine this question thoroughly to realize that this attempt, too, misses its goal.

Third: the attempt to establish a relation between the act and a rule.

Some say that morality consists in a relation between the act and the rule of right. The act is called good or bad, depending upon whether it is in accord with the rule or not.

But how are we to understand this rule of right? How is it determined? By reason, you will say, which investigates the moral relations of actions. Thus moral relations are established by comparing acts to a rule, and the rule is established by taking into consideration the moral relations of acts. A fine sort of argument! Stop, you will shout; all that is metaphysics, and this in itself is sufficient to raise a strong suspicion that it is false. Yes, I answer, it is metaphysics, but it is all on your side; you set up an abstruse hypothesis that can be neither clarified nor applied to any concrete example. The hypothesis I propose is, on the contrary, very simple. It is that morality is established by our feelings. It defines virtue as that species of spiritual activity or disposition which arouses the pleasant feeling of approval in those who contemplate it, while vice arouses the painful feeling of disapproval. Then I enter into the path of experience in looking to see which acts have this influence. I look for every circumstance in which these acts are in agreement, and from this I seek some general determinations about these feelings. If anyone wishes to call this metaphysics, and finds something abstruse in it, we can only draw the conclusion that his mind is not suited to philosophical study.

2. Up to this point I have reproduced Hume's train of thought practically word for word. For the rest I shall summarize at least the essential contents.

Next Hume seeks to destroy an apparent similarity that could mislead us into ascribing the establishment of moral principles to reason. If someone is deliberating about how he should act, whether in a particular situation he should stand by his brother or his benefactor, he must consider each aspect in itself, with all the circumstances and relations pertaining to the persons involved, in order to determine where the preponderance of duty and obligation lies. Do we not have a similar case when we wish to determine the relation of the square of the sides of a right-angle triangle and undertake for this purpose an investigation of the nature of this geometrical figure and the relation of its parts? Hume replies that there are essential differences. For the mathematician concludes upon the basis of given relations that a new one exists, which depends upon them. On the contrary, he who is to decide a moral issue must already have achieved a knowledge of all the relations involved; only when he has the whole before him can he form his moral judgment of choice or approval. At that point no new relation is uncovered, no new fact presented. Rather, the ability to make a decision proclaiming approval or disapproval presupposes a knowledge of all the circumstances relevant to the case. Up to this point reason is active and the moral decision remains suspended. But once the preparatory work of the undertaking is finished, it is followed by approbation or rejection, which is nothing more nor less than a feeling, inasmuch as the soul receives, by contemplating the whole, a fresh impression of love or aversion, respect or scorn, approval or disapproval.

3. Hume places beside this misleading comparison one which corresponds to it but is, he thinks, correct: that between moral and natural beauty. All natural beauty depends upon the relations of the parts to one another, yet it would be quite perverse to conclude from this fact that beauty is grasped solely by the understanding, as is the truth of the propositions of geometry. When we are to decide whether something is physically beautiful or not, the relations lie from the first clearly before our eyes; depending upon the nature of these relations and that of our own organs, we feel either emotionally drawn to it or repelled by it. The beauty of a pillar manifests itself to us by means of an agreeable feeling connected with the relations between the base, the shaft, the capital, the frieses, the architrave, etc. It is by means of this feeling, not by his reason, that the observer of taste comprehends the beauty of the pillar. The activities of the mathematician are exhausted as soon as he has determined the new relations that he sought; whether he feels pleasure or displeasure, whether or not the circle, for instance, is beautiful, plays no role here. Euclid, in investigating geometric relations, never speaks of beauty.

Moral beauty is just like physical beauty; approving or disapproving is not an activity of the understanding, but of the faculty of emotion. It is not a speculative assertion, but a feeling.

46

4. In order to make it yet clearer that morality is not itself a particular kind of relation, Hume points to various cases in which, although the understanding discovers the same relation, morality or immorality is given in the one instance but not in the other. Some might wish to seek the moral ugliness of ingratitude in contrasts; Nero, the matricide, destroyed the life to whom he owed his own life. However, a young tree which overtops and destroys the plant from which it stems demonstrates the same contrast between the receiving and depriving of life, yet inanimate objects are never an object of love or hate, and therefore not of approval or disapprobation.

5. Hume presents one more argument, probably the most important of all. Reason never accounts for the ultimate ends of human action; they recommend themselves exclusively to our feelings and inclinations, without depending in any way upon the activities of the understanding. Try asking someone why he does exercises. He will reply that it is in order to maintain his health. If you further inquire as to why he wishes to remain healthy, he will tell you that illness is painful. If you go still further and ask why he hates pain, he cannot give you any reason. Remaining free from pain is simply an ultimate end for him and is not referred to something else as a means. Not everything can be desired for the sake of something else. Something must be intrinsically worthy of desire inasmuch as it accords directly with the feelings and inclinations of man. Now among our ultimate goals virtue is also to be found. It, too, is loved for its own sake; it furnishes immediate satisfaction without respect to rewards and punishments. We must already have a faculty of feeling which is moved by it— an internal taste or sense of beauty which differentiates between good and bad in turning to the one and being repulsed by the other.

6. It is easy, then, to distinguish between the domain and functions of the understanding and of the taste. From the understanding flows the knowledge of truth and falsehood, from the faculty of emotion that of beauty and ugliness, including the morally beautiful as well as the good and the morally ugly as well as the bad. Because of the subjective origin of this knowledge the rules of approbation and disapprobation are not, even for the will of the supreme being, eternal and unchanging, as are the propositions emanating from the understanding. Rather, they are

ultimately derived from that being, who has given to every creature having a soul its special nature and has established the various classes and orders of existence. So Hume ends his inquiry in his usual roguish manner. He acts as though he were teaching divine sanction, whereas he is in fact very far from sharing the theistic world view of the great thinkers of the golden age of philosophy. Hume reaches this conclusion: In ethical deliberations, the understanding (judgment) alone makes the decision so long as it concerns the choice of means, but the understanding does not have the ability to make any decision about the merit of the ultimate end.

16. *Refutation of the argument that the principles of ethics must be cognitions because there are disputes about ethical matters*

As paradoxical as the thesis may sound that the principles of ethical knowledge are not themselves cognitions, but feelings, the reasons presented in support of it are so weighty that they incline one to accept the doctrine. I allowed Hume himself to be the advocate of his doctrine, which is held by a number of other significant thinkers. And where Hume speaks, there speaks a clear head and a keen understanding. It was not without reason that Kant admired his acuteness above that of all other philosophers. Hume was certainly not caught napping in the case at hand. He presents us with a plethora of penetrating arguments, and whoever has followed his arguments cannot fail to have been impressed by them. But must we really agree with Hume that the principles of ethical knowledge are not cognitions but feelings? Before we do so, let us return to the arguments which we gave at the beginning for the opposite doctrine. They also appeared to be sound, and if they really are Hume cannot possibly be right, be all appearances to the contrary. But if what Hume says is conclusive and his view is the right one, then our earlier arguments must be merely spurious: *aporiae* which dissolve upon closer inspection.

According to the first argument, a principle of knowledge is nothing but an ultimate cognition from which it follows. If the conclusion is a judgment, the premises must be also. Hence it is absurd to claim that feelings are the principles of ethical knowledge.

According to the second, matters of taste are not subject to dispute, but ethical questions are disputed.

But when we recall what Hume said about the false analogy between ethical and mathematical relations, it is easy for us to see that this second argument is not conclusive. Hume himself took account of it and demonstrated that it was inadequate. In order to explain how it is possible to argue about what is morally good and bad, he said, it is not necessary that the understanding issue the last word as to which acts and which kinds of character are worthy of praise or reproach or that it place the seal of approval or disapproval upon them. That there are ethical disputes can also be comprehended from the viewpoint of those who hold the final sentence to be the expression of a feeling implanted in the nature of our species. However, we must not go so far as to exclude reason from taking any part in ethical decisions. Hume claims he is far from doing any such thing; even though, according to his doctrine, reason does not pronounce the final sentence, it does have a preparatory influence. 'It will fall to reason to make fine distinctions, form correct conclusions, draw remote comparisons, follow up the threads of compounded relations, set up and secure general laws, and thus set the object about which the feelings are to decide in its proper light, which determines in an essential manner the correctness of the decisions.'*

17. *The impossibility of refuting the argument that the principles of ethical knowledge must be cognitions, because these principles are the cognitions from which it is derived*

The second argument has been set aside. But Hume does not refute the first; he clearly never thought of it. Can we perhaps answer it? That does not appear easy. Let us recall it yet once again. It runs as follows. The first, immediate assumptions of a science are the first cognitions from which all other are deduced. There can be no conclusions which do not rest on judgments as premises, and if the conclusions are to be certain the premises must be judgments that are certain. To deny this in some cases and to assert that the

* Although this sentence is given by Brentano as a quote, I am unable to find any passage which corresponds to it exactly. However, it is approximately a portion of the *Enquiry* quoted under sect. 15, B in this chapter (op. cit., p. 173).

principles of some particular science are feelings is consequently simply absurd. This objection requires serious thought; indeed, it leaves no room for doubt, for it is conclusive. The light shed by this objection is such that it cannot be extinguished, not even by such a thinker as Hume. It has the clarity of evidence.

Thus it is Hume who is mistaken. There must be some error in his argument. In fact, it is quite easy to attack him by applying to his thesis the same distinction he applies to his opponents. He granted them that reason plays some role in distinguishing between good and evil; it does not make the final judgment, but is a precondition for it. However, it might instead be the case that feelings are merely a prerequisite for the coming into being of moral judgments. And, in fact, this is all that follows from his arguments. They are fully satisfied if the emotions are viewed as a precondition for the first principles of ethics. These principles themselves are not feelings; they are, rather, cognitions, as are the principles of all other sciences.

There is nothing paradoxical in the claim that emotions are a necessary condition of a particular cognition. All cognitions, even those that are immediate, have certain preconditions; in this respect they differ from derivative cognitions solely in that their preconditions are not themselves cognitions. This holds for both the classes of immediate cognitions that we have distinguished, for the axioms as well as for the evident perceptions. The condition necessary for the axioms consists of certain concepts, for an axiom is a judgment that is clear from the concepts, and in order for a judgment to be clear to us from the concepts we must possess these concepts and really be thinking about them. On the other hand, certain activities of consciousness are the condition required for evident perceptions. For it is possible to have an external perception that is blind, a perception of what is not (a colour, a tone, etc.), but internally we can only perceive with evidence what is really there.

If Hume is right in defining virtue as a spiritual activity or disposition that arouses in the observer the agreeable feeling of approval, it is clear that anyone who recognizes an act as virtuous must establish the presence of this feeling of approval. The feeling, then, is a precondition of moral knowledge. If someone wants to object that the feeling is the cognition itself, he has made a confusion similar to the one involved in holding that geometric axioms are ideas of straight lines, angles, etc., or that the first principles of the natural sciences are events in the physical world.

18. *A proof that Hume's arguments are satisfied so long as the emotions play at least some role in the establishment of ethical principles*

1. Let us examine Hume's arguments once again.

Suppose we begin with the comparison between moral goodness and physical beauty. A being without emotions could have no concept of beauty, for it cannot be discerned by the understanding alone. Mathematicians do not discuss the beauty of the circle. 'Beautiful' denotes, rather, a relation between the idea of a thing and our feelings. To call something beautiful is to indicate that the idea arouses pleasure of a particular kind. If the same is true of virtue, it follows that the concept of the good first breaks upon us when the feeling of approval is aroused. The concept signifies a relation to such a feeling; hence this feeling is a condition necessary for the knowledge of virtue.

But the same conclusion follows from the other arguments, too, and in particular from the most impressive one, which concerns the ultimate end: 'It appears that reason can never give an account of the ultimate aims of human action. Why are health, work, money, and pleasure called goods? Because they please us, because we are fond of them. Of course, many things which please us in this way are loved purely as means, but others, virtue in particular, are themselves ultimate ends, i.e. they are desirable in themselves, without regard to reward and punishment. They immediately arouse our approbation.'* From this Hume concludes that virtuous—that is, morally good—acts are to be defined as those which arouse our liking in and of themselves. What follows? That the faculty of emotion is a necessary condition for acquiring ultimate moral knowledge, i.e. for forming immediate judgments as to whether something is good or bad. A good act and an intrinsically pleasing act are the same thing. We cannot tell *a priori*—by means of pure understanding—that an act is pleasing. We have to have experienced the pleasure.

If we inquire further as to how it is possible for feelings to be

* Although this is given as a quote, I was unable to locate any such passage in the *Enquiry*. However, it largely summarizes what is said in op. cit., p. 293.

the precondition of cognitions, the answer is, as objects of those cognitions. There is no difficulty involved in distinguishing between feelings and the knowledge of feelings. For we often have a knowledge of feelings without having the feelings themselves: whenever we discern the emotions of our fellow men. For instance, we know that someone hates something that we love, or that something towards which we feel indifferently is loved by some and hated by others. Likewise, we may recall having harboured a feeling which we no longer have. The distinction may become yet clearer if we confine ourselves entirely to judgments. We must similarly distinguish between the forming of a judgment and the acknowledgment of it. If I know, for instance, that someone is mistaken, his judgment is an object of my knowledge, but I do not share this judgment. It is not my judgment.

Now if emotion and the knowledge of which it is an object are to be distinguished in these cases, they ought also to be distinguished when it is I myself who have both, i.e. my emotion and the internal perception that I have of it are to be distinguished conceptually. Needless to say, the relation is of a particularly intimate sort in this latter case. The knowledge of my feelings—my internal perception of it—is not a second act, in addition to the feelings; they comprise one and the same act. The philosophers of the unconscious fail to see this point. They hold that we sometimes have a consciousness of something without having an internal perception of it. But the only accurate claim they can make is that we sometimes do not perceive it *clearly*.

Thus we seem to have found the correct solution to the dispute. The principles of ethics, like those of all other sciences, must be cognitions; they cannot be emotions. If feelings play a part in these principles, it is only as objects of the cognitions. In other words, feelings are the necessary conditions of ethical principles.

This cautious phrasing may seem surprising after all that has been said. Have we not already established with certainty that feelings participate in these principles? No matter how probable this has come to seem, we must not leave caution behind us, for we have not yet mentioned all of the arguments against this theory. Let us not forget Kant's accusation that our moral knowledge would fail to be universally binding if we permitted pleasure and displeasure to be its standard. Now we in fact believe that what is morally right for us must be so for all, whereas tastes may vary from species to species. We will occupy ourselves with the merits of this argument further on; here I wish only to explain the motives behind my cautious statement of our results thus far.

2. The refutation of an error frequently lacks the power to prevent its repetition. (I am thinking only of the cases in which the refutation has actually succeeded, for a refutation which fails is no refutation at all.) The history of the sciences, and particularly of philosophy, shows that errors which have been refuted often reappear. In order to prevent this from happening, we would be wise to uncover the sources of the error.

Hume deceives himself because of the imperfections of his psychological analyses. His descriptive psychology leaves much to be desired. The following are factors leading to his errors.

(*a*) The intimate relation, previously mentioned, between emotion and the perception of it makes it difficult to distinguish them. Hume overlooked the distinction and did not differentiate sharply enough between emotion and the knowledge of it, as can be seen from the fact that our objection never occurred to him.

(*b*) Another cause is his sorely deficient classification of psychical activities. His primary distinction is only between impressions and ideas, between sensations on the one hand, and phantasms and concepts on the other, the latter being faint copies of the former. If we inquire where feelings belong in this scheme, we are told that it is with the impressions (or at any rate those feelings that are called passions [Affekte]). Hume confuses sensations with the pleasure and displeasure we take in them. If we were to ask where willing belongs, we would get no explanation at all. Judging, however, is characterized in a variety of different ways at different places in his works. Sometimes he speaks as if it belonged to the class of ideas; in this case, a judgment would be found where certain ideas have become so closely connected that they can no longer be separated from one another. In other places he says it is the tenacity of an idea which makes it into a judgment. And even this is not his last word on the subject, for we also find in his writings a remark to the effect that judging is a kind of feeling. In the face of such confusion we can no longer find it surprising that he overlooks the distinction between a feeling and the knowledge of it.

(*c*) Yet a further ground of the confounding of feelings and the knowledge of feelings is the general confusion of thinking and feeling which takes place because colloquial speech frequently uses the same terms in describing judgments and emotions. Agreement, approval, granting are used with reference to decisions made by judgment, or understanding, as well as those made by the emotions and the will. (We grant an argument.) Pleasure and displeasure are termed emotions, yet it is also correct to say we have a feeling that something is so in cases where we believe something but are unable to prove it. No one who is clear as to the peculiarities of judging will be disturbed by such equivocations, but they hold dangers for those who have not yet mastered the basic analyses of psychology. Hume himself falls into this group.

3. Once all this has been clarified, the matter seems simple. We can replace the dispute as to whether the principles of ethical knowledge are cognitions or feelings with the question whether feelings are the object of the cognitions that are the principles of ethics. I believe that Hume would have agreed, had he been presented with this precise formulation. He would have consented to modify his thesis to the claim that the principles of ethics are cognitions of feelings. His basic idea, that the emotions are participants, would be preserved, and he would probably have admitted that this was all he had in mind.

But why this lengthy investigation, why this piling up of arguments and counter-arguments, if the whole difference finally turns out to be so insignificant anyway? My answer is that a small error at the beginning leads to a large one at the end. Certainly, we could have avoided the lengthy investigation by immediately drawing the necessary distinction; but the very fact that such a clever thinker as Hume was unable to make it demonstrates that analysis is indispensable here. It is frequently this way, and perhaps particularly with the principal questions of philosophy: once we have the solution, it seems as though we have always had it, and yet its discovery may have been preceded by centuries of confusion, cleared up for the first time by the analysis at hand. The peculiarities of the gift for philosophy are nowhere more clearly to be seen than in the interest which is aroused by elementary analyses such as these.

19. Investigation of the argument that the principles of ethical knowledge cannot be feelings, because what is good and bad must be so for all rational beings

Three arguments were brought against the champions of the emotions.

(*a*) Emotions cannot be principles of knowledge or cognitions, because they are not themselves cognitions—as is required of genuine principles of knowledge.

(*b*) The principles of ethics are a subject of dispute, but there can be no disputes about matters of emotion and taste. These two arguments have been disposed of by means of our compromise: moral principles, we said, are not feelings, but cognitions of feelings. But how about the third argument against emotions as principles?

(*c*) We generally assume that what we hold to be good and bad is so for every rational being of whatever sort, even for God. This claim to universality, which in this instance is equivalent to being obligatory for all kinds of rational beings, seems meaningful only, however, where we are concerned with truths of reason. It is impossible for any being to have a logic different from ours, such that the principle of contradiction or the law of the excluded middle are replaced, in their understanding, by opposite principles. Matters are quite different when it is a question of emotions. What is pleasing or displeasing, beloved or disliked, often depends upon the constitution of the species in question. Different kinds vary greatly in the directions taken by their tastes. Now if the principles of ethics are cognitions of feelings, they are tied up with incidental features of the way in which we happen to be constructed; then how can they claim to be universally obligatory? Yet if they are not, ethics loses its true dignity and authority, especially if we consider that other, more lofty creatures, and perhaps God himself, may approve and disapprove of the opposite principles.

This consideration seems of great weight. How are we to confront it? Is it true that the principles of ethics lose their universal validity if their subject is feelings? Hume himself, the staunchest advocate of the sentimental theory, is no less of this opinion than those who attack him. They see the sacrifice of universal validity as an inevitable consequence. 'Whether the foundations of morality are determined by reason and insight or by emotion and consequently rest entirely upon the particular constitution of the human species, whereas in the first case they would be the same for every rational being, as are all correct judgments about truth and falsehood . . .'* This is how Hume conceives the controversy from the very first.

But is it not also true that, along with its universal validity, the great dignity and authority of ethics is lost, particularly since the possibility is not excluded that God might disapprove of what we approve as morally good, and since there would be as much to be said for this situation as for one in which his judgment and ours coincide? Richard Price, Thomas Reid and Kant are of one mind in this matter, and that was one reason why they rejected any morality based upon the emotions, and rightly so. To be sure, there has been no lack of attempts to reconcile such an origin with the sanctity and dignity of morality.

First attempt. Some rest their claim on the idea that God made us a certain way; because he activates our nature, these ethical laws, which are in accordance with nature, acquire a sort of divine, sanction. Hume, atheist as he was, expressed this sentiment— but not seriously, of course. However, some held this view in earnest, for instance, Adam Smith. In the case of Hume it was a piece of sophistry, but Adam Smith was taken in by a deceptive paralogism.

Certainly it is true that if God exists the constitution of every species, including human beings, is given by him; thus if they depend upon this constitution, moral taste, or the moral judgment, are also determined by him. But what follows from this? Does the fact that God created our characteristics vitiate the previous argument?

(*a*) Someone may say, 'A God-given moral taste is good.' But if there is a God, everything comes from him: illness as well as health, ugliness as well as beauty, blindness as well as insight, stupidity as well as wisdom. And yet they are opposed to one another as evil to good. Or should we agree with those who say that divine providence is not so petty that it concerns itself with everything, but looks only to things in general?—But this is an

* Again, Brentano does not quote precisely, and I have translated Brentano's words. The passage excerpted occurs in op. cit., p. 170, which appears in this chapter, in sect. 15, B, para. 3.

absurd distortion of theism; no sparrow falls from the rooftop, no hair from our head, without God knowing of it and willing it.

(*b*) Someone might remark that moral taste presents a quite special case. If God determines the manner in which we form approvals and disapprovals, he must approve of this manner; therefore our approval is in harmony with his. But then why should we not carry this argument over into the fields of logic and aesthetics? Consider an affected poet: his taste is given him by God, therefore it is in agreement with the divine taste; therefore we are to conclude that he is a divine poet. But our critical tastes, which condemn his, arise ultimately from the same source. How can two contradictory judgments be in agreement with one and the same judgment? Or suppose someone makes an incorrect inference or becomes a victim of sophistical reasoning, so that he asserts what our insight tells us is nonsense? He, too, is judging in the way that he must under the particular circumstances, given his constitution. If we are to draw this conclusion in the first case, then we must draw it here as well: we must conclude that God even approves of contradictions and absurdities. But no one ever dreams of drawing such a conclusion.

We can see what a distortion is involved in inferring from the fact that our moral taste depends upon our constitution, which springs from God, that what God approves always agrees with what we approve. What pleases us may well displease God.

(*c*) Some may say that at least one thing is sure in any case: if God gives us our taste, he must make it suitable for us, and consequently he must counsel us to be led by it. But this, too, misses the point. There are natural instincts that drive their bearers on to ruin: among some species of animals, the male dies in the act of procreation, and among others the female is eaten by her offspring. It may be true, as Darwin says, that instincts serve the best interests of the species, but not those of the individual. And not even the former claim is universally true.

(*d*) Very well, some may say: even if God has not arranged everything for the good of the individual or the species, he has at least ordered the universe as a whole for the best. But if God exists, this applies equally to all things: not only to knowledge but also to error, to crime as well as to virtue. Thus if it is only its participation in the divine world order that sanctions our moral taste, it is in no better a position than delight taken in what is harmful. God may have arranged the whole with divine wisdom, but our taste could nevertheless be utterly perverse, taken in itself. We should also mention another point. Although we may be motivated by an internal feeling of moral approval to do some things and not others, we feel at the same time other drives which resist this feeling. They, too, come from God, as does everything in the universe. They are so powerful that we measure our moral strength by the degree of resistance we are able to maintain against them. A victory over them is considered heroic and, under certain circumstances, even superhuman ($\mu\epsilon\tilde{\iota}\zeta o\nu$ $\dot{\eta}$ $\kappa\alpha\tau'$ $\check{\alpha}\nu\delta\rho\omega\pi o\nu$) and commands the greatest admiration. All attempts to justify our moral principles by means of recourse to their divine origin must similarly fail, for they rest upon circular reasoning. We have no immediate experience of God; we conclude that he exists from his works and attribute perfection to him, which includes moral perfection. In order to do this we must already have a concept of moral goodness and already have acquired insight into the principles of morals independently of the idea of God. It will not do for us to place trust in God's goodness that what we find good really is good, on the one hand, and to attribute goodness to God on the basis of what we find good, on the other.

Thus the first attempt has failed. It is impossible to deduce divine authority for our moral principles from the fact that we are a part of what God has created.

A second attempt views the universality of our moral taste among men as the source of its authority and universally binding force. Humanity, the '*grand être*' of Comte, replaces God as the authority, as being in some sense infinite compared to the individual.

But this attempt, too, is fruitless.

(*a*) To begin with, is there in fact universal agreement among men concerning their moral taste? It would be rather remarkable, as differences in taste are quite conspicuous with respect to other matters. In truth, complete accord is lacking here, too, for some are quite sensitive, while others are less so. Even direct contradictions occur. Relativists point to them as a proof that there are no universal ethical principles. Among the Arabs, the kin are expected to avenge the murder of a relation with blood. He who does not carry out the precept of paying for blood with blood is considered morally despicable. Buddhists and Christians forbid revenge and hold it proper to repay hate with love. Certain primitive tribes consider it the duty of the children to kill their aged and feeble parents, whereas our peasants reserve a place for them and follow benevolent rules and customs concerning the proper manner of treatment of the elderly who are no longer capable of working. As for the relation to one's own people and the state, some people approve of everything that is useful to these, while others place the interests of larger communities above theirs and demand that the smaller ones sacrifice their independence and commit suicide, as it were. Some abhor all lies, while others praise as staunch patriots those who know how to lie successfully in the interests of their party or country. Some hold that it is wanton to kill any animal, while others approve of dissecting living animals. Some condemn suicide as a cowardly flight from life, while others praise it as heroic. Some scorn every war as being mass murder; others consider it the highest blossoming of masculine virtue and, far from considering eternal peace an ideal state of affairs, condemn it as enervating and as leading to decay.

Thus there is no more harmony among men about moral tastes than about other tastes. The influence of habit is particularly powerful in this matter and produces very great differences with respect to pleasure and pain.

(*b*) But let us set all this aside and suppose, for the moment, that the universality of moral taste among men is more certain than these examples would suggest. Would such universality be sufficient to give moral taste a kind of sanction that the particular taste of an individual fails to lend it? What would be the actual ground of such a sanction? Apparently the fact that a large number of people share the same taste is felt to offer some guarantee that it is the correct taste. But if so, it would surely make a very great difference whether this generally accepted taste were confined to mankind or were extended to all rational beings. What if another group of rational beings does not share our ethical taste, and the species that disagrees with us so outnumbers us that the whole of mankind taken together stands to it as a single man to the entire human race: how would our moral taste appear then? Clearly, the obligating force of our moral principles, and with it the whole of morality, would be badly shaken if the opinion of the majority were the sole criterion for correct moral taste.

20. *Attempts to establish the agreement of all rational beings about moral taste as probable or even certain*

I. Some thinkers have attempted to show that the human race must eventually reach complete accord with respect to moral tastes—indeed, that not only all rational inhabitants of the earth but all rational citizens of the universe must reach such accord.

1. They admit that at present accord does not reign even among men, but they claim this state of affairs will change over the course of history, that it must change, according to natural law, in the direction of increasing assimilation. Men are approaching closer and closer to a state in which they are pleased solely by what furthers the collective good. In the course of evolution moral approbation comes to be given to what is truly general, and this unanimous taste, because of its generality, is ideal and correct.

2. Why should tastes that initially take such opposing directions eventually come into harmony? Two main reasons are given.

(*a*) Because of the law that men eventually come to desire the means independently of the end. Each person discovers that what is useful for all also serves the individual best and cherishes it, to begin with, as a means to his own good, but eventually he comes to love it without regard to his own advantage, in accordance with this law.

(*b*) The struggle for existence also co-operates in this harmonization. He who fails to respect life and property is hanged; he who proves himself useful to the whole gets ahead. Thus opponents disappear in time, and only those who make themselves amenable to the more progressive taste survive, just as the harmful species disappear more and more from the animal world while the useful species multiply without restriction. In other words, the struggle for existence in human society breeds the utilitarian disposition.

3. Assuming all this is true, it appears justifiable to draw the conclusion that other species must also eventually form the same taste as the inhabitants of earth, for:

(*a*) the law of causality is universally valid,

(*b*) the world is constructed throughout of the same basic elements, as spectrum analysis has shown, and

(*c*) the struggle for existence belongs to the general laws of all species.

Thus there must be a universal ethics, just as there is a universal science of physics that applies to all physical bodies (cf. Note 34). And along with astrophysics, there must be astroethics (Gizizky).

II. Doubts about the attempt to make the existence of universal agreement in moral taste appear probable.

Can we really expect, with certainty or with probability, that the taste of the human race will develop constantly in the direction of the utilitarian goal? Both inductive and deductive arguments have been given for this view.

1. Let us consider first the inductive proof. It rests upon the testimony of history, which supposedly displays a constant progression in this direction. Is this true? At present, certainly, the goal has not been reached, and that makes it questionable whether we may justly conclude that the goal ever will be reached, even if a movement in that direction is discernible. The evolution might be arrested at a certain distance from its goal; perhaps the acceleration of the process decreases constantly, so that it can never progress beyond a certain boundary. But suppose a state in which all tastes were the same were finally attained: would that necessarily be the end of the process? Further developments might take place. Many people whom we revere for their moral rectitude are not utilitarians. They consider a world of happy nobodies to be less valuable than one in which there are many stupid people who suffer but also a few select people who are moral heroes or geniuses of scientific research or artistic creativity. The resolving of humanistic ideals into nationalist ideals that Grillparzer forecast was considered by him to be a step backwards; he clearly felt no taste for the proclamation of the well-being of one's own nation as the highest moral goal. The regression might go still further: egoism might become, once again, the sacred principle of private morality. Perhaps a change in the evolution of moral taste takes place from time to time, just as it does in aesthetic tastes.

2. Thus the inductive argument, based upon the evidence of history, is not decisive. Let us turn to the deductive argument.

(a) The psychological law concerning the love of the means does not give sufficient proof that all men will eventually be united through a love of the general good because each has come to find it desirable as a means to his own interests. After all, not everyone becomes a miser, even though we all learn to value the worth that money has as a means to an end.

(*b*) The struggle for existence does not tend to have an equalizing effect in other respects. Quite the contrary, it generally makes differences still greater. Ought it to lead to similarity in this instance? It is more apt to breed differences if, on the one side, honour has the advantage while on the other knavery has it. The saying that honesty will win out in the end is more a pious dream than a truth in politics and social life in general. For the survival of the individual as such it seems more advantageous never to allow the disposition to sacrifice oneself in the service of another to blossom, rather than to cultivate it. In any case it is an exaggeration to say that the gallows serve the function of weeding out, for the saying goes that petty rascals are hanged while the big ones run free.

3. But suppose it were an established fact that all men are striving for the collective good with increasing harmony. Would this give us a right to suppose the same process is taking place among other species and to expect there could be a science of astroethics? It is far from clear that such a generalization is permissible.

ad 1. The inductive arguments become weaker and weaker the further we get from the field of experience, as is demonstrated by physics. If a law is established for the transmission of sound through the air, we cannot simply assume that it will hold true for other media, such as water. It depends upon the circumstances. If we presume to apply what we learn from our own species to species of rational beings with whom we are entirely unfamiliar, the inductive arguments are reduced to mere vague analogies.

ad 2. Thus we can only seek refuge in the deductive arguments, which we already found deficient when we applied them to the field of our experience. But it is clear that they offer no security.

(*a*) That the law of causality applies equally to all spheres favours in no wise the assumption of a universal moral taste; indeed, it is consonant with the existence of endless variations upon earth.

(*b*) The uniformity of the elements proves just as little. All animals are constructed out of the same chemical materials: yet how different is their taste with respect to food, and how greatly their dispositions vary in other respects!

(*c*) The psychological law concerning the love of the means is related to human weakness and would consequently prove less forceful among creatures of superior rationality. But even if it did apply here and there, it would offer no guarantee that all moral tastes would eventually harmonize.

It is common for moral philosophers of the historical school to make the mistake of taking a general movement that is clearly headed in one direction to be aimed at a goal worth seeking. Think of how, in two countries with opposing interests, public opinion is drilled for years into favouring war. The opinion eventually becomes general within each country, and yet each believes that the aims of the other are evil.

III. We are still occupied with the attempt to defend the sentimental theory against the accusation that it does not adequately fulfil the demand that the ethical law bind all rational beings. Two lines of defence were presented.

The first attempt points to our divine creator. What he creates, it runs, is necessarily good, and since, in particular, he is the originator of our moral taste, it must accord with what he approves of himself. But both these points proved to be sophisms. The argument is also question begging, for in order to declare that God is a good principle we must already know what is good.

The second attempt places the sanction of our moral taste in its universality among the human species. By analogy, it is said, we can assume its existence among all conceivable types of rational beings. A variety of attempts have been made to prove this universality, all of them unsatisfactory. The arguments turned out to be defective in every point. Let us take up the problem once again, viewing it in an entirely different manner. The entire attempt to ground the sanction of moral taste upon its being universally disseminated failed from the first, and would have failed even if we could be sure that moral taste is in fact universally accepted, for it suffers from a gross equivocation.

1. The opponents of the sentimental theory claimed that it failed to account for the universal validity of the moral law, but the arguments mentioned were attempts to establish its *de facto* universal acceptance, which is an entirely different matter. A principle can be universally valid without being universally accepted; every evident judgment is universally valid even if only a single person makes it and all others fail to have the insight. Each such judgment is valid for the whole universe just as surely as it is valid for the individual. There is only one truth for everyone. It would be absurd if I could discern a judgment and someone else

could discern its contradictory. One and the same judgment cannot be true for one person and erroneous for another; if true, it can at the most be incorrectly held to be false.

On the other hand, some opinions are universally held, at least temporarily, and are none the less false; therefore they are not correct and valid for everyone, but rather for no one at all. Just think of the initial trust we place in external perception. We take all sensible appearances to be real, but it turns out afterwards that nothing really existing is fashioned like the objects that sense perception simulates for us.

Certainly, universal acceptance can in some cases serve as an index of validity and correctness; for instance, when all the occupants of a street in which a murder was committed agree as to who the murderer was. But in other cases it is not, and under certain circumstances one solitary man may have the truth, in opposition to all others. It never occurs to any reasonable person to establish the truth of facts or of theories by taking a vote.

Now how do things stand with the universality—real or supposed—of moral taste? Clearly, universal acceptance as such gives no guarantee of intrinsic superiority, any more than it makes the proof of a mathematical law superfluous. Indeed, if moral sentiment were based upon feelings or the knowledge of feelings it would be doubtful whether we could speak of its having an intrinsic advantage over other conceivable tastes—a point much emphasized by the opponents of the sentimental theory. After all, if someone prefers sour things to sweet we do not say that the one taste is intrinsically superior to the other, or that one is justified and the other not.

2. Some thinkers, perplexed by such difficulties, wish to give the inquiry an entirely new turn. They say we cannot demand that the moral law be accepted as widely as required here; we cannot demand validity for all times and places. It suffices for the individual if within his society harmony reigns among everyone's feelings of approbation. From that he can tell what is right for the present time.

I would scarcely consider this doctrine worthy of mention, were it not so widely held. Many think it the greatest wisdom to accommodate themselves to the *status quo*, believing that the whole of history has shown a belief in the constancy of ethical convictions to be historically unsound. But if, as we have demon-

strated, not even the agreement of every age can suffice to conse-
crate so-called moral taste and save its dignity, what are we to say
of this new limitation? It is almost inconceivable how anyone
should have chanced to hit upon such a belief. Adaptation, as
such, far from sanctioning our moral feelings, seems more likely
to degrade them altogether. If I am capable of making judgments
myself, why should I be impressed by the fact that a certain opinion is widely held at the present? If, without degradation, I
permit myself to judge differently, why should it lower me to feel
differently from the others? Is there something intrinsically valuable in adapting oneself to other people? Of course, he who conforms will not give offence; if Socrates had been adaptable he
would not have drunk the hemlock. But here we are not concerned with such advantages. It is Socrates as not conforming
whom we honour as morally elevated and whose ethical sentiments and judgments we respect as being superior and most
noble. Thus those who advocate this view are only passing judgment upon themselves. They demand that we judge each person
in view of the ethical feelings and judgments of his contemporaries
and that we think and form judgments in harmony with them;
yet they themselves oppose the generally held opinion and feeling.
For now, as always, people do not feel and judge differently in
considering the far-distant past than in judging the present. They
will simply be more indulgent towards an action which is not in
accordance with our present feelings of moral approbation if it
was performed during a stage of development that has long since
been outgrown.

3. Hence the advocates of this doctrine are forced to make a new
modification, intended to get around this flaw. We cannot, they
say, disregard moral progress and focus our gaze too narrowly
upon the present; we must also consider what is apparently to be
the general moral feeling for the immediate future. We frequently
recognize in which direction the present is heading and also, consequently, which forms of feeling and willing will predominate in
the immediate future. Such a position may do more justice to the
case of Socrates. He can be recognized, and honoured, as a man
who had progressed somewhat further along the path that his
contemporaries had just begun to take.

But how am I to know what the general feeling will be, and
what sort of a criterion should I employ in taking a position with

regard to such predictions? Until they have been fulfilled, how can I know, or even know to be probable, that something will make its appearance that has never before occurred in history? Even the period of conformity will pass away, and what will take its place? A strange doctrine! According to it, our moral position should be like our behaviour at the stock exchange, where the players must act in accordance, not with how the stocks stand now, but how they will stand later. In playing the market, however, we are justified in considering the future inasmuch as we can get rid of our stocks at the proper time and, indeed, intend to do so. Is similar behaviour appropriate in moral matters? If so, of course, only in those cases in which I can hope to see the day when I can with advantage renounce those of my ethical feelings that have progressed beyond present tastes. According to this view, however, figures such as Socrates are still to be condemned, despite the immediately following victory of a feeling favourable to them. No such morality—if such blatant degradation deserves the name—can be approved of by a worthy man, today any more than yesterday, and this will always be true. Only subservient minds can take pleasure in it.

If we wish to avoid such erroneous paths, we must, it would appear, take back the confession that we were disposed to make to Hume. It looks as though the first ethical principles must be established completely independently of feelings, as though moral law must be purely a matter of knowledge gained by perception and understanding. But how can knowledge alone establish such principles? Hume was convinced that it could not in any way, either *a priori* or *a posteriori*. And as for establishing the examples by means of experience, my investigation leaves no doubt, unless feelings can be brought in in the manner indicated previously.

It appeared to be impossible to establish them *a priori*, too, but here there might be a cause for hesitation, especially since *a priori* knowledge became the object of a new sort of discussion after Hume. Let us turn once again to this possibility. Since at least one point has become clear from our inquiry—that the principles of ethics are cognitions and not feelings—the only possible remaining decision is whether they are established *a priori* or by experience. Thus we wish to take up once again the inquiry into whether morality can be grounded upon principles of the understanding.

IV

Are the Epistemological Principles Underlying Ethics Synthetic a priori *Cognitions?*

---

21. Explication of the concept of a synthetic a priori *cognition*

1. Our investigation has established that the principles of ethical knowledge are not feelings, whatever they may be. Indeed, it began to seem that they must be entirely independent of the emotions if they are to be universally valid. On the other hand, it looked as though Hume had demonstrated quite adequately that the principles of ethics cannot be found in experience. He examined the realm of experience with great care, but he was not so thorough in his inspection of *a priori* cognitions. In opposing Clarke, he attempted to show in detail that there are no analytic judgments which could offer a suitable basis for ethics. But here his investigation ended. Like most thinkers before him, he believed that all *a priori* cognitions were analytic. Not until after his time did the doctrine that there are synthetic *a priori* cognitions find numerous and well-known supporters. Here, apparently, lies our greatest hope of finding the foundation we are seeking.

2. As a matter of fact, many significant moral philosophers have held the principles of morals to be synthetic *a priori* cognitions. The name did not come into being until after Hume; it stems from Kant. But long before Kant, Cicero acknowledged essentially the same variety of principles, which he held to be implanted by nature. In modern times, many Cartesians have held the doctrine (cf. Arnauld). Locke appears to have such principles in mind in his polemic against innate principles of morality. Among English thinkers, Ralph Cudworth (1617–88) held that prior to all

action certain moral truths are to be found in the mind, anticipating morality and springing forth from a vital principle found in intellectual beings in virtue of which they are naturally determined to do some things and avoid doing others.

Wollaston's principle of honesty (see Part I, chap. 2, sect. 12) is also synthetic and would be a synthetic *a priori* cognition if it were really self-evident. After, and in reaction to, Hume, the advocates of the synthetic *a priori* as the basis of ethics became more numerous. To name just a few of the more famous, they include Bishop Butler (1692–1752); Thomas Reid (1710–96), whom we have already mentioned, and many of his followers; and, in Germany, Kant and his many followers.

3. To begin with, we must clarify the concept of synthetic *a priori* cognitions. A cognition is a judgment. Although it may seem superfluous, let us begin by determining the concept of a judgment.*

A judgment occurs where there is truth in the sense of correctness, or falsehood in the sense of error. In every judgment, something is either recognized as existing or rejected as not existing.

A cognition is a sure judgment, an insight—expressions which admittedly can only be comprehended by those who have experienced within themselves the peculiar characteristics of judgments possessing certainty.

In order to provide clarification and to avoid a confusion that is sometimes made, let us note that every cognition is a true judgment, but not every true judgment a cognition. A cognition is not a judgment that is certain in the sense of being subjectively convincing. There are judgments that are formed without admission of a single doubt but which turn out to be erroneous after all. But cognitions are judgment seen to be, discerned as, correct.

Analytic and synthetic judgments. These terms come from Kant. By means of them he hoped to give an exhaustive classification of all judgments. He explained them as follows. An affirmative judgment is analytic if the predicate is included in the concept of the subject, a negative judgment analytic if the predicate affirms the

* For a more complete exposition of Brentano's views on judgments, see his *Psychology from an Empirical Standpoint*, Book II, chap. 7. A translation of this chapter appears in *Realism and the Background of Phenomenology*, ed. R. M. Chisholm (Free Press, 1960), pp. 62–75.

contradictory of something included in the concept of the subject. An affirmative judgment is synthetic if the predicate is not included in the concept of the subject but introduces a new element; a negative judgment is synthetic if the predicate does not express or include the contradictory of something included in the concept of the subject.

These are Kant's stipulations, but developed somewhat further, for as regards the negative judgment he contented himself with indicating briefly the oppositional character of the predicate.

He said that analytic judgments are only explicative and do not contain any genuine addition to knowledge; but synthetic judgments expand our knowledge.

However, these explanations do not quite accord with what Kant has in mind when he speaks of analytic and synthetic judgments. They do not suffice for his real purpose. A few brief remarks will fully illuminate this point. Kant distinguishes between categorical, hypothetical, and disjunctive judgments. A connection between the subject and the predicate exists only in the first sort; in hypothetical judgments there is, rather, a connection between the premise and the conclusion, and in disjunctive there are several elements, all having the same status. If we direct our attention to the definitions just given of an analytic and a synthetic judgment, we see that they refer to subjects and predicates. Thus they are suited to the first class that he distinguishes, but they are clearly not applicable to hypothetical and disjunctive judgments, which he co-ordinates with categorical judgments.

Furthermore, there are assertions that are neither hypothetical nor disjunctive and which also do not contain any connection between a subject and a predicate, viz. the so-called existential propositions already touched upon by Kant and before him by Hume. But even today little attention is paid to them by logicians, who none the less could learn a great deal by studying them. Examples of such propositions are: 'There is a tree'; 'There is a flash of lightning'; 'There is a shortage of money.' We know that Kant believed he could count existential propositions as synthetic judgments. Just as the concept of the predicate is synthetically added to the concept of the subject in categorical judgments, the object is synthetically added to our concepts in existential judgments.

But that is clearly impossible. How can I bring something that is outside my mind together with one of my concepts in the same way in which, in other cases, I add one of my concepts to another? And is an existential judgment not also capable of being false? But how, if no objects exist? How can I couple it together with my concept? And what about negative existential propositions? 'There is no temperature of one million degrees Fahrenheit'; 'There is no such thing as a griffin'; 'There are no unicorns.' Kant would say that these propositions, too, are synthetic. But can this be generalized? Take, 'There are no four-cornered triangles.' I think we would have a tendency to pronounce this proposition analytic, just as is 'No triangle has four corners.' The same is true of, 'If something is triangular, it is not rectangular,' and 'Any given object is either not triangular or not rectangular.'[10]

Thus, if the grouping of assertions into analytic and synthetic is to be exhaustive, as Kant wished it to be, we must formulate the definitions somewhat differently from the way he did, as follows. A negative judgment is analytic if it denies something containing incompatible determinations; an affirmative judgment is analytic if it is equivalent to a negative judgment of this sort. (Kant himself states that the law of contradiction is the principle of all analytic judgments.) A synthetic judgment is one of which neither of these is the case. (I chose to speak of incompatibility rather than contradiction because positive antitheses are to be rejected as impossible, along with contradictions.)

We can now understand the difference between the conceptions of *a priori* cognitions prevalent before and after Hume. Before him, they were confined within the limits corresponding to our definition, but afterwards people did not keep them strictly within these bounds. But we can also understand the special case at hand. When Hume criticized Clarke and other thinkers, he thought of them as wishing to build upon principles that they believed to be denials of a contradiction, or else equivalent to such denials; but others, such as Butler, Reid and Kant, had in mind principles of which this is not the case and which are nevertheless confirmed independently of experience. It is with such principles that we must occupy ourselves.

[10] To put it more clearly, 'A given object is triangular and therefore it is not rectangular.'

22. *Two kinds of moral philosophers who wish to make synthetic* a priori *cognitions the foundation of ethics*

There is one striking difference to be found among the thinkers who claim that ethical knowledge rests on *a priori* principles: one group posits many such principles, the other a single one. The first group includes Cicero, the Cartesians, Cudworth, and the Scottish philosophers, while the second includes Wollaston and Kant.

1. Criticism of the first group. If such principles are discernible *a priori*, they must be absolutely valid, without exception. But if there are many of them it may come about that one conflicts with another in some given case. How are we to decide between them? If they are of equal status, then the answer must be at the same time both right and wrong inasmuch as it accords with the one and conflicts with the other. But if the principles are ranked, the highest one must be absolutely binding and, consequently, the only one that deserved to be called a principle. No one has set up any such order of precedence, and it would be better to establish only one principle, as Kant and Wollaston intended; indeed, this would be the only correct move.

2. Criticism of the second group. We already established that Wollaston's doctrine, like Kant's, suffers from two defects, each of which appears quite devastating, even without the other. The first is that the principle he proposes is not evident, the second, that we cannot deduce ethical precepts from it with certainty. Thus the principles which these philosophers place at the summit do not fulfil their task. May we hope to find another synthetic *a priori* insight suitable as a basis for ethics? I can predict that such hopes would prove idle. An argument that we used against Kant's categorical imperative comes into play once more: it could not have remained undiscovered so long, although it might have been left to Kant to clarify its characteristics as a synthetic *a priori* principle. But as only the name is new, and investigators of note have looked around carefully for what is, in essence, a synthetic *a priori* principle pertaining to the field of ethics, they must long since have established both the existence of a synthetic *a priori* cognition of this kind and its contents, were there any such thing.

PART ONE: THE PRINCIPLES OF ETHICAL KNOWLEDGE

23. *There are no synthetic* a priori *cognitions within the realm of our knowledge*

Furthermore, we may take it as established that synthetic *a priori* principles exist neither within the realm of ethics nor anywhere else within the sphere of our knowledge.

1. In order to convince ourselves of this fact, let us call before our minds the characteristics a synthetic *a priori* cognition would have to have. It would have to be more than a confident assumption which we feel compelled to believe even though it is not backed up by experience. An assumption that is a consequence of blind impulse is not a cognition, for it is not evident. The impulse as such does not justify the assumption before the tribunal of logic. On these grounds many people have rejected out of hand the possibility of synthetic *a priori* knowledge, declaring it to be discernible from the concepts involved that a proposition which contradicts itself is to be rejected. Analytic cognitions, they say, are merely explicative judgments, but synthetic judgments, inasmuch as they genuinely expand our knowledge, can never be certified by the concepts, for they go beyond them. But this pronouncement, if it be made straight from the first, seems to me self-contradictory. It is synthetic and would have to be *a priori* if it were intrinsically justified, but it is not. The following consideration will serve to illustrate this point. According to the views of most theists, God is a being necessary through himself. Philosophers, with but a few exceptions, do not admit the possibility of absolute chance; they teach that everything which is is necessary, whether it is unmediated or caused. Supposing that a being with a sufficiently capable understanding found himself in possession of an adequate idea of God, he would discern immediately from this idea that its object exists. Should we call his judgment that God exists analytic? By no means, for it is neither a denial of something incompatible nor an affirmative equivalent of such a denial. Therefore it could only be a synthetic *a priori* cognition, a fact many thinkers have overlooked. They—and most particularly Descartes—believed that we could derive the existence of God analytically from our idea of him by means of the so-called ontological argument, which runs as follows. God is, by definition, an eternal and intrinsically necessary being. What is clearly and distinctly contained in the concept of an object can with certainty

72

be attributed to that object. Now the concept of God includes eternal, necessary existence and perfection. Therefore God exists. But this argument overlooks the ambiguity of the word 'is'. The proposition, 'A is A', does not mean, 'There exists an A which is A'; it simply denies that there exists any A which is not A. Again, the statement, 'A triangle has three sides,' means simply that there can be no triangle that does not have three sides. The function of 'is' is not the same here as in sentences such as 'A tree is green', which certainly asserts the existence of a tree. It is the same with the instance in question: the *a priori* discernible proposition, 'God is something that exists necessarily', does not assert that there is such a being as God, but that God cannot exist unless he be a necessarily existing being. If the proposition were discernible in a positive form, it would be a synthetic *a priori* cognition. The same objection applies to all those who do not believe in God, yet hold that the existence of the world is not a mere coincidence. They claim that atoms are intrinsically necessary things, which is as much as to admit that anyone who had at his disposal the requisite mental powers and an adequate idea of atoms would discern their existence by means of a synthetic *a priori* judgment.

2. Thus we may not go so far as to hold synthetic *a priori* cognitions in general to be impossible. But certainly, we do not possess many. No one has ever found one, not even Kant. The very way he expresses himself bears testimony to this fact, for after he thinks he has established that certain propositions are of this kind he poses the question, 'How are synthetic *a priori* cognitions possible?' Indeed, this question is the basic problem of his famous *Critique of Pure Reason*. What is the point of this question? In what sense is it intended?

(*a*) Does Kant perhaps wish to know what the nature of a being would have to be in order for him to have cognitions of this sort? If this were the import of his question, Kant would be asking after something which eternally escapes our knowledge. Or is it not obvious that in this sense we cannot even account for analytic *a priori* cognitions? Do we then truly have insight into the nature of beings that are capable of judging, thinking, willing, and other psychic activities? Suppose that what we are speaking of is an occurrence in the brain; are we sufficiently acquainted with its inner nature to be able to say how it is possible for such a being to have sensations, feel pleasure or displeasure, and form judgments

—analytic judgments in particular? No, and here we shall stand before a secret into all eternity, for we know no being in such a way that we can derive his activities from his nature. We are incapable of doing this for even the simplest mechanical occurrences; we cannot do it for gravitation, or even for movements caused by pushing or pulling. If Kant had intended the question in this way, he might just as well have asked it respecting analytic cognitions, which he did not. In either case it would have been an unreasonable question.

(b) But what, then, is the sense of Kant's question: what made him pose it? Clearly he detects in synthetic *a priori* cognitions a paradox, a puzzle, that he does not find in those that are analytic. The latter appear to him to be justified in themselves and to be perfectly clear and intrinsically comprehensible. But this is not true of synthetic judgments, for it is not evident that they are universally and necessarily true. The only reason for assigning to them the same stature as analytic judgments, which are immediately discernible, would be that a natural impulse makes them immediately convincing and that consequent experiences are in accord with them. Thus the heart of the question is this: How does it happen that I trust with such certainty while having no genuine insight? The conviction, no matter how strong, is not logically justified. How does it happen that experiences do not immediately contradict such preconceived convictions?

Now if, indeed, it was this circumstance—that experience does not immediately contradict these convictions, even though they are not logically justified—that led Kant to put his question, then it was occasioned by their lack of evidence. The impulse to agree with these propositions may be implanted by nature and be invincible in a way which only the clearest insights are otherwise, but the insight is lacking—which is as much as to say that they cannot be instances of genuine cognitions. In the very framing of the fundamental question of his *Critique*, Kant testifies that we do not in truth possess any cognitions that are synthetic and *a priori*.

(c) The fact of the matter is that, of the propositions he cites as being synthetic *a priori* cognitions, all those which are really synthetic are not evident, while all that are are so only because they are analytic cognitions. To be sure, Kant fails to recognize their analytic character because he does not succeed in analysing them correctly, and this clouds his insight into the justification of these judgments.

Mathematical axioms are an example of this latter sort of cognition. They are evident; even Hume, sceptical as he is, thought so, but he held them to be analytic, and rightly so. Or is the proposition, 2 + 1 = 3, not analytic? Is the relation of equality not given with the fundamental elements, 2 + 1 and 3, inasmuch as both are the same as 1 + 1 + 1? And does it not follow, therefore, that the concept of a 2 + 1 and a 3 that are not equal to each other is self-contradictory? Clearly it is. If Kant failed to make this simple analysis, it can only have happened as a result of the faultiness of his definitions of analytic and synthetic judgments, which we touched upon previously. He always looked for the predicate in the concept of the subject, and if he failed to find it he declared the judgment in question to be synthetic. In the proposition, '2 is less than 3', the predicate is not included in the concept of the subject; nevertheless, it is analytic, for this relation between their sizes is clearly to be seen in the concepts of 2 and 3.

Thus mathematical axioms are evident but not synthetic. However, the other examples that Kant presents are synthetic but not immediately evident. Take the proposition, 'Every change presupposes something permanent.' It may be true, but it is so little evident that even today many people believe the contrary, and their view is certainly not downright absurd. Another example of this sort is the proposition with which we already most particularly occupied ourselves, the categorical imperative. Kant says that reason presents it as legislation: *sic volo sic jubeo*. [Inasmuch as I will it, I command it.] But many have responded quite correctly that he might have added: *sit pro ratione voluntas* [if my will is rational]. The proposition cannot in fact be clearly discerned, for it is not analytic. Thus if our reason were really impelled towards immediate agreement, this demand, arising from the nature of our reason, would be no less than a rational demand.

The result: there are no synthetic *a priori* cognitions. Therefore ethics is not to be based upon them.

24. *The attempt to establish a relation between Kant's doctrine of synthetic* a priori *cognitions and Darwin's law of hereditary transmission*

The examination of the doctrine of synthetic *a priori* cognitions is of particular significance in our time. Kant is held in great esteem, and so, consequently, are his teachings. He has followers even in circles where one would least expect it: among scientists working in distinctly empirical subjects. Of course, these men generally modify the theories they accept from him in such a way that they conform completely to the views that they have attained by other means; they simply admire Kant because he closely anticipated these views. But even the anticipation appears to them to be a great achievement.

The same phenomenon is to be found in the attempt to be discussed here. The thinkers in question relate the doctrine of the synthetic *a priori* to one of the cornerstones of the Darwinian hypothesis, the law of hereditary transmission. They claim that, as a consequence of their heredity, men born today possess a stock of synthetic knowledge quite independent of their own experience, i.e. synthetic *a priori* cognitions. And, they say, we not only inherit *a priori* cognitions but also ideas (concepts)—just as Kant assumed we have ideas which are not derived from our experience.

It is worthwhile lingering at this point to demonstrate, first, that this doctrine of hereditary transmission of ideas is false and, second, that this supposed modification of Kant's teaching is utterly unrelated to it.

According to this doctrine of heredity it is supposed to be possible to contemplate concepts which we could not in any way put together from our own experience, either as wholes or in separate parts, for the experiences of our ancestors can replace our personal experience as a source of concepts.

But this hypothesis is purely fictitious. Not a single concept is to be discovered which is not made up of elements with a perceptual basis in our own experience. We possess none without abstraction that we ourselves have undertaken. If we were able to operate with elementary concepts not culled from any perception, it would be incomprehensible that, e.g., a person born blind never grasps the concept of colour. But quite aside from the fact that this theory of heredity is untenable, it is not related in any but a superficial manner with Kant's theory. For he teaches that there are concepts which are not given in any experience and cannot be culled from any experience, e.g. the concept of causality.

We might try giving the theory of heredity a somewhat different cast by claiming that we inherit, not ready-made concepts and cognitions, but ready-made dispositions.

Clearly these must be immediate cognitions that would not be directly discerned if they were not inherited from our ancestors; otherwise the hypotheses would be quite vacuous. And they also must be such that an immediate knowledge of them would not be impossible as such without heredity, for otherwise no one would have been able to attain them earlier and pass them on to us.

But in that case, they once again lose all connection with Kant and lead, furthermore, to the complicated question of how we are to conceive of hereditary knowledge.

We can recall to consciousness knowledge which we have acquired during our lifetime in one of three ways.

(1) We re-establish the basis for it; or

(2) we at least have a clear recollection of having discerned, at an earlier time, grounds for holding it and cherish a reasonable conviction that our judgment is true, even if we do not at present review its basis; or

(3) we no longer recall the foundation, but our earlier knowledge inclines us to agree with it, just as dispositions to perform similar acts are built up by habit. We form judgments out of force of habit.

To which of these would a conviction which we have a hereditary disposition to hold be analogous? Not the first, or the second, but the third. But that is as much as to say that it is not a question of cognition. In just the same way, with an equally strong impulse, we could hold what is false to be an *a priori* truth, as well as what is true; we could claim, e.g., that ghosts exist. And that even this third case does not occur is to be seen from the fact that not even associations are hereditary. The Chinese have ancestors who have spoken the same language for thousands of years, generation after generation, but each descendant has to learn it from scratch.

Just as surely as there are no synthetic *a priori* cognitions, so surely is it impossible for the principles of ethical knowledge to be counted among them.

V

The Concept of the Right End

---

25. *Definitions of ethics that do not agree with ours*

1. What strange results! The examination which Hume inspired us to take up has come full circle, and ethics has returned to the same position in which it was before he made his attack. For a while we were inclined, with Hume, to consider feelings the principles of ethical knowledge. Then this theory showed itself to be clearly impossible, for only cognitions can be the principles of cognitions. Indeed, we found some yet more important reasons why the emotions cannot play any role in the establishment of ethical principles. We still hoped to find these principles in that realm of knowledge which was unknown to Hume but became an object of intense investigation after his time: the realm of the synthetic *a priori*. But behold! It turns out that this entire region is a mythical land quite unknown to geography. There is nothing of this sort to be found in the entire realm of human knowledge.

Thus we are back with our old hypothesis: the only remaining possibility is what seemed most likely in the first place. The principles of ethical knowledge must be either experiences or analytic *a priori* cognitions. No other kinds of principles exist in ethics or in any other body of knowledge. But for precisely that reason the possibilities are boundless, and we still lack any indication that some particular concept or fact is the starting-point of ethical proofs. Hence we must start from the very beginning in a different manner and determine how we are to find the point at which ethical investigations are to begin.

But where should we find this information, if not in the definition of ethics itself? It certainly tells us the difference between ethical cognitions and other kinds of cognitions. How did we define ethics? We said it was the practical discipline which teaches us about the highest end and the choice of means for attaining it.

Clearly, the former task must be performed first. Ethics must first determine which ends are rightly to be striven for as the highest ones. Whereas other practical disciplines only tell the right means to any given end, ethics is primarily concerned with telling which ends are right and which not. But if establishing the right end is the main task of ethics, it must begin with an explanation of the concept of the right end. After all, ever since the time of Aristotle logic has demanded that every science begin by giving a definition of its object, at any rate in so far as the concept is not clear and comprehensible without further explanation.

Such a definition is precisely what we appear to lack with respect to ethics. Everyone understands what is meant by 'the correct means', viz. the means which, when utilized, actually lead to the end in question. But what is meant by 'the right end?'

2. However, before I commence upon an investigation of this question, I wish to disclose the fact that not everyone defines ethics as I have. Ours is no doubt the original definition; it is essentially the same as the one given by Aristotle in the *Nicomachean Ethics*, and it reappears in similar dress fairly often during the history of philosophy. Nevertheless, some quite different definitions have come up over the course of time; moral philosophers disagree as much in this point as they do in others.

In the Middle Ages, for instance, we find ethics defined as the science of the morality of human actions or alternatively as the science of human actions inasmuch as they are recognized to be good or bad, correct or incorrect, on the basis of the highest practical principles of natural reason. This is the definition given by the Thomists.

Thomas Brown (1778–1820) mentions three formulations of the fundamental problems of ethics: (*a*) What constitutes virtue or morality? (*b*) What constitutes the moral obligation to perform certain actions? (*c*) What does the agent have to gain? He himself prefers yet a fourth formulation: What is the basis of moral approval and disapproval?

Another English moralist, Paley (1743–1805), defines moral

79

philosophy as the science which instructs men as to their duty and its grounds.

In his *Grundlegung* (IV, 338) Kant, too, gives a definition of ethics. 'All rational knowledge,' he says, 'is either material, observing some object, or formal, occupying itself solely with the form of the understanding and reason itself and of the general laws of thought as such, without regard to distinctions between objects. Formal philosophy is called logic, but material philosophy, which has to do with concrete objects and [the] laws to which they are subject, is itself divided into two parts. For these laws are either laws of nature or of freedom. The science of the first is called physics; that of the second is ethics. The former is also known as the theory of nature, the latter as the theory of morals.' He goes on to say that the laws of ethics are laws in accordance with which everything ought to happen, while those of physics, on the other hand, are laws in accordance with which everything really does happen.

Although we have listed a sufficient number of dissenting definitions, let us in conclusion mention one formulated by a thinker who lived closer to our own times: Herbart (1776–1841). He sees philosophy as a threefold treatment of concepts: logic works them over in order to make them clear; metaphysics, in order to make them comprehensible; aesthetics, in order to complete them through the stipulation of values. Ethics belongs under aesthetics. What is beautiful presents something permanent, of indisputable value, and that is why the moral is to be classified with the beautiful. But it is to be distinguished from other things of beauty as that which not only possesses value as an object but which also determines the absolute value of the person himself. In this definition we can see clearly the viewpoint peculiar to Herbartian ethics, but it is not far from some others, in particular the Scholastic point of view, inasmuch as Herbart also conceives of ethics as the science of what is moral. On the other hand, his definition seems to have as little in common with ours as do the others mentioned previously.

3. Are any of these definitions such as to put us into a state of confusion about our own? In general, the determination of concepts is not a subject for dispute. Anyone can attach different meanings to the same word at will, yet there are certain cases in which one usage shows itself preferable to another. Thus it is

advisable not to depart without reason from the established usage. Furthermore, the dispute about a definition acquires significance and takes a firm hold as soon as the parties to it agree that its object has certain peculiarities shared by no others. This is the situation in this instance, and I hope to be able to demonstrate that our definition merits preference.

To begin with, it has the advantage of being the original definition. It goes back as far as Aristotle, who gave the first systematic presentation of ethics, and it has never fallen completely into disuse. But there is another factor that is more decisive. Only when understood in this way is ethics the architectonic art; that practical wisdom which holds a position among the practical disciplines similar to that which metaphysics holds among the theoretical disciplines. It concerns itself with the first grounds of action just as metaphysics concerns itself with the first grounds of being, for the stipulation of the end determines that of the means.

Now if other people want to define ethics differently, e.g., as the science of the morality of actions, their definition can only be correct if it says, in different words, what we want to say, i.e. if by 'moral actions' they mean those which pursue the end which is, or is held to be, correct. In such a case our definition has the advantage of being clearer. But many moral philosophers suffer from far more significant defects and are hindered by certain false assumptions from accepting our definition.

Thus Thomas Brown, who holds that ethics teaches us the grounds of moral approval and disapproval, believes that it is not the difference between ends which determines the essential moral differences between actions. Indeed, he goes so far as to say that under certain conditions it would be better to prefer that the lesser good be realized, even if more evil consequences than good consequences can be expected to follow. For instance, justice must be fulfilled under all circumstances, no matter what comes of it. *Fiat justitia, pereat mundus!* [Let justice be done, though the world perish!] He would doubtless protest against our definition, but he would be wrong. It is self-contradictory to say that it could be morally better to choose a lesser good over a greater. For choice is a sort of preference, and 'better' means nothing other than 'preferable'.

No one can appeal to the disrepute of the dictum that the end justifies the means, for it deserves to be condemned only when it is used with reference to a certain end without regard to all the circumstances or to the consequences that would flow from its realization. If we subsume under the end the totality of foreseeable consequences, then it is morally right to use means not desirable in themselves for the sake of the better end. Think of the painful methods a doctor must sometimes use in order to effect a cure or of the suffering the judge must inflict for the protection of society.

But let us suppose for the moment that it is praiseworthy in some instance to realize a lesser good. Under what circumstances could this be the case? Only if the moral character of the choice in question were so sublime that the preponderance of the greater good which it slights is no longer of any account. But in that case the nobility of this choice is itself to be weighed into the balance on the other side, and in accounting for it the person making the choice could certainly say that he was preferring the better over the worse.

Kant would have a different reason for not agreeing to our definition. Of course, he himself relates the morality of actions very closely to the right end inasmuch as he holds that he who does not degrade to a mere means what is to be handled as an end in itself acts morally. ('So act, that you at all times treat mankind, in your own person as well as in that of every other, as an end and not as a mere means.')* At the same time, he does not in any way include the concept of the right end in the concept of morality. Indeed, he forbids all consideration of ends in determining the highest principle of action.

The greatest philosopher of the Middle Ages, Thomas Aquinas (1225–74), who put much care into the development of ethics as the *opus plane aureum* [the most excellent work], would have yet another reason for refusing to exchange his stipulation for ours. In his view, as in that of other Scholastics, we are able only to choose among means, but not among final ends. All men pursue their own happiness as their sole ultimate end. They are incapable of striving for any other end. They are distinguishable from one another only by their choice of means, so that the sole task allotted to ethics is to instruct as to the means that lead directly to the universally sought end.

Once again, the objection rests upon a fundamentally defective

* *Grundlegung*, IV, 429.

point of view. It is not correct that everyone always pursues his own happiness as a final end. For one thing, the person making the choice often knows or believes he knows that he cannot attain it, no matter how much he may desire it. (In the same way we cannot will to grow wings.) In such cases, the person can at most strive for a portion of happiness or of some state similar to it. Now someone might say that we should still call happiness the final end because people strive for what they believe to be the attainable portion of it or the nearest thing to it under the given circumstances; thus they do, after all, keep their eye on happiness itself as the highest good and make their choice with it in mind. But we can counter that the concept of an end has been changed, for by 'end' we commonly understand the same as 'what is striven for', a πρακτὸν ἀγαθόν, as Aristotle put it. Hence the portion approximation of happiness cannot really be called a means, for that refers only to what serves the realization of the end. Consider, for instance, the case where we have to choose between pleasure and knowledge. Clearly, the criterion for our choice is not which of the two is better suited to the realization of our happiness. Or consider choosing between a momentary present and a later, greater pleasure; both may show up as a part of happiness, but neither is chosen as a means.

Furthermore, Aquinas says that different people place their happiness in different things, some in riches, some in knowledge, others in sensual pleasure. Thus they are the same only in name but not in fact, and in the last analysis people clearly do not pursue a single goal, but rather various goods for their own sake.

There have been many recent attacks on the view, so common in ancient and medieval times, that the ultimate end is happiness. The attacks have been made not only by theologians like Fénelon and Bossuet but also by philosophers. They consider those who are willing to buy their own happiness at any price to be despicable egoists. Even positivists like Mill, Comte, and Bain are fortunately better in their practice than in their theory in this respect, as Hume once said of a similar case. And this is to say nothing of the idealists. The facts are so obvious that even Aquinas cannot remain consistent. In one place he poses the peculiar question how we ought to decide if we had to choose between our own eternal damnation and offence against the love of God and answers that we ought to pick the first alternative. This case seems highly paradoxical, for how could such moral heroism be coupled with eternal damnation? But the inconsistency into which Aquinas finds himself to be driven exposes the untenability of this doctrine.

4. Thus we have also averted this attack upon our definition, and we may lay it down as the original and also as the flawless one, for all those which disagree in essentials rest upon errors and those which do not are inferior with respect to clarity. Ours best characterizes the discipline, ethics, and its essential task. If this is true, there arises, as we mentioned earlier, another legitimate demand: it is now incumbent upon us to clarify the concept of the right end.

26. *Classification of the attempts to define the concept of the right end*

We have already indicated the peculiar source of difficulty here. There are neither disputes nor any disagreements about the concept of a correct subordinate end, i.e. one which is sought as a means. Here it is clear what is meant by 'correct'. But we cannot speak of correctness in this sense with reference to the highest good. Hence there are many different formulations contained either explicitly or implicitly in the statements made by moralists. (For after what we have noted about the various definitions of ethics, it is to be expected that some will not explicitly mention the concept of the right end.)

It will be both interesting and useful in making our own decision if we take a quick look at the most important formulations. (Where the definition is not explicit we will ascertain it through other definitions.)

The definitions are so numerous and varied that we are in danger of losing our prospective in the confusing array of possibilities. Consequently it is wise to arrange them into groups under certain general viewpoints.

There are three closely related factors in ethics: the objects which are striven for as the right ends; the justified endeavours, i.e. those directed towards right ends; and the rules that determine which ends are to be pursued and which not. Anyone who is familiar with one of these is familiar with the others, and each can be determined from the others, i.e. they are dependent upon one another. Yet there is only one order of definition that is natural and suitable. The others are circular, explaining nothing.

In point of fact, all three orders of definition have been tried. Some have established the correctness of the end by means of the correspondence between the endeavour for certain objects and a certain precept. Others construct the definitions of the concept of the highest end out of characteristics found in the very objects that are striven for. Still others take the middle road; they believe they can discover a distinguishing characteristic of certain endeavours that marks them as justified and then determine the right end as the object of such endeavour. Thus we get three groups, each of which presents, in turn, a variety of views which can themselves be divided into groups. We shall order them in such a way that we first present those definitions of the concept of the right end that depend upon the establishing of the rule, then those which establish directly the concept of the right end, and finally those which first distinguish endeavours directed towards the right end from other endeavours.

I. THE ATTEMPT TO DEFINE THE RIGHT END THROUGH ITS CORRESPONDENCE WITH A RULE

27. *Definition by means of external rules (heteronomous ethics)*

1. Under this heading belong the views of those who say that an end is right if the endeavour towards it corresponds to God's command. But there is no standard for this law itself; whatever God chooses to command is right because he commands it. If he commanded us to hate him, it would be right to hate him. Nominalists such as William of Ockham (1270–1347) taught that divine commands are arbitrary in this way. In more recent times the view has been taken by Crusius (1712–76).

2. Others leave God out of the picture and declare that end to be right which corresponds to the command of the ruler or the state. Hobbes (1588–1679) deduced this doctrine from egoism.

3. Others say that end is right which accords with the public opinion among the bourgeoisie, a view held by, e.g., Sextus Empiricus (*c.* A.D. 200). Many matters are not determined by the law of the state but by custom. If a law contradicts public opinion, the bold offender is often held to be the representative of true justice, freedom, and progress towards a better way, indeed, a saint and martyr.

4. The end is right if the endeavour has the approval of all, or at least the majority of men, or would have their approval if they had a sufficient knowledge of the relevant circumstances and relations. This was evidently the view of James Mill (1773–1836) and, at times, of John Stuart Mill (1806–73), who was enabled in this way to defend his derivation of utilitarianism from egoism against the accusation of being a crude paralogism. Similarly, some hold the end to be right if the endeavour accords with the conventions of men and their opinions about laws and morality, e.g. La Rochefoucauld (1613–80) and Mandeville (1670–1733), who have the distinction of trying to show that no one does what everyone ostensibly demands. Everyone acts wrongly; vanity, selfishness, and impurity are universal. But they praise what is good with their words and attempt to deceive themselves and others into believing that they practice it.

These four approaches agree with each other not only in starting out with a rule but also in that this rule is an externally derived, or positive, precept.

28. Definition by means of internal rules (*autonomous ethics*)

Others make their starting-point a rule given internally by nature, an *a priori* rule of reason. Here, too, I shall list the main examples, but I can be briefer, as I am largely repeating familiar material.

1. The end is right if the endeavour is in harmony with one's conscience, i.e. is acknowledged, approved of, as good by a peculiar faculty that reacts in accordance with certain general moral truths. This view was held by Socrates, representatives of Christian ethics (including particularly Abélard and Aquinas), Bishop Butler, Thomas Reid, and in a certain sense Cudworth.

2. We must be honest; that is an evident precept. The end is right if the endeavour is honest, as the precept demands (Wollaston).

3. The end is right if the act accords with the *a priori* demand of reason, the categorical imperative. Kant, like the Scottish philosophers, calls this *a priori* demand conscience, but he does not teach that there are a variety of such precepts, but only one. 'Two things excite my admiration: the starry heavens above me and the moral law within me.'*

Critique of Practical Reason, V, 161.

4. Finally we must include here a thinker who, unlike Kant, was not inclined towards *a priori* proclamations in any other matters. Without characterizing it as such, he bases his morality upon a sort of synthetic *a priori* principle. A. Comte (1798–1857) starts out from the thought that reason demands uniformity and systematization of personal and social life. Hence, among ends desirable for their own sakes, that one is right the endeavour towards which is compatible with the uniformity and systematization of personal and social life.

Clarification of the derivation: egotistical and sympathetic inclinations lie in our nature. At the outset the former are predominant, but the result is chaos, for one inclination is contrary to another and the present is contrary to the future. But it is different with sympathetic inclinations. Although very weak to begin with, they gain strength with cultivation. Hence the motto: *vivre pour l'autrui* [Live for others]! None the less the egotistical inclinations have their domain; for instance, we must nourish and take care of our bodies and souls in order to serve others. This is how unity is brought about.

Comte attempted to anchor his ethics in a church. He founded a sort of religion, but a religion without God. This did not seem self-contradictory to him, for he considered only the following elements essential for religion: first, a dogma concerning the purpose and duty of mankind, and second, an emotion which attaches itself to this dogma. It seemed advantageous to him to have the emotion directed towards some concrete object, crystallized around some real ideal. This *grand être* is humanity. Mankind is eternal; we can genuinely love it, and we owe it gratitude. Contrary to the God of the theists, this ideal offers the additional advantage that we can promote it ourselves. It embraces all beings who have sensations.

II. ATTEMPTS TO ESTABLISH THE RIGHT END DIRECTLY BY REFERENCE TO THE NATURE OF CERTAIN OBJECTS

29. *What sort of objects are these?*

In accordance with our plan, we shall now proceed to the stipulations of the concept of the right end which have been attempted directly with reference to the nature of certain objects.

1. By 'the right end' is meant the greatest degree of good and the greatest possible freedom from evil that are attainable under given circumstances. But 'good' here is equivalent to 'pleasure', 'bad' to 'pain', of which we personally partake. These words are supposed to have no other meaning whatsoever in contexts concerning what is good or bad in itself and not merely what is useful or harmful. This view was held by Bentham (1748–1832).

2. Some other thinkers also stipulate that the right end is the highest degree of good and the greatest freedom from evil which can be attained under given circumstances, but they do not identify the concept of good with pleasure or that of bad with pain. By the greatest quantity of good and the greatest possible freedom from evil they understand the greatest attainable personal perfection. Examples are Christian Wolff and Schleiermacher (1768–1834).

But if we go on to ask what perfection is, they list such a variety of characteristics and activities that it is difficult to determine a univocal concept.

3. For Plato, the right end is the greatest possible participation in the Idea of the Good, where participation is to be interpreted as similarity or imitation. To make ourselves more and more like the Idea of the Good is the proper object of our endeavour. We might be tempted to include this formulation in the first classification inasmuch as the Idea of the Good is supposed to be inherent in us rather than won from any experience we could have in this life. It thus becomes a rule for our behaviour. Yet its relation to the formulations mentioned earlier is not so close after all as it might appear to be. The Idea of the Good is also an object, one the vision of which we bring with us from an earlier life. And consequently the imitation of the Idea is something that we perceive in objects of experience, which we comprehend as being similar to the Idea of the Good. Hence the Platonic version belongs to those which define the right end in terms of the objects striven for. It bears a special relation to the following determination, which is also historically connected to it.

4. The right end is the one peculiar to human nature. In nature, there is a recognizable endeavour towards ends, even to some extent in inorganic bodies, e.g., crystals. This striving of nature for certain ends becomes still more clearly visible in living creatures. And the extent to which these ends are fulfilled is the extent of their perfection and goodness. The bird is more perfect than

88

the egg, the nightingale flying and singing more perfect than the one resting and being silent, regular growth more perfect than stunted growth.

The concept of the end aimed at by nature and the concept of the right end are identical:

(*a*) Aristotle, in particular, starts from this point of view, which was represented already by Socrates and again by Plato, who believes that nature is constructed with a view to the Idea of the Good, as an imitation of it. Aristotle holds the noblest task to be activity, specifically, that activity peculiar to a species. For men, this is the theoretical and practical life of reason.

(*b*) But sometimes Aristotle speaks as though the true natural end of man were not within himself but in a greater whole. Man is not, he says, self-sufficient but is a political being (ζῷον πολιτικὸν).

(*c*) Inspired by Aristotle, others have seen the right end in humanity, but not only in those men living at present; for man is not only a creature fitted out by nature for life together within a state but also one who undergoes historical development. See, for instance, Trendelenburg (1802–72).

(*d*) The Stoa extended in another way the scope of the end in considering the uniform ordering of all things in the world to a whole. Man is a cosmologically political being (ζῷον κοσμοπο-λιτικὸν); the right end, they say, is the good of this whole. It goes beyond our own personal good. It follows that we have a duty to surrender and sacrifice our own advantages in the interests of the whole. None the less, the highest practical good lies within ourselves. Whatever we may further outside ourselves in the course of this pursuit does not itself attain the value of these pro-ceedings and ways of behaving. Thus the highest practical good is virtue. (Cf. Adam Smith's nice observations about the Stoa.)*

5. The right end is the application of things to one another in such a way that they suit each other. The aforementioned thinkers said the right end is the one pursued by nature; these thinkers say it is the one outlined by the nature of the objects of choice. The most prominent representative of this interpretation is probably Samuel Clarke. A reminder will serve as sufficient clarification.

* No reference is given here. Brentano may be referring to the last paragraph in the short essay entitled, 'The Principles which Lead and Direct Philosophical Enquiries, Illustrated by the History of the Ancient Physics', in Smith's *Essays on Philosophical Subjects*.

Clarke teaches that certain relations lie in the nature of things. The same is true of actions and persons, and among the relations included here we find those of fittingness, or suitability, and unsuitability. From these tenets Clarke derives our obligations to God and our fellow men. (Cf. Part I, chap. 2, sect. 10.) One of the relations bestowed upon things by nature is the way they are suited to be applied to one another. Reverence with respect to God shows a greater degree of congruence than does one triangle with respect to another that coincides with it.

This exhausts the most prominent formulations of the second classification.

III. ATTEMPTS TO ESTABLISH THE RIGHT END ON THE BASIS OF JUSTIFIED ENDEAVOUR

30. Endeavour as characterized by an accompanying consequence or effect

We now come to the third class of attempts, which we have generally defined as those that begin by establishing what constitutes justified endeavour. Moral philosophers of this group believe that they can find in certain endeavours distinguishing characteristics which mark them out as justified, and they consequently define the right end as the object of such endeavour.

Like the first, this group is divisible into several parts.

Some find the distinguishing characteristic in a consequence that accompanies justified striving. According to some this effect is a sensation; according to others it is a feeling awakened both in the person who makes the endeavour and in the passive spectator.

Others find the distinguishing characteristic, not in a phenomenon accompanying the endeavour, but in the endeavour itself.

A. The following are the principal definitions of the right end.

1. The end is right if the endeavour towards it strikes our moral sense as good.

Proponents of this view think of the 'moral sense' as something similar to the external senses. The understanding, they say, would not discover colour, heat, etc., in material objects, but the sensations which they arouse disclose these phenomena. Similarly, the understanding cannot discover any such characteristic as 'goodness' in an endeavour, but it appears good in the sensations of a certain inner sense, the moral sense. This is, in particular, the view of Hutcheson.

2. More common is the view that justified endeavour is characterized by an accompanying feeling.

The end is right, it is said, if the endeavour arouses certain pleasant feelings of approbation, not only in the actor but also in those who perceive it. One example is Hume. He claims that those endeavours, activities, and characteristics that are suited to furthering happiness within a greater or smaller sphere arouse such emotions within us, whether or not we belong to this sphere. He concludes that they are a pleasure we take in the ordering of affairs in a manner appropriate to such an end.

3. Adam Smith also thought the right end was to be defined as one the striving towards which arouses certain pleasant feelings of approval. Verbally, this definition sounds just like Hume's. But the agreement between them is not so great as it would appear. Smith has an essentially different understanding of the feeling of approval and traces it back to different sources. In one place in his work, *The Theory of Moral Sentiments*, he summarizes his teachings on the subject in the following terms. '. . . the sentiments which we feel are, according to the foregoing system, derived from four sources, which are in some respects different from one another. First, we sympathize with the motives of the agent; secondly, we enter into the gratitude of those who receive the benefit of his actions; thirdly, we observe that his conduct has been agreeable to the general rules by which those two sympathies generally act; and, last of all, when we consider such actions as making a part of a system of behaviour which tends to promote the happiness either of the individual or of the society, they appear to derive a beauty from this utility, not unlike that which we ascribe to any well-contrived machine.'*

The last element is the only one that Hume recognized. Without wanting to deny that it has some influence, Smith deems it the least significant of the four. The knowledge of this usefulness, he says, is not the original source of our approval and disapproval, but it may enliven and intensify it. The feelings are of a kind

* *The Theory of Moral Sentiments*, Part VII, sect. III, chap. III; the second paragraph from the end. Here the translation given in Brentano seems quite accurate, so I have simply quoted the original English.

different from those we have when approving of a well-arranged building. When we give our approval, we by no means think first of the usefulness of the state of our emotions. The other three elements in our feeling of approval are all of greater, though not equal, importance. It is they that give it its peculiar character; without them there is no genuine moral feeling, no truly moral judging. But among them the third is most prominent; thus we might say that Smith sees the feeling of approval which decides if an endeavour is justified as a certain sort of delight in the agreement of the endeavour with the general rules which sympathy ordinarily supports.

But this will scarcely suffice to clarify completely Smith's views, which are somewhat complicated and are often conceived of incorrectly. Hence I want to illustrate his train of thought somewhat more closely.

(*a*) It is a fact that we sympathize with others. This can be seen in joy and sorrow and is a consequence of our picturing to ourselves the state of the person experiencing joy or sorrow. Sympathy appears in its clearest and purest form where he who feels it is not in any way directly affected by that which brings joy or sorrow to the other person. Of course, we are not always able to imagine the situation of another with equal perfection, and hence we cannot be equally sympathetic at all times. For instance, it is beyond the limitations of our imagination to intuit perfectly the sensible pleasure or pain of someone else.

(*b*) It is well known that we are glad when others sympathize with us. But it also affords us a special pleasure when we are able to feel sympathy with other people. If we feel repelled by someone's behaviour, this feeling of antipathy is itself painful. Our approval of the actions of someone as being suitable or meritorious is related to this joy in sympathizing.

(*c*) To find someone else's behaviour suitable means simply to sympathize with it, or with his motives, or to recognize that one would sympathize under the proper conditions. (An example of unsuitable circumstances is the case where I see a son sorrowfully following his father's casket, but I have just won the grand prize.)

To find the behaviour of another not only suitable but also meritorious is to feel a double sympathy, inasmuch as an indirect form of sympathy is added to the immediate sympathy just mentioned. This happens when the behaviour which is fitting has beneficial consequences for a third party. We then sympathize also with the gladness of the person who benefits from the act.

What it means to find impropriety or demerit in something follows directly from the foregoing.

(*d*) To find something suitable or meritorious is itself to make a moral judgment in the real sense of the term. It is the first moral judgment we make; thus we judge first with reference to the action and character of others. Consequently Smith thinks there can be no knowledge of a difference between what is morally good and what is morally bad without prior observation of the acts of other people.

These are the first two sources presented by Smith.

(*e*) Nature teaches us to acknowledge such jurisdiction when others exercise it over us. For as everyone knows from experience, we are glad when other people sympathize with us, while their antipathy pains us. The approval of others arouses within us satisfaction with ourselves; their disapproval distresses us and puts us to shame.

(*f*) But in order for this court of justice to have genuine authority over us, it may not issue decisions upon the basis of deficient or incorrect information or, as often happens, against the natural rules of sympathy. A number of things may cause us to fall into such errors. It is admittedly perverse to allow the bestowal of our approval to be influenced not solely by a person's intentions but also by the effects of his acts. Nevertheless it happens very frequently. Similarly, it is supposed to make no difference whether we are judging the actions of a rich man or of a poor man, of a prominent or of a lowly person. But we are more inclined to sympathize with cheerful people and, consequently, with those who are comfortably placed and are respected. Thus it is that people make a great show of their wealth and carefully disguise their poverty. Distinctions of rank are also connected with this. And, here as in other domains, fashion and habit occasion to a certain extent irregular and discordant opinions.

(*g*) Now if we observe ourselves being judged by others in an irregular manner, the impression their opinion makes upon us is not the same as it would be otherwise. Unfounded praise does not give us any satisfaction; likewise, unfounded blame does not leave us without consolation. We picture to ourselves what totally different sentiments people would have to harbour upon observing our behaviour if they saw into affairs more correctly and weighed matters more thoughtfully. We place ourselves under the gaze of an impartial spectator, not subject to confusion or error, and, no matter how irregularly praise and blame are dispensed, we shall not fail to feel shame and embarrassment in the one case and gladness in the other. A superior judge dwells within our breast, though his view of matters may stem in essence from the view of the initial judge.

But even the pronouncements of the internal judge are not always reliable. We are inclined to be partial to ourselves. Two occasions are at our disposal for observing our actions from the viewpoint of the impartial observer; before and after the act. At both times we show partiality and are subject to self-deception.

(*h*) There is only one remedy against these tendencies. We derive general rules of morality from our observations of other people's actions. If they are abstracted from experience and are approved by the general sentiment of mankind, we often look to them as a guide line for our judgments. In particular, they are often very useful in correcting the delusions into which our self-love entices us.

(*i*) The respect for these general rules is, according to Smith, the real sense of duty, so called. He who follows them loyally is a man of principle and honour.

(*j*) In order to elevate their dignity yet further, we declare these rules of conduct to be divine commands. And rightly so; our moral faculties are given to us by God for the purpose of guiding our conduct during this life. They plainly are intended to be the governing principles of human nature. In consequence of this position they are to be regarded as divine laws.

We are confirmed in this view by the experience that good conduct is followed by internal rewards, bad by internal punishment, and yet further confirmed by the fact that the happiness of mankind, which is the purpose aimed at by the creator, is furthered by the following of these laws. And virtue finds external reward even here, although it may not be granted so regularly and in such sufficient quantity that there remains no place for vindication in the next world.

(*k*) Thus the rules of morality acquire a new degree of sacredness. For the man who believes in God, respect for his will is without question the supreme rule of conduct.

We now understand what Adam Smith lists as the third source

94

(of the feeling of approbation) and also the predominant significance of this factor. According to Smith, the right end is that one
the striving towards which excites our approbation in that it
conforms to the rules in accordance with which sympathy generally operates.

4. The end is right if the effort directed towards it is aesthetically pleasing, i.e. if it is beautiful. The morally good is what is
beautiful within the realm of striving. Even the Greeks spoke of
moral beauty. The good (ἀγαθόν), they say, is also beautiful
(καλόν); κάλλιστον τὸ δικαῖον.

Many of the British moralists also make great use of this expression, although they may not have employed it with precision.
A thing is to be called beautiful if the idea of it is pleasing and
desirable. In Hume, the pleasure appears to be directed more
towards the existence of the action itself.

But in Herbart's ethics the aesthetic viewpoint is adhered to in
a strict and obviously conscious manner.

31. *Herbart's doctrine of the moral as a special case of the beautiful*

Herbart makes ethics subordinate to aesthetics, but does not
wish to surrender it to subjective caprice in so doing. He holds
that the end is right if the efforts directed towards it are beautiful.
This beauty, however, is established by an evident judgment of
taste.[11]

(*a*) According to his theory, the beautiful and the ugly—and
those special varieties of them, the praiseworthy and the shameful
—possess a primal evidence in virtue of which they are clear,
without having been learned or proven. While the pleasant is
present only in momentary feelings from which nothing follows,
the beautiful, on closer observation, gives us something to think
about and offers something that is permanent and has undeniable
worth. But that which is moral singles itself out from everything
else beautiful as that which not only possesses value but determines the absolute value of the person himself.

Because ethics, or practical philosophy, constitutes a special
part of aesthetics, it is the task of a moral philosopher to adopt the

[11] Compare the presentation of Herbart's theory that Brentano uses
here with that in Trendelenburg's treatise (for the Berliner Akademie),
'Herbarts Praktische Philosophie' (1856).

stand of an independent observer with respect to the moral and immoral behaviour of mankind. From his observations he makes sketches of the various types of voluntary action in such a way that the observer involuntarily approves of some acts of will and finds displeasure involuntarily aroused by others.

One fundamental law governs aesthetic taste: each part of a thing which, put together, is pleasing or displeasing, is of indifferent value taken in itself; the beauty does not lie in the separate parts but in their relations. Nowhere is this more clearly true than in music. No one of the tones which are sounded together in a third or a fifth is able, taken by itself, to arouse the feeling which attaches itself to the combination. A judgment of taste does not take on an object until we imagine the relations between a majority of its elements in their finished form. In other words, material is aesthetically neutral; aesthetic judgment can be passed only on the basis of the form. (This is formal aesthetics.)

Thus sketches that are to be drawn by the moral philosopher are of harmonious and disharmonious relations constructed of acts of will or judgments. Herbart gives the name *idea* to any formal concept that arouses a never-changing judgment of approval and thereby becomes a model for all future relations between the elements in question.

He outlines five practical ideas as types of harmonious relations in the activities of the will: the idea of freedom, the idea of perfection, the idea of benevolence, the idea of justice, and the idea of approval. (There are also five derivative social ideas.)

The idea of (internal) freedom is given when the will corresponds to the insight, i.e. when they affirm or reject in unison. 'If a desire or resolution is awakened in a rational being, the image of his desire or resolution immediately arises before him. To discern it and to pass judgment are one and the same thing. The judgment remains suspended over the will; while the judgment perseveres, the will strides into action. Now, either the person asserts in willing what he spurns in judging, or he neglects in willing what he prescribes in judging, or the will and the judgment have unanimously made either an affirmation or a denial.'* Accord arouses aesthetic pleasure, the contrary displeasure.

* Herbart, *Allgemeine Praktische Philosophie*, Book I, chap. I (1808). Reprinted in his *Sämtliche Werke*, ed. Kehrbach (Hermann Beyer u. Söhne), vol. II, pp. 355–6.

The idea of perfection emerges when the proportions of an endeavour are in harmony. The moral philosopher observes only the form and not the matter of the will, as beauty is a merely formal concept; that is, it must be abstracted from concrete objects. Their relations are not peculiar to the will; that which is willed must be mentally set aside. All that remains are acts of will as mere endeavours, among which we are to find the relations pertaining to ethics.

Inasmuch as they are endeavours, all acts of will are the same, except with respect to their strength. Perfection is to be determined in purely quantitative terms. Simply in its proportions, what is stronger is more pleasing than what is weaker. And, to put it the other way, what is weaker is displeasing in comparison to what is stronger. We here compare the greater to the lesser in three ways. Among individual endeavours, we are pleased by a greater strength of will; with respect to the sum of all endeavours, we are pleased by the presence of a greater variety of endeavours; with respect to a system, we are pleased by concurrence of several endeavours made by a single person.*

These two ideas are based upon a harmony between the elements that can be given in the will of an individual. Three further ideas emerge when we imagine the relations between endeavours of several different persons.

We encounter first of all *the idea of benevolence*. We imagine a will that makes the satisfaction of some other will its immediate goal for its own sake, not from any egotistical motives. The image of this relation is pleasing, that of its opposite, the idea of malevolence, displeasing. Malevolence is the ugliest relation of all.

This agreement between one's own will and that of another is not the same thing as involuntary sympathy, in which we feel and strive with a person. This latter is only the repetition of the same striving that another has already made. A simple condition of this kind does not constitute a relation. The required approval is missing.

We must not imagine the value of benevolence to be independent of the value of the projected alien will. Goodness is goodness because it is kind to another will directly and without motive. But we must imagine this other will to be unblemished, in order

* Ibid., chap. II (pp. 358–60).

97

that no objections may be lodged from the other side to interfere with the benevolence of the person who is internally free.*

The idea of justice. It sometimes happens that several wills reach into their common sensual realm and wish to dispose of the same object in incompatible ways. If both of two wills know that they are standing in each other's way and nevertheless pursue their goal, then each wishes to negate the other. They are at odds, and disputes are displeasing. Now how are we to avoid the displeasure? The practical path to pursue is to yield. This applies to both parties. If both sides yield, each will leave something to the other.

Once the concession has been made, the one who has yielded must recognize it as a rule, as a boundary that he may not overstep.† Thus a boundary is erected between the two parties, delineating their rights. Justice consists of unanimous agreement between several wills, conceived as a rule intended to prevent all disputes. From this derivation we can discern that, in respect of its material, justice is always positive, for it originates in the arbitrary determinations of several wills which have been brought into agreement with one another. Nevertheless, it is not a matter of indifference how the boundaries delineating our rights are drawn, for not every will is equally suited to avoiding disputes. Thus the conventions governing justice have differing degrees of value, which vary in inverse proportion to the strength of the provocation to the dispute, regardless of what other characteristics the provocation may have.‡

The idea of approval. The act, conceived as a good or a harmful deed, leads to the idea of approval or of fitting retribution.

1. The act is displeasing in that it disturbs the former state of affairs. This displeasure applies to the relation of the new conditions to the former ones, which were opposed to them.

2. If this displeasure had the power to affect the act, this power would work in the opposite direction and, by moving backwards, wipe out the act.

3. But since the displeasure as such does not possess this power,

* Ibid., chap. III (pp. 361–4).

† Brentano omits one step described by Herbart. Ideally, both sides yield to begin with, but then one may proclaim a right to the object once again, and without dispute this time. Sometimes, only one gives way. Thus Herbart can speak of the *one* who has (ultimately) yielded.

‡ Ibid., chap. IV (pp. 364–9).

it is only possible to regress by making comparisons [in thought].*

Herbart considers that these five practical ideas, which are supposed to emerge as types of harmonious relations in the activities of the will, constitute a complete list of moral elements; if more than two wills come together, on purpose or accidently, the same relations will reappear, though they may be intertwined with one another.

This latter contingency finds fulfilment in the state, which gives rise to derivative, or social, ideas originating in each of the five elementary ideas: the idea of justice gives rise to that of legal society; the idea of approval to that of the system of recompense; the idea of benevolence to that of the system of government (that seeks the greatest possible well-being of society through suitable administration of the means at hand); the idea of perfection to that of the system of culture; and the idea of internal freedom to that of a society with a spirit (general obedience over against general insight: a society animated by a single spirit, living in all members).†

All five ideas retain the character of an harmonious relation, and Herbart's principal presupposition, that moral goodness is in essence beauty and beauty the same as harmonious relations, has been fulfilled.

32. Definitions of the right end by internal characteristics of endeavour

B. We still have the task of discussing those conceptions of the right end which seek the distinguishing characteristic of endeavour not in a consequence which follows from it but within itself. The following attempts at a definition belong in this category.

1. The right end is the most desirable of those that can be attained. Hence it is the end that will in fact be chosen by any person who is sufficiently acquainted through experience with the objects among which he can choose and is also well informed about their relation to his own situation. In other words, the right end is the object of the desire which wins out in the man of experience.

* Ibid., chap. V (pp. 369–75).
† Ibid., chaps 7–12 (pp. 385–408).

This formulation appears from time to time in J. S. Mill. He makes no distinction between what is desirable in the sense that it is possible to desire it and what is desirable in the sense that it is worthy of desire. And even Socrates taught essentially the same doctrine, for he holds that no one who has knowledge will do wrong and that virtue *is* knowledge.

2. The end is right if it is esteemed more highly than every other end by a correct and *normal* act of the emotions. The right end is the one preferred by normal love. In contrast to every incorrect evaluation, a correct evaluation, conceived in this manner, carries with it duty, moral necessity, obligation, on the grounds that it springs from the essence of the soul. This view is held by Beneke (1826–71), who in essentials follows Überweg. He claims that we evaluate objects according to the ascending and descending moments which we experience in our psychical development because of them. They manifest themselves in the form of feelings and desires. The height reached during an ascent is determined by the nature of the native capacity of the emotions, by the stimuli, and finally by the associations and fundamental principles of human development. The worth of an object to which a moment of ascent pertains and which it evaluates becomes generally greater in proportion to the height reached by that ascent, as determined by the aforementioned universal laws of human development. Here we have a practical norm that is valid for all men. Morality demands that which is perceived as loftier in virtue of the norms grounded in human nature and is accordingly desired. But it is also possible for disturbances to take place that lead to evaluations diverging from this standard. Correct evaluations, as opposed to divergent, announce themselves by the feeling of duty, moral necessity, and obligation.

3. The previously mentioned British moralist, Cudworth, whose analyses of morality echo in some ways the Scholastics, taught the following principles. Man possesses a faculty of knowledge, superior to the senses, that concerns itself with the immutable, eternal essences and natures of objects and the eternally unchanging relations between them. The moral distinctions between good and bad belong to these essences. They pertain to particular natures, viz. to the actions and souls of men. They dwell within them as characteristics of them, but they also exist already *a priori*, as anticipations of morality in the spirit. If our endeavour

possesses this essence, the 'verity' of goodness, the end towards which it is directed can be recognized as right.

Let us conclude our survey here. We have not noted every nuance, but all the significant distinctions, all the genera and species have most likely been taken into account: the image is quite colourful enough. Now the question is, what position are we to take with respect to the many diverse conceptions of the right end. Can we accept one? And, if we can, which one? Within which genus, and which species, is the correct definition to be found? We cannot answer these questions until we have subjected the conceptions presented in this chapter to a critical examination.

VI

Critique of the Various Definitions of the Right End

How should we proceed in order to find out whether any of the interpretations given to the term 'right end' are proper?

To begin with we shall list some conditions that the true definition of 'right end' must indisputably meet. Then we shall determine whether the conceptions which have been discussed fulfil them. If not, they are to be rejected. The requirements are as follows:

1. If some given end is recognized to be the right one, there remains no place for the question, 'Am I doing the right thing, acting reasonably, if I pursue it?' Given the knowledge that it is the right end, there is no question about whether it is good to pursue it. Thus we possess one criterion in the demand that the concept of the right end cannot be formulated in such a way that any such question can still arise once something has been established to be that end.

2. Another equally justifiable demand is that the definition of the right end may not presuppose anything that does not exist.

If we review, in the light of these demands, the theories discussed, we recognize that they are all deficient.

I. CRITICISM OF THE ATTEMPTS TO ESTABLISH THE RIGHT END BY ITS AGREEMENT WITH A RULE

33. *Rebuttal of the definitions by means of an external rule*

We were able to distinguish two groups of definitions based upon the establishment of a rule. The first four definitions were based upon an external rule, and none of them meet the first requirement.

ad 4. 'The end is right if the endeavour towards it is such that all men, or at least the majority of men, approve of it.'

Why? I certainly do not believe everything that commands the assent of the majority.

ad 3. 'The end is right if the endeavour towards it accords with public opinion within bourgeois society.'

Here it is yet more appropriate to ask why. Perhaps my own example* will be conducive to a change in public opinion. Indeed, this idea is the main argument for civil liberty. Experimentation and mobility lead to progress (cf. J. S. Mill).

ad 2. 'The end is right if the endeavour towards it accords with the law of the ruler.'

Why? Because he is powerful, or because it is advantageous to maintain the regime? Even if these were relevant grounds, the right end would merely coincide with the law; the concept as such would remain distinct.

ad 1. 'The end is right if the endeavour towards it accords with the law of God.'

Why? Because, it is said, he created us, and we consequently belong to him. But the question of possession is itself a special question of ethics; furthermore, we would have to look into whether the right of possession falls without further ado to the producer.

Similarly, every other reason given includes the admission that the concepts 'commanded by God' and 'right end' are not identical.

34. *Rebuttal of the definition of the right end based upon an internal rule*

The second group of determinations belonging to the first class begin from an internally given rule, an *a priori* order of reason. We presented four such determinations. Determinations 2, 3,

---

* Brentano, a deeply religious Catholic priest, was opposed to the dogma of papal infallibility. When the dogma was declared, he resigned his priesthood and left the Church, which cost him his university post at Würzburg. He then assumed a professorship in Vienna, but had to resign that position when he decided to marry; he continued to teach, but at a low rank and without salary. Thus he sacrificed a successful career to be true to his own beliefs.

and 4 do not in any case meet the second demand. For they are all supposed to be *a priori* but not analytic, and we have already established that there is no such thing as synthetic *a priori* knowledge. Not only are these rules not immediately evident; they are not suited to be genuinely regulative. (Cf. what is said in Part I, chap. 2, sect. 12, against Wollaston and in sect. 13 of the same chapter against Kant's categorical imperative.) As for the first determination, which is based upon the 'voice of conscience', it depends upon what is understood by this phrase. If what is meant is an *a priori* order of reason, the same objection applies.

The law, laid down by Comte as an immediate demand of reason, that we should act and make efforts in a way that harmonizes with the uniformity and systematization of the whole of life alienated J. S. Mill, and not only because it is supposed to be immediately evident, and hence an axiom; he even disputes that it is a correct principle. We shall not go into whether or not he is right, but his denial is at the very least an indication that the law is not evident. It could be evident only if it were analytic, i.e. if 'right end' *meant* the same thing as 'the end, the endeavour towards which is consistent with the uniformity and systematization of the whole of life'—but who would want to claim the identity of these concepts! They are distinct and consequently leave room —for the time being, whatever the final decision may prove to be—for the question, 'Should I act in this way?'

Thus we have summarized and set aside the first class of determinations.

II. CRITICISM OF THE ATTEMPTS TO DETERMINE THE RIGHT END DIRECTLY WITH REGARD TO THE NATURE OF CERTAIN OBJECTS

35. *These attempts are deficient, either because they leave room for the question why we should strive for such an end or because they involve fictitious objects*

We listed five main determinations of the right end, viz. as:

(1) the greatest attainable degree of pleasure and the greatest attainable freedom from pain;
(2) the greatest attainable degree of personal perfection;

(3) the greatest possible participation in the idea of the good;
(4) the end peculiar to human nature; and
(5) the application of things to one another in such a manner that they suit one another.

Here, too, we can easily see by applying our double criterion that none of these determinations are correct.

ad 5. The fifth view was rejected previously. Hume has already given an adequate demonstration that relations of congruence such as Clarke claimed to find in things and in the concept of things are not, in truth, to be found in them. Thus this interpretation does not meet our second criterion. The same error also lies at the root of the third determination. And the Platonic ideas have been generally abandoned.

The other three do not meet the first criterion.

ad 1. Pleasure may be the right end, but the concept of pleasure is distinct from that of the right end; hence it is proper to ask whether I ought to aim at my own greatest pleasure in every case, and this is something many moral philosophers have emphatically denied.

ad 2. The concept of one's own perfection also does not coincide with that of the right end. Here, too, the question, 'Why?', can be meaningfully asked; so, indeed, can the question whether it *is* so. He who sacrifices his life to some great cause can scarcely have in mind his own perfection as his final aim. It is much more likely that he is bringing to a halt a promising development of his existence on earth. Of what human perfection consists is also a subject for dispute.

ad 3. Participation in the idea of the good. Quite aside from all the considerations that speak against 'ideas' in Plato's sense, the concept of the good first requires clarification, particularly with respect to whether it contains anything pertaining to an end—as it must, if it coincides with the concept of the right end. Neither of the two previous determinations of the concept appeared to contain anything pertaining either to an end or to an endeavour. They also do not coincide even partially with these concepts.

ad 4. The determination which identifies the right end with the 'natural end of the human species', with what nature itself in man strives for, sounds more plausible. But not everyone admits that ends are pursued in nature. And if they are, why should those be the right ends? Schopenhauer denies that they are. The will he believes to rule nature is supposed to be blind and, accordingly, the world the worst of all possible worlds. And what if the Manichaeans, who place a bad principle opposite the good principle, are right (James Mill)? What if the author of nature himself lacks perfection (J. S. Mill)?

Furthermore, if nature really strives for the best that is possible, how are we able to know it, upon which criterion should our judgment about it rest? The mere fact that such doubts can arise shows that the concept, 'the end striven for by nature in man', does not coincide with the concept, 'right end', even though they may ultimately coincide with respect to content.

So none of the determinations of the second group are to be approved, either. And the same is true of every other which could be tried upon the hypothesis that 'end' means the same as 'the object of an endeavour'. 'Endeavour' here is taken in its real sense, not in the figurative sense in which we permit ourselves to say that the falling body strives for the centre of the earth. And, just like the concept of endeavour, the concept of the right end must most particularly be gained from our own inner experience; after all, it means neither more nor less than that which is the object of a justified endeavour. We must proceed from this point; and this is in fact done by the representatives of the third class, to whom we shall now turn.

III. THOSE WHICH SEE THE PREFERABILITY OF RIGHT ENDEAVOUR
IN SOME PHENOMENON ACCOMPANYING IT

Here we distinguish two groups, according to whether the distinguishing peculiarity of justified endeavour is supposed to lie in an accompanying sensation or an accompanying feeling. We listed Hutcheson, Hume, Adam Smith, and Herbart as representatives of the latter theory. To begin with we will concern ourselves with the first three; then we shall discuss more thoroughly Herbart's theory, which has gained such renown.

36. *Criticism of the definitions of Hutcheson, Hume, and Adam Smith*

1. Hutcheson, among others, holds that the right end is to be recognized by the fact that endeavour towards it affects our moral

sense. This sense, it is said, reveals to us that the endeavour has a certain quality, 'moral goodness'.

How are we to interpret this claim? Does it mean that inner perception, just as it enables us to recognize endeavour, in general, also reveals its various characteristics, among them that of goodness? If so, it would not be a question of a mere accompanying phenomenon, but of an internal characteristic, and the theory would belong to group B of this third class. But it looks more as though what is intended is a physical sensation that necessarily accompanies the endeavour; good, like colour or sound, is being grouped with the sense qualities, as an object of a special sense: the so-called moral sense.

Interpreted in this way, the explanation meets neither of the two criteria. There is no such thing as a sensation having as its object a quality called moral goodness; it is an *ad hoc* invention.

But even if there were a sense directed towards moral qualities, we could question, just as justly as we do of colours or tones, whether the objects of these sensations are real or are mere appearances. In other words, the goodness of the endeavour could be just an illusion flashed before our eyes, and we would be justified in asking why we should make a given endeavour.

2. According to Hume, the rightness of an end is revealed to us, not by a physical sensation accompanying the endeavour towards it but by a *feeling*. The end presents itself as correct when the endeavour arouses certain pleasant feelings of approval which upon close inspection turn out to be just that pleasure that we take in the appropriate ordering of things to the happiness of a greater or smaller circle of people, whether or not we belong to it ourselves. Adam Smith also appeals to pleasant feelings of approbation, which are supposed to consist essentially in the delight we take in the agreement of the endeavour with the general rules, in accordance with which sympathy ordinarily acts.

Here, as before, the question, 'Why?' is appropriate. Is the pleasantness, as such, supposed to give sanction to the endeavour? It may be weighed into the balance as a motive, but there are, after all, other sorts of pleasure, which frequently fall on the opposite side and prove to be a stronger motive. Hume's explanation that these feelings of approbation are peculiar to the human species does not cancel out the question why we ought to allow ourselves to be guided by them. Suppose there are other, and perhaps more sublime beings who do not share these human feelings but, on the contrary, disapprove of what pleases us? And suppose that reason is on their side? Or is it really on ours? The question is appropriate, and that is a sufficient ground for rejecting the definition. The same objection can be raised against Smith, especially as he himself differentiates various rules of sympathy and admits to widespread irregularities. These, too, rest on laws of human nature; why may they not also be included in the laws of sympathy? Why, for instance, should our partiality for the rich and prominent be excluded? And why should our tendency to sympathize with those who are successful not be counted among these rules? Of course, Smith says it is generally recognized that the consequences are not to influence our sympathies. Why not? Our sympathies may go astray if we allow them to run their course without regard to consequences. And if the consequences exercise a legitimate influence over our sympathies, then the principle does not lie within the laws of sympathy as such.

In finding it necessary to bring in grounds of usefulness, Hume has admitted himself that the question 'Why?' remains open and, consequently, that the true concept of the right end cannot be equivalent to that of the endeavour that arouses pleasure.

37. *Criticism of Herbart's definition*

Let us examine Herbart's formulation to see if it meets the two standards. Anticipating our conclusions, we may say that it fulfils neither.

1. (*a*) The very concept of a 'judgment of taste', which Herbart employs, is a *contradictio in adjecto*. He himself says, rightly, that the judgment is not the will. Willing and judging are two distinct entities. But feeling is also not judging. Hence his concept, taken literally, transgresses against the second criterion. Nevertheless, this criticism does not strike the theory at its root, and it can be rescued in its essentials by making a single modification.

(*b*) A more decisive consideration is that the theory does not meet the first criterion. It is quite appropriate to ask, 'Ought I necessarily to endeavour in a beautiful manner?' Beauty is a matter of appearance. It seems almost idolatrous to place so much weight upon appearance. Beauty may constitute some motivation, but should it be absolutely decisive? That is unthinkable. Ihering, in *Der Kampf ums Recht*, also expresses misgivings, and Lott,[12] in criticizing Herbart's theory, expresses essentially the same doubt. To be sure, Herbart thinks that every beautiful thing represents something of eternal and indubitable value and that what is moral differentiates itself from everything else of beauty as being that which determines the absolute value of the person himself. But if the beautiful represents something of value it is with reference to an appearance. It does not matter whether the thing which appears really exists, but only whether the idea of it is aroused within us and excites pleasure. This would have to be true of what is moral, too, if it is beautiful in the real sense, i.e. in the same sense as are artistically beautiful objects. And this is explicitly Herbart's doctrine: Moral taste, as a taste, is no different from poetic or musical taste or a taste for sculpture. He considers ethics, in its true sense, a part of aesthetics, and compares it to the thorough-bass. The only difference is that in the latter simple tones are sounded, while in the former, 'concepts of acts of will are to be determined with speculative caution, so that their relations, like the relations of the tones, fall into those that arouse absolute approval and those that excite absolute disapproval'.* If

---

[12] R. von Ihering (1818–92), one of the most prominent German lawyers during the latter half of the nineteenth century, was given an appointment in Vienna in 1868. Franz Karl Lott (1807–74) held the chair in Vienna just before Brentano.

* This quote seems to be pieced together out of several sentences from the following passage. 'Must we say that, up to the present time, the only correct model for a genuine theory of aesthetics is the musical theory that carries the curious name Generalbass [thorough-bass]? The thorough-bass demands, and procures, the passing of absolute judgments upon its simple intervals, chords, and transitions, without any proofs or explanations.—To continue: relations of will should be presented in the same way, so that, like the relations between the tones, they fall into those that arouse absolute approval and those that arouse absolute disapproval. Let us set aside in this case, as we do in that, all questions as to the possibility of making such judgments. It is enough that they are made. The only difference between them is self-evident: the musician has only to let the tones sound in order to present the relations, but in order to fulfil the same end, concepts of volitions must be determined with speculative caution, for the relations between *them* can only be perceived mentally, not physically.' Herbart, op. cit., Introduction, p. 345.

morality were beauty in this sense, then it is clear that it, too, would offer something of value with respect to appearance. And the moral would be superior to other beautiful things only in that it establishes the worth of the person—let us say, of the whole person—with respect to appearance. But perhaps there is another value to be distinguished, one that pertains to the person as such, not with respect to appearance. That every correct evaluation is aesthetic is to be absolutely denied. If Herbart is of this opinion, he has strayed into it by confusing concepts. He mistakes the pleasure taken in a thing on the grounds of a mere idea of it with the pleasure taken in it inasmuch as it brings about the idea. In the latter case the thing is pleasing as a means; thus it is with what is beautiful. If we had to decide, with respect to the beautiful, between the appearance and the reality, i.e. the existence of the object, we would choose the appearance. But if we had to make this choice with respect to the good, we would make the opposite choice. A mother loves her child's happiness more than the idea of it.

2. I have already had to oppose one fundamental idea of Herbart's aesthetics. It fails to recognize its boundaries. But there is yet another point in which I cannot share his conception of aesthetics. Herbart thinks all beauty is based upon relations: each part of what, in combination, pleases or displeases, is indifferent, taken in itself. In music, for instance, no one of the separate tones, the relations between which form an interval—say a fifth or a third—that is recognized in music, has by itself anything of the character it takes on when they all sound together. Thus, he says, the matter is indifferent; only the form determines the judgment of taste. 'Just as the ground carries with it its consequences, the perfected idea of a relation carries with it the same judgment in all beings who form ideas: [just as] at all times, so also under all accompanying circumstances and in every connection and complex . . .'*

What reasons does Herbart have for his opinion that nothing but relations determine beauty? Does it rest solely on the handful of examples that he cites from music and other arts and employs in his induction? By no means; rather, his theory is connected with

_____

* Though this was not in quotes, it is a quotation from Herbart, op. cit., Introduction, p. 350. It appears again below as a quotation.

the determination of the difference between what is beautiful and what is merely pleasant. With the feeling of pleasure and pain, what is felt cannot be conceived of in separation from the feeling. On the other hand, what we have an idea of in judgments of taste is something of which we can have a purely theoretical imagination. It is this characteristic which, according to Herbart, distinguishes it from what is pleasant or unpleasant. Now how is it possible, he asks, for us to conceive purely theoretically, and consequently as something of indifferent value, the imagined object to which the approval or disapproval pertains? It is only in so far as that which is pleasing or displeasing in judgments of taste consists of relations constructed of several elements, of which each is indifferent in itself.

But this argument seems to me to miscarry from the first. It is false that pleasure and pain have no other object besides themselves. Psychology proves the opposite. In this respect, the pleasure we take in a single tone is not different from that we take in a chord. What Herbart calls the merely pleasant also has the characteristic that he attributes solely to the purely beautiful. The feeling that is *not* directed to combinations also does not have only itself as an object; therefore any conclusion to be drawn from this characteristic applies equally to both combinations and simples. It does not follow that all beauty lies in relations.

No matter how we look at it, the explanation does not work. Is it true, then, that only the matter, and not the relation, is an object of theoretical contemplation? Clearly the relation must be such an object, too; how otherwise can the indifference of the value of the matter serve to make this theoretical contemplation comprehensible? If, under certain circumstances, I imagine the relation without aesthetic enjoyment or aesthetic displeasure, this only goes to show—if it is correct—that another among Herbart's opinions is not, viz. that such contemplation is necessarily, without exception, accompanied by aesthetic approval or disapproval. And there are indeed occasions when, e.g., scientific interests exclude all others. But we cannot in any way conclude from this that the matter is of indifferent value. Thus the proof that judgments of taste are determined by nothing but the forms of relations manifestly fails.

What is the true solution to Herbart's difficulty? Answer: Correction of the error he makes in speaking of judgments of taste. As I said already, taste is not judgment, nor judgment taste. But they have the same object. The difficulty does not exist in the first place for anyone who keeps feeling and judging distinct, as two separate species of mental relations.

Not only is the claim that beauty is determined by relations alone unproven; in my opinion, it is obviously false. A melody does not arouse the same aesthetic feeling regardless of whether it is played slowly or quickly, loudly or softly; imagine, for instance, the Marseillaise played pianissimo or Zerlina's aria sung fortissimo. Similarly, the same colours in the same relation to one another arouse a different feeling, depending upon whether they are lighter or darker, more or less vivid.

3. This leads us to another point in Herbart's principles of aesthetics, a point that is of the greatest importance for his ethics but is as far from the preceding point from being either proven or tenable. We have frequently remarked how much depends upon the fact that ethical precepts must be admissible as models not only for mankind but also for all other rational beings. Hume and Smith ran into difficulties as a consequence of this point. How, in this respect, does it stand with Herbart's theory, which comprehends all moral approval as aesthetic pleasure in relations?

Herbart declares decisively that his ethical laws, like aesthetic laws in general, are valid for all beings who form ideas.

For, 'just as the ground carries with it its consequences, the perfected idea of a relation carries with it the same judgment in all beings who form ideas: [just as] at all times, so also under all accompanying circumstances and in every connection and complex . . .'* This, then, is his proof: In contrast to the feeling of pleasure or displeasure, the judgment of taste refers to an imagined object, or, to put it more precisely, towards an imagined relation. The imagined relation gains my approval. The idea of the relation is the ground, the approval the consequence. Now whenever the same reason is given, the same consequence follows. Therefore the same judgment always attaches to the idea of any one relation, no matter in what connection and complex and in which of the beings who have ideas it occurs.

Now, is the course of this argument correct? Far from it! Assuming that, as Herbart claims, our aesthetic pleasure were

* Herbart, loc. cit.

always directed solely towards the form of relations, it would by no means follow that everyone who has an idea of this relation must feel the same aesthetic pleasure. Let us illustrate this by comparing it to a conclusion—more specifically, a sophism—by which someone gets taken in. The sophism leads him into an error. The premises are the ground; the erroneous conclusion is the consequence. But will everyone who believes the premises be ensnared? No, for in every case in which the conclusion actually comes into being certain accompanying conditions play a role, and it is only when all of these occur together that the conclusion really enters our consciousness; otherwise it does not. Furthermore, the conclusion is not even always drawn from correct principles. Its unconditional validity does not lie in, or follow from, the fact that it is always drawn in this way, for it is not. The case at hand is similar. The idea of the relation is the ground, the approval is the consequence. But here, too, certain accompanying conditions are always required in order for the approval to actually materialize. Our inner nature, the most essential aspects of which are hidden from us, makes it possible for us to have ideas, to acknowledge or reject the object of the idea, and also to find it beautiful or ugly, to desire it or flee from it. No one is able to explain in any individual case how it is that the one or the other thing happens. Opinions also differ widely in so far as some think that physiological processes play a part and others that they play no part; some thinkers conceive the physiological processes to be of a different sort from other thinkers.

Thus we see clearly that Herbart has not proven his aesthetic principles to be valid for all beings who form ideas. The same hesitation that we had about other moral philosophers remains standing with respect to him.

4. Indeed, not only has he not proven that in general the same judgment of taste attaches to the idea of the same relation; experience shows us the very opposite.

(*a*) We indicated this already in disputing his claim that the matter is of indifferent value. Loudness and softness, slowness or rapidity in music makes a difference with respect to aesthetic pleasure, even if all the relations are preserved. It is wrong, then, to state that it remains the same 'under all accompanying conditions'.

(*b*) Moreover, in earlier times certain relations between tones in music were held to be beautiful which now arouse no aesthetic pleasure; conversely, certain relations were considered discordant which are now generally acknowledged to be pleasing. The keys were different from ours. The ear had to get used to them, and did. And in more recent times it has had to change its habits again; we are still getting used to *Tannhäuser, Tristan und Isolde,* and the *Nibelungentrilogie.* The form of the relation is by no means something which at all times, under all circumstances, and in all beings who form ideas awakens the same approval or disapproval. Consequently we have no guarantee that this will be the case with relations, which, according to Herbart, call forth moral approval. But that was the only way he knew to establish their validity for all rational beings. Thus this validity is not confirmed by his efforts, and the old objection to the sentimental theory has not been disposed of.

38. Further criticism of Herbart, using his idea of justice as an example for discussion; the fundamental error in his ethics; an indication that it contains a grain of truth*

I. After these critical comments on Herbart's fundamental view of ethics, we can spare ourselves the trouble of going into the details of his theory, particularly as we are concerned here only with the concept of the right end as he develops it. Nevertheless, we may gain a not unwelcome support for our general criticism if we demonstrate, using as an example one of his five 'practical ideas', that his basic idea in particular cannot be carried out. Let us select for the purpose the so-called idea of justice.

A. How does what Herbart says about it fit in with the facts?

1. Is conflict aesthetically displeasing?

(*a*) In his famous work, *Der Kampf ums Recht,* Ihering denies this decisively. And indeed, all the games, e.g. chess and card games, which include opponents are a convincing proof that, on

* This section on Herbart has been much abridged by the German editor. The reader who is interested in Brentano's discussion of Herbart should consult the manuscripts of his lecture notes: *Ethikkollege,* MSS., Eth. 21, pp. 20563–613. These are available on microfilm.

the contrary, conflict arouses pleasure. The English take such delight in boxing that anyone who prefers to cry 'Peace!' and separate the opponents, rather than to follow the fight as a spectator, is sure to become entangled in fights himself.

(*b*) And is the pleasure we derive from conflict not of an aesthetic nature? If it is not, why do the poets show such a predilection for the struggle between the Trojans and Aegeans? And think, too, of the Roman gladiator fights and Spanish bullfights. They are performances for spectators, however bloody they may be. And in our imagination we associate these dramas with dramas in nature; we are able to picture fire and water as conflicting powers. We stand enthralled before the drama of the seething of the sea, and, following an ancient tendency in our nature, we conceive of the elements as analogous to our inner soul, as genuinely conflicting forces, raging and then repelling the storm.

(*c*) To be sure, displeasure also attaches to conflict; we do have the proverb, 'Blessed are the peacemakers'. But this displeasure is not actually directed towards conflict as such but towards the motives, which are displeasing under certain circumstances, and, even more frequently, towards the consequences of dispute. Thus we may be repelled by particular forms of conflict, but it cannot be claimed that conflict in general displeases.

2. Is displeasure at conflict the basis of the idea of justice? Is the sole aim of justice to avert dispute?

(*a*) The answer is no, if only because, as already discussed, conflict is not displeasing as such but displeases for other reasons, if at all. Consequently, bringing conflict to an end cannot be an ultimate goal.

(*b*) Justice is not the sole, or the most effective, means of averting or ending conflicts, especially as regard for the general good, but not compulsion, is a part of the essence of justice. Otherwise, pleasure in the concluding of a conflict would appear even when it results from complaisance, cowardice, or a servile spirit. These are surely more effective means of averting conflict than justice, and justice does not follow in their wake, but rather the sacrifice of justice.

(*c*) If this were the end of justice, displeasure at an offence against justice would have to disappear once the danger of conflict was over; we could only feel displeased for other reasons, but that would not be displeasure at injustice.

(*d*) Moreover, if conflict is displeasing, the use and even the exercising of justice must be displeasing where it gives rise to conflict. But resistance to injustice is pleasing.

(*e*) And doing what is just often causes conflict, e.g. when important persons persecute the judge who has issued a just decision against them.

(*f*) If justice were pleasing solely because of the avoidance of conflict, conflict would have to displease more than injustice.

(*g*) Lott also raises the point that the order not to begin any disputes concerns both parties, although it may apply more closely to the person who has given his assent. (But it appears to apply even more strongly to the party whose submission seems most plausible and most persistent. However, this person is not always the one who ought by rights to yield. Herbart recognizes this point himself and expresses it in the part where he places restrictions on the arbitrariness of justice.)

3. Not every positive law of justice is just, even though it may avert conflict for all time. It may be flagrantly unjust. Positive justice is a compound concept, formed out of justice, in the true sense, and power. According to Herbart, all justice is positive, a view which obliterates the distinction between good and bad laws. All laws, he says, are instituted, either by settlement or by power, in order to bring conflict to an end in one way or another. Consequently all laws are good in so far as they suppress conflict; despotically repressive laws often succeed in doing this just as well as humane laws. And if there is any distinction between laws, in this view, it is highly questionable whether precisely those laws are best which come the closest to making conflict impossible; this might rather be a consequence of their being bad laws, viz. laws that are repressive and unreasonable. In other words, if we consistently hold Herbart's theory we must put power before justice, as more certainly averting conflict. Suppose the Franco-Prussian War (1870–1) had been concluded by a peace treaty which permanently destroyed the French people. Would that have been just? Yes, according to Herbart's principle, for it would have permanently disposed of the danger of war; but in fact, only the most extreme nationalist could make such a judgment.

How does what Herbart says about the idea of justice fit in with his aesthetic principles?

Which is the object of approval: the establishing of justice—the limits it sets—or the doing of justice? Assume it is the first. Is the pleasure we take in the limits set by justice an aesthetic one? They are supposed to be pleasing as a means to averting conflict or disharmony. But pleasure taken in something inasmuch as it is a means cannot properly be called aesthetic; if so, any pleasure we may take in a violin inasmuch as it is a musical instrument would be aesthetic. Indeed, this alternative is unthinkable here for another reason: the limits set by justice are not a means to harmony, but to the avoidance of disharmony (Trendelenburg). Now let us assume it is the second, that the object of aesthetic pleasure is the doing of justice, the observance of just limits as such. Then the relation to conflict is still more remote. According to Herbart, what distinguishes the doing of justice is concurrence with a rule which serves to avert disharmony. This rule cannot itself be conceived of as a unanimous agreement among wills, but only as the consequence of such agreement. Thus the rule is not itself a relation among wills, and consequently the pleasure taken in it is not, according to Herbart's principle, an aesthetic pleasure.

II. No matter how carefully we examine Herbart's ideas, including those which have not been mentioned separately here, we cannot find any useful guidelines for our behaviour. We cannot gain any clarification from them respecting the ultimate end. But this is not the greatest fault in his system. It also suffers from the same defect for which we had to admonish the Scottish philosophers. Just as they claimed there were a number of moral rules, Herbart propounds five ideas; here, as there, each is supposed to be absolute and valid without exception. But while a given relation may be derivable from one idea, an opposing relation can just as easily be derived from another. Trendelenburg already noted that every deed can be justified by the idea of perfection, or accomplishment, and every omission by the idea of fairness (in that it does not disturb current conditions). How are we to decide when the ideas become so entangled with one another and so conflicting? Herbart has no means of instructing us as to which relation deserves preference, for the idea of analogous relations is always supposed to carry along with it the same judgment of approval or disapproval, in any connection or complex. Hence, when two ideas come into conflict with one another, approval as well as disapproval must set in; in other words, the act must be both good and bad. Where no unitary standard commands, we cannot decide what takes precedence. We lack a supreme idea to decide and resolve the conflicts between the several ideas.

In Herbart's theory we have found some causes of contradiction. But it would be unfair for me not to indicate here that it also deserves recognition, not only as a product of earnest mental efforts and because of its noble propensities, but also because it contains a grain of truth. In one point Herbart came nearer to the truth than many another thinker; but the ingredient of truth is so overgrown with errors that the seed does not sprout and come to fruition. For just this reason we must fight our way through to greater clarity with the help of further investigation, until we find it possible to give a justification of this admission.

B. Criticism of the definitions of the right end by means of the internal determinations of endeavour.

39. J. S. Mill, Beneke, and Cudworth

Certain philosophers have considered justified endeavour itself, rather than its consequences, to be the distinguishing mark by which we are able to recognize the right end. Let us turn now to a critique of their conceptions of the right end.

1. The right end is the most desirable of the attainable ends; consequently, it is the end striven for by the man who has experience both of the objects and of the means his circumstances offer. Thus the actual endeavour of the man of experience becomes the standard. From time to time J. S. Mill expresses this view; in ancient times it was represented by Socrates. In more recent German philosophy we can also find statements which seek to explain all moral differences by means of differences in knowledge.

The first thing to be said against this view is that it is false. *Scio meliora proboque, deteriora sequor.* This becomes particularly clear where a choice is made between a momentary pleasure and later, more perfect and permanent possession of the same good. One person makes this choice, another the other, although neither of them lacks an adequate knowledge of the objects of choice or of his own situation. Mill himself does not hold to this idea consistently. To be sure, he expresses on occasion the thought that no one who is familiar with nobler pleasures and who has retained the capacity to enjoy them would prefer the lower; on the other hand, he mentions that in cases of temptation a person succumbs with a consciousness of having chosen what is worse. After that Mill tries once again to seek a standard more in consciousness than in actual behaviour.

When Socrates identified virtue with knowledge, he underrated the power of habit and education. But Mill lays a great deal of weight upon these factors, so much that, disregarding his own claim that only pleasure is desirable, he holds it to be possible, and to be virtuous, to sacrifice all our pleasure, our whole selves, for the well-being of others. As a consequence of ethical training it is possible for us to reach a state in which we always have the well-being of the whole in our gaze.

Second, even assuming the proposition that we always endeavour towards the most desirable of the objects which seem attainable is correct, the concept of what is most desirable does not coincide with the concept of the right end. We must ask why we ought in fact to desire what is most desirable.

2. Beneke clearly seeks something which Mill omits. But in making efforts to find it he gets no further than thinking of certain impulses as characterized as normal or, let us say, as healthy products of development. That which is perceived as higher and is desired in accordance with the norms based in human nature is supposed to be what is morally required. Why? Is it certain from the very first that the tendencies of human nature are directed towards the good? To be sure, Beneke goes on to say that the correct evaluation makes itself manifest by means of the feeling of obligation, and if this is so there remains no more place for the question, 'Ought I to?' But what is meant by the 'feeling of obligation?' And are there not imperatives issued by separate authorities? It depends upon whether someone says, 'You ought', with justification. Beneke thinks the correct evaluation announces itself by the feeling of obligation because it is grounded in the fundamental essence of the soul. This leads us back to the question of how we recognize that this essence is directed towards the good.

3. If Beneke's opinions excite doubt and scruples, whatever are we to say of Cudworth's manner of metaphysical expression? How are we to conceive of his endeavour, which includes the

essence, the 'verity', of moral goodness? In any case, the right end must at least be attainable. How are we to recognize this from the endeavour?

Thus none of the formulations belonging to the third genus are satisfactory, either.

VII

A New Attempt to Give Ethics a Foundation

40. *The origin of the concept of the good, and the analogy between it and the concept of the true*[13]

1. Our historical survey and our evaluation of it have produced negative results. We have not been released from the need to make our own investigation. Nevertheless, this investigation was not made in vain. It has got us into practice and, more important, steered us in certain directions. All indications are that the truth is to be sought in the third genus, i.e. in that group of ethical systems that proceed from justified endeavour. At first we were disappointed that we could not find anything tenable even here, but nothing can mislead us into giving up our trust that we are on the right track. It is not the same as with the other groups, where we recognized that no further attempts could succeed. And this trust is confirmed on other grounds as well.

For in the course of our observations we have hit upon something to which we can without a single doubt adhere as valid. Philosophers who in other respects set about working on the basis of ethics in quite different ways were unanimous in their opinion that the right end consists in the best of what is attainable.

---

[13] Sections 40–4 have been edited by A. Kastil with an eye to Brentano's more developed analyses. Cf. *The Origin of our Knowledge of Right and Wrong* (trans. Chisholm and Schneewind, London: Routledge & Kegan Paul, 1969), *The True and the Evident* (trans. Chisholm *et al.*, London: Routledge & Kegan Paul, 1966), and Kastil, 'Ontologischer und gnoseologischer Wahrheitsbegriff' (see note 3 above).

If there is any just accusation to be made against this definition, it is that it is obscure. For the concepts certainly coincide. If something that is striven for is not attainable, then it certainly cannot be the correct ultimate end, no matter how good it may be. Conversely, if something that is striven for is not good or is not better than what is omitted or set aside in order that it may be realized, it is not the correct ultimate end, even if it is attainable; the greater the discrepancy between the values, the further it is from being the right end. Only the end that exceeds all others in value can be the correct ultimate end, i.e. it must be the best, but only in so far as it is attainable.

Now, what is it that is obscure about the concept and prevents it from fulfilling the task of any definition, viz. to explain a name? Clearly, the obscurity comes only from the terms 'good' and 'better'. For here, too, there were great discrepancies between the determinations given by philosophers, which led to a great variety of formulations of the correct ultimate end.

How are we to go about establishing the concept of the good? This is the first and the most urgent question, and everything depends upon its being answered. The task of determining a concept is very closely connected to the question as to the source from which we attain it. The explanation of a term is in the last analysis a reference to certain phenomena. Thus Hume was quite right when, in his famous investigation into the concept of causality, he introduced the question as to the origin of the concept. For this reason we already distinguished in a certain way the various views according to their origin, at the point where we discussed, not the simpler determination of the concept of good, but that of the ultimate end.

2. Where does the concept of the good come from?

Some thinkers teach that there are certain *a priori* ideas, in addition to concepts gained from experience. They are said to be innate, to be imprinted upon the soul prior to all experience. But such an assumption is totally unnecessary. For every general concept we can point to certain concrete ideas, or images, from which it or the parts of which it is constructed are abstracted.

What are these ideas in the case of the concept of the good? Does this concept originate in inner or in external intuition? External intuition or perception always shows us localized qualities in temporal duration and apprehended, therefore, either in a state of rest or in the act of changing, be it abruptly or continuously. This is the origin of the concepts of the coloured, the sounding (sound making), the warm, the big, the small, the spatially removed, etc. But none of our senses deliver to us the concept of the good. The concept of the 'moral sense' was erroneous.

Thus the concept of the good must be abstracted from inner intuition or perception. This does not show us localized, spatially extended objects, but mental occurrences, the consciousness of something, i.e. we perceive ourselves as having an object. We can have an object in three ways: merely as having an idea of it, as judging it as well, or as also taking an interest in it, viz. as feeling and willing.

3. That the concept of the good stems from inner perception is also supported by its similarity to the concept of the true. These concepts appear to be analogous, not only in content but also in origin.

Now, the concept of the true undoubtedly arises from inner perception. But in order for this to become quite clear, attention must be drawn to the fact that the word 'true' is employed in several meanings which are to be distinguished from one another. Aristotle was aware of this ambiguity. It is no merely accidental ambiguity such as occurs when two things happen to have the same name and by virtue of which, e.g. the name 'Bauer', in German, is sometimes given to a bird cage and sometimes to a farmer, or an ocular disease and a bird are both called 'Star' (in German). Rather, the various meanings of the word 'true' are related in much the same way as the various meanings of the word 'healthy'. We speak sometimes of a healthy body, sometimes of a healthy complexion; at various times we use 'healthy' with reference to food, to a district, to medicine prescribed by a doctor, to a walk, etc. Aristotle made use of this example himself in order to show how a certain relation, a certain connection between the meanings sometimes exists with respect to expressions having a variety of meanings. For everything called healthy here bears this name in reference, with regard to the health of the body. It is the body which is to be called healthy in the genuine sense; anything else is to be so called only in derivative senses which are to be distinguished from one another according to the various relations in which the objects referred to as healthy stand to the body: one because it demonstrates the health of the body, another because it assists, maintains, restores, etc., the health of the body.*

It is the same with the expressions 'true' and 'false'. They are ambiguous because of a variety of relations to something to which these terms apply in their real sense.

At times we call ideas true or false, e.g. false ideas in dreams or hallucinations; we also apply the terms to suspicions, apprehensions, hopes, etc. But we also call external objects true and false: expressions, letters of the alphabet, various signs or signals, money.†

Now, what is the one thing to which we are relating all other things in calling them true or false? What, in other words, is the one thing that is referred to as true or false in the proper sense?

Here, too, Aristotle has already given us the right answer. Truth, in its proper sense, is found in judgments. It is with reference to the truth or falsity of judgments that things bear one or the other of these designations: some things because they induce us to make a false judgment (an hallucination, a word written in by mistake, a piece of copper that we erroneously take to be gold because of its lustre); still others because they are intended to induce a false or a true judgment; and yet others because anyone who holds them to be such will make true, or false, judgments accordingly (a true scholar, a false friend).

The question is this: when are we to call a judgment true, and when false? That—as the law of contradiction declares—every judgment must be either true or false, makes clear that these

* There is no single English adjective that is suitable in all these cases. In some we might use 'wholesome', in others 'salutary'. Yet the point can be comprehended.

† Here again, these expressions are not all admissible in English, as they are in German; we do not generally speak of true or false expressions, etc. For 'true' we could substitute 'real' or 'genuine'. For 'false' it is impossible to find a single applicable term; try 'insincere', 'spurious', 'counterfeit'. But the point can still be made; we can speak, e.g., of true and false friends. The reader should also be reminded that the German term, 'Vorstellung', which is being translated as 'idea', has the sense of something presented to the mind. It sounds odd to speak of a false idea in a dream, but we must think of it as an image of what is not, an illusory image.

determinations must be essentially bound up with the nature of judgment. Hence Aristotle gave his answer in accordance with his own conception of the nature of judgments.

He holds that a judgment consists fundamentally of a complex of thoughts; it is a combination of ideas, and that is what distinguishes it from mere ideas, involving no opinion. Someone who contemplates the concept of the red or the round does not thereby form a judgment. But a judgment is formed by the person who combines them by pronouncing that there is something round which is red.

A judgment, he says, is that particular synthesis of thought in which something is held to be either bound up with—one with—something else, or divided off from—separate from—something else. If we hold what is really bound together to be combined and what is really separated to be separate we make a true judgment; on the other hand, we make a false judgment when we judge things to stand in the opposite manner from the way they do. Thus Aristotle.

Does this definition fit all true judgments? If I say that a dog is not a cat, I have certainly separated a dog from a cat. But the judgment that he is not a dragon is also correct. Yet there is no dragon, either united with the dog or separated from him. In order to do justice to such negative judgments, Aristotle's definition must be slightly altered. We would have to say that a judgment is true if it ascribes something to a thing which is united with it or if it denies of it something from which it is separate.

But still the definition does not fit all judgments. For some judgments neither attribute a subject to a predicate nor deny that it has such a predicate, but simply accept or reject something. In making them we do not judge that some S is P or some S is not P, but simply that there is an S, or no S, e.g. 'There is a God', 'There are no ghosts'. In his theory of judgment Aristotle overlooked these simple acknowledgments and rejections, which do not have predicates; his definition of true and false is of no use for them. We need a definition which is applicable to all judgments.

In order to achieve a unitary definition, we could point out that we can introduce predication into existential propositions by replacing, e.g., 'Some person is sick', 'Some triangle or other is right-angled', 'No circle possesses unequal radii' with 'There exists a sick person', 'There exists a triangle that is not right-angled', and 'There exists no circle with unequal radii'. If we did this, then the definition of truth that is applicable to simple acknowledgments and rejections would suit all judgments; an affirming judgment is true if its object exists, a rejecting judgment true if its object does not exist.

Whoever says this is not speaking incorrectly, but also is not making the concept any clearer. Treating this definition seriously, we would have to have established previously that A exists in order to recognize the judgment, 'A exists', as true, i.e. we would have to recognize the judgment, 'A exists', as true before making it. Clearly, this definition leads us around in a circle, and we have need of a different one.

4. It happens not infrequently that all efforts to analyse a concept fail. It cannot be otherwise if the concept is elementary, for a thing which has no characteristics cannot be dissected. No one would be illuminated by an analysis of the concept of the coloured if he had not already abstracted it from the intuition of individual colours. Perhaps we are faced, in the case of the sense of the term 'true', with a fundamental difference between judgments which can only be clarified by means of examples from our inner perception.

Now of course this conjecture assumes that the truth of a judgment is a characteristic that can be perceived, and it is precisely this that we could question. Imagine someone who judges, correctly, that there still exist specimens of a certain species of animal. Must the person who makes the judgment undergo some change if, during the time he still maintains his judgment, the last specimen dies and the entire species dies out? Surely not—yet his true judgment has turned into a false one. Similarly, a correct denial, e.g. 'There exist no dragons', does not become false by undergoing some change itself but because the objects the existence of which was correctly denied come into existence.

True judgments, then, do not seem to be really different from false ones as such. The difference is not one which can be perceived and illuminated by examples from perception. Apparently there does not exist any intuition from which the meaning of the word 'true' could be culled; the word itself seems not to have any meaning.

In reaching clarity, we shall not be able to avoid enumerating every characteristic with respect to which judgments in our inner perception can vary. In doing so we can exclude those characteristics common to all judgments, for the characteristic peculiar to truth cannot lie in them.

Anyone who forms a judgment about something has an idea of a thing, even if it is not perfectly definite. Some thing is the object of his idea and, consequently, of his judgment. For instance, the judgments, 'There exist people' and 'There exist fish', are to be distinguished by their objects. But judgments that have the same object can be distinguished in other respects. The believer and the atheist both have as their object an infinitely perfect creator, but the former makes a judgment with the quality of affirmation, the latter, with the quality of rejection. Since both true and erroneous judgments are to be found among the affirming as well as among the rejecting judgments, the characteristic truth cannot lie in the quality of the judgment as such.

We judge what we judge either as a mere fact or as a necessity. This difference is called a difference in the modality of the judgment; in the first case we speak of an assertoric judgment, in the second of an apodictic judgment. Truth cannot lie here, either. Columbus' opponents judged apodictically that the Antipodes could not exist, and Materialists think nothing can exist that does not take up space. And both are as much in error as the man who believes that coloured bodies do in fact exist, but denies that they must exist.

We do not find the characteristic that distinguishes true judgments from false in their quality and modality. But our judgments point to another sort of distinction. Let us compare the judgment of external perception that acknowledges something blue or something sounding, or making noise, with the judgment of internal perception, in which we recognize ourselves as seeing something blue or hearing tones. Both judgments are positive, and both are assertoric, but the second is distinguished from the first by a basic difference: it is evident, discerning, while the former lacks evidence. When I see, I acknowledge what is coloured instinctively and with complete conviction; but if I make the consequences of this affirmation clear to myself, I immediately find myself entangled in contradictions with certain facts, which teaches me that my judgment is false. But this is not true of the judgment that I see something coloured. This is an immediate certainty, not to be refuted by any argumentation. It is not a subjective conviction, which could be an error; it is infallibly true. I may be deceived in many of the judgments that I hold with conviction. While convinced that I was standing in a certain place, I could in reality be dreaming. As Descartes puts it, an all-powerful being might have ensnared me in an inescapable web of errors, so that everything outside that I hold to be real would be mere appearance; but that I myself exist, doubt, think, hope, see, hear, love, fear, etc.—about these things no omnipotent being can deceive me. With the exception of the judgments of inner perception, that is, the affirmations of our own mental activity, our own acts of consciousness, there are no positive judgments possessing immediate evidence.

It is only among negative judgments that we find others that are immediately discernible. For instance, we can discern that a thing cannot both be and not be at the same time, or, more precisely, that I cannot correctly both affirm and reject something at the same time. Such insights have the advantage over those of inner perception inasmuch as they are apodictic: what is rejected apodictically is rejected as impossible. On the other hand, such judgments do not offer us any positive information; they do not allow us to acknowledge anything as existing; they do not reveal to us what is, but only what cannot be.

These two forms of immediate cognitions, the assertoric cognition of our perception of ourselves and the apodictic, negative cognition, exhaust the sources from which we obtain our concept of the true. It can only be culled from such instances of evident judgments. They must be pointed out to anyone who wishes to understand the import of the word 'true'. But no rhetoric, no analytic acumen, can teach their significance to someone who has never had the experience of an evident judgment and who is therefore not in a position to compare it with other judgments which lack this characteristic.

41. *Truth and evidence*

Is it really the evidence of a judgment that contains what is called its truth? It might be objected that many judgments lack evidence without being false. For instance, someone may fully understand the significance of a mathematical proposition and continue to believe in it with conviction, even though he has forgotten the proof. His judgment is true, but it is no longer evident.

I want to touch upon this objection because some people who have already become quite clear about the matter have been led astray by it. I shall make use of an analogy to deprive it of its force. Suppose we are defining the word 'healthy' and list, among the features that form the concept, a certain blood temperature. Would the fact that a medicine or a food are called healthy,* even though they contain no blood, show the definition to be false? Clearly not, for these are called healthy in another sense: not because they are healthy themselves, but because they promote the health of the body.

Likewise, a blind judgment is not called true in the same sense of the word as an evident judgment, i.e. it does not bear this name because it is itself discernible, but *because it can be derived from evident judgments or because*, though it does not share the characteristic of evidence with immediately evident judgments, *it agrees with them in every other respect, in particular with respect to its object and its quality as a judgment.*

Difficult as it has been for philosophers to analyse the concept of truth, and often as they have strayed from the right path, no great philosopher has failed to notice the phenomenon of evidence. It is to be noted even in the designations contained in common speech. They are graphic and have a distinctive character, the images being taken mostly from seeing or from light: illuminating [*einleuchtend*], evident (from *videre*), insightful. And the picture of a judgment which is not evident as a 'blind' judgment is related to them. In considering the elementary character of the phenomenon, philosophers, too, frequently make use of such figurative paraphrases. Descartes speaks of a natural light, which he opposes to natural but obscure impulses to believe (*lumen naturale, non impetus naturalis*). Leibniz says that certain truths establish themselves as valid '*dans une manière lumineuse* [in a luminous way]'. Yet scientific terminology could get along without any such images. It is of greater importance that we reserve the name 'cognition' or 'knowledge' for judgments that are evident or are deduced from evident judgments; unfortunately,

---

* Here again, the example does not work in English: medicine and foods might be called 'wholesome' or even 'healthful', but not 'healthy'. Nevertheless the point is clear.

this proposal is frequently disregarded. But let us set aside this question of terminology. We are now clear about the essentials. Only an evident judgment is certain. If a judgment lacks this character, we must try to elevate it to the rank of an evident judgment by means of proofs; that is, by deriving it from judgments. No such proofs, no sciences, can exist at all unless we possess, among our judgments, some that are immediately evident.

With evidence is given universal validity of the judgment; it is conceivable that we should believe the opposite of it, but not that we should know it.

42. *The concept of the good originates in the experience of acts of the emotions that are experienced as being correct; the analogy between these and the evidence of judgments*

The preceding investigations into the concept of truth were intended solely to throw light upon the concept of the good, which was formerly obscured from our view. The light I mean is the light of analogy, which has put us in a position to continue our investigation.

Like 'true', 'good' also has several meanings. We speak of a good will, of a good breakfast, of a good sign, and so forth, as well as of good as an object of our desire and of the goodness of this desire itself.

And among objects that are good, not all are good in the same sense. We call a stock of provisions a stock of goods, but we also call the knowledge of a scientific truth a sublime good.

The variety of meanings of the goodness of objects is easily explained. Some are called good in the sense of useful, viz. those that are means to a good end, as medicine for health.

Such an end can itself be useful, that is, it can serve a yet higher end, but ultimately we reach something we call good, not because it serves something else, but in itself. We learned that the various meanings of the true all pointed to something which bears the name in its real sense: the true judgment. The ambiguity of good is analogous. In calling an object good we are not giving it a material predicate, as we do when we call something red or round or warm or thinking. In this respect, the expressions good and bad are like the expressions existent and non-existent. In using the latter, we do not intend to add yet another to the determining characteristics of the thing in question; we wish rather to say that whoever acknowledges a certain thing and rejects another certain thing makes a true judgment. And when we call certain objects good and others bad we are merely saying that whoever loves the former and hates the latter has taken the right stand. The source of these concepts is inner perception, for it is only in inner perception that we comprehend ourselves as loving or hating something.

But is an act of loving or hating really able to reveal itself to us as correct? Does this constitute a real perceptible difference in such acts?

We no longer need be embarrassed by this question. For if we pose it in a manner analogous to the way in which we posed the question whether a true judgment is perceptibly different from a false one, we shall find an analogous answer.

Among our judgments we found some that are distinguished by possessing evidence and others that lack this characteristic. A blind judgment may coincide with an evident judgment in every other respect, but as long as we fail to judge something with direct or indirect evidence we can make no decision as to whether it is true or false. However, in the case of an evident judgment we need make no such decision. It is experienced as being correct. It is only inasfar as we discern certain judgments that the word 'true' takes on significance. Without this sort of standard or guide for our judgments, which is offered solely by evident judgments, no logic or science would be conceivable. There would exist no distinction between innate or acquired impulses to believe and that more sublime aspect of our intellectual nature that determines us to form correct and discerning judgments, no difference between stupid animal expectations stemming from instinct or habit and human intelligence, which because of its superiority has been likened to light as opposed to darkness and vision as opposed to blindness. The situation which the Sceptics believe to exist would in fact be realized.

But inner experience also reveals an analogous distinction between our lower and higher selves with regard to our being pleased and desiring. Our feelings of pleasure and displeasure are often, like blind judgments, merely instinctive impulses, arising from the particular situation or from habit. This is true, for instance, of the pleasure or displeasure we take in certain tastes or smells and of the pleasure the miser takes in hoarding money. The innate instincts of the various species often conflict, and even those of different individuals of the same species. But are such pleasurable or displeasing impulsive emotions the only kind of pleasure or displeasure? Many psychologists mention no other variety. They overlook the existence of a higher class of emotional activities. But other psychologists have long recognized these more exalted emotions; they have said, for instance, that we are naturally constructed to take pleasure in clear insights and feel displeased at obscurity and error. At the beginning of the *Metaphysics*, Aristotle says that all men by nature desire to know. This desire may serve us as an example: *It is a pleasure arising from a more exalted form of acts of consciousness and is analogous to evidence in the sphere of judgment.* In so far as our spiritual life operates normally—that is, is not disturbed by disease or completely spoiled by the influences of the surrounding world—this higher form of emotion is common to all men. If there existed men, or some other kind of being, having the general capacity to exercise this higher form of judgment and evaluation, yet taking a position opposed to ours, we would not say that it was a matter of taste, as we do of the preference for certain sensual qualities (*De gustibus non est disputandum*). Rather, we would declare that such love and hate are fundamentally perverse, that the species in question hates what is without doubt good and love what is bad. Why is everything so different in this case? It cannot be because of the strength of the impulse, for under certain circumstances our enjoyment of sensual pleasure can be as strong. It has quite different grounds. In the case of ordinary feelings the violence arises from an instinctive impulse; here, the natural pleasure we take is a more exalted form of love, experienced as being right. *In discovering this love within ourselves we recognize the object not only as being loved and lovable, but also as being worthy of love.*

These examples can be multiplied. But it is not until later that we will be saddled with the task of setting up a table of goods; here it is not our business to give an exhaustive account of the realm of the concept good, but only to become clear about its contents. And we have attained this goal. *We call something good in view of the fact that the love directed upon it is experienced as being correct, just as we say that an object exists if the acknowledgment directed upon it is directly or indirectly evident.*

132

43. *The concept of the better*

But we have not yet answered exhaustively the question as to the principles of ethical knowledge. We know not only that things are good or bad, but also that some are better than others. And here the analogy to the correctness of judgments deserts us, for everything true is equally so. How do we recognize that something is better? And above all, what does 'better' mean?

Some people have attempted to give the following answer. If A is a good and B is a good, then the sum of A and B is a greater good; this is discernible *a priori*, just as is the fact that one existing thing plus another existing thing add up to a greater quantity of existing things. Everything that is better consists of a greater quantity of good and is to be recognized by means of addition.

But this explication appears to be unsatisfactory. Is it true that in every case where we find something to be better the difference in question is merely quantitative? Does not quality also bring about differences of value? And quite aside from this, is having a greater quantity of good really the same as being better? If so, having a greater quantity of existence would have to be equivalent to being truer. Whence the difference?

This question makes us aware of a peculiarity of the life of the emotions in which that of the intellect does not take part. That I love good A more than good B does not mean that I love it more intensely but that I *prefer* it. This preference is a special species of the class of the phenomena of interest. It is a love directed upon an object, which is known in all its peculiarities to everyone through his inner experience and is distinct from simple love. The fact that not everything good is equally good, although everything true is equally true, is connected with the particular character-istics of this variety of interest. Saying that something is better is simply saying that it is preferable as over against some other thing, i.e. that it can correctly be preferred to this other thing.

But how do we recognize the preferability? Not as a real determinant residing in the object. Just as 'existent' does not designate a predicate that pertains to a thing along with other predicates, 'good', too, is not such a predicate. And like 'good', 'better' is not a real determinant. When someone acknowledges something with evidence, we say that he recognizes it as existing; when someone who loves with a love experienced as being correct perceives himself as loving correctly, we say that he recognizes something as good. Thus, to recognize something as better means simply to recognize oneself as someone who prefers it with a preference experienced as being right.

For, like the simple acts of love, those acts that involve preference include some of a higher and others of a lower order. Some preferences result purely from instinct, blindly, whereas others are experienced as being correct. It is not only correct to love knowledge and recognition, but they are also to be preferred to mere belief or, indeed, error with a preference experienced as being correct. Here, too, our stand is not left to our taste or our will but finds its standard in preference experienced as being correct; any position that is opposed to this preference is wrong, perverse. For instance, the person who prefers joy along with knowledge to mere knowledge without joy prefers rightly, and in recognizing himself as someone who prefers in a manner experienced as being correct, he recognizes the entirety of these goods as better than each part taken in itself.

44. Conclusion of the investigation, begun in section 19, as to how the participation of the feelings in the realization of ethical knowledge fits in with its universal validity

1. We have now answered the question we designated as being prior to the question regarding the right end. We know now what it means for something to be good or to be better than something else: the former means that it can be loved rightly, the latter, that it can be preferred rightly. In recognizing ourselves as loving something with a love experienced as being correct, we recognize that thing as good; in recognizing ourselves as preferring something with a preference experienced as being correct, we recognize that thing as being better.

Our suspicion that the principles of ethics are cognitions of feelings has proven to be correct. And this result has also brought us close to the solution of the problem as to how the participation of the feelings in the realization of fundamental ethical knowledge is to be reconciled with its validity for all rational beings.

Only a person who has failed to notice the difference between instinctive, blind emotions and emotions experienced as being correct can have any doubts about the universal validity of the knowledge of good and bad on the basis of the part played by the emotions. Ethical subjectivism based on these grounds is in the same position as subjectivism with respect to truth and falsity. When the Sophist Protagoras declared man to be the measure of all things—of the things that are, that they are, of the things that are not, that they are not—he betrayed the fact that he had never been struck by the difference between evident and blind judgments. Anyone who grasps this difference recognizes that no more than one of two contradictory judgments can be discerned. What one man discerns may be hidden from another, but no one can discern the contrary. Protagoras extended his relativism to good and bad as well. But what is true of evident judgments is also true of emotions experienced as being correct. When I recognize my acts of loving and preferring as correct, I also recognize that it is impossible for anyone to recognize the opposite stand as correct. Of two opposed positions taken by the emotions, only one can be experienced as being correct.

2. This universal validity of the good would not in itself explain how we come to recognize the goodness of an entire class of objects. For if an act of love experienced as being correct had reference solely to a concrete object falling within the range of our perception, say, to a particular act of cognition, it would signify that this cognition is worthy of everyone's love, i.e. that anyone whose emotions stand in the right position to it must love it. However, this act alone would not involve recognition of the goodness of the entire class. But when we number knowledge among the things good in themselves, we clearly wish to say not simply that this particular act of cognition is a good but that knowledge as such is a good. How do we achieve this general recognition?

Aristotle himself gave the right answer to this question when he pointed out that our emotions, like our judgments, may direct themselves upon universals. We feel anger, he says, only towards the particular thief who has robbed us or the particular sycophant who has deceived our innocence, but we hate thieves and sycophants in general.

In fact, we must enlarge upon our previous remarks about emotions experienced as being correct by pointing out that all acts of loving and preferring that are so experienced are universal in this sense, i.e. they are directed upon conceptualized objects.

When we contemplate, for instance, knowledge in general or—which is to say the same thing—when we contemplate the general concept of knowledge and this concept forms the basis of our act of emotion, the emotion manifests itself as analogous, not to assertoric knowledge, but to apodictic knowledge. Just as axioms arise from the contemplation of general concepts, are discerned from the concepts (*ex terminis*), acts of interest that are experienced as being correct originate directly in general concepts. When we perceive within ourselves such an act of love, we perceive clearly at a single stroke, without any induction from particular cases, the goodness of the entire class in question. The difference between these cases and those in which we recognize, upon the basis of the general concepts of 2 and 3, that 3 is greater than 2 lies solely in the greater complexity of the assumptions involved in an ethical principle. We must be in possession not only of the concepts of the things we recognize as good but also of the experience of a love directed upon these objects and experienced as being correct. Even if he has command, on the one hand, of the concept of the relevant object, e.g. of the concept of knowledge or of joy, and, on the other, of the concept of an act of love experienced as being right, the person who lacks this experience is incapable of recognizing the objects as goods. In order to recognize something as a good,[14] i.e. as worthy of love, we must ourselves have loved it with a love characterized as being correct.

3. It might be asked whether this theory about the principles of ethical knowledge places us among the advocates of empiricism or of the *a priori*.[15]

In answering this question, we must make a number of distinctions. If, by the doctrine of the *a priori*, we mean that the concepts

---

[14] Here Brentano disagrees with George Katkov, who holds that anyone who has gained, from his own experience of it, the concept of an act of love experienced as being correct is thereby enabled to recognize, in conjunction with the conceptual idea of certain objects, the goodness of these objects; that is, he is capable of recognizing their goodness in a purely analytic *a priori* manner without the experience of a special act of love directed upon them. See Katkov, *Untersuchung zur Werttheorie und Theodizee*, p. 148.

[15] Sect. 3 has been added by Kastil, taking account of 'Loving and Hating' and 'The *a priori* Character of Ethical Principles' which appear as appendices in *The Origin of Our Knowledge of Right and Wrong*.

of the good and of the better are *a priori*, then we are far from holding it. The concept of an emotion experienced as being right originates in a perception, as do all our elementary concepts—in this case, in the inner perception of acts of this kind. In the entire realm of ideas there is nothing that is *a priori*; the distinction between empirical and *a priori* knowledge belongs entirely to the sphere of judgment, and only judgments discernible from the concepts are *a priori*, as we noted already in our refutation of so-called synthetic *a priori* cognitions.

We need not stress further that the perception of acts experienced as being right does not constitute *a priori* knowledge. But how do things stand with other cognitions having a universal scope, e.g. the cognition that joy as such or knowledge as such is a good?

We have already noted that they are not simply discernible from the concepts but require, as experiential premises, a love, experienced as being correct, that is directed upon these objects in general. Thus what we have here is actually a conclusion, one premise of which consists in this experience and the other of which consists in the analytic knowledge that only one of two opposed emotions can be experienced as being correct.

However, the ultimate source of our knowledge of the good and the better are inner perceptions of acts of love and preference, directed upon universals and experienced as being correct, and in view of this fact we must profess ourselves members of the empirical movement.

4. For the present, enough has been said of the principles of ethical knowledge. So far we have only discussed them in general terms, from the formal aspect, as it were, for I have confined myself to examples when it comes to the contents. In what follows it will be our business to present, in as complete a form as possible, those cases in which we recognize something as good, or as better than something else, on the basis of acts of interest experienced as being correct. Only when the foundation has been laid in this way can ethics be constructed in a logically cogent manner.

But first let us anticipate some objections that could be raised against our conception of the principles of ethical knowledge.

VIII

Objections to the Theory of the Principles of Ethical Knowledge Presented in the Previous Chapter, and Replies to the Objections

---

45. *Do emotions experienced as being correct really exist?*

1. The doctrine presented is based upon the assumption of a distinguishing characteristic of certain acts of interest, analogous to the insight that accompanies the apodictic judgment. But suppose somebody disputes the existence of such a characteristic? How are we to refute him? Defence appears impossible, and the question arises whether this objection does not remove the supports from under the entire ethical system.

2. We have claimed that the distinguishing characteristic is something completely new, but how could this be so if the characteristic actually exists? We would have had to notice it long since. It cannot be denied that the theory is simple, but for that very reason it would not have had to wait for us to discover it if it were indeed based upon fact.

3. Others declare that there is another reason for having doubts about such a theory of ethical principles. If a person is not acquainted with the principles, how can he reach the conclusions? Ought we perhaps to call all previous ethical decisions into question? Or do we acknowledge them? But if so, how is it to be explained that people have already attained the correct conclusions? Is it a coincidence, or a wonderful instance of pre-established harmony?

Answer: ad 1. Experience reveals directly the distinguishing characteristic of certain acts of love and preference; thus their existence cannot be rightly denied. Here we have everything needed in order to build upon firm ground. We need not be worried if the foundation is merely erroneously called into doubt.

The distinguishing characteristic of evidence also can be, and has been, a matter for dispute; some have denied that evidence is a guarantee of truth. To be sure, the people who make this claim are usually so inconsistent that they do not want to be sceptics. For they wish, at the same time, to know how to distinguish true judgments from false, and if we ask them what constitutes the distinction, they reply that it is universal correspondence in judging. Where this correspondence is present, the judgment is to be termed true, where it is absent, false. If we inquire further how we are to recognize this correspondence, they do not know what to say, or else they become ensnared in a vicious circle. In any case, general correspondence, even where it exists and its existence can be established, can be no substitute for insight. Thus more consistency was displayed by the ancient sceptics, with their doctrine of the arbitrariness of our principles. But even they were not consistent; no sceptic can possibly be. For if there is no such thing as insight, we can also have no insight into the impossibility of knowledge. We would not even be justified in asserting that our principles are arbitrary; indeed, every claim would be a defection from the basic thesis. Hence it was that Aristotle said silence was the only suitable stance for a sceptic— and silence deprives him of the possibility of teaching scepticism.

But, as previously mentioned, there are among those who recognize no distinction between evident and blind judgments also some thinkers who nevertheless do not wish to be sceptics. They also reject the imputation of wishing to make agreement among the judges the criterion of truth. If we then ask what they mean by true and false judgments, the only remaining answer they can give is: the judgment 'A exists' is true if I acknowledge A without harbouring any doubts; the judgment 'A does not exist' is true if I reject A without harbouring any doubts. They call a judgment false if it is opposed to their own judgment. The atheist says that whoever believes in God makes a false judgment; the theist says that whoever rejects God makes a false judgment.

According to this theory, of course, contradictory judgments can both be false; thereby the law of contradiction is abrogated and extreme scepticism is attained. And it is also questionable whether, from this point of view, it makes sense to want to prove something. According to the common conception, to prove something means to deduce a judgment from evident judgments. For the man who recognizes no judgments as evident the distinction between judgments that require proof and those that do not is obliterated. The only distinction remaining would be that between judgments that convince us and those that we form with misgivings. But what is meant here by misgivings, or doubts? What is it that we doubt: that we have made the judgment, or that it is true? The last, clearly. But in that case it is useless to define a true judgment as one that we form without having any misgivings about its truth, for the concept of doubt presupposes the concept of a true judgment.

More recently, the theory of evidence and its analogue within the realm of the emotions has been designated 'psychologism'. It was Husserl, the founder of phenomenology, who coined this name. Thinkers guilty of psychologism conceive of evidence as a 'feeling of conviction'. But, say its enemies, a feeling of conviction is no guarantee of the truth of the judgment in question, and this theory would lead to relativism, since every judgment that is provided with this mysterious feeling of evidence would be true and, consequently, judgments contradictory to those we call evident could bear this mark of consciousness in other beings. However, it is utterly perverse to describe the phenomenon of evidence as a 'feeling of conviction'. Every man in the street is convinced of the truth of external perception, i.e. he attributes as a matter of course everything that he sees, hears, and touches to the external world, but he lacks inner insight. A compulsion to agree is not the same thing as knowing.[16]

In pointing out to those who at first are unable to note the distinction between evident and blind judgments the extent of their oversight, we lay down a condition, as is shown by experience, under which they must acknowledge the distinction. This is easily comprehensible. In order to understand what we mean in speaking of this consequence, they must themselves make repeated use of the distinction, for that is the point of the whole discussion. We can proceed in the same manner when it is a question of the distinction between blind phenomena of interest and those that are

[16] This paragraph was introduced by the editor in accordance with Brentano's *Psychology from an Empirical Standpoint*, Appendix I, sect. II (On Psychologism).

experienced as being correct. First we present examples both of love and preferences that are experienced as being correct and of love and preferences that are blind. If this proves fruitless, we must make clear the import of our opponents' denial.

In the case of judgments, the phenomenon of evidence, once rejected, cannot be replaced by the distinction between true and false together with universality, i.e., agreement among all those who judge. Likewise, denial of the phenomenon of love and preferences experienced as being right obliterates the distinction between what is worthy of love and preference and what is in fact lovable and preferable, between what is in fact desired and what is worthy of being desired. The attempt to validate the distinction on the grounds of the universality of certain loves and preferences among the human species does not lead to our goal, as we came to see earlier. A psychological law to the effect that everyone loves certain objects and hates others would be no law in the ethical sense.

While in the former case no knowledge at all would be possible, in the latter no ethical knowledge would be possible. Only certain basic laws of the psychology of desiring would be left. If anyone considers this sufficient, we can have no quarrel with him; but he ought to refrain from talking about ethics and thus introducing confusion through the equivocal use of this term.

46. 'Such a simple fact would not have had to wait so long to be discovered'

ad 2. To those unfamiliar with the history of philosophy, it may seem improbable that a distinguishing characteristic could remain unnoticed for so long, that such a simple truth should not have been established long ago. But this objection carries no special weight with those who know their history. In many cases philosophers have overlooked the simplest points right up to the present time, even when their oversights have entailed the most amazing consequences. This has happened even in spheres where they have worked with the greatest industry. They have dedicated themselves more to logic than to ethics, and many thinkers believe that they have attained full certainty and completeness in this area. And yet it can be demonstrated that even the logicians have committed great blunders and overlooked vital problems.

For example, there still today prevails almost universally a false conception of the nature of the judgment, to the effect that it consists in a synthesis of concepts. People still fail to recognize the negative character of the so-called universal affirmative proposition. Moreover, words such as existence, possibility, and law are taken to be genuine names because of the substantival character of their appearance. As a consequence many futile efforts have been made to specify and analyse the concepts corresponding to these terms, whereas it is in fact not a matter of names at all, but of syncategorematic symbols. One of the most peculiar defects is the fact that innumerable textbooks of logic completely overlook the phenomenon of evidence with respect to judgments.

Thus the fact that a certain distinguishing characteristic has been generally misunderstood or overlooked by no means gives any proof against its existence; it simply demonstrates the difficulty of noticing what is perceived internally and of determining its concept.

But is the theory of the evident judgment and its analogue in the sphere of the emotions really new? In a certain sense it is, but in another not; many thinkers have asserted something similar. No one could claim that the characteristic we have pointed out was entirely unnoticed before, but only perhaps that it had not previously been exhaustively analysed and that erroneous opinions entered into its determination.

Good in the sense of what is valuable in itself is generally distinguished from good in the sense of the useful. And being valuable has been connected with evaluating, which, it has been recognized, is a phenomenon of interest. Furthermore, what is lovable, capable of being loved, has been contrasted with what is worthy of love, just as, with reference to judgment, a distinction is made between what is believed and what deserves to be believed. Indeed, people have spoken explicitly of the morally right and morally wrong. Aristotle speaks of ὀρθῶς and οὐκ ὀρθῶς ὀρέγεσθα; he even goes yet further and finds the former to be present in a special species of desire, to which he gave the name βούλησις, in opposition to ἐπιθυμία. The former, he says, is directed towards a ὂν ἀγαθόν, the latter towards a φαινόμενον ἀγαθόν.

But we also encounter the recognition of the existence of things worthy of love and things worthy of hate, i.e. of good and bad, in the voice of conscience, which is presupposed by Christian ethics and is regarded by many philosophers as the crucial element.

Indeed, we will not go wrong if we trace back Hume's 'inner taste' and Leibniz' 'moral instinct' to the acknowledgment of value, even if these concepts have been obscured because of a confusion between instinctive and discerning love.[17]

47. *'How is it possible that, though ignorant of these principles, people nevertheless arrive at correct moral knowledge?'*

ad 3. (*a*) What view do we take of everything that men have previously held to be good and bad? Do we wish to set up an entirely new morality? By no means; it will turn out, rather, that our principles, though they may necessitate some corrections in detail, will in general lead to the justification of the precepts commonly acknowledged to be moral.

Does this mean that other people have come to a knowledge of the conclusions without premises? What a coincidence this would be, or what wonderful pre-established harmony! But it is neither, for the same premises were at work in the establishing of their conclusions, even if they were not explicitly recognized as such. There is much that is to be found in our store of knowledge and that is fruitful in the production of new knowledge without this process being brought clearly to our consciousness. People had been drawing correct conclusions for centuries before they made this method and the principles determining the formal validity of conclusions clear and distinct by means of reflection. Indeed, when Plato reflected upon the matter for the first time, it happened that he set up a completely mistaken theory. He thought that every drawing of a conclusion involved an act of reminiscence; what we perceive and experience on earth, he thought, recalls to our memory cognitions won in a previous life, where everything was viewed directly. And it is still true today that if we ask a man who has never explicitly concerned himself with logic to give the premises of a conclusion he has just drawn he usually will not succeed but will give utterly false replies. The same is likely to occur if we have him define a concept that he habitually employs. We can see that thinking and the accurate description of the process of thought are two separate matters. It has even occurred

---

[17] This paragraph has been inserted by the editor. Cf. O. Kraus, *Die Werttheorien*, p. 44 ff., p. 32 f., p. 104 f.

that mathematicians have failed to take sufficient account of the principles they employ while doing their proofs: hence the dispute about the principles of mathematics.

For example, a proof of the proposition that a straight line is the shortest distance between two points can only succeed if we make the assumption that there can only be one straight line between two points.[18] But mathematicians usually pay no attention to the use of this proposition. Furthermore it cannot be directly discerned, but only when we lay down as its basis the proposition that lines pointing in the same directions, if altered in the same manner, result in lines pointing in the same directions. Yet this proposition is not to be found anywhere among the principles; there have even been mathematicians who have deluded themselves into thinking that they have no need of the concept of direction in order to carry out their geometrical proofs. It is only in circuitous ways that we can make them comprehend that they need it. The most effective manner of doing this is to seize upon the fact, admitted to be such by almost everyone, that we have no special concept of absolute places, but are always referred to relative determinations of place. But this means nothing more than that we possess only concepts of spatial intervals and their differences with respect to size and direction.

In much the same way, ethical principles are effective, even where we are not able to account for each separately. Their presence can be demonstrated in both laymen and philosophers, without their being perfectly aware of them, and their traces are betrayed in a variety of ways. Where is the man, for instance, who would demur at declaring joy to be an evident good, unless it be delight in what is bad? And few men will deny the intrinsic value of knowledge. Indeed, some philosophers have exalted precisely this to the position of the principal good, superior to all other goods, although they attributed a certain intrinsic value to every act of virtue. Others have considered such acts the highest good.

Let us turn our attention to the principles of preferring. How

18 This section was added by A. Kastil. Cf. Brentano, *Versuch über die Erkenntnis*, p. 65 ff. Concerning the lack of absolute determinations of places in our spatial intuition, see *Psychology from an Empirical Standpoint*, Appendix, sect. 13, para. 2.

often is the principle of summation[19] taken into account? Who would deny that it is the quantity of happiness over our entire lives, not that of a single moment, that is to be considered? Even Epicurus had to make that admission, even though it did not exactly harmonize with his own theory. And Aristotle held the happiness of all the people to be a higher end than one's own happiness. The effects of this principle of preference are displayed even in the yearning for personal immortality. Thus, in a lecture concerning the origin of the planetary system, Helmholtz says, 'So long as what we achieve will ennoble the life of our descendants, the individual can bear without fear the thought that the thread of his own consciousness will someday be broken. But even such free and noble spirits as Lessing and David Strauss could not reconcile themselves to the idea of an ultimate destruction of living beings and, with it, an end of all the fruits of the endeavours of all past generations.' If it were to be scientifically established that the earth will some day be incapable of sheltering living beings, Helmholtz believes that the need for personal endurance would irrepressibly reassert itself, and we would feel driven to look around to see where some possibility of it might be lurking.

Popular religion also does justice to the principles of correct preference. In counselling us to love our neighbour as ourselves, Christianity is teaching us that, where the correct preference is made, the same good is given equal weight in the balance, be it our own or another's. From this principle it follows that the individual is to be subjugated to the collective whole. It is also employed in the command, 'Love God above all else', for we conceive God as the sum total of everything good in perpetual enhancement.

Thus the principles we have mentioned have shown themselves to be operative, and this at least partially explains the general agreement in results which appeared so paradoxical at the outset.

(*b*) But even if the correct principles of knowledge were not operative in people, or were far less effective than they are, an at least superficially similar development could have taken place. For

[19] In his *Untersuchungen zur Werttheorie und Theodizee*, G. Katkov gave a presentation of the laws of preference completely leaving out the principle of summation, which he subjected to penetrating criticism.

there are other forces which work in the same direction. Many ethical maxims have come into being on grounds that are logically and ethically inadequate. They stem from inferior impulses, selfish desires, and the transformation which they have undergone during the course of history in the direction of taking account of the collective whole has by no means always come about because of superior insight. The force of habit led to this result. Utilitarians correctly make the point that even egoism recommends us to make ourselves pleasing to others, and that such behaviour, when carried out continuously, leads ultimately to a habit that has lost sight of its original purpose and is consequently blind. The so-called limitations of consciousness participate in this process in that they do not permit us always to keep the more remote and ultimate end clearly before our eyes while we are considering the question immediately at hand.

This has made possible a phenomenon frequently encountered over the course of history. It has often happened that a powerful man, motivated by egoism, has forced weaker men into subjection and, assisted by the influence of habit, reared them to be willing servants. After this has taken place, their slavish souls have reacted to the command of their master as though it were a compelling 'Thou shalt', as though it were justified on the grounds of an immediate insight. Every time they have violated a command they have felt inner torment, much as a well-trained dog. Where such a man of power has had many subjects, he has on the grounds of egoism issued commands conducive to the maintenance of his herd. These commands have become second nature to them. And thus concern for the collective whole has become something to which they felt driven. And, on the other hand, he who holds the power in his hands has sometimes over a period of time come to hold dear the welfare of his herd, so that he has even sacrificed himself to it, as the miser sacrifices himself to his treasure. This entire process can take place without the influence of any ethical knowledge. But we can see how the process produces results that coincide, with respect to their contents, with the correct ethical precepts.

An analogous process is to be found in the intellectual sphere. For example: from our earliest childhood, we all believe in an external world that surrounds us and which we at first identify completely with the objects of our sense perceptions. Gradually we reach the point where we undertake some corrections of this picture, but the belief in the existence of a physical world remains intact. Logic has here very little effect. We are guided by instinct and habit in our judgments as to the origins of our changing sense perceptions. And yet we would reach essentially the same conclusion if we made an induction in accordance with the fundamental principles of probability theory.

And so it seems that the third difficulty has also been satisfactorily resolved. It would be encountered, incidentally, not only by ours but also by every other ethical system. For no matter how strongly philosophers may oppose each other with respect to the principles of ethical knowledge, they are all in agreement about particular precepts and prohibitions.

PART TWO

THE SUPREME PRACTICAL GOOD

I

Hedonism[20]

---

48. *Bentham's classification of goods and evils*

The first application to be made of the results of our investigation into the principles of ethical knowledge concerns the question as to the right end of action, which remains unanswered. We know that it must consist of the best that we are able to attain; we know what is meant by 'good' and by 'better' and how to recognize something as good or better. But we must still look into the individual constituents of the right end. In order to determine them, we must investigate the following.

1. What kinds of goods and evils there are, i.e. we must set up a so-called table of goods, along with a table of evils, making a particular point of finding out whether only those things which lie within the sphere of our own spiritual activities are to be considered as goods or evils or whether objects lying outside this sphere can also be viewed under these categories.

2. We must compare goods and evils in order to determine their relative values, setting out the laws of correct preference in as complete a form as possible.

3. Then we must discuss the highest good, both the absolute highest good and the highest practical good.

---

[20] It would be better to call this theory eudaemonism rather than hedonism, for utilitarians generally use the word 'pleasure' in such a way that it includes more than merely sensual pleasure. Inasmuch as it is a theory that stipulates happiness to be the basic good, eudaemonism embraces hedonism.

4. This last question necessitates an additional investigation into the useful and harmful, in which we will have to specify some of the most important classes.

There have been moral philosophers who have not concerned themselves in the least with the theory of goods. But those who have usually proceeded directly to determining the supreme good, not concerning themselves at all with a classification of goods. Yet it is easy to see that the inquiry into the supreme good cannot be thorough without the benefit of this classification, for by 'the supreme good' we can only mean the best among all the goods.

Jeremy Bentham (cf. part I, chap. 5, sect. 29) is almost the only exception worth noting. Even in his earliest work on ethics, *An Introduction to the Principles of Morals and Legislation*, he presents a thorough classification of both goods and evils. The same classification is to be found, with minor alterations, in the *Traité de la legislation civile et pénale* (Theory of Legislation), which Dumont compiled from Bentham's manuscripts,* and again, in precisely the original form, in Bentham's posthumous work, *Deontology* (ed. Bowring, 1843).

Bentham says that he reached his classification upon the basis of an analysis of human nature, which, however, he neglects to disclose. But since, as we know already, the intrinsically good is the same as pleasure and freedom from pain, while the intrinsically bad is equivalent to their opposite, his classification contains nothing but instances of pleasure and pain.

To begin with Bentham separates into simple and complex those impressions† that interest us as being pleasing or painful. They are simple if they cannot be further analysed, complex when they include a multiplicity of (simple) pleasures or (simple) pains, or both. What causes us to regard several pleasures as a single complex pleasure is the fact that they spring from the activity of one and the same cause. Thus everything depends upon the classification of the simple pleasures and pains.

---

*Trans. into English by R. Hildreth (London: Trübner, 1864). Future references will be to this edition.

† Brentano uses 'impression' [*Eindruck*], but Bentham actually uses the term, 'interesting perceptions'. Cf. *Introduction to the Principles of Morals and Legislation*, chap. 5, 1.

A. Simple pleasures

1. Pleasures of sense: those of taste, of smell, of sight, of hearing, of feeling (touch); those that arise from our sexual make up; the pleasant feeling of being healthy; finally, the stimulation of curiosity.

2. Pleasures of wealth, i.e. in owning something that is a source of enjoyment and security. This pleasure is most intense at the moment when the object is won.

3. Pleasures of skill. The man who plays an instrument himself derives from it an enjoyment of a kind different from that he would experience if he merely heard someone else playing. This sort of pleasure appears where difficulties have been overcome, where proficiency has been acquired. Bentham apparently includes here delight in one's own scientific discovery: think of Archimedes shouting 'Eureka!'

4. Pleasures of friendship, conjoined with the conviction that we possess a man's goodwill and therefore can expect his good services.

5. The pleasures of a good name, conjoined with the conviction that we possess the respect and goodwill of an extensive circle of people, from whom, consequently, we may expect good services under certain circumstances.

6. Pleasures of power, i.e. the pleasure in ruling over other men and in being conscious of the means whereby we can make use of others by manipulation of their fears and hopes.

7. Pleasures of piety, which result from the conviction that we possess, or are acquiring, God's grace and will consequently be worthy of special mercy in this life or in another.

8. Pleasures of benevolence—in other words, of sympathy or of the social inclinations. We enjoy them when we think of the happiness of people dear to us. Depending upon their strength, these inclinations may extend to a smaller or a greater circle or, indeed, to all mankind. Our goodwill may also be directed towards animals.

9. Pleasures of malevolence—in other words, the pleasures of the angry passions, of antipathy, of antisocial inclinations. They result from viewing or from imagining people or animals whom we hate.*

*Bentham says these pleasures result from viewing the objects of our malevolence *in pain*, which seems to make more sense. Ibid., 11.

10. Pleasures of memory. When we have enjoyed something, and even, sometimes, when we have suffered pain, we love to picture it to ourselves in our memory. These pleasures are as numerous as the things we remember. (In memory, objects can be arranged in an altered and beautified form.)

11. Pleasures of the imagination. New ideas in arts and sciences, which engage our hunger for knowledge, are pleasures for the imagination, which views them as extending its sphere of enjoyment.

12. Pleasures of hope, at the thought of an imminent and anticipated pleasure.

13. Pleasures of association. Certain objects, which would afford no pleasure taken in themselves, are connected in our mind with pleasant objects and consequently partake of the pleasantness.

14. Pleasures of relief or release. They originate in pain. If a pain from which we are suffering ceases or abates, we experience pleasure, and often an intense pleasure. These pleasures are as manifold as the pains from which they stem. (Think of Socrates in the *Phaedo*, or Aesop's fable.)

According to Bentham, these fourteen elements comprise the entire material of which our pleasures are composed. All others are made up of them, but it requires attentiveness and practice to be able to analyse out the constituents in the individual case. 'The pleasure afforded us by the view of a country landscape is comprised of the pleasures of the senses, the imagination, and sympathy. The variety of objects, the flowers, colours, the beautiful shapes of trees, the combination of light and shadow delight the eye; the ear is caressed by the song of the birds, the murmuring of the spring, the soft rustling of the leaves in the wind. The air, filled with the scent of fresh vegetation, brings pleasant sensations to the sense of smell, while its purity and lightness quickens the circulation of the blood and eases movement. Imagination and goodwill make the scene yet more beautiful inasmuch as they awaken in us images of wealth, plenty, and sumptuous fertility. The innocence and the quiet happiness of the birds, herds, and domestic animals contrast pleasantly with our memories of the struggles and excitements of city life. We attribute to the rural population all the pleasures of which we partake because of the novelty of this experience. Finally, our feeling of gratitude towards the highest being, whom we honour as the author of all these benefits, augments our trust and our admiration.'*

B. *Simple pains*

1. Pains of privation and deprivation, where the lack or the loss of a pleasure gives us grievance. There are three main modifications:

(*a*) The pain of desire, i.e. of unsatisfied desire. (This occurs, for instance, where the fear of failing to attain a pleasure one desires outweighs hope.)

(*b*) The pain of disappointment, when a confidently held expectation is suddenly destroyed.

(*c*) The pain of regret upon suffering a loss, including the disappointment regarding a good that we believed ourselves to possess. (The pain of boredom does not relate to this or that particular object, but rather to a general lack of pleasant feelings.)

2. Pains of the senses. Bentham distinguishes nine kinds: hunger, thirst,† bad taste, bad smells, painful impressions from touching, painful impressions of the hearing, painful impressions of sight (which offend us independently of any association), excessive heat or cold, diseases of all varieties, and, finally, spiritual or physical exhaustion.‡

3. The pain of awkwardness, from fruitless attempts or difficult exertions in using the various means that serve our pleasures or needs.

4. The pain of enmity, arising when we believe ourselves to be the object of somebody's ill will and must expect evil at his hands.

5. The pain of a bad reputation (also the pain of dishonour or of the popular sanction), arising when a person believes himself to be the object of the ill will or displeasure of the world about him or to be in danger of incurring them.

6. The pains of piety, arising from the fear of having offended the supreme being and of incurring his punishment in this life or the next. (If the fear is harboured on good grounds, we call it the

---

* *Theory of Legislation*, chap. 6, sect. 1, p. 24.

† Bentham lists these two as one kind; cf. *Introduction to the Principles of Morals and Legislation*, chap. V, 21. Presumably Brentano meant to do so as well; otherwise there would be ten kinds listed.

‡ Actually, Bentham speaks of 'the pain of exertion . . . or the uneasy sensation which is apt to accompany any intense effort', not of exhaustion. Loc. cit.

fear of God; if it is harboured without foundation, we speak of superstitious anxiety.)

7. The pains of benevolence, sympathy, or the social inclinations, occurring when we view, or contemplate, the suffering of fellow men or animals.

8. The pains of malevolence, antipathy, or the antisocial inclinations, i.e. the pain felt upon contemplating the happiness of those whom we hate.

9. The pains of memory.

10. The pains of the imagination.

11. The pains of fear.

12. The pains of association.

The pains listed under nos. 9 through 12 correspond exactly to the pleasures of the same names.

The simple pains are compounded in much the same way as the simple pleasures and are viewed as one complex pain when a number of them are brought about by a single cause. They are to be analysed by means of the catalogue; examples are exile, imprisonment, confiscation. Taken together, the two catalogues also include the means for the analysis of mixed feelings that are neither pure pains nor pure pleasures.

Here, then, is Bentham's classification of goods and evils (not including the many detailed subdivisions he gives).

We may note that no corresponding pain is listed for some of the kinds of pleasure, for instance, the pleasure of wealth or acquisition and the pleasure of power. The corresponding numbers are missing; so, too, among the pains of the senses, are any corresponding to the pleasures of novelty or the pleasures based upon our sexual structure. Bentham omitted them on purpose; he says that the absence of riches and power over other men is not a positive pain, except in cases of seizure or of disappointed expectation. He declares explicitly that not every pleasure has a pain corresponding to it.

We may note further that the goods and evils, the pleasures and pains, listed by Bentham are almost all purely personal; only those of benevolence and malevolence bear any reference to other people. Bentham does not classify as a good or an evil the well-being or misfortune of others, but only our consciousness of it, our belief in it—or, more accurately, the pleasure or pain attending the belief.

49. *Bentham's arguments for limiting the table of goods to pleasures*

1. Bentham's classification is noteworthy, not only as the first thorough attempt to set up a table of goods but also because it displays the fruits of the astute, careful, and time-consuming exercising of one of the most significant philosophical minds. And it is also notable because of the consistency with which Bentham applied it. The whole of Bentham's renowned system of legislation is based upon it, a fact that thoroughly justifies the fascination which it held for J. S. Mill, and which he expresses in his *Autobiography*. Bentham held a knowledge of pains and pleasures to be the principle of all clear thinking in matters of morals and legislation. Virtue, vice, innocence, crime, systems of rewards and punishments—what do these all come down to in his eyes? Pleasure and pain, and nothing more. Any argument concerning morals and legislation that cannot be translated into the simple terms of pleasure and pain is unclear and sophistical; nothing is to be gained from it. 'If we wish to explore, for instance, the sphere of offences, that vast object dominating the whole of legislation, our study will essentially consist of nothing but a comparative weighing, a calculus of pains and pleasures. If the investigation concerns the evil to be found in a certain action, then it concerns the pain that has arisen from it for this or that person; if it concerns the motives of the delinquent, this means that we will search for the attraction that a certain pleasure holds for him and that led him to commit a crime. Again, if we inquire after the advantage stemming from the crime, it is as much as to ask what pleasure was gained as a result of the crime. And if we are concerned with what legal punishment is to be imposed, we are asking what, and how much pain the guilty person should be forced to endure. Thus the present theory of pleasures and pains is the basis of this entire science.'*

Inasmuch as he himself makes such a sweeping application of his principles and erects an edifice that is certainly far more inhabitable and useful than any work done by philosophers on questions of law either before or after him, Bentham appears to have contributed a new standard by which to measure laws.

2. Certain as it is that Bentham's catalogue of pleasures and

---

* *Theory of Legislation*, chap. 6, sect. II, p. 26.

pains is not without advantages for moral philosophers and legislators, we may nevertheless question whether it has the significance that he himself attributed to it. The answer will depend, of course, upon whether both the fundamental idea and the psychological analysis upon which the working out of the catalogue is based, and which Bentham unfortunately does not reveal to us, are flawless.

The fundamental idea is that all pleasure, and nothing other than pleasure, is in itself a good, while all pain, and nothing but pain, is in itself an evil. Hence, instead of saying that pleasure is *a* good and pain *an* evil, we ought rather to say that pleasure is *the* good and pain *the* evil. And if that is not the case, Bentham's classification obviously has great deficiencies as a classification of goods and evils. Furthermore, the table would also require some corrections as a catalogue of pleasures and pains. For instance, we would have to revise Bentham's definition of the pleasure of hope as a pleasure that grows upon the contemplation of approaching and anticipated enjoyment.

Certainly, if Bentham's claim that the concepts of pleasure and good are identical were correct, everything else would follow easily, but we recognized previously that it is false. Furthermore, we have established, at various times, that the concepts are not even interchangeable. Insight is a good, but not itself a pleasure, while, on the other hand, delight in another's misfortune is a pleasure but not a good.

3. Other people have felt these qualms; indeed, they were familiar to Bentham himself, but he rejects them energetically. He thinks that a lack of clarity would become pervasive, were we to give up this foundation. Legislation would become a matter of sympathy and antipathy; that is, it would become the prey of moods and arbitrary whims, of the imagination and of taste, which varies, here favouring one thing, here another. In place of a secure, unified political principle would come the destruction of all principles, an anarchy of ideas. This might please aesthetes, superficial men of letters, and people who suit their thinking to the fashion and do not allow it to be directed by reasons of substance, but the philosopher cannot accept it. Think how many follies would have been avoided by governments, had they not been so devoid of principles. One government, he says, may direct all its thoughts towards trade and wealth, seeing the entire state as

nothing but an enormous factory and citizens as nothing but tools of production, and having no conscience about tormenting individuals, provided only that the wealth of the nation is increasing. Their mind is absorbed by the customs, exchange banks, and the treasury. They remain indifferent towards a host of injuries which they could heal, taking care only that a goodly quantity of the instruments of pleasure are produced, while at the same time continually presenting obstacles to the possibility of enjoyment. Other governments seek the public fortune only in power and fame. Full of disdain for states that understand how to exist happily in peace and quiet, they require constant intrigues, cabinet negotiations, wars, and conquests. They do not take into account how much suffering has gone to form this fame or how many victims of battle have prepared their bloody triumph. In the glory of victory, the acquisition of a province, they close their eyes to the forlorn state of the country and fail to recognize the true aim of a government: the happiness of the people. Still other people feel no concern with whether the state is well run or whether the laws protect life and property; they care only for political freedom, for the most equal possible division of political power. Where they do not find the form of government to which they are attached, they see nothing but slavery. And if the supposed slaves feel comfortable in their condition and have no longing to change it, these people despise and rebuke them for it. In their fanaticism they would be prepared to risk the entire happiness of the people in a civil war in order to place power in the hands of men who, because of the invincible ignorance resulting from their condition, will only be able to use it for their own destruction. 'Here we have', concludes Bentham, 'some examples of phantasies that in politics commonly replace the proper striving for the general good; [. . .] people forget that all that is only a means and only happiness is of intrinsic worth.'*

Certainly there is a great deal of truth in this candid criticism, and it would not be difficult to supplement this list of the phrases in which statesmen dress up their false goals with examples of new ones that have come into being since Bentham's time. (But according to Bentham, the same thing is true of every goal that is

* The above passage recounts almost word for word the last four paragraphs of chap. 6 of the *Theory of Legislation*, pp. 14–15. The quotation is from p. 15 (my translation).

not pleasure. He places insight, justice, good morals, and religion on a par with wealth, power, liberty, and equality.)

4. However, he adds a warning concerning a possible misunderstanding to his observation that legislation which is not guided by a regard for the happiness of the people must stray into the path of sympathy and antipathy and fall into arbitrary ways. In a certain sense, he points out, sympathy and antipathy may, and indeed ought, to set a standard for legislation; that is, the legislator ought to take into account that of the people, not his own. Are we to believe that there have been monarchs who preferred to lose provinces and to pour forth streams of their own blood rather than to spare the particular sensibility of a people, to tolerate an intrinsically innocent habit, to leave untouched an old bias, or to preserve a certain costume or certain forms of prayer? Yes; Joseph II, an enlightened monarch motivated by a desire that his people might be happy, undertook to reform everything in his state—and everyone rebelled against him. Looking back over all the troubles of his reign on the eve of his death, he pronounced that his epitaph should be that he had been unlucky in all his undertakings. But for the instruction of future generations it would have been better to write on his grave that he had never comprehended the art of reckoning with the inclinations, partialities, and sensibilities of human beings. Even where peculiarities and superstition have harmful effects, they are a factor that must be taken into account. And only when we fully appreciate the attention due to these factors can we hope for change and improvement. This, then, is the way in which sympathy ought also to regulate legislation—as follows logically from the basic principle. Any other way leads to arbitrariness and invites all sorts of foolishness.

5. Bentham took it as a clear sign of the correctness of his principles that only pleasure is used as a reward and only pain as punishment. And, one might add, every sort of pain. For instance, the sublime pain felt when gazing upon the shocking consequences of a crime counts as a punishment, while Esther and Herodias stipulated that the pleasure of revenge was to be their reward.

These are the reasons why Bentham, while not exactly equating the concept of pleasure with that of good, believes that only pleasure is intrinsically worthy of love.

50. *Other hedonists*

Bentham does not stand alone in more recent times. Even if no other philosopher has drawn up such a detailed catalogue of the varieties of pleasure, there are nevertheless many others who have also considered each man's own pleasure as the only intrinsic good. We encounter this doctrine particularly often in the empirical school of thought, as for instance in Fechner. And Kant, who himself demands a completely different motivation for our action, nevertheless explains that from the empirical standpoint no other good can be discovered. Hedonism was also represented in ancient times, not only by Epicurus, who said he could not think of anything to call good except pleasure, but also during the ascendency of Greek philosophy. Here we think not only of such a man as Aristippus, who as a Sophist and a man of the world led a life of pleasure in the royal courts, but also of the worthy Eudoxus, an astronomer and a pupil of Plato. Aristotle, who recognized the importance for ethics of an investigation of pleasure and devoted a thoroughgoing discourse to the subject, explains his reasons to us in Book X of the *Nicomachean Ethics*:

1. Eudoxus says that pleasure is *the* good, and this is supposed to follow from the fact that all beings, both rational and irrational, strive after pleasure. Every creature knows how to find what is good for himself, just as he can find the nourishment that suits him. Hence that which is the good for all and for which everything strives must be the absolute good.

2. This conclusion follows no less clearly, he says, from the fact that all beings flee from pain and reckon anything to be fled from as pain. Hence the contrary thing must be intrinsically desirable.

3. Eudoxus does not dispute that objects other than pleasure are desired and objects other than pain shunned; he only denies that they are desired or shunned in and for themselves. True good is not desired for the sake of something else; no one asks to what end we yearn for pleasure.

4. Finally, Eudoxus points out that every good is rendered yet more valuable by the addition of pleasure, even temperance and justice. Consequently this addition must be a good, for a good can only be enhanced by something good.

Aristotle himself notes that this last argument shows no more than that pleasure is a good alongside other goods. However, what Eudoxus probably had in mind was that just action is value-less if it is performed without joy, or with positive distaste; there-fore, he reasoned, the good really lies in the component of pleasure in this instance, too.

According to Aristotle, Eudoxus' teachings made a great im-pression because he was a man of excellent character, which had far more effect than his arguments. This could also be said of Bentham and other modern hedonists.

Many thinkers hold that our own pleasure is not only the only thing worthy of desire, but also the only thing that is desirable, that can be desired. They claim that it is ultimately impossible to strive for anything but our own pleasure.

51. *Reasons for rejecting hedonism*

1. Numerous and energetic as are the representatives of the doc-trine that our own pleasure is the sole good, this view neverthe-less has fared much the same as every other one with which philosophy occupies itself. Some deny the doctrine, while others exclude pleasure from the realm of the good altogether. Kant considered a concern for one's own pleasure to be precisely the opposite of moral. The term good, he said, has two meanings; in the one case it is equivalent to well-being as opposed to distress, in the other to moral as opposed to immoral, but there is no re-lation between the two meanings. Pleasure should in no way be a motive determining our actions, which ought to arise solely from a respect for the categorical imperative. (However, in the course of his exposition and application of the categorical imperative Kant reaches the conclusion that we ought to promote the plea-sure of others, but not our own. This is a most curious con-clusion: if the pleasure of others is worthy of pursuit, it is not because it is not our own but because it is pleasure. But our own pleasure is pleasure, too.)

2. Opposition to hedonism is nothing new. Antisthenes, one of Aristippus' fellow students, declared pleasure to be a positive evil (μᾶλλον μαγείειν ἢ ἡσθέιειν). Diogenes saw the good only in a freedom from wants. Christian ascetics shunned the incitement of pleasure as being the work of the devil.

Aristotle, in his day, was already presented with extreme opposites, and it is interesting to see what position he adopts towards them. He does not give his approval to either.

(*a*) He rejects Eudoxus' view (which, as we have seen, coincides with Bentham's) that nothing is good but one's own pleasure. Pleasure, he says, is not *the* good. 'We would be fond of, and consider important, many things, such as sight, memory, knowledge, and virtuous action, even if they brought us no pleasure. And no one can object that pleasure is necessarily attached to these activities; for we would desire them even if they were devoid of pleasure.'*

(*b*) But he also clashes with those who wish to exclude pleasure from the list of goods altogether. He sees genuine force in the argument that everything strives for pleasure and flees its opposite. Anyone wishing to deny this argument would find it difficult to offer a sounder substitute. And he thinks there is something to the argument that the value of a thing is increased by the addition of pleasure; it shows that it is a good. But no argument demonstrates that pleasure is *the* good.

And here, too, he makes a distinction. The question is, to what does pleasure attach itself. Pleasure taken in what is bad is not a good, but is bad and harmful, and pleasure in what is mean, childish, or bestial is in any case of small value. 'No one would wish to live his entire life with the understanding of a child, taking the greatest delight in the things children enjoy. Similarly, no one would wish to rejoice in perpetrating a crime, even if no harm should ever follow from it.'†

In contrast, he says, the pleasure that attaches to a noble deed is a true good.

3. The points raised by Aristotle coincide with our earlier comments and doubtless accord with the truth.

(*a*) The criterion that we attempted to set forth clearly in our preliminary investigation demonstrates decisively that pleasure is not to be excluded from the sphere of the good. Delight taken in doing good, for example, is a pleasure loved with a love experienced as being correct. A being who hated joy and loved sorrow would be perverse.

(*b*) But the criterion also vouches for other goods, e.g. the entertainment of sublime ideas, insight, noble acts of will. When

* *Nicomachean Ethics*, Book X, chap. 3, 1174a.
† Loc. cit.

philosophers of the empirical school claimed pleasure was *the* good—when they claimed, indeed, that it was not only the only thing worthy of love but also the only thing capable of being loved—their claim did not harmonize with what experience shows, but was, rather, opposed to it. One point at least is clear: some things that at first we loved only as means to acquiring pleasure eventually become dear to us in themselves. The miser becomes fond of money as such, and if he starves to death amidst his money bags, we surely cannot say that pleasure was his motive for acquiring it. Nor is it so for the martyr when he ascends to the stake as a witness to his beliefs. He may be sacrificing himself for his ideal without even having a belief in vindication in a world beyond.

(*c*) Furthermore, the thesis not only contradicts experience but also contradicts itself. To feel pleasure or delight is an emotional act, a taking pleasure or a loving; it always has an object, is necessarily a pleasure *in* something which we perceive or imagine, have an idea of. For example, sensual pleasure has a certain localized sense quality as its object. Now if nothing but pleasure could be loved, this would mean that every act of loving had an act of loving as its object; but the beloved act of loving would have in turn to be directed upon an act of loving, and so forth *ad infinitum*. No; in order for pleasure to exist at all, something other than pleasure must be capable of being loved.

But it follows further that pleasure is not the only thing worthy of love. If it were, any pleasure would be pleasure taken in something unworthy of love and hence unworthy of being an object of pleasure. And in that case, pleasure could scarcely be worthy of love; the danger would be that nothing at all was worthy of love.

If pleasure is a good, then there must also be other goods.

(*d*) Consequently pleasure is not *the* good. However, it also cannot be the good for the further reason that not every pleasure is a good. Aristotle was right in saying that we must distinguish good pleasures from bad, according to their object. Delight taken in the suffering of a benefactor is not truly worthy of love.

52. *Refutation of the hedonists' arguments*

If, with this preparation, we look back over the reasons presented in favour of hedonism, we see that they prove either nothing at all or simply that pleasure is to be accounted among the goods.

1. Bentham's reasons are partially of a practical nature, as

(*a*) when he points out that, without hedonism, everything would be unclear and the door would be open to sympathy, antipathy, and every other sort of nonsense.

Assuming that such undesirable consequences do result, this would nevertheless not constitute a proof. In the same way we could prove that it is necessary to decide all questions in ethics and the philosophy of law by means of positive legislation or by appeal to human and divine authority. Someone might say that speculation gives free rein to caprice. And certainly the history of free-ranging speculation reveals many errors and confusions, endless disputes, and unsettled doubts. Indeed, some might prefer not to settle lawsuits by means of reasons but to leave them to the discretion of a divine tribunal, just as Otto the Great decided by means of a duel whether grandsons should be heirs. No one does this any more, but the inclination to settle theoretical questions by force has not entirely vanished from the face of the earth. It is betrayed, for instance, in the complaints that positive theologians register against philosophical and even historical exegesis.

Philosophy rejects the criterion arising from an externally imposed decision; it appeals to reason. Theologians of understanding give philosophy its due, for they realize that without it the whole edifice of church doctrine would lack a foundation capable of supporting it. Hence we find that we are directed towards rational criteria also when it comes to the question of whether there are other intrinsic goods besides our own pleasure. The difficulties are the same here as in all other questions concerning principles, and the man of understanding will admit here, too, in particular, that not even pleasure can be recognized as a good without such a criterion.

(*b*) Bentham makes a further appeal to the fact that only pleasure and pain come into consideration as rewards and punishments, but it is doubtful whether this is accurate. Is there no reward to be found in helping someone, out of love, to realize an idea in which he has a purely disinterested concern, involving no thought of gaining pleasure? Aeschylus would have remained in Athens if he had been rewarded by staying in the Aeropagus instead of being crowned. As elsewhere, the close connection between pleasure and the object of love does not blur the clear distinction between them. The realization of the object of love may be accompanied by pleasure, but this is not its purpose; hence it is that some do not shrink from offering their own lives in order to attain their ideal.

The claim is also not true for punishment. Even if it consisted solely in the infliction of pain, this would not prove that no other evils exist. Stupidity and moral turpitude are evils, too, but we do not inflict them upon the delinquent, both because they are despicable and because the end of punishment—the protection of society—has in pain a tested deterrent at its disposal. Yet even those who wish to hold the theory of retribution nevertheless have to admit that the retribution consists primarily in the fact that what is realized is the opposite of what is desired by the delinquent and in his consciousness of this fact. After trying to realize what he loved and wanted by overstepping the boundaries of justice, he then sees the opposite take place (Aquinas). To be sure, this is related to pain, but the punishment does not consist solely in the pain.

2. Eudoxus' arguments can be refuted in much the same way.

ad 1. As Aristotle said, the fact that all beings, both rational and non-rational, desire pleasure does not prove that pleasure is *the* good, but only that it is *a* good; and it does not strictly prove even this. It merely seems improbable that all creatures desire what is not desirable, and only that. However, anyone who takes a closer look at experience will be forced to qualify both the 'all' and the 'only', for, he points out, we do not always strive after pleasure, nor are our efforts directed solely towards gaining pleasure.

ad 2. Even if we fled from any sort of pain, it would not follow that every sort of pleasure is good. Just as the single state, health, is opposed to many diseases, there can be a variety of reasons for the absence of the characteristic, good. But not every pain is evil by any means. Noble suffering is an object of love experienced as being correct.

ad 3. Certainly, we aspire to joy for its own sake, but this is not to say that it is worthy of our aspiration. It may be absurd to ask, 'To what purpose are you feeling pleased?', but it is not absurd to ask, 'How can you take pleasure in the suffering of your benefactor?'

ad 4. It is wrong to look for the value of an object in the pleasure taken in it rather than in it itself. If it were the pleasure we take in justice that gave it its value, pleasure taken in injustice would make it valuable, too. And think of the case where we feel sad about an injustice that we were unable to prevent. *Here, our love of justice expresses itself in pain.* We must not confuse the higher emotions, whether pleasure or pain, with the sensual feelings of pleasure and pain that redound from them, giving them the character of so-called affects.

Thus the doctrine of hedonism reveals great defects, and we cannot consider the theory of goods to be completed with the investigation of pleasure and pain.

II

The Good within the Sphere of our own Mental Activity

---

53. The good within the sphere of judgment

In considering the fundamental divisions of our mental activity, we found the most pertinent ground of classification to lie in the nature of the relation between objects. We distinguished, accordingly, three basic classes of mental activity: presentation (ideas), judgment, and emotion.

As we have already had occasion to remark, experience reveals within each of these three classes something that is intrinsically valuable, i.e. good in the true sense of the word. Let us begin the construction of our table of goods with the class of judgments.

1. In ancient times, Aristotle included knowledge in the table of goods, and both ancient and modern thinkers have assented to his view. And certainly, to ask why we prefer knowledge to error would seem as absurd as asking why we would rather experience pleasure than suffer pain. But there still remains open the question whether knowledge or joy is a more exalted good. For the love of knowledge is also experienced as being correct.

This does not exclude the possibility that under certain circumstances knowledge may be painful to us, being knowledge of something that will cause us sorrow. But taken in itself it remains a good.

And it is a proportionately greater good the more important it is, the more general and penetrating, the greater the range of things that it illuminates, the more difficult the questions that it clarifies, and the richer the springs that it opens up for the discovery of new truths. Fundamental principles, such as Newton's law of gravitation, are more valuable than the knowledge of the characteristics of a particular variety of plant or mineral. Yet these latter are, in turn, more valuable than completely concrete pieces of information.

The value also varies according to the quality of knowledge—whether it is affirmative or negative. For instance, inasmuch as it is a system of analytic and hence purely negative principles, mathematics occupies a position inferior to that of the natural sciences, which contain propositions applying to things that we recognize to exist. So-called applied mathematics belongs to the natural sciences, inasmuch as it has reference to the physical world. But the value of a particular piece of knowledge also depends upon the value of its object. Consequently psychology, which concerns psychic states and activities, occupies in turn a higher position than the natural sciences. And from the viewpoints both of generality and of the relative perfection of the object, metaphysics, which deals with the laws common to all existence and its first, divine cause, holds the first place.

2. Just as knowledge is a good, error is an evil as such, and the magnitude of the evil varies in proportion to the goodness of the knowledge corresponding to it and to its distance from the truth. An error that is not far short of it has a certain value as an approximation to the truth.

But no error is to be called a pure evil, for as a judgment it includes an idea, and every idea is a good as such, as we hope to demonstrate later. The man who errs is of greater worth than the man who makes no judgments and who is therefore incapable of error, but the good in this instance is coupled with the evil of a disharmony, for the erroneous judgment acknowledges what is evidently false or rejects what is evidently true.

3. Because knowledge is a good, and an exalted good, inquiry is also of value. Even the first speculation, the first clearing of the way—not only the knowledge (sophia), but the love of it (philosophia)—is a good. Lessing went so far as to say that if he had to choose between the complete and perfect truth and investigation, he would prefer the latter. The kernel of truth at which he was groping was probably that knowledge is a double blessing when it follows vagueness and error, as is health when it follows illness. And even if our delight in the fully revealed truth is the most

sublime, our pleasure in inquiry is more lasting. Progress and change are necessary if happiness is to persevere. The pleasure of a game consists of hope and disappointment, exertion and conquest. Yet in spite of all this, investigation is only of value because it leads to knowledge. Unhappy the investigator who has not discovered that it is sweeter to find than to search. The destination is more than the path.

54. *The good within the sphere of the emotions*

1. This sphere embraces a still greater variety of activities than the sphere of judgment. The latter includes distinctions according to the object, and in particular between sensible and intellectual judgment; distinctions according to the quality of judgment (acknowledgment and rejection); the distinction between thetic and predicative judgment, between blind and evident judgment, and between motivated and unmotivated judgment; the distinctions of modality, whether assertoric or apodictic; and finally the temporal distinctions, according to which something is judged to be present, past, or future. Within the sphere of the emotions there are distinctions corresponding to each of these. Here, too, there are differences according to the object, particularly that between the sensible and the intellectual; distinctions of quality, whether love or hate; and the distinction between what is blind and what is characterized as being correct, and between what is motivated and what unmotivated. But alongside these come still others, according to the position in which the person who loves believes himself to stand *vis-à-vis* the thing he loves. They are the distinctions between joy, sorrow, longing, hope, and willing. The most advantageous situation is that in which we feel joy, which is unique in being the form in which our love is manifested when we believe that its object is realized.

2. Our criterion now enables us to recognize what is good within both spheres of emotional activity: among sensations as well as among intellectual acts.

Sensual pleasure is an act of sensation which is directed upon a certain sensible, localized quality and which possesses, in our secondary consciousness, not only the characteristics of presenting and accepting, but also that of intense loving. To be sure, this loving is in itself purely instinctive and blind, yet it belongs to the class of objects which call forth love experienced as being correct when they are contemplated under their universal aspect, i.e. it is something good in itself. Its opposite, that intense, sensible hatred which we call pain, is the object of a hate experienced as being correct, i.e. sensual hate is an evil. However, such acts of blind, instinctive love do not occupy the highest place among the goods of the emotions. Unless further goods are added to it, a blind sensual pleasure of this kind has a value inferior to that of spiritual joy. Who would care to compare the pleasures of smoking a good cigar with the sublime joy we feel when listening to a Beethoven symphony or gazing at one of Raphael's madonnas?[21] Moreover, habituation to sensual pleasure curtails our capacity for loftier pleasures. An instrument upon which trivial dance music has been pounded out day and night cannot reproduce the pure and sublime melodies of one of Beethoven's compositions.

3. Among the intellectual emotions, we can once again distinguish the blind from those experienced as being correct. Intrinsic good is to be found in both categories. As with sensations, a blind, purely habitual pleasure is to be considered a good, and blind sorrow an evil, quite independently of their objects. In contrast, all emotions that are experienced as being correct are intrinsically good. This is true of love and hatred in all their forms. There is intrinsic value to be found in noble pain, such as sorrow over the victory of injustice or at a failure to recognize the truth. It is a good in that it is a hatred of something deserving hatred; nevertheless, hate in any form is inferior to loving. Schopenhauer was mistaken, if only because he placed sympathy at the summit of all emotions. Nietzsche, in whose works we again and again find flashes of insight in spite of all the defects in his groundwork and deductions, showed superior insight on this point.

4. Even if blind sensual love is an inferior good, at least it is not pleasure in what is bad. And even that sort of pleasure contains some good, simply because it is pleasure, but it is an evil inasmuch as it is a perverse emotion. Who would will to be a Nero, lapping up the pleasures of cruelty in long draughts from a goblet of blood? Here we can really say: $\mu\tilde{\alpha}\lambda\lambda o\nu\ \mu\alpha\nu\epsilon\acute{\iota}\epsilon\iota\nu\ \mathring{\eta}\ \mathring{\eta}\sigma\theta\acute{\epsilon}\iota\epsilon\iota\nu.$*

'No one', says Aristotle, 'would wish to live in such a way that

[21] This section has been expanded by the editor, following *The Origin of our Knowledge of Right and Wrong.*

* Cf. Part II, chap. 1, sect. 51.

he retained the understanding of a child for his whole life and took the greatest delight in childish things. And similarly, no one would wish to take pleasure in committing a crime, even if no harm were to come of it.'*

5. Love activated by a belief in the existence of the beloved is of a joyful nature and consequently possesses a superior value; nevertheless, if we take a different viewpoint, there is another prerequisite for value. For if the belief is erroneous, the value of the joy is diminished. Not only do I desire not to take pleasure in my father's misfortune, but I also wish not to delight in grand mental achievements and acts of virtue that I erroneously imagine myself to have accomplished. In these instances the pleasure takes the wrong form, even though the love is correct. In such a case I would be grateful for information that would cause my delight to disappear. The real error here lies in our judgment, for the object of our love deserves it—but not our recognition of it as really existing.

6. Thus the correct emotion is a good in all of its forms, even if it is not always an unmixed one. Likewise, incorrect emotion is an evil, yet one containing some admixture of the good where it is of the nature of love or, most particularly, of joy. And not even wrong hatred can count as an unmitigated evil. It, too, is a mental activity and as such contains an idea; and the same category, ideas, also contains good in a variety of degrees. We shall now turn our attention to this group.

55. The good within the sphere of ideas

Of the three classes of acts of consciousness, we have so far examined the judgments and the emotions from the viewpoint of the table of goods. The fundamental class, ideas, still remains for investigation. There is no doubt but that we love some ideas, and certain of them in a very great degree; even children delight in seeing and hearing. We read the works of the poets, contemplate paintings, and listen to music, all because we delight in the ideas that are thereby presented to us. Whether or not their objects really exist does not trouble us. Merely possessing the idea of such

* This is clearly the same passage as was quoted on p. 178 (*Nic. Ethics*, book X, chap. 3, 1174a), but Brentano gives a slightly different translation here.

things is enough to make us take pleasure in them. Now, is this pleasure in ideas justified? Certainly ideas belong to what is intrinsically valuable; indeed, I venture to declare that each and every idea is of value, taken in itself. This is not to deny that there are some we should wish to be rid of; it is, rather, to claim that we should wish them gone because they take the place of some other, more interesting and pleasurable idea, not because they are themselves worthless. For our consciousness has definite limitations. At any one time we are unable to harbour more than a certain number and variety of ideas; much less can we give them our attention and equal amounts of our interest. And there are other conditions under which we may not wish to dwell on an idea, viz. when we find it repulsive, either instinctively or because of its associations. Nevertheless, aside from such consequences and incidental circumstances, having ideas is good and is recognizable as such. Certainly, anyone who had to choose between a condition of unconsciousness and the possession of at least some ideas would welcome even the most trivial of these and would not envy inanimate objects. Thus every idea appears to constitute a valuable enrichment of our lives. If we conjure up an idea of an ideal being (God), we cannot attribute to him every judgment and every act of love, but we must certainly confer upon him the possession of every conceivable idea.

56. *Objections to the thesis that every idea possesses value*

1. This thesis may sound strange to some simply because of the contrasts to what we found in the other two classes.

But this difference is comprehensible.

(*a*) The class of ideas has no opposite in the sense that the other two classes do. Judgment is differentiated into acknowledgment and rejection, the emotions (acts of interest) into loving and hating. That only one of the two can be right at a given time, that, indeed, there can be attributed to them any distinction between correct and incorrect, i.e. between true and false or between good and bad, is connected with these distinctions. But ideas are neither correct nor incorrect. If we none the less speak of incorrect ideas, we are referring not to the presenting itself but to a judgment that attributes the characteristic presented to an object which does not possess it. Or we may be thinking of the incorrectness of relating this idea to a particular word, which in turn amounts to saying that someone who uses the word has made an incorrect judgment about common usage. In this derivative sense we can also speak of morally bad ideas, perhaps in connection with the fact that they are liable to lead people astray into immoral desires and behaviour.

(b) The fundamental class is the class of presentations, or ideas. Judgment rests upon presentation, and particular acts of the emotions—e.g. hope, fear, sorrow, joy—are connected with judgments as well as with ideas. As a consequence it may happen that an act of love or hatred appears defective because the judgment upon which it is based is erroneous, as in the case of a foolish hope and the like. Simply because of its basic character nothing similar is possible in the case of presenting.

2. A second possible objection to the claim that every idea is a good is that we hate certain ideas; they fill us with revulsion, arouse our displeasure.

Answer: But here, as was noted earlier, we do not feel a hatred experienced as being correct but an instinctive or habitual aversion, based partially on special circumstances and partially on associations. A decision as to worthlessness is only to be made by a hate experienced as being correct.

3. The ideas of the pleasing and the beautiful stand out among all other ideas. Ideas of the beautiful appear to be distinguished by being loved with a love experienced as being correct, i.e. by being good. But if this is their distinguishing feature, all ideas are intrinsically valuable.

Moreover, the beautiful is the opposite of the ugly, or hateful. But what can this be except that the idea of which is hated with a hate experienced as being right? Therefore, certain ideas are bad.

Answer: This is no doubt the most significant objection. What is its basis? It rests upon a definition of the beautiful and the ugly that seems to have much to be said for it. The beautiful is defined as something the idea of which can be loved with a love experienced as being correct, the ugly as its opposite, i.e. as what can be hated with a hatred experienced as being correct. (To be more precise, it is not the idea of the thing that arouses our love or hatred, but the idea aroused in us by the influence it exercises upon our senses (and our imagination): its look, its sound.) Where, on the other hand, love for an idea is not experienced as being correct or incorrect, we speak simply of the pleasant or unpleasant rather than of the beautiful.

In what other way is it possible to construe these distinctions?

Kant and Herbart would probably agree with this definition of the beautiful. For in designating the 'necessity' of the pleasure it gives, and not simply its universality, as that which distinguishes the beautiful from the merely pleasant, they seem to be aiming at the distinguishing peculiarity of what is experienced as being correct. I say 'aiming', because the idea is false as they frame it. It is precisely with the beautiful and the ugly that taste and judgment diverge. Like many others, these philosophers commonly confuse necessity with correctness. But in endeavouring to establish a difference between the beautiful and what in fact happens to please, they are trying to associate with the former feeling a consciousness of universal and necessary justification, which shows that they have in mind the peculiarity of a pleasure experienced as being correct.

Now if we accept this definition, our investigation will have the embarrassing consequence that there is no class of ugly things standing in opposition to beautiful things, inasmuch as every idea is beautiful to some extent. Nevertheless it would still not be true that all differences between the beautiful and the pleasing would be erased. On the contrary, the concepts would remain different in their content and domain.

(*a*) They are different in content, for commonly pleasing people as a matter of fact is quite a different matter from being capable of arousing pleasure experienced as being correct. (In the former case the concept 'experienced as being correct' does not apply; in the latter, the concept 'actually arousing' does not apply.)

(*b*) They are different in domain, for the sphere of what actually arouses pleasure is smaller. Some things are in fact matters of indifference to us; others are positively displeasing. (The concept, 'being capable of being acknowledged by a correct judgment', does not presuppose anyone's actually making such an acknowledgment or, indeed, anyone even having a disposition to do so.)

(*c*) Furthermore, even when we are only speaking of things the ideas of which are actually pleasing, it is demonstrable that the beautiful and the pleasing do not coincide entirely. For the variations in degree with respect to what is actually pleasing do not correspond to those with respect to what is beautiful. The latter hold universally, whereas we encounter conflicting preferences of taste in different people. Hence with one of the opponents it is necessarily the case that what is the more pleasing does not coincide with what is more beautiful.

(d) And yet another point: one and the same person may, in virtue of his constitution or the habits he has developed, be afforded greater pleasure by one of two phenomena, while having to admit that the other possesses the advantage of beauty. He might, for example, recognize a visual phenomenon as the more beautiful, taking in it a pleasure experienced as being correct, while nevertheless getting greater enjoyment from a phenomenon involving touch.

4. Thus if we equate the beautiful idea with what is capable of being an object of a pleasure experienced as being correct, we are left with just one difficulty, that of accounting for the difference between the beautiful and the ugly.

We could attempt to assist ourselves by saying the same thing about the concept of the beautiful as can be said about the concept of the big, viz. that it has both a broad and a narrow sense. In the former sense every person is big, for every body has a certain size; in the latter, only certain people are big, i.e. they are of a size greater than the average. And this is what we usually mean when we speak of big people.*

And we might make a similar claim for the word beautiful. Beauty, it would run, is also predicated sometimes in a broad sense and sometimes in a narrow. In the latter sense it denotes a mark distinguishing certain things from others; this is its ordinary use. Understood in this way, not every idea is an idea of something beautiful.

The ugly would also be a relative concept. Taken in itself, its opposition to the beautiful would only be like the opposition between big and small. Ugly would not be positively opposed to the beautiful, but would only be a relative deficiency. An idea designated as ugly would not be an actual evil, but simply some-

---

* Brentano's analogy makes clearer sense in German because 'gross' (big) is obviously related to 'Grösse' (size); every person is 'gross' because he has a 'Grösse'. But the point can be put across in English by remarking that we can ask of anybody, 'How big is ——?' and can say of anybody, '—— is this (that) big'; hence everybody must have a 'bigness'.

thing that, because of the limitations of consciousness, interferes with the idea of the beautiful and is therefore displeasing to us.

57. Definitions of the beautiful and the ugly; the beautiful in art

But these definitions do not seem quite suitable either, if we are trying to capture what is commonly meant by beautiful and ugly. According to the ordinary conception of things, what is ugly is a downright evil. It might be countered that this is a result of confusion; after all, people commonly fail to distinguish clearly between feeling pleasure and feeling pleasure experienced as being correct, and confuse what displeases with what rightly displeases. The concepts of beautiful and ugly are, it will be said, in general wavering and indistinct; every idea to which pleasure attaches itself is at times called beautiful. (It is beautifully warm, etc.)*

1. This is all undoubtedly true. Nevertheless it may be possible to give a definition of the beautiful and the ugly that accords better with the ordinary use of the word than does the one mentioned previously. When we say things such as, 'It's beautifully warm', we feel them to be anomalies. On the other hand, regard to what actually pleases and displeases is normally and universally of such great influence that no one would call something beautiful if the idea of it gave rise universally to a feeling of displeasure—even if that displeasure be purely instinctive and not experienced as being correct—or if no pleasure could arise in connection with it or at any rate could not develop into any more significant sort of enjoyment. In ordinary life we use 'beautiful' with reference to any phenomenon which can be rightly preferred for its own sake to ordinary phenomena and which presents itself in such a manner that it in fact arouses love and delight in a particularly high degree in the man of proper disposition—the man endowed with good taste. But in order for this to happen, it is not sufficient for the idea to have value; a number of other conditions must be fulfilled.

Thus the concept of the beautiful also has reference in ordinary

* The other example Brentano gives—'it smells beautiful'—obviously does not work in English. We could employ synonyms: 'It smells gorgeous', 'That feels lovely', etc. However, no single English word with a meaning similar to that of 'schön' can be used with respect to so many kinds of things.

life to actual pleasure, while the ugly, in particular, bears an analogous reference to what is in fact displeasing.

2. And how do matters stand with the fine arts? We remarked that what is called beautiful in ordinary life is any object the idea of which can correctly be preferred for its own sake to ordinary ideas. The pleasure of observation in such a case must not be destroyed or disturbed by any actual displeasure at the idea, even a displeasure not experienced as being correct. Is the beauty that the artist strives for totally unrelated to what is actually pleasing or displeasing, whether or not it be experienced as being correct? By no means; the artist aims at arousing not only ideas of particular value but also a great degree of pleasure in them, pleasure experienced as being correct.

Hence the artist tries to avoid as much as possible anything that is displeasing, in order that he may not disrupt our enjoyment. But when he does make use of an idea to which displeasure attaches, he does so in order that a more intense pleasure may proceed from it, as, e.g., when a composer resolves a disharmony. Our interest is intensified; the harmony, in any case pleasant in itself, becomes more pleasant as being the resolution of something that can only be artistically justified as a preparation for it. Or, to take another instance, the harmony becomes pleasanter because of the way that various series of notes run along side by side, each glittering through the other. This phenomenon becomes even clearer with disharmony, for here the multiplicity of tones is more conspicuous and consequently becomes more comprehensible in the harmonious places as well. What would be disharmony taken in itself is not disharmonious in the relevant place in the melody.

It is a fact that what is pleasing affords special pleasure in the moment of attainment, and most particularly when it is preceded by something unpleasant. After a while the feeling becomes, as it were, exhausted. Hence an alternation between the pleasant and the unpleasant is appropriate in art. The fluctuating feelings of fear and hope play a special role, as Hume remarked, while the joy of having attained satisfaction is the highest crown. Perpetual suspension reaching no satisfactory conclusion becomes torture.

We find something similar in the sphere of scientific research. As previously remarked, Lessing and some thinkers after him declared that they preferred the striving for truth to the full possession of it. This is a curious confession; we feel inclined to say that whoever is of this opinion cannot really be striving for truth. The knowledge is undoubtedly the greater good, but the joy in approaching it step by step, the excitement of the alternation between hope, disappointment, exertion, partial success, etc., is constantly regenerated, so that the pleasure in the research is kept alive longer than the pleasure in the completed, concluding discovery, even though this latter pleasure is certainly the greatest of all in the first moment of its attainment.

It is out of these and related considerations that the artist, while intentionally mixing in some elements that displease, or are rather less pleasing than some others might have been, generally avoids what would displease.

3. Furthermore, the artist not only avoids what is in fact displeasing, but also prefers and chooses what in fact affords pleasure, even if the pleasure is blind and instinctive or is based solely upon habit. For instance, that pleasure attaches more to one colour than to another may turn out to be a reason to give the former preference. Undoubtedly artists do allow such considerations to hold sway, but they do so in varying degrees. Some works of art display a greater wealth of genuine beauty, while others arouse a greater degree of pleasure. Thus we have, on the one hand, art that is rich in content and free of frills and, on the other, art of little substance that aims to soothe and charm us.

The artist is justified in displaying a concern with pleasure. Indeed, he ought to aim at uniting the beautiful and the pleasing. But why? Do the fine arts, too, aim at exciting a blind pleasure in ideas? Hardly. On the contrary, their sole end is to present the most perfect possible image and to induce with respect to this image the highest possible degree of pleasure experienced as being correct. What, then, is the point of bringing in instinctive and other blind forms of pleasure felt in certain ideas? The answer is, to serve to intensify that pleasure that is experienced as being correct. And it can achieve this influence in much the same way that a simultaneous instinctive displeasure can cause disturbance.

This alternate fostering and restraining of the emotions is a very striking phenomenon, of considerable importance for art. Once something has put us into a gay mood, we take delight in many things that otherwise would appeal to us only slightly or not at all. And, on the other hand, the man who is in a melancholy frame of mind sees the sad side of whatever he looks at. One pleasure arouses in us a disposition to feel further pleasures.

Certainly, this is not unconditionally true. Sometimes, instead, pleasure diverts our attention from other things. Think of a boy who, while he is studying, is distracted by a dog he has just acquired or a bird in the room or by his pleasure in a jolly piece that an organ grinder has begun to play in the court outside. But in other cases one pleasure does not detract from another in this way. Instead, a number of objects of pleasure may stand in such a relation to each other that they can easily become conjoined by a unified act of attention, which enhances the delight taken in each. Consider what Aristotle says about pleasant smells in a dining room, which are supposed to stimulate the appetite, viz. that an odour of roses would detract from it, but the odour of a roast stimulates it. Yet in certain cases, he says, even the former odour might assist our appetite, viz. when an association has been formed on the basis of habit. Thus when we find virtue and charm coexisting in a single person it increases our pleasure in both, and similarly when beautiful poetical images are expressed in beautiful verses and corresponding metres. Goethe's remark that we should translate a poem into prose in order to evaluate it is accurate in so far as this process would assist us in giving an explicative analysis of the motives of the pleasure we feel in it. Suppose there are two sorts of delight, each of which we are able to take in a variety of ideas. Even if only one of them is delight of the sort directed upon an idea of something that is distinguished by being beautiful —that is, delight experienced as being correct—while the other is a blind pleasure, it is nevertheless in the interests of art to call forth this instinctive pleasure, too.

4. These remarks serve to elucidate several matters concerning the tasks of aesthetics. If aesthetics is intended to be a theory of art—i.e. to instruct the artist—or even if it is only meant to analyse works of art and make them comprehensible in the light of his motives, then it has a great deal more to do than just to present the laws determining high degrees of true beauty. It will also have to deal with the laws that determine the greater pleasure that we in fact take in what is beautiful and, indeed, all the actual pleasure that is taken in various ideas; it will, that is, have to deal with the laws of instinctive pleasure, as well as the laws of habit, which wield a great influence both in cases of pleasure experienced as

being correct and in cases of instinctive pleasure. This influence proves to be of such significance that some philosophers have gone so far as to think that all beauty is determined by habit; they say, for instance, that regular features are considered beautiful because they represent the average, and similarly for certain proportions of the body, etc. According to what we established earlier, this could not possibly be true; but it is undeniable that the laws of habit, like some other psychological laws that are not, as such, laws of beauty, must be taken into account in order to make comprehensible the more exalted pleasure aroused by a phenomenon that is beautiful.

5. But we are still left with the question that is the real object of our present discussion. I believe that the preceding remarks make comprehensible why it is that the artist not only excludes what is displeasing from his works but also includes, for the sake of making the beauty more impressive, elements the ideas of which arouse blind pleasure.

This same purpose can easily take him still further afield. Artists are fond of reaching out beyond the sphere of delight in the imagination and employing for similar purposes other sorts of pleasure. They may even attempt to elicit aesthetic pleasure by an admixture of flattery, be it of an individual or of a whole people. This is indicated by such turns of phrases as 'telling a person fine tales' or 'using a thousand fine phrases'. But they would rather not touch upon what would cause displeasure, even if not relating to an idea. The target of a satire seldom finds it agreeable, and when it insults the entire public no one enjoys it. (Think of how blue-stockings dislike Molière and shrews Shakespeare. An old man clinging to life takes no pleasure in works of art that remind him of death.)

In taking into account his public, the artist is able nevertheless to act with a truly artistic purpose and in accordance with aesthetic standards.

6. It is a different matter when the beautiful is sacrificed to what in fact happens to please or when pleasure in ideas having great value is subordinated to more lowly ideas or other interests. Unfortunately this happens frequently, as when art places itself at the service of sensuality. At that point it ceases to be fine art and descends to the level of cookery, aiming at cleverly preparing pleasure for our palate. Similarly, when the principal pleasure in a

eulogistic poem focuses upon the flattering phrases it contains, this pleasure is not aesthetic. Plato called the art of cookery an art of flattery. And when a noble art is diverted to such an inferior aim, this reproach is all the more justified. Indeed, by degrading what was intended for a higher calling, such art strikes the man who really loves what is beautiful as positively repulsive. Even didactic literature is alienated from the true aims of art, although it is of greater ethical value than the works just discussed.

7. Art is also deflected from its true mission when it indulges in so-called *tours de force* and, in general, where our attention is concentrated upon the artist's craftsmanship rather than upon the beauty of what is presented. Pleasure may be aroused in such cases, and it may be justified, but it is not pleasure directed upon the beautiful.

Such errors are made in every branch of art. We find poets who weave together the most artistic rhymes and assonances and display an astonishing command of language; yet none of this perfects in any way the image of his subject or the feeling attaching to it. We find composers who assign outbursts of frustrated sorrow or a mad passion for revenge to a coloratura—who dispels any solemnity we may feel with her deftly executed leaping and trilling. We find painters who make excessive use of linear perspective in order to display their mastery, e.g. Mantegna. We find architects who, instead of putting a tower upright on a church, place it crooked, at the greatest, most daring angle permitted by the laws of equilibrium. We find expert dancers who have not the slightest notion of that beauty of motion which makes Terpsichore truly worthy of a place among the muses; they consider the most violent distortions of their arms and legs to be the greatest triumph of their art. And the public is sufficiently barbaric to take pleasure in this human torment. It is questionable whether pleasure in the mobility and masterful control of the body offers a substitute for the lack of aesthetic appeal. But even if it does, it is in each and every instance like the cases mentioned previously; they all constitute a falling away from the true purpose of art, even when executed by such ranking masters as Mantegna and Mozart.

It also happens frequently that a portrait is pleasing primarily because of the artist's craftsmanship, as, for instance, in the cases where only the likeness is held to be of value. Aristotle tries to explain the pleasure we take in a likeness by the analogy between making a comparison with the original and the mental activity involved in drawing a conclusion. But this would also not be aesthetic pleasure, and in any case the explanation is insufficient. A comparison between two natural objects—two eyes, two hands, or two legs—does not afford us the pleasures that we derive from a successful portrait. Rather, our pleasure derives from the virtuosity. 'How natural he has made it look!', we exclaim. Our pleasure and admiration are justified, yet they do not arise from the beauty, but from the mastery.

Conscious of the many respects in which all artistic beauty is inferior to the beauty of nature, an artist friend remarked to me that he was frequently puzzled as to how we are to comprehend the great delight that men take in works of art. He thought the ultimate explanation was to be found in their vanity—in their pride in the beauty of the works of man. This would be something like pleasure in craftsmanship. But it is not what the artist ought to aim at, for the true artist considers it his greatest triumph when the person enjoying his work forgets the artist and even himself for the beauty.[22]

8. Let us return to our reply to the last objection: that the thesis that every idea is intrinsically valuable contradicts the fact that ugly ideas exist, too. I did not in the least intend to equate the beauty of an idea with its value. It is not only beautiful ideas that are justifiably pleasing; beauty is the narrower of the two concepts. We assign the appellation 'beautiful' to ideas that are of such very great value that we are justified in taking a particularly high degree of pleasure in them. It is not enough that they deserve to be found highly pleasing; in order to be beautiful, they must be presented to us in a way that actually arouses such pleasure. In order for this to happen, inferior and distracting ideas must be avoided; above all, displeasure, even blind displeasure, must not emerge, unless the contrast it displays induces a delight in what *is* valuable. To make use of displeasure only where it will serve this purpose, while employing blind pleasure, not for its own sake, but solely

---

[22] One might add that the artist extracts the essence and is able thereby to produce a stronger impression than the natural formation, in which the essentials are often obscured by secondary qualities. The relation in question is similar to that between the intuition of an object and its concept.

for the purpose of supporting aesthetic pleasure, is one of the niceties of artistic creation. How this is brought about in individual instances is a subject for aesthetics. Our concern was simply to establish the position of ideas in general among those things good in themselves and to defend this portion of the table of goods against objections, the last of which we disposed of by means of our explication of the concept of beauty. Later on, when we discuss the general laws of correct preference, it will be appropriate to examine in greater detail the relative values of particular ideas.

Thus we have upheld the claim that every idea is something good in itself and that every extension of our life of ideas increases the good within us. And as ideas lie at the basis of all other mental activities, it follows that every mental activity is a good.

III

The Good outside the Sphere of our own Mental Activity

---

58. *Not only our own mental activity is capable and worthy of being loved*

1. Many people think our own mental activity is the only object deserving love, while everything else is to be loved only as a means to it. Indeed, they go further and claim, not only that our own mental activity is the only object worthy of love, but also that it is impossible to love anything else for its own sake. Needless to say, all those who hold that our own pleasure is the sole good and the only thing that can be loved belong to this number. But still others can be counted among them, in that they make a similar claim for our own perfection.

How should we reply to these claims? One thing is certain: if it is true that only our own mental activity is lovable, the whole world is deceiving itself, for the reverse is constantly being asserted.

And if both theses are correct—that we can only love what pertains to ourselves as well as that only what is our own deserves our love—then people must be lying to one another in professing to love and desire that which is not worthy of love and desire. In telling such lies, they are charging themselves with loving and desiring wrongly.*

---

* This is a confusing passage. I take it Brentano means the following. If it is true that what pertains to ourselves is the only object capable of being loved and also the only object deserving of love, then people must be lying when they claim to love what pertains to another, e.g. a friend's success, for it is not possible for them to feel such love. Not

185

Even the first thesis seems harsh. Yet there have been philosophers who did not shrink from making it: Mandeville, La Rochefoucauld, Nietzsche (with his 'beautiful German beast of prey'), and Darwinians. But the second claim seems utterly implausible. It runs so completely counter to all human inclinations that even the aforementioned thinkers might have had qualms about drawing such a consequence. Yet, who knows?—Some bold investigator might rather make this concession than abandon his central thesis. He could explain it to himself in the following way: we do not always shy away from self-incrimination, particularly not when we make the self-accusation in front of someone whom it flatters and places under an obligation; think of Wolsey and other politicians before their monarchs, or Medea before Jason. Another thinker who wanted to defend this improbable view might give it a different twist by saying that we have simply made the error of holding what is bad to be good.

2. All these explanations seem rather contrived, and we would do well to request a proof before we accept a doctrine that leads to such paradoxical consequences. The grounds offered vary from thinker to thinker.

Some proceed deductively, setting out from the proposition that all being is fundamentally nothing but a striving for self-preservation. Inasmuch as all activity springs from being, it springs from this egotistical endeavour.

Others, and indeed, most supporters of this view, call in experience to their defence. But experience is precisely what bears unequivocal witness against the doctrine, as we saw earlier with hedonism. Let us demonstrate this in detail.

(*a*) First of all, it is most certainly false that only our mental activity is capable of being loved. People sacrifice themselves for other people and other things: the friend for his friend, the mother for her child, the patriot for his fatherland, the enthusiast for his pet idea. These facts are so undeniable that sincere men whose

---

only are they lying; they are also going out of their way to accuse themselves of loving what they ought not to love, given that what pertains to others does not deserve our love. All this makes the two claims quite implausible, for we can hardly be made to believe that all people make a regular practice of consciously telling lies that make them appear worse to each other than would the truth.

systems embraced the opposite view have gradually been forced to admit them. (Cf. Hutcheson's astute remarks concerning this point.) Mill, who originally held that only our own pleasure is lovable and always remained of the opinion that it alone can be the object of our love at the beginning of our life, admitted later on that in the course of our mental and spiritual development we attain to a love of our neighbours, just, he says, as the miser comes to love his gold. Nevertheless, he continued to claim that we love our neighbour and wish him to have pleasure really only for our own sake. Whether he is correct about this particular point does not concern us here; it is enough to know that even in this camp we find evidence against the doctrine that we can only love what pertains to ourselves.

(*b*) But the following observation may perhaps do more to illuminate the true state of affairs. How are we to construe the claim that only what pertains to ourselves, i.e. our own mental activity, is capable of being loved? Is this to include only the activity of the present moment, or of the future as well? Scarcely anyone would want to exclude future activity. Even the hedonists, for instance Epicurus, teach that our future pleasure is also capable of being loved; they point out that people are willing to sacrifice a smaller present pleasure with an eye to it. Yet, like Epicurus, many hedonists are materialists. From this viewpoint, the continuous change in the matter constituting our brain means that there is a continuous change of the object of mental functions. What is ordinarily referred to as 'I' over a period of years is at the present no longer a material part of myself, and it could quite possibly be standing outside and over against my present self, having been reconstituted in just the same manner as before. But behold! believing all this does not annihilate the hedonist's love of future pleasures. This might be simply because hedonistic materialists have failed to contemplate the consequences of this belief, so that it has been unable to have its due influence. But no; even if we make them aware of the consequences, they will have no less concern for their future, though at the same time it seems to me very doubtful that they will give up their materialism.

It is clear, then, that a man is in fact capable of loving the mental activity of others as well as of himself.

Somebody might make the following objection. Even if, strictly speaking, my future ego is not quite the same as my present one, this is surely a special case involving a quite special form of similarity such that we can consider them the same thing for all practical purposes; consequently it is still possible to maintain that our love is in fact confined to our own present and future pleasure.

Reply: (α) The alleged extensive similarity does not exist. The grown man differs far more from the boy than the boy from other boys.

(β) No matter how great the similarity, the boundaries of each ego would have to be set somewhere. But a similarity between things can gradually decrease, and this makes it impossible to indicate a specific boundary that is absolutely incapable of being exceeded.

Hence our own mental activity is not the only object that can be loved. Nor is it the only object worthy of love.

(*a*) No one seriously considers it an instance of self-incrimination when a person confesses to an interest in the happiness of other people. We often boast of our sacrifices for others before a third party. Indeed, our vanity sometimes leads us to stray from the truth in this regard—all of which would be incomprehensible if what lies outside ourselves were not included in the good. No one is surprised at such boasting; rather, everyone admires the sacrifice. In fact, when we make preferences and choices in such a way that we sacrifice a small personal good for the sake of incomparably greater benefits to an extended circle of other people, we perform an act of the emotions that is experienced as being correct. If any acts at all are right, surely this one is.

(*b*) Another way of clarifying the matter is by asking whether it is only our own present welfare that is supposed to be worthy of love, or our future welfare as well. It is practically impossible to find anyone who would not include the latter; otherwise, the greatest possible short-sightedness would be the ideal in all our dealings. Or rather, all acts and endeavours would be folly, since these are always directed towards future goals, which cannot possibly be a means to anything in the present. Thus the earlier argument for the possibility of unegotistical love can also be used to prove the correctness of such love.

What pertains to others, then, is not only capable of being loved but also worthy of love.

Even Bentham admits that instances of pleasure in another's

happiness do occur and are a good. To be sure, he believes there to be no such thing as self-sacrifice. However, once it is granted that we can love the happiness of others as well as our own, it becomes impossible to deny that there are also cases where something benefiting another is preferred to some smaller personal benefit, which is sacrificed. As we have demonstrated, the facts confirm this so strikingly that even Mill deviated from Bentham on this point.

Of course, all this holds for goods within every sphere of mental activity, and similarly for all the evils. Pleasure is not the only good capable and worthy of being loved, and goods pertaining to others are capable of inducing, and are deserving of love, just as are those pertaining to ourselves.

59. *Are there goods other than mental activity?*

So far, our acquaintance with goods has extended only to the mental activities of ourselves and others. The question now is whether there are other intrinsic goods or whether everything we call good is good only for the sake of these mental goods. Let us make the general question more specific.

1. Is a virtuous disposition preferable to its opposite? Actually, we love and admire people more on account of their character than because of isolated moral acts. We hold these in esteem inasmuch as they reveal moral character. The word 'Ethik' [ethics] comes from ἦθος (meaning custom or usage), while 'tugendhaft' [virtuous] comes from 'Tüchtigkeit' [ability] and 'taugen' [to be good for, of use for]. Does it follow that dispositions are also valuable in themselves? Or are they valuable only because of the acts that they give rise to?

2. Are plants worthy of love in themselves, for their own sake; are they to be regarded as an intrinsic good? Is the perfection of their organization valuable in itself?

3. Is each and every existing thing a good, quite aside from whether it is always useful?

Here, too, opinion is divided. Many people deny that anything not mental has inherent value; they say that we are not even capable of loving any of the objects in question for their own sake. but others disagree with this view. How should we decide?

One point is easily settled: it is an exaggeration to deny that people love anything other than mental acts. After all, the miser loves gold without motivation.

However, it is more difficult to decide whether the other things mentioned contain an element intrinsically worthy of love.

Our first inclination is to say, 'No'.

(*a*) Those mental acts of others that are worthy of love for their own sake are always such that they also deserve the love of the possessor. If plants are worthy of love for their own sakes, the same should hold for them. But plants themselves do not find their own nature lovable with a love experienced as being correct, for they are altogether incapable of loving. Therefore, it would seem to follow, they are to be loved not in their own interest, but in ours—that is, they are to be loved as a means—and their value does not lie in their essence itself.

(*b*) If, nevertheless, some people still show an inclination to number plants among the intrinsically valuable, we can explain this temptation by the fact that what deserves love as a means easily becomes associated with justified love and what intrinsically deserves it, so that we are led to view as an intrinsic good what is merely good as a means.

However, it is of some importance that the majority of significant philosophers have considered the sphere of the intrinsically valuable to be more extensive. Plato thought that every positive being was an imitation of the idea of the good, and Aristotle and the most important medieval philosophers agreed. So, too, did Leibniz, who in his correspondence with Wolff says that perfection is a degree of positive reality or—which comes to the same thing— of affirmative discernability (*intelligibilitas affirmativa*), so that what is more perfect is what contains more things worthy of esteem (*notatu dignae*). Pierre Janet took up this view. He says that good is to be found in all activities, especially those that are intensive, and in the harmony between the various elements, in the unity among the universe. He expressed both these tenets in the statement, '*Le bien d'un être consiste dans le développement harmonieux de ses facultés.*'* The question is of importance for theodicy, for if mental activity were the only intrinsic good, we would be faced with the problem of why God did not cast aside all indirect means and place, from the start, all mental beings in the most perfect

* 'The good of a being consists in the harmonious development of its faculties.'

possible state: knowing everything, loving only as is right, and experiencing the most sublime joys. It is precisely these metaphysical considerations which indicate that limiting what is good to what is mental is an untenable position. The world could not develop; like a bad play, it would consist of isolated, unrelated episodes. It would appear that causal connections and relations must be accounted among what is good.

Upon closer inspection, the counter-argument is seen to be weak. It rests on the proposition that everything worthy of love is in our own or in someone else's interest. What does the phrase, 'in our own or someone else's interest', mean? If it is equivalent to, 'as a means to certain mental activities, pertaining either to ourselves or to others', the argument begs the question. If, on the other hand, what is meant is that the good is the object of justified interest and consequently bound up with the existence of creatures capable of such interest, then we are confronted with a misunderstanding. That an object be good is the objective condition required for any love directed upon it to be correct. But this says nothing as to whether anyone is actually present who could possibly harbour such interest. This point can be clarified immediately by appealing to the analogy to the true in the sense of what exists. If we say that something is true if it can be acknowledged in a correct judgment of recognition, we are not saying that such a judgment must necessarily be made by someone. What exists would continue to do so even if no one were there to acknowledge it.

We could give the following argument with just as much justification. If one of the characteristics of another person is true for me, then it must be one that is true for its possessor also, and the same must hold for plants. But the characteristics of a plant cannot be true for the plant, for it is incapable of acknowledging them. Therefore the characteristics of plants hold no truth for us. And this is clearly sophistry.

(c) I have already stated that the question is of overwhelming importance for metaphysicians, and if we wish to view it from the metaphysician's viewpoint we cannot avoid a more thorough investigation. However, the question is not equally important for the moral philosopher, as for all practical purposes the opposite views lead to the same consequences.

For instance, whether we assume that virtuous dispositions are intrinsically preferable to their opposites or that they are preferable only with respect to acts arising from them, the acts are in any case of paramount value. Consequently the value that the disposition derives from the good proceeding from it is in practice of greater importance.

Similarly, it is a matter of indifference for ethics whether or not animal and vegetable organisms are valuable as such or only in so far as they are useful and are necessary conditions of aesthetic pleasure.

As far as the forces of inanimate nature are concerned, we can neither increase nor decrease their quantity in the physical world. Thus it is of no importance to ethics whether they are valuable as an end or only as a means.

The longer we study the matter, the more we find that mental goods have such rank and significance within our sphere of influence that any intrinsic value physical goods may possess is negligible in comparison.

This completes our investigation into the various species of goods. To summarize:

We discovered intrinsic good in the mental activities of both ourselves and others: every instance of presenting is intrinsically good; within the sphere of judgment, knowledge is intrinsically good; within that of the emotions, justified love and pleasure in the good are intrinsically good.

60. *Are the same things good for everyone?*

An incidental question, before we proceed to an investigation of the relative value of goods: Are the same things good for everyone?

We must clarify the question before we can answer it. It has two possible meanings:

(*a*) Is it to be desired that the same intrinsic good pertain to all creatures?

(*b*) Is it desirable for everyone that any given intrinsic good exists?

Taken in its first sense, this question is to be answered in the negative; taken in the second, in the affirmative. It is good for a horse to have four legs, but for a man to have two; it is good for a man to have a genuinely masculine character and for a woman to have a genuinely feminine character. On the other hand, it is good for both men and women for men to be masculine and women feminine. (Here I speak of good in the sense of intrinsic good, rather than in the sense of useful.)

This result follows directly from our previous discussion. We came to see that not only our own perfection is to be loved, but also that of others. And regarding the perfection of plants and other physical perfections, it is yet easier to recognize that diversity in the persons feeling the love cannot result in any differences as to the rightness or wrongness of the love.

The same things are good for everyone, just as the same things are true for everyone. And it is this that makes possible the peace of all who will the good. The angels are right in singing, at Christmas, 'Peace on earth to men of good will'—assuming, of course, that the men have understanding as well as good will.

IV

The Relative Value of Goods

61. *Immediate knowledge of what is better*

Our previous remarks about the concept of the better made it apparent that immediate cognitions concerning relative values, by means of which we recognize one good as greater than another, are always instances of preference experienced as being correct. Let us give as complete a survey as possible of these cases.

1. First, there is the case in which we prefer something that is good and known to be good to something bad and known to be bad, as when we prefer joy to sorrow or knowledge to error—both clear instances of an act of preference experienced as being correct.

2. Second, there is the case where, comparing the existence of a good to the essence of it, we give preference to the former. And we are equally right when, comparing the existence of evil with its non-existence, we give preference to its non-existence.

To be included here are:

(*a*) the case in which we prefer a good that is pure to the same good with an admixture of evil, and the case in which we prefer an evil with an admixture of good to the same evil in its unadulterated state.

(*b*) the case where we give preference to a whole good over a part of it or to a partial evil over the entire evil, in accordance with the principle of summation (cf. note 19).

Aristotle himself remarked that the sum of the good is always better than the individual constituents. This principle also applies where it is a question of duration; a pleasure lasting an hour is better than the same pleasure extinguished after but a moment. Epicurus disputed this point in order to comfort us about death. But how short-sighted he was! For if he were right, then an hour's pain would be no worse than an instant of pain, and a life of happiness with one single moment of pain would not be preferable to a whole life of pain with a single moment of joy. And Epicurus himself teaches the contrary doctrine.

Cases in which there are differences of degree are also to be included among those where the value becomes greater by being coupled with other things of value. If two pleasures are exactly alike except for the fact that one is more intense than the other, the intenser one is the better of the two; conversely, the more intense evil is the greater evil. (This has to do with the fact that genuine intensity is found only within the sphere of sensations and sensual affects, where it is measured by the density with which the field of our sensations is filled.)

3. A case very closely related to the one just mentioned is the one in which one good is given preference over another one which, while not belonging to it, is the same as one of its parts. Similarly, a greater evil is produced when one bad thing is added to another. It is better, for instance, not only to have an idea of something good, but also to love it; the sum of the mental relations produces a greater good.

4. Another instance of a preference experienced as being correct occurs when we give preference to the more probable of two equally valuable goods. Bentham remarked upon this, but made the error of supposing that the value of a good could be increased by temporal proximity, quite independently of the probability of its coming into existence, just as it can be increased by greater intensity or longer duration. It is possible to have a situation in which a greater good with a smaller possibility of coming into existence competes with a smaller good that is more likely to be attained; then we must take probability into consideration in making a correct choice. If A is three times better than B, but the chances of realizing B are ten times better, it is right to give preference to B.

Here, too, the principle of summation applies, for the more probable good will on the average be realized in more instances.

5. There are also cases of preferences experienced as being

correct in which what is better is not the greater sum of good. Rather, the preference is grounded on a qualitative difference. For instance, positive knowledge is better than negative, other things being equal. Advantageous as it is that geometry reveals to us universal laws, its value would nevertheless decrease significantly if it turned out that there were no physically extended objects and that, consequently, geometric propositions were without application.

6. An analogous instance occurs where we give preference to an emotion of love over an emotion of hatred, as we discussed when erecting the table of goods. Clearly, we are concerned here with special cases of preferences experienced as being correct.

7. A related, though not identical case occurs where pleasure in what is good is placed over against pleasure in what is bad and pain regarding the bad over against displeasure in the good. Pleasure in what is bad is good in so far as it is pleasure, yet at the same time it is bad in so far as it is a wrong emotion. It is preponderantly but not purely evil. In rejecting it as bad, we are not performing a simple act of hatred but, rather, executing an act of preference in which the freedom from evil is selected over the possession of good. This preference, experienced as being correct, justifies our revulsion at delight taken in evil: better to have no pleasure at all than to take pleasure in what is bad.

Turning to the second case, what must we say about displeasure experienced as being correct in what is evil? Once again, we have a preference experienced as being correct, as, e.g., in cases where we are pained at the sight of oppressed innocence or feel regret when, surveying our past life, we become conscious of having performed an evil deed. Here we find ourselves in a situation just opposite to the one where we take pleasure in the bad. Pain from regarding evil pleases on the whole, but not purely; it is not an unadulterated good, as would be the sublime delight we would feel upon contemplating the opposite of the evil at hand. Descartes was right when he counselled us to turn our attention to the good rather than to concentrate upon the evil.

8. Consider another case of preference experienced as being correct that cannot be subordinated to the principle of summation. Imagine a process that brings about evil out of good or less good out of greater good and compare it to one leading in the opposite direction; the latter appears preferable, even if the total sum of

good is the same in both cases. And this preference is experienced as being correct. This is what we mean by a *bonum progressionis* and a *malum regressus*.

62. *Cases where we cannot know what is preferable, and cases of indifference*

What happens when we compare goods belonging to different classes? This is a matter about which there is considerable disagreement. Most noteworthy is the well-known dispute as to whether pleasure or knowledge is preferable and whether correct love or knowledge is preferable. The problem is, how we are to compare the various classes. Clearly, if we are to establish the superiority of the one class over the other, we cannot arbitrarily select an example from each class, for each contains a range of goods, some better than others. Instead, we must compare the worthiest example from each class.

Both insight and correct love are goods, but how can we know whether this particular act of insight or that particular act of love is better? Some people waste no time giving their verdict; in their view, every act of noble love is intrinsically of such sublime value that it is better than all scientific knowledge put together. But this claim is not only dubious; it is positively absurd. For no matter how valuable, any single instance of noble love is a finite good. But every insight also constitutes a certain finite good, and if we keep adding on more and more of these finite goods, sooner or later the value of the sum must necessarily exceed any single given finite value.

Plato and Aristotle, on the other hand, place acts of insight higher than virtue, but their claim is also unjustified. The very clash of opinions makes clear that the criterion fails us here. (However, that says nothing against the instances previously clarified, where we are capable of holding a preference experienced as being correct.) Genuine determinations of quantity are impossible here, as with many mental phenomena. And where intrinsic superiority cannot be established, it cannot be taken into consideration. For all practical purposes, it is absent. (When we discuss the supreme practical good, we will see that this hiatus is of no practical significance.)

It is just as impossible to recognize in individual cases whether or not a given cognition is more valuable than a given pleasure. Not all insights are of the same value. On the other hand, the phenomenon of a preference experienced as being correct does offer us a criterion of a more general nature. For instance, presented with the concept of blind pleasure and the concept of a cognition in general, the preference experienced as being correct will tell us that it is better to give up all blind pleasure than all knowledge.

2. These cases where we fail to have a preference experienced as being correct and are therefore unable to tell whether any difference in value is present are to be clearly distinguished from those where comparison between the two objects demonstrates that no such difference exists. An instance of the latter occurs when we see that it is irrelevant whether a value pertains to ourselves or to another. We have already recognized that it is wrong to hold only what pertains to oneself to be worthy of love, or even capable of being loved, but we would also be making a mistake, i.e. an incorrect preference, if we held a good to be of greater value because it pertains to ourself. This is one of the fundamental principles of ethics, in the light of which we realize that the decisive choice is not the one between egoism and altruism. Neither is correct, taken in itself. *The only right thing to do is to give our love and preferences in accordance with the standard of true value;* that is, to give preference to the greater over the lesser good, even when this turns out to leave us with the short end of the stick —but also when we turn out to reap the greater good ourselves. The full significance of this proposition will not become clear until the next chapter, where we turn our attention to the question of the highest practical good.

63. *The relative value of ideas*

Finally, let us apply the laws of preference experienced as being correct to the realm of ideas. As I remarked earlier, these laws are fundamental for aesthetics.

1. A richer, more fertile idea is more valuable than a meagre one. Among other things, the aesthetic preferability of the ideas emanating from our imagination over conceptual ideas stems from this fact. The former always contains a greater wealth of ideas.

2. Ideas about the mental are more valuable than ideas about the

physical. Hence poetry is the highest of all arts, for no other is able to present the life of the soul so well. Music may appear to have a more immediate effect upon us; nevertheless, it appeals not only to our superior faculties but also to our affects, which are grounded in sensual faculties.

3. Ideas of what is better, nobler, and, in general, more valuable, are themselves of greater value.

4. The true idea of something is more valuable than a mere surrogate idea.

5. A distinct idea is of greater value in itself than a confused idea.

6. Composite ideas that are put together by intuition are of greater value than those put together by predication.

V

The Supreme Practical Good

64. *Making the correct choice*

1. Up to now we have been talking about correct loving and correct preferring. These may be directed upon something that lies outside our power, where it is not in the least a question of realizing or sustaining something. In such cases, we still prefer one object to another; this is a theoretical preference, so to speak. However, ethics is supreme among the practical disciplines. It demands that we perform or refrain from certain acts; its precepts and prohibitions are directed not simply towards our loving, hating, and preferring, but more particularly towards our willing and choosing.

Let us clarify the difference between preferring and choosing. Giving preference is the more general concept; making a choice is giving preference, but not all preferring is choosing. Two factors must be present for a preference to be a choice:

(*a*) It must be a decision.

(*b*) It must be directed upon something that it is our business to accomplish and that can be accomplished in virtue of our desiring it.

ad (*a*) Every emotion is principally distinguished by being one of love or of hatred, but emotions have many nuances, which constitute the specific distinctions within the two general divisions. They include, for instance, the distinction between simple loving and preferring and between the exclusive and the non-exclusive, by which I mean the following. It is possible for me to love two things that are incompatible, e.g. doing sums and writing. The love of one does not exclude the love of the other. But in any particular case I can opt for only one of the two. A decision in favour of one is not compatible with a decision in favour of the other.

Some wishes, too, involve a decision. For instance, I can wish decisively that the weather will be good tomorrow. Deciding is not always willing, but every act of will constitutes a decision.

ad (b) What is distinctive about willing? As remarked previously, acts of will always concern something that is to be brought about by ourselves. Hence we can only will what lies within our power or what we at least seriously believe to be so. This distinguishes willing both from wishing and from wishing that involves a decision.

Willing, then, can be defined as wishing, involving a decision, that has as its object something that is to be realized by ourselves and that we confidently expect to take place as a result of our desiring it. In other words, it is a wish for which we have opted and which we believe to be capable of being realized by our intervention.

Willing is not an elementary phenomenon in the sense that loving or knowing or being red or location are elementary. These latter cannot be analysed because they are themselves constituents. In contrast, the concept of willing is complex, containing a multiplicity of elements that could also be extracted from other phenomena: the concepts of loving, of judging with conviction, of loving involving a preference, and of realizing an end. But in pointing out this fact, I do not wish to give rise to any misunderstanding; it is not possible to acquire an intuitive idea by means of the definition without having experienced the particular phenomenon in question.

In this, willing differs markedly from judging. Once we have got quite clear about the concepts of affirming, or knowing, and rejecting, we are able to form an idea of any judgment at all, whatever its object may be. It is only in order to form an idea of an assertoric, evident judgment or an apodictic judgment that we require a more particular sort of experience. In any other case, it is easy to form an intuitive idea of a judgment, once we possess all the elements of which it is constructed. But it is different in the case of willing; a man may have exercised his faculties of loving and hating with great frequency; none the less, if he had never experienced an act of will, he would not be able to discern the phenomenon of willing, with all its peculiarities, from the analysis given here. However, this is not to say that willing is fundamental and irreducible. It is the same with composite colours and with chords. Furthermore, it would be a mistake to suppose this characteristic to be of a peculiarity of willing, as over against other activities of the emotions. Loving and hating, although common to all emotions, have in every case a different shade of character. A person who has experienced no other feelings besides those of joy and sorrow could not acquire an intuitive grasp of the distinctive character of hoping or fearing by means of analytic definitions. The same holds even with regard to the various varieties of joy.

There is a difference not only of quantity but also of quality between the delights of a good conscience and the pleasure of becoming comfortably warm, between the joy of gazing upon a beautiful painting and the pleasure of tasting good food, and unless we have had special experience of these, a description of the particular object will not help us to form an idea corresponding perfectly to it.

These differences of detail found in the phenomenon of interest might tempt us to divide this unitary class into two, feeling and willing, but these categories would be woefully inadequate. Making this distinction would be analogous to denying that there is such a thing as the unitary class, colour, on the grounds that there are various specific colours.

Ought we to make any further distinction between willing and choosing? As we have defined them, they coincide. But if we should want to distinguish them further, we might speak of choosing in cases where our preference applies to opposing objects and willing in those where it concerns simply whether a given object is to exist or not.[23]

2. When is a decision directed upon the right end? Answer: When the best among the ends attainable is chosen. Let us

---

[23] This section was edited by Kastil, in conjunction with the treatise, 'Loving and Hating', which appears as an appendix to *The Origin of our Knowledge of Right and Wrong*.

construct an ideal case in order to make clear how this can occur.

(*a*) To begin with, when we are to make such a decision we must investigate our sphere of influence; that is, the extent of the objects upon which we can have an effect. This survey must take into account not only the immediate consequences of the decisions in question, but also the long-range ones. Of course, past experience plays an important role here. The final judgment can only claim a certain probability, which may be greater or smaller but can never attain to perfect certainty.

(*b*) Next, we must establish which of these consequences are good and which bad.

Once we have gained a general picture of this, we must make a comparative evaluation, asking which of the mutually exclusive values (or disvalues) is the better (or the worse). As noted previously, whether or not these values pertain to ourselves or to others does not come into consideration in making these preferences. For instance, we have acknowledged that joy and knowledge are goods as such and that we should give preference to a greater quantity of these goods over a smaller, but there was no question of whether it was our own or someone else's good. These comparative evaluations must indicate what is the best within our sphere of power, i.e. what is the highest practical good in a given case. This, then, is the end to choose, and only this choice is correct.

In this ideal case, our choice is preceded by an act of preference that is not itself an act of choosing. Furthermore, making the correct choice of the best of what is attainable becomes the principal factor in making the decision. It is only when the decision is determined by a preference experienced as being correct that it can be considered morally right.

Needless to say, many cases of deciding do not accord with the ideal case that we have constructed. We frequently feel for an object a preference experienced as being correct, yet fail to give it practical preference. In other words, our correct preference lacks the power to determine our will, standing as it does in conflict with an opposing blind and passionate preference, stemming from instinct or from habit, that wins out in the end. In such cases we say that the correct preference has lost the battle to the blind preference. They are related to those cases pertaining to the sphere of judgment, where blind prejudices overwhelm discerning reason.

65. The supreme practical good

1. From our remarks about cases of preferences experienced as being correct there follows the important proposition that the domain of the supreme practical good includes everything subject to our rational influence; not only ourselves, our families, and the state, but also the whole living world of the present, and even of the far-distant future may come under consideration here. This is all a consequence of the proposition that a greater quantity of good is preferable to a lesser. Clearly, the right end of our lives, at which every action should aim, is to further as far as possible the good within this sphere. This is the single supreme precept, capable of being known by the understanding, from which all other precepts follow.

According to our analysis, this good that we are supposed to realize is the greatest possible spiritual good for all animate beings who fall within our sphere of influence. This is to be understood quantitatively as well as qualitatively. Since people who possess these goods in a high degree are called happy, we can also define the highest practical good as the greatest possible happiness for the largest number of living creatures over whom we have an influence.

Here we have established a supreme moral precept that is based neither upon giving preference to what pertains to ourselves nor upon giving it to what pertains to others, neither upon valuing pleasure and pleasure alone, nor upon disregarding pleasure—a precept, then, that can be regarded neither as altruistic nor as egoistic, neither as hedonistic nor as ascetic. If anyone wants to call it a utilitarian principle, he is free to do so. To make oneself as useful as possible to as many beings as possible *is* to strive for the best end attainable.

This fundamental ethical principle, that we ought always to strive for what is best—to love it, to further it, and to serve it—accords, in its full objectivity regarding the distinction between mine and thine, with the basic principle of Christian ethics: love God, who is the supreme good, above all, and love thy neighbour as thyself.

2. Yet objections can be made to this doctrine.

(*a*) Someone might claim that the principle makes superhuman demands and is consequently unjustified.

(*b*) Another might say that it goes too far: experience has shown that people who are forever carrying on about the happiness of mankind neglect their responsibilities to their intimates, while those who are always gazing into the dim future lose sight of what is present and close to them.

(*c*) Some people have even considered the command to care for the greatest happiness of the greatest number to be self-contradictory. For instance, Cassel wrote, in 1899: 'This proposition is just as senseless as every other proposition that attempts to reconcile two superlatives in this manner. In any problem dealing with the maximum our task is to establish the conditions under which a given variable has its greatest possible value, and it would be absurd to try, say, to distribute a thousand marks among a group of people in such a way that each person receives as much money as possible.'

However, I do not believe that any of these objections are viable. The last one is so obviously spurious that I would not have even bothered to mention it, were it not that so many people have permitted it to impress them.

ad (*c*) In what is the absurdity supposed to consist? Certainly, if I am to distribute one thousand marks among a group of people of a given size—consisting, let us say, of ten members—the question of how much is to be distributed is superfluous, for it has already been answered. On the other hand, there still remains the possibility of giving each person either more or less, and in giving each one hundred marks I am giving each as much as is possible under these circumstances. But there is another task that I might very well set myself: to earn, not one thousand or one hundred thousand marks, but as much money as it is possible for me to earn, and to distribute it, in some way or other, not among ten or one thousand persons, but among as many people as I can find. And this is precisely what our principle calls for: we ought to disseminate as much good as within our grasp among as many people as we can reach.[24]

ad (*a*) It is said that we must not demand more of the human will

[24] The third objection has been revised in accordance with Kraus's work, *Zur Theorie des Wertes, eine Bentham-Studie.*

than it is capable of accomplishing. Consequently, some people reject as too strict the precept that we ought to devote ourselves fully to the realization of the moral goal; even the just man, they say, falls short of the mark seven times a day. But this qualm, too, is unfounded, as may be demonstrated by analogy. No human being is in a position to avoid all error. Nevertheless, avoidable or unavoidable, every error is a judgment of an improper sort, opposed to the norm of logic. And just as the ends of logic are not altered by the weakness of our mental powers, morality does not permit our weakness of will to prevent it from demanding of man that he give preference to what is acknowledged to be the better, letting nothing take precedence over the highest practical good.

ad (*b*) The objection that the doctrine leads to the neglect of our own welfare and that of our family and friends rests upon a misunderstanding. We must take care not to conclude from the principle of loving our neighbour that each of us is to look after every other person just exactly as we care for ourselves. Far from promoting the general good, such behaviour would be fundamentally detrimental to it. This is a result of the fact that everyone stands in a relation to himself different from his relations regarding anyone else and is furthermore in a position to assist some people more and others less. If there are people living on Mars, we here on earth can and ought to wish them as much good as we wish ourselves and our fellow earth dwellers but not to try to attain as much good for them. Hence it is that every rational morality admonishes us to take care of ourselves to begin with: sweep your own doorstep, as the saying goes. It is also demanded on all sides that we attend to our own family and our own people. The reason for this will become still clearer further on, when we turn our attention to the differences between the duties of justice and the duties of love. There it will be a question of what division of labour is proper in the interests of the highest practical good.

Clearly, the care of oneself is fully justified—only it must be put to the service of the supreme practical good. Where it is, it is not egoism, i.e. that form of subjectivism in which our decisions are determined by what we possess rather than by the value of the good. No, indeed; the principle of giving precedence to taking care of ourselves makes not a single concession to egoism, which is the reckless seeking of our own advantage without regard to the needs and sufferings of others. But we shall hear more about this in connection with the doctrine of duties.[25]

Inasmuch as they have mental and spiritual lives, animals, too, are to be included within the domain of moral considerations. The utilitarians also acknowledge this point, though they quite correctly add the qualification that our obligations towards them are not so great as those towards our fellow men. They base this distinction upon the thesis that animals do not feel pleasure and pain to the same extent as human beings. But from our viewpoint, there is in addition to this difference of degree the most important matter of concern for those special varieties of goods of which men, but not animals, can partake.

66. *The useful and the harmful*

We must also discuss what is useful and what harmful, for most of our influence in bringing about the most prominent goods is only indirect. Consequently the doctrine of duties deals primarily with the useful and the harmful. If we subsequently examine, e.g.,

[25] Some critics have recently objected to Brentano's theory on the grounds that it does not contain the 'concept of duty', or obligation. It is true, they say, that the theory shows us the source of the concepts of the good and of the better, i.e. what deserves love and what can be the object of a correct preference, but it fails to demonstrate adequately why it is our duty to *choose* the good and the better. They claim that this can be done only by appealing to an authority: ultimately, the divine authority. But this accusation appears to be unjustified. For, as Brentano shows in the introduction to this volume, saying that you ought means simply that if you will a certain end you must act in such and such a manner. If, for instance, you wish to draw correct conclusions, you must follow the rules of logic. It is presupposed as a matter of course that you do aim at drawing correct conclusions. It never occurs to anyone to appeal to an authority who regulates the correct drawing of conclusions. The subordination of right action to the highest end, or that which is an end in itself, is just as natural. Once we have laid bare this end, the command, 'you ought', has been given a sufficient foundation and has become a moral duty, for the concept of duty is contained within the concept of the highest end. Of course, this moral duty is given further underpinnings when we acknowledge as highly probable the immortality of the soul and the existence of a supreme and best creator and ruler of the world; cf. sect. 67, in this chapter.

the decalogue of Moses, we find that it is mainly concerned with *means* to goods and evils (not killing, not bearing false witness, not stealing, and so forth). The same is true of other moral codes. Hence the doctrine of what is useful and what harmful is important for the doctrine of duties. However, for the time being we shall dwell on this point only briefly, for we may presuppose a knowledge of most matters that would come under discussion here.

The useful and the harmful fall partially within our influence and are partially beyond its reach, as with the seasons and the weather. We shall discuss only what we can influence, since we are concerned with the supreme *practical* good.

Some of the useful and harmful objects that we are able to realize can be expected with certainty to produce good, or bad, consequences; in other instances, it is merely probable that such results will follow. In these latter, the object may not be useful or harmful in particular instances, but may nevertheless be so in general. We must judge the individual case in accordance with the degree of probability we predict. If something which appears to us to serve our end promises to be successful three-quarters of the time, we will on the average be doing the right thing if we act each time as though it were certain to produce three-quarters of the good in question.

Furthermore, a thing may be useful or harmful either for a particular person or for a particular complex of persons, e.g. for a particular nation, or for an unspecified group. Similarly, the usefulness or harm is itself either clearly defined or indefinite.

The following are to be viewed as notably useful goods for the individual.

1. Personal goods.

(*a*) Physical goods: vegetative life, health, physical strength, the advantages of sex and age, physical capabilities, beauty.

(*b*) Mental and spiritual goods: a good disposition of the intellect and of the emotions, memory, the gift of being observant, the capacity for abstraction, positive cognitions, aesthetic taste, moral virtues.

2. Material possession of what is absolutely essential (the necessities for living) and of things that bring pleasure and serve as means to furthering worthy endeavours.

3. Social relations: a society that is well-ordered as such.

(*a*) This is a species of non-physical possession. Whether we possess it depends to a large extent upon what society we happen to have been born into or to have fallen into. The experiencing of encouragement and innumerable kind offices from childhood onward is of great importance in this connection.

(α) Above all, we must take into consideration the cultural atmosphere in a society: the predominant moral and intellectual upbringing, the artistic forces at work in it, and most particularly the virtue justice. We must ask whether society, in which we of necessity live, accounts in a just manner for the differences between people. For instance, do its moral views assure women a position demanding respect? The manner in which this is brought about is one of the most reliable standards for judging the cultural level of a society; where it has reached a high level, monogamy is the practice.

(β) The goods of order and security, as offered by a good legal code, which protects the fruits of honest labour from exploitation and preserves external and internal peace: national peace, religious peace, and peaceful co-operation between the various classes.

All these constitute good arrangements within society as such. It was they that prompted Plato to thank God that he was born a Greek and not a barbarian.

(*b*) A society that is well ordered with respect to ourselves.

(α) Love and friendship that we experience.

(β) Honour and respect of which we partake.

(γ) The particular position in which other people stand with respect to us in virtue of their moral obligations; and the freedom in which we rejoice. The individual is a citizen and a spouse, and has parents, children, a status, and an occupation. We must ask whether the society in which we live has a clear need of the values which, thanks to our abilities, we are able to offer it. What is an artist if no one longs for his works? Men often lack insight even into what they need most and consequently do not desire it. Thus it happens that their true benefactors frequently are condemned to the life of a martyr. In certain eras, nothing has been called for more than the resolution of the evils resulting from feuds among various nationalities. Yet that has not stopped society from honouring as a patriot the fomenter of hatred and ostracizing as a traitor the man who preaches reason and justice.

67. *The attitude of ethics towards the question of the existence of God*

I have included, along with other things, vegetative life and physical health among secondary goods, or what is useful. What I had in mind here, of course, was that they are the necessary conditions for the existence of the goods of consciousness. My tacit assumption was that we can expect more good than evil to result from the continuation of life of both individuals and mankind as a whole. Otherwise, we would have to account life positively harmful. Now, how are we to decide whether this presupposition is correct? On the basis, perhaps, of the present and of that small segment of the past that we call human history? A number of people have tried this and have reached opposite conclusions, depending upon their personal experience and their temperament. Quite a few have been pessimists; indeed, pessimism has been widespread precisely at times of great intellectual education. In ancient times, suicide reached epidemic proportions among philosophers during an age resembling our age of enlightenment, and certainly we can assume that these men were more in the habit of contemplating the meaning of life than other people. And we today also have our poets and philosophers of *Weltschmerz*. Some are still under the spell of Schopenhauer, the effect of whose view of life upon the emotions and energy deserves the predicate he applied to the world: it is the worst conceivable. And if we turn our gaze from this atheist to the Christians we again find pessimists. Many of them consider the world to be a vale of tears. If this view were flatly contradicted by experience, would we not dispute their claims more energetically than we in fact do? Were we to cite as a point against pessimism the fact that suicide takes place far less often than would be expected on their view, the pessimists could reply that nature took care to restrain by means of a powerful instinct any inclinations so inimical to life and go on to point out that this does not make it reasonable to submit to the instinct to maintain life.

But suppose we assume for the moment that experience speaks in favour of optimism: that the history of the world reveals more joy than sorrow, more knowledge than superstition, more contentment than unsatisfied longing, more virtue than vice, more love than hate. Even so, the question of how we ought to order our lives depends primarily upon what we are to expect from the future. This is as true for the individual as it is for the collective whole. A person who knows himself to be incurably ill and who must reckon on dying soon will find that his duties undergo a change. What used to seem important loses its interest for him, while what appeared to lie in the distant future takes on immediate significance. The same thing happens with a race who live in the expectation that the world may end at any moment, such as the early Christians. They were unable to make far-sighted plans; the consistent among them even felt it inappropriate to undertake a marriage. Indeed, a moral system that places value on effects is unsuitable in such circumstances, and any ideals of progress lose all meaning.

But an end is in store for the entire human race, for the earth will not always house living creatures. As we mentioned, Helmholtz once remarked that a cheerful concern for future races might perhaps be found in conjunction with a renunciation of personal immortality but never alongside the idea that the entire human race is inevitably going to come to an end. The person who wishes to place his life in the service of progress requires an answer to the serious question, 'What then?' But the answer presupposes that he has taken up a definite stand concerning the purpose, the end, of the world, which in turn embraces the question of its first cause.

This is the point at which ethics must turn to metaphysics. Here the two paths separate, according to how we happen to answer the question as to whether God exists. If we give a positive answer, we continue on our way, rejoicing in life; otherwise, we fall into resignation and nirvana.

Before pursuing these thoughts further, let me give a reminder of what has gone before in order to forestall a misunderstanding. In making ethics dependent upon the position we assume towards the question of the existence of God, I wish neither to recall nor to deviate from my earlier statement that the principles of moral knowledge are not affected by the dispute between atheists and theists. It is untrue to say that there must be either a theistic morality or none at all. We recognize what is good and what is better than something else quite independently of any metaphysical considerations. But we cannot set aside these considerations when deciding what is useful and what harmful, i.e. what advances or detracts from the best that is attainable, and consequently not when treating questions as to the usefulness or purpose of life.

Natural philosophical knowledge is sufficient for the construction of the correct moral system. If someone who does not believe in religion as revealed truth and does not even believe in God also happens to be bad, it is to be charged to his own character. There are some very noble people to be found among the unbelievers and atheists. The man who acts wrongly cannot make the use of his reason responsible for his action; he deserves blame, not for following reason, but for failing to follow it.

But although the same principles are to be recognized by atheists as by theists, the consequences to be drawn from them vary according to who is right.[26]

The consistent atheist is a pessimist. The world, he thinks, has arisen out of blind necessity; that in it which appears to be purposeful is illusory and is more correctly called a happy coincidence than a purpose, for there is no one who could bestow upon the world a meaning or a goal. I am speaking of the consistent atheist; certainly there are many who inconsistently wish to be optimists. But such optimism without God is a world view based upon blind instinct rather than insight and deserves the scorn in which it was held by Schopenhauer, who is distinctly superior as regards consistency to the would-be atheists with their professions of the ideals of progress. They are just as much in the power of a blind instinct as those who loftily dismiss everything transcendent in epistemology and believe in things because they grasp them.

How, on the other hand, does the consistent theist view the world? He believes in a creative cause of the world, an infinitely perfect understanding and will. Here he finds the guarantee that all things, in arising from a rational cause, are also aimed at a rational goal. In particular, it can be demonstrated that it is overwhelmingly probable from the theistic standpoint that our spiritual life does not come to an end with the death of our body.

[26] In his book *Albert Schweitzer: Sein Werk und seine Weltanschauung* (Panverlag, Charlottenburg, 1926), O. Kraus discusses the practical consequences for the agnostic, who does not dare to decide between atheism and theism.

The correlate of theism is the individual's conviction that he will continue to exist after his life on earth.

Thus Helmholtz's doubt vanishes. The history of mankind may end at the same time as, or even long before, the downfall of the earth, but the real history is the history of souls. In this universe guided by divine wisdom they outlast the planets. The theist sees his life as subject to a law of responsibility that is grounded in the eternal. He knows that in acting he stands in the service of an unending development. I once expressed these thoughts in the following dialogue.

One man will say, this world must be the best possible,
For, in creating, the best must choose the best.
Another man says, No; for if it were,
It would present the measure of God's power.

Oh, listen to me, you two disputants!
Can we say the world is?
No; *becoming*, it oversteps all measures of good,
And strives endlessly, from likeness unto likeness,
Towards the supreme and unattainable image of the Lord.

PART THREE

THE FREEDOM OF THE WILL

I

Freedom in the Sense of the Supremacy of the Will

---

68. *Freedom of the* actus a voluntate imperatus

1. We have moral insights, and we know what is the good and what is the best that we can attain. But do we, in addition, have the power to follow our insight; are we free? The knowledge of what is morally right, of moral rules, is not enough to make us behave morally. For this we must have the capacity to employ this knowledge as a standard for our human actions. Hence the question, 'Are we free?'

David Hume deplored the serious confusion that reigns with respect to this question owing to the ambiguity of the term, 'freedom'. True enough, various concepts are to be distinguished here, and such outstanding philosophers as Locke, and even Plato and Aristotle, did not keep them sufficiently distinct.

Above all, we must distinguish the act of will itself (*actus elicitus voluntatis*) from the effect or consequence we desire it to bring about (*actus a voluntate imperatus*). The former is always a mental activity, while the latter in certain circumstances takes a physical form. The difference seems clear enough, yet the two concepts are frequently confused. It was as a consequence of this confusion that Spinoza came to misunderstand Descartes' theory of judgment, taking him to consider the *judicum a velle*—whereas Descartes in fact merely held the opinion that every judgment is made on the basis of a choice between a yes and a no.

2. Let us next inquire into *freedom with respect to the actus imperatus*. The question is, can I do what I will to do, what I want to?

Almost the whole world agrees that we frequently can do what we wish and could do the opposite if we so wished. And, on the other, everyone agrees that we frequently cannot do what we would very much like to. We possess the freedom to do what we want, but only within certain limits. The will has a twofold power.

A. Control over the external world:

(*a*) over the members of our body. This control can be limited by positive force, as, for instance, when we want to walk but have had our legs bound together, but it can also be increased by practice; for instance, by doing gymnastics, swimming, playing the piano, riding a bicycle, or dancing.

(*b*) over the forces of nature.

(*c*) over the powers of other people.

B. Control over what is internal.

(*a*) Control of our thoughts when we are conscious of ourselves and when we are contemplating. (Contemplation involves, on the one hand, seeking out thoughts and, on the other, retaining them.) Under certain circumstances it also lies within the power of our will to banish thoughts, whether simply by means of an effort of will or by using other means suitable to that end.

When certain religions order us to believe something and forbid us to harbour doubts, they are taking into account this power that the will has over our judgments.

The man who has gained greater power by means of such control, both positive and negative, of his thoughts is better qualified to be a thinker and a scholar. But we do not always succeed in retaining or banishing thoughts as we wish. (Themistocles said to the experts on memory, 'Teach me, rather, the art of forgetting'.) Memories keep returning to torment us. Many a hardworking student has discovered during an examination that we can fail to recover an idea. If we are exhausted, it becomes difficult and sometimes even impossible to remember something. Then we are no longer capable of concentrating or of paying attention.

(*b*) Control over the *emotions*, whether in order to arouse them or to suppress them.

It is possible for us to *arouse* emotions, in others as well as in ourselves; for instance, anger can be kindled or courage built up. This can be done in part directly—by conjuring up appropriate images, holding a monologue, talking ourselves into something—and in part indirectly: by going through the motions of

anger, by adding fuel to the fire, we can become genuinely angry—
or we can fire up our courage by drinking (the James-Lange
theory of affect). We also exert an indirect effect when, for instance,
we increase by the promise of reward the incentive to do a piece of
work that is satisfying neither to our understanding nor to our
imagination.

But we also *suppress* feelings and emotions, directly and indirectly.

We suppress them *directly* by seeking out distracting and opposing thoughts, thereby banishing those that foster the emotion we
wish to suppress. Here, too, monologues play a role. In misfortune we attempt to present ourselves with the comforting side
of our situation. We counteract the superior strength of a passion
by pursuing other matters that engage our interest. Even sensual
pleasure and pain can be eliminated or alleviated by considering
that they are blind instincts, the full submission to which is
undignified, and by diverting our interests towards objects of
greater value. This is similar to the case where we correct by
logical reflexion our instinctive belief in the reality of everything
we perceive with our senses. Here, as there, the instinctive impulse remains in existence, but it loses the upper hand.

Many people recommend suppressing the emotions *indirectly* by
means of asceticism. But this must be done with care. Reason
demands moderation even in restraint. In general, we should not
approve of carrying asceticism so far that it weakens our natural
powers. It is possible to produce artificially the condition of an
old man, but it cannot be done without also causing harm to our
capacity for doing good. Great weakness positively deprives us of
control over our ideas and emotions and leads to delirium and
hallucinations. *Mens sana in corpore sano.* That is, it is better to
strengthen our nervous system by avoiding injury to it. Asceticism
is similar to the limitations of freedom in despotic states; in both
cases, the ability to do good can easily suffer.

It seems to me that other means are to be preferred to asceticism.
To begin with, we can flee from circumstances likely to cause outbursts of emotion. In some circumstances fleeing is the weapon
most likely to succeed. A clever general does not take on a superior
enemy at a place disadvantageous to his own forces. Another
method worthy of recommendation consists of suppressing the
expressions of the emotion. If we master the external gestures of

anger, we also dampen the flames of our ill humour. Press the angry man into a chair, and he will calm down; lend external support to his agitation, and you support the passion within him as well.

Clearly, then, there falls to each of us a certain power, partially for the control of external events and partially for the regulation of our own spiritual life. Some philosophers, such as the Stoics, emphasize only the latter, teaching that we have power solely over our own thoughts and wishes and that it is consequently just a question of practising and securing our power over them. But they are wrong; the man who wishes to serve the supreme practical good is able to exercise control within a certain external sphere. That is the point of having private possessions. Nevertheless, it is true that the finest victory is the victory over ourselves. The man who cannot master himself is a slave, and would be a slave even if he occupied the throne of an Oriental despot. But it is to be hoped that no external power will fall to the lot of a man who is a slave to his passions, for he would use it more for evil purposes than for good. Enough has been said of the *actus imperatus*; to a certain extent it is at our disposal.

69. *Freedom from compulsion and freedom in the sense of self-determination* (*freedom of the* actus elicitus voluntatis)

1. What about willing itself, the *actus elicitus voluntatis*? This question, too, can be taken in several senses.

Sometimes people speak of freedom and mean thereby the absence of compulsion. That our will is free in this sense is beyond doubt. Our action may be subject to coercion, but we cannot strictly speaking be compelled to will anything, for that would be willing against our will. Practically no one has supposed that such compulsion exists. Nevertheless, thinkers who have in fact held that willing is necessary in quite another sense have been accused of taking this view. Opponents have charged these determinists, so-called, with subjecting our will to coercion.

What is true is simply this: under certain circumstances that have been forced upon us, we find ourselves determined to make a decision that is opposite to our usual inclinations and habits. This is, to be sure, not willing against our will, but it is willing contrary to our intention, i.e. contrary to our previous willing.

2. To a certain extent, we also possess freedom of the will in the sense of self-determination. That is, we are not so totally determined by external circumstances that our self is not a causal factor; it is, rather, always a determining element alongside others. This explains why different people make the opposite decision in the same circumstances. Our intellectual and emotional decisions, the experiences that we have gained and mastered, always maintain their role among the causes. This is not to say that external circumstances do not influence us; it is simply a question of more or less, of degree. Our freedom of self-determination is greatly decreased when we are on the rack or in prison or have been denied nourishment and sleep for days on end.

Freedom in this sense does not have many opponents, either. But there are impassioned disputes about freedom in a broader sense, with which we will have to deal thoroughly.

II

The Dispute between Determinism and Indeterminism

---

70. *Three versions of the doctrine that the will is free from internal necessity*

1. Freedom of the will is spoken of in a third sense by those who say that the acts of our will do not occur by necessity, unlike all other physical and mental events. Acts of will, they maintain, are *not causally determined*.

What do they mean by this?

(*a*) Some mean that the will is self-caused: 'I will because I will to will.'

(*b*) Others define acts of will in such a manner that the will has no cause at all, either within me or without.

(*c*) A third group is of the opinion that, although the will is caused, the causes are not such that the effects occur necessarily and without exception. Circumstances may arise which, without the addition of further conditions, could have a certain act of will as an immediate effect; yet it is possible, under these same circumstances, for the act of will not to take place. Furthermore, even if it did take place, it would still be the case that it did not have to take place. The will, they claim, is different from, say, a physical body, where all the conditions are stipulated if it is to move in a certain direction at a certain speed. Given the relevant circumstances, the body has to move. But the will, given the sufficient conditions, sometimes acts and sometimes does not.

These are the three possible ways in which the will might be said to be free from necessity. How do they bear up under close scrutiny?

2. The will is its own cause. To say that I will something because I will to will it either means that I am free from external compulsion or is nonsense. We must guard against making the will into a person, into a soul within the soul. The soul wills, just as the soul thinks.

Thus the only question can be whether the will has no cause at all, or at any rate no determining cause. And this question it was that initiated the celebrated dispute between the determinists and indeterminists. It has dragged on through the centuries. Traces of it are to be found as far back as Aristotle, but because the problem had not yet been clearly laid out it is open to question which side he took. Even since then it has not always been possible to draw reliable boundaries between the two camps, for the opponents in this dispute frequently talk right past each other inasmuch as they fall into using the term freedom in different senses, quite unremarked by themselves or their opponents. Determinism has clearly been upheld by, for instance, Spinoza, Leibniz, Hume, J. S. Mill, Alexander Bain, Herbert Spencer, and, among German philosophers, Schopenhauer, Herbart, Trendelenburg, and Fechner. The indeterminists include, for example, Descartes and the Scottish philosophers, especially Thomas Reid and Hamilton. Nevertheless, the point in question often gets displaced. It is not only Plato and Aristotle who cannot clearly be counted on the one side or the other; Locke and many others have not conceived the problem clearly enough for us to be able to place them definitely with one group or the other. Even Kant cannot be absolved of confusion; his 'autonomy' means that necessity holds within the realm of phenomena and freedom within the realm of noumena. Nevertheless, it would be an error to dismiss the quarrel as merely verbal; there are enough arguments around and about that are to the point or at least aim at it.

Let us now let both sides present their most important arguments, beginning with the indeterminists, as their views may be accounted the older and more popular.

PART ONE: THE ARGUMENTS OF THE INDETERMINISTS

71. A. The direct evidence of consciousness

The indeterminists appeal above all to certain pieces of direct evidence offered by our consciousness.

1. Immediate perception, it is said, allows us to recognize that when we are awake and healthy we could act differently from the way in which we actually do. This appears to have been Descartes' view.

2. Experience teaches us that we do take action in cases where equally strong motives pull us in opposing directions. If the act of will were a necessary result of motivations, no decision could result in such cases. If our motives for and against stand in equilibrium, then forces working in accordance with necessity could not turn the scale in one direction or the other. It is the same as when a body is pulled in opposite directions by equally powerful forces: it remains stationary, the forces acting upon it cancel each other out. But experience shows the opposite to be the case with the will. Here motives of equal weight do not prevent our forming a decision, for the reason that the decision is freely formed.

In scholastic disputes the opponents of determinism seized upon an analogy with which they tried to make it appear ridiculous. Imagine a hungry donkey placed between two bundles of hay that are of equal size and smell equally good, so that there is no reason at hand for him to nibble at the one rather than the other. According to the determinists, they said, he would be unable to reach any decision and would have to starve to death between the two bundles of hay, in spite of his hunger and the abundance of food. This illustrious donkey has gone down in the history of philosophy as Buridan's ass, after the philosopher Jean Buridan, who occupied himself with the problem of the freedom of the will. If determinism were true, its opponents claimed, we humans would in all seriousness find ourselves in the same position as this unhappy animal in every case where equally strong reasons make an act appear advisable in some ways and inadvisable in others. We should have to remain permanently in a state of indecision— but experience quite unequivocally demonstrates the opposite. We do make decisions, even when the grounds for action are in a state of equilibrium.

3. We discover that we sometimes act in opposite ways in exactly the same circumstances: this way today, another way tomorrow. This, too, is taken to be a disproof of the necessary efficacy of our motives. When people talk about the same circumstance, they are, of course, not referring solely to external factors; circumstances

DISPUTE BETWEEN DETERMINISM AND INDETERMINISM

may be the same with respect to mental factors also, inasmuch as the objects of choice are the same and the same reasons are taken into consideration.

4. The indeterminists believe another confirmation of freedom is found in our frequent experience of choosing between two possibilities only after going through a prolonged conflict. If the decision necessarily followed the stronger motive, it would have to be made at the same moment in which the motive entered our consciousness. A necessarily efficacious cause acts as soon as it is able. But a free will may, after initially not permitting itself to be determined by a certain motive, follow it after all, even though the motive has not changed with respect to it. The existence of such states of indecision, during which the battle between the motives continues without any alteration in their strength, together with the fact that a decision eventually does arise, demonstrates that the decision can only be a free one.

5. When I resist a desire, I am aware of making an effort, and if the exertion lasts long I feel exhausted by it, just as when I make a continuous physical effort. But this could not be if the will were determined by the stronger desire; the scales do not need to exert themselves in order for the man with the heavier weight to go down. If our will were not free, it would have to be analogous to a pair of scales; like the heavier weight, the stronger motive would have to turn the scales, immediately and without any effort.

6. Finally, the indeterminists appeal to the so-called *opinio communis* as a direct witness to the truth of their views. We all believe that both we ourselves and others have free will. The opposite opinion arose solely as a result of philosophical speculations.[27]

So much for the so-called immediate proofs of consciousness to which the indeterminists make appeal.

72. B. Indirect evidence for indeterminism

1. We distinguish between what is morally good and morally evil. The capacity to make this distinction is given us by nature, and with it is given the consciousness of our obligation to perform

---

[27] This paragraph has been expanded in accordance with the ethics lectures of F. Hillebrand.

the one thing and to leave the other be, which presupposes freedom. Only if we are conscious of freedom can we feel under an obligation; the ability, the freedom, to do something is included in the obligation to do it. You can, for you ought to, as Kant rightly put it.

2. If determinism were true, it would follow that in every case only one line of action is possible, i.e. everyone would act just as well, or as badly, as he was able. But if people act in the only way they are able, why should we praise them when they act well and blame them when they act badly? In fact, we feel guilty when we have done wrong; we feel that we deserve punishment, and when we are punished we feel that we have been treated with justice. Indeed, we punish ourselves by giving ourselves up to remorse. This consciousness of guilt, this knowledge of responsibility disappears when we have to tell ourselves that we could not have acted differently.

3. Faced with the moral defects of other people, we are overwhelmed with a feeling of indignation at their badness. Why is this feeling directed solely upon moral evils and not upon others, such as illness, error, and stupidity? Why do we harbour this feeling only with reference to grown-up persons, and not to minors or animals? Clearly, it is because we hold ourselves, but not irrational beings, to be free, and because we find this freedom to be present only in the case of willing, and not in judging or acknowledging.

It is easy to see that the indeterminists' arguments include accusations against determinism which make it appear to them not only false but also pernicious.

(a) First, there is the accusation that determinism obliterates the distinction between good and evil.

(b) Second, there is the accusation that it makes praise, blame, and punishment senseless.

(c) Finally, there is the accusation, brought up again and again, that determinism ends up by being fatalism, which throttles all effort and ambition. The logical consequence of determinism would be for us all to sit with our hands in our laps, doing nothing —but no determinist does this. Even the most convinced determinist feels outraged at moral depravity, shares the yearning for recompense, opens himself to feelings of regret, makes plans and in so doing bears witness against his own theory.

PART TWO: THE ARGUMENTS OF THE DETERMINISTS

I. *Criticisms of the arguments for determinism*

The determinists do not feel themselves to be defeated by any of these arguments. According to them, all alleged experiences are worthless as proofs of indeterminism, and all the accusations that the indeterminists bring against them are unjustified. They quickly move over from defence to attack, for they believe themselves to be in a position not only to produce for their doctrine proofs of experience in every conceivable manner, but also to bring the charges made against them against the indeterminists.

73. *I. A. Criticism of the so-called direct evidence of consciousness for indeterminism*

In what follows, we will give the determinists an opportunity to take up a position against the reproaches of the indeterminists. This will be done partially in the form of a direct dialogue between the two sides.

1. Indeterminist: We are conscious of being able to do the opposite of what we in fact will to do.

Determinist: Good enough; we'll admit that. We will even admit that we could often really *do* the opposite of what we are now doing—if we willed to, that is. I can lift my hand if I will to, just as I have let it fall because I willed to do so. But that is not the issue of our dispute. We are not inquiring into the freedom to do something that we will to do but into the freedom to will something. Your argument confuses the *actus imperatus* with the *actus elicitus*.

Indeterminist: But I can will what it pleases me to will!

Determinist: No one denies that, but you made a different claim that you are also able to will what you are not willing now.

Indeterminist: Yes, I maintain that view as well and will prove it to you on the spot. Just tell me what to will, and you will see that I am able to will it just as easily as what I just willed.

Determinist: Certainly you can do that, for the commission you gave me has somewhat altered the circumstances under which you are making your choice. But the question is not whether you could will differently under different circumstances but whether you could will differently under the same circumstances.

Indeterminist: I could will differently even under the same circumstances, for my immediate consciousness tells me that I can act differently even here and now.

Determinist: Is that what your immediate consciousness tells you? All that means is that you are deluding yourself into thinking that you have an internal perception of it. You are deceiving yourself, for we can only perceive what is real, not what is merely possible. We recognize something as being possible by deriving it from reality. But what that is real could have led you to the conclusion that you could, here and now, will the opposite of what you willed? In fact, you will only the one thing and not the other. If you now will the other, the circumstances have changed, for now you will to show me that you can also will the opposite.

2. The indeterminists say that there are cases where a decision comes into being even though there is not a preponderance of motives on one side or the other. The reasons for and against are equally strong, neither possibility attracts us more than the other, yet we choose the one and not the other. Clearly, they say, the choice is not necessarily determined.

This supposed experience also fails to impress the determinists. They find the arguments fallacious in a number of ways.

(a) It would prove too much, viz. it would also prove that animals have free will, which the indeterminists certainly do not want to claim. 'If you were right,' the determinists say, 'animals would also be unable to make a decision when the opposing motives have equal weight, yet no donkey has ever yet starved between two bundles of hay. Are we to say that the donkey, too, possesses freedom of the will? Why do you not do so—or do so only when you are constructing an impossible example like that of Buridan's ass? It is because you yourselves recognize the argument as untenable; but in that case it is as untenable for people as for donkeys.'

(b) 'The reason', they continue, 'is that the entire set of presuppositions is imaginary. There never is such a perfect balance between the motives for opposing decisions. We can no more assume that these circumstances occur than we can assume the occurrence of those in the following proposition: if a perfect cone is placed on its point on a flat surface, it will for some time remain in equilibrium in that position. Neither proposition is absurd, yet it is so highly improbable that we can say with assurance that things like that do not happen.'

Leibniz, a determinist, was thus quite right in giving the following retort to the argument of Buridan's ass. If such a case were realized, he admitted, the donkey would certainly have to starve; but what conditions would be required for its realization? Not only must the two bundles be precisely similar, but also the donkey's two eyes and two nostrils. Furthermore, the entire donkey would have to be symmetrically constructed. And not even this would suffice; the entire universe would have to be divided into two absolutely symmetrical halves, the vertical plane between them dividing the donkey in half as an ellipsis is divided by its bisector.[28]

But the indeterminists are not to be put down so easily. Cases of perfect equilibrium do not occur in the animal world, they admit, but they do among human beings.[29] That can be seen from the fact that people often say, 'It is a matter of complete indifference to me', and nevertheless make a decision, which, it follows, cannot be considered determined.

The determinist's reply will be, 'You are wrong in concluding from this sort of remark that there actually is complete equilibrium between mental factors. In fact, the differences have simply not been remarked. In such circumstances the decision is not to be called an act of choice, for we use this term more accurately in cases where the preponderance is clearly distinguishable. There are differences here in the balance that the person willing is not aware of or that are too minute to offer a rational motive. (After all, we can occasionally make a decision by counting down our buttons!)

'The behaviour of people in these circumstances varies according

[28] It is perhaps interesting to note that modern science is able to produce examples of situations very similar to that unhappy one in which Buridan's ass found himself. If some lower species of marine animal which ordinarily turns energetically towards whatever light is at hand is placed between two equally distant light, it can be observed that he swims towards neither the one nor the other but moves back and forth midway between them or remains quavering in the middle. Here equally strong motives actually do suspend any decision.
[29] Which is false, as was just shown. It is precisely, and solely, among simple organisms that such cases can occur, not among men.

to their temperament. Some people try harder than others to establish a clear preponderance of reasons on one side. Indecisiveness can become an habitual defect. A man like Fabius Cunctator will search for rational pros and cons even where no more are to be found, whereas another will rashly indulge his mood and leap in resolutely.'

3. The indeterminists appeal to the fact that when the same circumstances occur the second time we do not always make the same decision as the first time.

The determinists reply, 'Exactly the same circumstances never occur twice. The absolute similarity of two situations temporally removed from one another is as much a chimera as the alleged similarity in the previous argument. Once the soul has taken action, it never again returns altogether to its former state. Nothing passes over it without leaving its mark; every act leaves so-called engrams behind; changes in our mental substance and in the "background" constructed of all our associations, out of which every new activity arises. Because the past is efficacious in every mental state that follows after it, the ego never repeats or makes a new decision as exactly the same decision that it was before.'[30]

Still less can the indeterminists make appeal to the fact that different individuals make the opposite decision under the same circumstances. Even if the circumstances themselves were the same, the choosers are not; and to assume that the same circumstances can exist for several choosers is to be deluded. Furthermore, it does not depend solely upon the external circumstances but also upon the light in which we see things and how they act upon us. And this, in turn, depends upon a thousand and one factors which never occur together in one person in precisely the same way as they do in another.

4. The indeterminists point out the frequently lengthy conflict that takes place between the motives for and against a certain decision. If one or the other side immediately becomes preponderant, we nevertheless do not decide in favour of it at once, but often only after a period of time. If, like the heavier weight on the scales, the stronger motive tipped the balance within our soul, hesitation could not set in.

The determinist will counter, 'Let us stick with the example of

---

[30] This paragraph has been expanded by the editor.

the scales; it does not tell against us. If the scales are well constructed, they, too, waver, and their wavering can be reconciled with the fact that they are determined by the weights. For if one of the objects is just slightly heavier than the other, even the smallest impulse from outside can cause a movement, and then oscillation sets in. All sorts of imponderables exercise an influence, one after the other. The more precise the construction of the scales, the more easily the play of the weights is complicated by disrupting factors and the greater the precautions we take against them; we suspend the scales from a column that is independent of the building, and so forth. The scales present quite a good picture of what happens in the mental sphere when a so-called conflict of motives holds up the decision, but here the advance and retreat of new impulses is even easier to imagine. Images are constantly flitting in and out, and one motive drives out another and is driven out in turn as long as none having a considerable preponderance is present. Clearly, matters are not as the indeterminists represent them. It is not with unchanged motives that hesitation sets in, to be ended at the last by a spontaneous decision. The motives do not in the least remain equal; their relative strength changes, the person considering them keeps having new thoughts and discovering new aspects of the objects of choice; new considerations occur to him, new points of view reveal themselves, the old appear in a new light—in a word, our opinion on the matter changes. And when we are finally determined by a motive that was there at the beginning and yet did not turn the scales at the time, it has become in the meantime a new motive, relative to the others, for the motives tending in the opposite direction have been weighed more closely and lost some of their weight. In the end, perhaps, our decision is brought about solely by the knowledge that, while no decision is better than another, a decision must none the less be reached. But in that case the decision is not undetermined, but is reached on the grounds of indiscernible differences, just as the man who loses his way in a fog sets off at random in one direction.'

Incidentally, we must not be led astray by the equivocation. The term 'motive' does not have the same meaning in the following two sentences, 'Greed was the motive for the act', and 'Fear was too weak a motive to determine his will'. In the first sentence, 'motive' denotes a force that has in fact been efficacious in bringing about the act of will, if not by itself, then in consort with all the other factors concerned. In the second, on the other hand, 'motive' denotes that which, coupled with a different set of circumstances, would have determined the will but which lacked the requisite accompanying conditions in the case at hand. It is only by confusing the second meaning with the first that people come to say that the will is not determined by our motives.

5. The indeterminists believe it to be a point in their favour that our will occasionally withstands a passionate desire with resolution and energy, but then leaves off the battle in a state of exhaustion, only to renew its resistance after a pause. Once again they draw the conclusion that the will is not determined by our motives.

The determinists answer, 'This, too, is an incorrect presentation of the facts. What is meant here by a will that resists our motives and thus bears witness to its own freedom? The ability to will? That is not a thing and cannot act; consequently it also cannot put up a resistance. It is simply a potentiality. The act of will? The act cannot do battle, for it is supposed to come into being only later, and is not yet present. No, it is not the will that struggles against the motives; rather, one motive battles against another, e.g. a blind desire against a preference experienced as being correct, short-sighted passion against a considered appraisal of genuine goods, consciousness of our duty against laziness. Once again it is as with the scales. The scales do not contend with the weights; the weights contend with each other.'

'What is correct is simply that we are glad to identify ourselves with one of the motives, one of the two opposing inclinations. We say, "I have overcome my passion (or my pain)", but we would be more precise if we were to say "My inclination to do my duty overcame my leanings towards pleasure (or my self-pity)" and still more precise—for abstractions are fictions—if we were to say, "One part of my self gained a victory over another part of myself". For my sense of duty is just as much mine as my yearning for pleasure or my sensitivity or my laziness. It is simply that we flatter ourselves more when we identify ourselves with that part of ourselves that has greater worth. Nevertheless, other viewpoints can serve as a measure of this *pars pro toto*. Out of the mass of our inclinations we extract those that have come to be fairly strong habits, that have proved to play a role in the majority of our decisions, and we find in them "our true self". This is, so to speak, what has the greatest durability within us.

'The indeterminists have also pointed out the weariness and exhaustion the will experiences in battles between motives, but I must confess that I do not comprehend how this is supposed to speak in favour of the theory that it is free. Furthermore, it is quite wrong to say that the will operates in a way that exhausts us in any direct sense. It is true, however, that affects with sensual redundancies [*Redundanzen*] attach themselves to acts of will, as to every other phenomena of interest of a higher order, and it is these that cause our nervous exhaustion.

6. 'Finally there was cited the opinion of the common man, who, it is claimed, generally believes in the freedom of the will. But the characteristic, genuine opinions of people can be recognized far better on the basis of their action than of their words, particularly within the mental sphere. If we observe the *opinio communis* from the standpoint of people's behaviour, we see that it is precisely opposite to that of the indeterminists. We observe that we trust ourselves to predict with the greatest certainty what people whom we know well will do under certain circumstances. What does that signify? From our experience we construct an opinion about the person's character and are convinced that his future acts will also be guided by his dispositions. Thus human behaviour is deterministically disposed, even among people who are champions of free will.'[31]

The determinists, then feel, themselves to be fully armed against the arguments of their opponents. All the appeals to the proofs of our immediate consciousness fell short of the mark. Either the presuppositions were illusory or the facts contain nothing that tells against determinism.

74. I. B. *Critique of the indirect proofs for indeterminism*

These proofs have been considered to have particular weight, for they contain serious accusations against determinism; it is supposed to make nonsense of morality and all the institutions that serve it.

[31] This portion has been expanded in accordance with the lectures of F. Hillebrand.

1. The indeterminists say it is only from their standpoint—only, that is, on the presupposition of freedom—that the distinction between moral good and evil can be justified; but this distinction is indubitably valid, for we possess an innate consciousness of it.

The determinists, on the other hand, point out that there are to be found among their ranks, too, thinkers possessing a most subtle faculty of distinguishing moral good from moral evil. Think of Leibniz, Spinoza, J. S. Mill, or Fechner. Moreover, some religious sects that observe great moral strictness take a decidedly deterministic viewpoint, e.g. the Calvinists, the Puritans, and the Independents. The question is whether this does not simply demonstrate a lack of consistency on their part.

'Not at all,' says the determinist, 'it is completely justifiable. The distinction between moral good and evil makes sense for the determinists, too. If not, the indeterminists would be equally guilty of inconsistency, for they have no hesitation about drawing a distinction between good and evil within spheres which they themselves do not suppose to be free from necessity. They, too, consider, e.g. knowledge a good and error an evil. Yet the indeterminist claims that freedom is grounded in the very consciousness of obligation; "You can, for you ought to." The determinist retorts: "In order to counter the objection, we must clarify the meaning of obligation, and we discover that 'you ought' means simply, 'If you decide differently, you make the wrong decision.' 'You ought' is a rule of right behaviour. Similar rules are to be found elsewhere, e.g. logic lays down obligations for our judgment. That a conclusion is logically correct means that it is as it ought to be. The only difference is that obligation is conditional in other spheres whereas it is unconditional in the moral sphere—as we already made clear." ' (Cf. note 24).

The question how we recognize moral obligation is just the same as the question how we recognize the correctness of an act of will, a preference. This question we have already answered. Now, does the moral ought always include the ability to follow it? In other spheres, the ought does not assume the ability. If so, people would never draw erroneous conclusions in logic. Why should it be different here? 'You ought' does not mean 'you must'. Nevertheless, it is not to be denied that the moral 'you ought' in fact contains a 'you can'; that is, it implies an ability in the sense of the freedom of the *actus imperatus*. What is morally bidden must be of a kind such that it depends upon my will whether or not it comes to be, and to just this extent the ability to carry it out has something to do with the correctness of the act of will. In the strict sense, only acts of the will can be called good or bad. Transferred to actions, these terms make sense only if they are conceived of as a result corresponding to the act of will, i.e. if freedom consists in the *actus imperatus*. It must be granted to the indeterminists that in this sense freedom is the necessary condition of morality, for clearly an act could not be called either morally good or morally bad if it were possible for an act totally different from the one intended to come into being. However, the argument has no application to freedom of the *actus elicitus*.[32]

It is clear that Kant, too, did not make a sufficient distinction between freedom in the sense of the *actus imperatus* and freedom in the sense of the *actus elicitus*, as is illustrated by his pronouncement that only actions, not love, can be commanded. The only situation in which love cannot be commanded is that in which a person could not love even if he willed to do so.

As for the claim that the ability to distinguish good from evil is innate, we have already established that this is false and have revealed the true source of good and evil.

2. The indeterminists feel that, if every act of will followed from necessity, no feelings of guilt, no consciousness of responsibility, no moral reproach would be justified. How can we blame, indeed punish, a man for an act of will that is wrong if he could not have done otherwise under the given circumstances?

The determinists answer, 'But we also criticize and find fault within spheres where no one would want to champion indeterminism. For instance, we reproach a bad painter, a shallow poet, and a boring orator even when we know that they cannot manage to do any better. And we criticize people for faults in their thinking or in their judgment without wishing to ascribe freedom to human judgment. We reproach them because we conclude from the failure of their products that there are defects in their disposition. The products are displeasing, and the disposition displeases in that it is the source of the displeasing product. Indeed, we blame ourselves

---

[32] This section has been expanded in accordance with F. Hillebrand's lectures on ethics.

and are ashamed to be caught in faulty thinking. When we blame someone for performing the wrong act of will, our blame once again is directed at his disposition, at the moral faults in his character as being the source of his bad willing and bad behaviour. And he himself heaps reproaches upon himself for his moral weakness inasmuch as he feels guilty and confesses to it. Because of his imperfect character, he had to succumb under the given circumstances. Hence the consciousness of guilt and the self-reproach; they have nothing to do with freedom as conceived by the indeterminists.'*

3. The indeterminist will object, 'A person may accuse himself, on the grounds of having made an inaccurate observation or drawn a false conclusion, of having an inferior intellectual disposition; a cleverer person would have been protected from such failures. Nevertheless, neither the man who has failed nor others harbour any desire that he should be punished for his fault. Now, why is it different within the moral sphere? Because of the special character of moral evil, which is fundamentally different from every other variety of evil. Unlike other human failings, it does not call forth pity or scorn. Instead, it arouses our indignation, a desire that the bad person should suffer, and satisfaction when he comes to harm; if this desire is not fulfilled, we find ourselves hoping fervently that he may find his just deserts in the world beyond. The intensity of this longing is revealed by the fact that most religions teach future, and even eternal, punishment. This teaching accords completely with our natural feelings, and philosophers also bear witness to these feelings. They were so powerful in Kant that he dared to ground upon them the belief in Divine Providence and in a future life, in contradiction to his own theoretical tenets.'

The determinists answer, 'It must be admitted that moral evil has a special character—and how could it be otherwise, since the will is different from judgment and imagination? Moral evil is simply evil within that sphere upon which, more than any other, the value of the person depends. Virtue and a noble disposition are superior to intellectual and artistic gifts, misdeeds and an ignoble disposition worse than a weak judgment and poor taste. But these

---

* The sentence as it stood had no clear reference; I have tried to give it an intelligible construction.

facts have no consequences that speak in favour of indeterminism.'

Above all, protest is to be entered against the claim that moral defects and moral depravity are not suitable objects for sympathy. If the indeterminists were indeed inclined to this view, it would be a strike against them; the determinists are of the opposite opinion. They urge sympathy even with the person possessing a poor moral character, and humility on the part of the man who knows himself to be morally superior. The consistent determinist will ask himself what he himself would have become had he grown up under the conditions in which the guilty person was raised. It may appear at first glance that punishment cannot be justified from the deterministic standpoint, but this illusion vanishes as soon as the purpose of punishment is made clear. To be sure, some determinists have thought it necessary to give up punishment because of certain results of moral statistics, and, needless to say, this was grist for the mill of the indeterminists. But it can be confidently assumed that these determinists have not given enough thought to the point of rewards and punishments.

We speak of reward and punishment in a variety of senses.[33] Sometimes—and here we use them in what is not their strict and proper sense—we mean the natural good and evil consequences which in every sphere result from our deeds and omissions; everything offers rewards and takes revenge, people say. Talent calls forth admiration, while stupidity leads itself into misfortune. Willing, too, has natural consequences: the pain of a bad conscience, the feeling of torment that accompanies the consciousness of moral inferiority, the bad habits that arise from repeated lapses. The individual act is a link in a chain that can become the fetters of slavery. Passions develop that constantly call forth new desires, and these become harder and harder to satisfy and to suppress. In addition, we must endure the displeasure of our fellow men, especially those of high moral character; the mistrust which bad people encounter; and the reputation that goes before and follows

[33] Cf. Kraus, *Das Recht zu strafen* (Stuttgart, 1911), and Brentano's essay, 'Strafmotiv and Strafmass', published as an appendix to *Vom Ursprung sittlicher Erkenntnis* (*The Origin of our Knowledge of Right and Wrong* trans. Chisholm and Schneewind, Routledge & Kegan Paul, 1969). Later, Brentano tended more and more towards the view that the desire for retribution is not purely instinctive; see his unpublished commentary on Martineau.

after him. To be sure, there are enough cases where punishment appears not to take place: where the industrious and virtuous go to the wall while the inferior and the evil triumph. But this appearance is to be explained partially by our defective insight and partially by the limits of the period of time surveyed.

We speak of reward and punishment in the true sense where, with rationally motivated intent, something good is awarded or something evil inflicted upon a person. This intent always bears reference to the will or the act that ought to be improved, whether by means of the punishment itself or through other persons (corrective punishment and exemplary punishment).

There is another way in which two kinds of punishment can be distinguished:

(*a*) Punishment that would be eliminated were it known that the misdeed arose, not from immoral desires but rather from an innocent error accompanied by noble motives.

(*b*) Punishment that ought to be inflicted even under these circumstances. The first sort of punishment is corrective in the narrower sense; it aims at improving behaviour and desires. It is made use of in training, in educating—taking these terms in their narrower, and best, sense. The educator attempts to support the attraction of what is recognized as superior by an ulterior motive and thus to improve the disposition of his charge. It is for this reason that parents punish their children. In contrast, to punish simply for the sake of venting one's anger is barbaric. The second sort of punishment is protective; that is, it aims at protecting society while improving the performance of the wrongdoer. It is used in training animals and, generally speaking, in situations in which concepts of what is morally wrong and repugnant to justice do not play a role. Here the aim is to create a motive, not for preferring what is acknowledged to be superior to what is acknowledged to be inferior but for choosing what really *is* better over what really is worse, even in cases where the worse is erroneously held to be better or where no evaluation has taken place. Aversion to the threatened evil of punishment is to constitute this motive. The state punishes even where there appears to be no hope of educating; the purpose is to protect society as a whole.

The person who in one way or another rationally metes out punishment adds to the evil in the world with the intention of bringing about a greater good. If this were not their purpose, human beings would forfeit the right to create additional evil, to inflict suffering or death. This applies to the state as well as to the individual, for the state exists in order to channel evil, not in order to hold people tyranically in fear and trembling. These indications concerning the purpose of punishment should be sufficient to show that it is completely in harmony with determinism. The thought of the threatened evil is intended to determine the will to make the right choice.

If, after all this, someone were still to ask how we can punish or blame a man when he could not do otherwise, he would betray the fact that he had still not learned to distinguish between freedom of willing and freedom of action. If the man does not have the latter sort of freedom—that is, if he does not possess the power to carry out what he desires even if he wills it—his will is certainly not to be reproached. But if he does have this freedom, he ought to be blamed when he has made a wrong decision.

Just as punishment can be reconciled with determinism, so, too, can our consciousness of responsibility.

(*a*) In its broader sense this consciousness is the conviction that punishment is justified in the case of a certain act. A person who has been at fault through error can also have this consciousness of being responsible, once he has recognized his error. It is different with the consciousness of guilt, for the person who was moved by noble motives and failed only because of error may tell himself that he strove for the best.

(*b*) In its narrower sense our consciousness of responsibility is the knowledge that the case at hand is one of justified punishment. And here we find appropriate the feeling of guilt; the consciousness of having earned the punishment because of the guilt of our will; self-reproach; and remorse.

Neither in the one case nor in the other is indeterminism to be called in as an explanation. The consciousness of a moral debt, the knowledge that we deserve punishment, are as compatible with the fundamental principles of determinism as is the distinction between moral good and evil upon which they are based.

But still the indeterminists are not satisfied. They believe that the explanation of punishment given above applies only to punishment that is administered for a purpose. However, they go on to say, it is a mistake to think that the desire for punishment is based solely upon comprehension of its usefulness; our immediate consciousness teaches clearly that in many instances no such motive is present at all. The desire has far more to do with revulsion in the face of moral evil, which is a variety of badness fundamentally different from every other kind. That this is so, the indeterminists claim, is demonstrated forcefully by those cases where our unsatisfied sense of justice finds its comfort in the idea of retribution in a world beyond, an idea which the bad person who has aroused my indignation perhaps does not share or allow to bother him. It is not, they say, considerations of usefulness, but simply an abhorrence of the wrongdoer that causes our outraged sense of morality to demand punishment, and to demand it purely as retribution.

The determinist's answer: 'Here the indeterminist makes an appeal to the so-called desire for retribution. But no matter how strongly it asserts itself, this impulse lacks moral justification inasmuch as it is a blind instinct. Certainly, it is rational to feel displeasure and revulsion towards a bad person, but the yearning to couple suffering with guilt, and delight in seeing them joined together, are as such blind impulses. Like other instincts, they may serve a purpose in that they were of assistance in making sure that punishments were inflicted, even before rational reflexion produced the idea of punishment. But there is nothing intrinsically noble about the desire for revenge; it is to be accounted rather among the meaner passions of the human soul. And just as it precedes a rational justification of the institution of punishment, we also encounter it as a consequence of this institution. Once the infliction of punishment in accordance with a rule has proven to be useful, whether because it improves us or because it frightens us away from doing evil, it is possible for us to fall into the habit of demanding punishment even where it serves no justifiable end—just as the miser loves money without any thought as to its use. But we cannot call such a desire justified.'

And there is still more to be said. Assume that we were justified not only in being displeased at moral evil but also in yearning for retribution, independently of any regard for its usefulness, and that purely vindictive punishment were deserving of moral approval: would that be a good reason for giving up determinism? By no means; this would not constitute a proof of freedom. Suppose there were beings who were so powerfully attracted to evil that they always gave preference to what is worse. The inherent revulsion typically felt towards moral evil, and our indignation, would be directed not only towards these creatures themselves but also, as Mill so aptly remarks, against him who invented such devils. And if a justified hankering for vindication is indeed linked with our moral revulsion, then we will feel the same yearning here as elsewhere. We would hope to see these beings, who are necessarily determined to be evil, punished in accordance with the extent of their depravity, while wishing luck and happiness to the virtuous beings who are opposed to them.

Concerning the idea of just deserts in the world to come, we can agree with Kant's assertion that only theism can be reconciled with our faith in the general tendency of the world's development towards harmony between virtue and happiness and between evil and suffering, a harmony that we often find lacking under present circumstances. For if there exists a holy will in whose infinite power the entire universe rests and finds its foundation, this will will only permit evil, and particularly moral evil, in ways and to the extent that it will further the life of the whole, although the connection may be largely concealed from our will. Suppose there were powers that, in so far as it was up to them, willed only evil; in a world guided by a divine will and understanding they would, like Mephistopheles, simply form a part of that power which 'is forever willing evil and forever doing good'.

But let us return to human concepts and human standards. When we punish, we are not guided by the thought of the good that may lie in the harmony between guilt and suffering but by the idea of the service that punishment may perform by acting as a corrective and as a deterrent. And the more strongly the thought of this service is able to motivate the human will, the more likely it is to be performed successfully. Hence punishment can be completely reconciled with determinism.

4. It is also a mistake not to differentiate between determinism and fatalism. There are two kinds of fatalism.

(a) There is pure, or Asiatic, fatalism, which was the variety asserted by Oedipus. This is the view that what we do and omit to do does not depend upon our will at all; no matter what our own inclinations are, a superior power or a blind fate, being stronger than they are, will compel us to act as we are predestined to act, rather than as we are inclined to. Our love of the good and our aversion to evil have no influence. They may be intrinsically virtuous, but nurturing them is fruitless, for they exercise no influence upon our behaviour.

(*b*) The other sort of fatalism, what we might call modified fatalism, acknowledges that our behaviour depends upon our will and that our will is determined by the combined efficacy of our motives, which in turn have their roots in our inclinations—in what is called our character. But, its supporters contend, this character itself is not a result of our own choice; it is given us once for all. We are not responsible for it, and consequently not for the acts that it allows us to carry out. To try to change our character is a fruitless endeavour. This doctrine has most recently been upheld by Schopenhauer, and indeed, it fits perfectly into his vision of the worst of all possible worlds.

In contrast to these two systems, determinism holds that not only our behaviour but also our character is partially dependent upon our will. We are able to improve our character by applying suitable means, in accordance with Aristotle's contention that habit can become second nature to us. His perception in this matter was far more accurate than Schopenhauer's. If a man's present character determines him to do evil, that is a good reason to try to influence him in a way that will create better motives and thus gradually to free him from this necessity by replacing it with a more desirable necessity. Along with acknowledging that the human character can be moulded, the determinist recognizes the moral duty to work at its perfection. It may be fair enough to accuse the two forms of fatalism just discussed of throttling all forms of activity and effort, but this criticism leaves determinism untouched.

75. II. A. Attempts to prove determinism

The arguments of the indeterminists have proven to be untenable, and their accusations against determinism have turned out to be unjustified. But the determinists are not satisfied with mere criticism; they wish to adduce positive proofs of their own conception. They claim for their side the proofs of experience to which their opponents appealed with so little success.

To begin with, the determinists say, the very fact that necessary causation has been established in every other sphere speaks in their favour. There is not a single exception to the law of causality,[34] neither in animate or inanimate external nature nor within the mental sphere. Indeterminists suppose that the will offers the sole instance of freedom—which claim itself suggests that the will is not an exception. In fact, what appears prima facie to be extremely probable is definitively established by our particular experience with the sphere of the will.

1. In every instance of an act of will, inner perception reveals to me that I am determined by motives to make that particular decision. But where the will is determined by motives, it is necessarily determined, and there can be no question of indeterministic freedom. To be sure, Thomas Reid thought we ought to distinguish between motives and causes, for motives can move us to act, but cannot themselves act. But was this anything more than a mere sophism? If motives impel us to action, they are clearly working in conjunction with other factors; that is, determining along with other factors. Hence, as motives, they are operative causes of the will.

2. Observation demonstrates that we are always determined by the stronger of two opposed motives—just as with scales, where the preponderance of weight on the one side is decisive. Given the choice between one piece of gold and two pieces, everyone would choose the second. And if a connoisseur of wines is given the choice between a Johannisberger and an ordinary Pfälzer, he will choose the former, unless there is some special reason for preferring the other.

3. Regarding his own acts of will, everyone notices that he makes the same sort of decisions under similar circumstances and is consequently enabled to form reliable judgments about his future course of action.

4. But we can also predict what decisions other people will

---

[34] This point has been called into doubt in modern physics; consider Heisenberg's uncertainty relations. Yet physicists of note have taken the opposite stand.—However, these developments did not begin until after the time at which Brentano wrote his ethical treatise. The earlier unity of physics throughout the world has been so upset by them that it is now scarcely possible for modern physicists to agree upon a 'universal physics', which for Brentano was a matter of course (cf. Part I, chap. 3, sect. 20, I, 3c).

make under certain circumstances, and the more closely we are acquainted from past experience with their opinions, inclinations, and habits, the more accurate our predictions will be. If this knowledge is sufficiently thorough and extensive, the reliability of our expectations approaches the certainty of those predictions about external nature that we make upon the basis of our knowledge of physical and chemical laws. However, if we do turn out to be mistaken in our predictions about behaviour, we do not say that matters just happened to be resolved in this unexpected way. Instead, we say that we erred as to the strength of one of the motives and as to the character of the person about whom we formed a premature judgment; we misjudged his susceptibility to certain enticements. The cases in which acts of will seem too uncertain to be predicted reliably are precisely those cases in which our knowledge of the influences that operate as causes is so incomplete that equally inadequate data would introduce the same uncertainty into the predictions of astronomers and chemists.

5. Finally, the determinists verify their view with the results of statistical investigations that have been initiated with groups of people and carried out continuously in order to exclude from groups containing sufficient numbers influences that only operate effectively upon a few and which in the long run and over a broad range of cases cancel each other out. The aim of these investigations is to get a final result approximately equivalent to what it would be if the acts of will of the entire group of people were influenced solely by the moving forces common to all the individuals included. The observations resulting from these investigations have exhibited a uniformity in no way inferior to that found in the physical sphere. For instance, it has been remarked that the same number of unaddressed letters are mailed every year in post offices in London and Paris. Likewise, the government expects that under similar conditions it will receive the same yield from taxes and can prepare for the same number of marriages, births, crimes, and so forth.

These are the reasons why determinists assume that there is a necessary connection between causes and effects in human acts of will as well as in external nature and the rest of the physical sphere.

76. II. B. *Counter-attacks by determinists against indeterminists*

The determinists are convinced that no manner of appeal to experience can refute them. On the contrary, they think experience supports their claims; the weapon used by the enemy is knocked out of his hand and turned victoriously against him. Moreover, the determinists do not feel themselves to be touched by the accusation that determinism is a destructive hypothesis. Indeed, they undertake to turn this accusation, too, against the enemy.

1. The determinists were accused of nullifying the distinction between acts that are morally good and acts that are morally bad. Quite the contrary, they reply; it is indeterminism that is guilty, for an act is called good or evil according to our motive in performing it, and if the will is not determined by motives it can be neither moral nor immoral.

2. The determinists have been accused of rendering punishment senseless, a consequence highly dangerous for social order. Once again they reply that it is in fact indeterminism that is at fault, that makes punishment appear unjustified. As pure revenge, punishment would not be morally justified; it can only be justified by its usefulness, be it for the actor himself or for the population as a whole. But this usefulness depends entirely upon its power to motivate, which is denied by indeterminism.

3. Determinism has been accused of being fundamentally the same as fatalism. As such, it is said, it cripples all activities of the will and all endeavours towards improvement. But this accusation also falls back upon the attacker.

(*a*) The person who does not believe that his will is determined by motives and that it is the necessary result of the circumstances at hand and of our intrinsic disposition, which is constructed primarily by previous exercises of the will, has no good reason for avoiding opportunities to do evil or to work on his character by forming good habits or by improving his natural inclinations. Why flee certain opportunities or work on our dispositions if the former do not work as external causes of our acts of will, the latter as internal causes? So it is not determinism, but rather indeterminism, that leads to moral inertia. In teaching us that it is not within our power to influence the will, it restrains us from making any effort towards self-improvement. Making no preparations, we just let the hour of temptation approach and succumb to it when it arrives.

(*b*) It can be demonstrated in still another way that indeterminism, to be consistent, would have to cripple our efforts and abilities.

If events in external nature did not turn out in accordance with necessary laws, could we count on them? Could our mighty technological achievements have taken place without our utilizing the laws of nature? Certainly not; only our knowledge of these laws gives us such power, and this power grows in proportion to our knowledge.

We would be powerless in the face of the phenomena of the will if they did not unfold in accordance with necessary laws. We would then neither know such laws nor be able to employ them in order to achieve our aims. No matter how long we were acquainted with a person, we could feel no certainty as to his future behaviour. Everything we experienced previously would be merely coincidental. Correspondence among the cases observed would not rest upon a single underlying cause, nor would a habit that has arisen construct incidentally a concomitantly determining principle. Promises that we make or that are given us would not offer any security, for regard for a particular agreement would no more be a determining ground for future action than would habit. But along with the possibility of rational expectations about our mutual relations we would also lose every sort of orderly union between people. The whole of human society would be destroyed. No long-term undertaking would be possible; the most powerful force on earth, the human will, would become unpredictable, and everything would be so completely veiled in doubt and darkness that no one would be able to form a plan even for himself, let alone one requiring assistants for its fulfilment.

It would appear, then, that indeterminism, rather than determinism, leads to a variety of fatalism, or at any rate to the same harmful consequences as fatalism. Possessing power neither over the external word nor over his own future acts of will, the consistent indeterminist has no choice but to watch idly as fate takes its inexorable path.

77. *A. The experiences to which determinism appeals appear equally compatible with modified indeterminism*

We have gained an acquaintance with the determinists' arguments from experience, and certainly, they deserved a hearing. They seemed to have great force, both where they destroyed the arguments of their opponents and where they wished to establish their own doctrine. But did they have equal success in both enterprises?

There is scarcely anything more to be said against the criticisms of the attempts to prove indeterminism, which demonstrated even the most popular of them to be untenable. No defence was possible. But matters stand quite differently when the determinists wish to prove that the doctrine of their opponents is not only unproven but also false, and also that their own doctrine is true. Here they seem to fall into the same error of which they were able rightly to accuse their opponents. It appears that they are refuting tenets that are not identical with those held by their opponents, but are merely an imperfect form thereof.

What is the indeterminists' thesis?

1. Do they teach that there are no motives for our acts of will? No, inasmuch as they know even just a little about psychology, they teach the opposite. Their thesis is simply that the will is not subjected to motives that *necessitate* its actions.

2. Do they teach that all motives have the same degree of strength and significance? No, anyone who acknowledges the existence of motives at all will allow that some are of greater weight, others of lesser. Suppose—which is certainly not the case —that all simple motives were equivalent; we would still have to assume a difference between the strength of the various motives in cases where several are found together.

Indeterminists are equally ready to admit that the same motives will not carry equal weight with persons of differing dispositions.

They only deny absolute necessity. The preponderance of the one motive over another, they say, simply implies a greater possibility and reveals itself by the fact that on the average it works out to be the determining factor more often than the motive opposing it. It is the same as with throwing dice, but with dice-throwing the probability is merely subjective, whereas there is both subjective and objective probability in the case of motives. That is to say, in the former case it is simply our ignorance that keeps us from knowing the determinants for every throw.

The indeterminists also hold that an increasing incongruity between motives can render a decision more probable or less so, or can even make it into a moral necessity. Aristotle remarks that a life of sin deprives us of freedom in a certain sense.

3. Do the indeterminists believe that there are no cases of willing in which necessity is to be found? No, they have always distinguished between cases where freedom is to be found and cases where necessity is at work.

(*a*) They hold that the will is not free where there is only one motive at work, unopposed by any other. Here the motive really does determine, and of necessity; there is no question of choice, and therefore none of freedom.

(*b*) But even where we have a choice, it is not always free. For instance, our choice follows necessarily when a motive A is working on the one side while the same motive A is working on the other, in consort with another motive B. Putting it in general terms, our choice is necessary when one of the two goods between which we are to choose includes the other; consider, for instance, the choice between one dollar and two dollars.

(*c*) On the other hand, choice is free when one motive is opposed to another of equal strength. We measure the strength of motives by our experience; we consider to be of equal strength those motives that, pitted against a certain other motive, predominate in the same number of cases. If a motive A, competing with motive C, wins out just as often as motive B does when it competes with motive C, they are to be considered as of equal strength. But if a case ever arises in which A is competing with B, then two equally strong, equally weighty motives stand in opposition to each other. Then a choice follows freely.

(*d*) It is doubtful that we have freedom of choice where nothing comes into consideration except pleasure and habits based upon it.

(*e*) On the other hand, our choice is certainly free where we choose between what is morally good (καλόν) and what is pleasant and advantageous (ἡδύ). Here there is less question than anywhere else of one motive including another.

(*f*) If the choice is to be made only between two moral goods (καλά) the greater good is necessarily the determinant.

By modifying their views in this manner, the indeterminists believe themselves able to hold their ground, for, they say, all the experiences to which determinism appeals are also compatible with modified indeterminism and consequently give no greater proof of the one than of the other. We shall test this claim in detail against the determinists' attempted proofs.

ad 1. The indeterminists say, 'Certainly, inner perception shows us that in every case we are determined by motives, but it does not show that we are determined necessarily.'

The determinist will perhaps answer that we have an immediate perception of the compulsion. But this answer would be erroneous. Here we can pose an argument similar to the one the determinists put earlier. It is just as impossible for the determinists to perceive that we cannot do otherwise as for the indeterminists to perceive that we can. Only concrete facts can be perceived; not possibilities, impossibilities, or necessities.

ad 2. The determinist made appeal to the experience that the stronger of two opposing motives always wins out. But has that really been established? In order to make clear who is right on this point, we must first understand the meaning of the phrase, 'the stronger motive'.

(*a*) Is the stronger motive the one that has more power to move the will? Reid defines it in this way, and attempts to make the determinists' argument absurd. 'How do we know', he asks, 'which motive has the greater power in moving our will? You yourselves say, only through the manifestation of its preponderance. Your supposed fact of experience, that is to speak decisively against us, comes to nothing more than that the motives that predominate are the ones that are predominant.'* This would be

---

* I was unable to find precisely these words in the relevant work: *Essays on the Powers of the Human Mind*. But the point is made in Essay IV, chap. IV, sect. 5: '. . . by what rule shall we judge which is the strongest motive? . . . If we measure their strength merely by their prevalence, and by the strongest motive mean only the motive that prevails, it will be true indeed that the strongest motive prevails; but the proposition will be identical; and mean no more than that the

an empty tautology and would of course be true no matter what hypothesis we hold. The error would be quite similar to that made by various indeterminists when they said, 'I can do what I will to do; therefore . . .'

(b) What do the determinists reply? A good many say, 'You are misconstruing our words. When we say experience teaches that the stronger motive always prevails, we do not mean the one strongest with respect to the will, but the one strongest with respect to the pleasure and displeasure that the objects between which we are to choose offer us.'

But the indeterminists are not satisfied with this answer. 'Which do you mean?' they ask. 'A pleasure, or displeasure, that we feel as we are making our choice, or one that we are to expect as a consequence of our choice through the coming into existence of what we have chosen?' If the first of these is meant, then the greater pleasure or displeasure would seem to be simply the manifestation of the greater love or hatred, the greater desire or aversion, i.e. a manifestation of the act of preferring, just as is the act of choosing. In that case, it certainly goes without saying that we choose what we prefer. But this tautological proposition says nothing as to whether this choosing is determined or not. If the second is meant—as in fact seems to be the case—it is not tautological; but does it accord with experience?

Not at all. It is, quite the contrary, refuted by experience. Here I need only remind the reader of what we have already said. We established that people love not only pleasure but also other goods, such as knowledge and virtue; that they love not only their own good, but also that pertaining to other people; and that they are able to sacrifice their own good for that of other persons. The same phenomenon that appears in these cases of noble self-sacrifice is also to be found among misers, who eventually come to love for its own sake what at first was only loved as a means. And there are also cases in which people, choosing between pleasure and displeasure, have chosen a smaller but temporally more immediate pleasure, thus preparing for themselves a future of incomparable misery. Incidentally, experience cannot demon-

---

strongest motive is the strongest motive. From this surely no conclusion can be drawn.'

strate that the greater pleasure is always given preference, if only because it is frequently impossible to determine the relative quantities of two pleasures, especially if they are qualitatively different. Because all this was noted earlier, I do not wish to dwell upon it further. Instead, I shall point to the testimony of J. S. Mill, who was a confirmed determinist. 'When the will is said to be determined by motives, a motive does not always, or solely, mean the anticipation of a pleasure or of a pain. . . . It is at least certain that we gradually, through the influence of association, come to desire the means without thinking of the end; the action itself becomes an object of desire, and is performed without reference to any motive beyond itself. Thus far, it may still be objected that, the action having through association become pleasurable, we are, as much as before, moved to act by the anticipation of a pleasure. . . . But granting this, the matter does not end here. As we proceed in the formation of habits, and become accustomed to will a particular act or a particular course of conduct because it is pleasurable, we at least continue to will it without any reference to its being pleasurable. Although, from some change in us or in our circumstances, we have ceased to find any pleasure in the action, or perhaps to anticipate any pleasure as the consequence of it, we still continue to desire the action, and consequently to do it. In this manner it is that . . . the habit of willing to persevere in the course which he has chosen, does not desert the moral hero, even when the reward, however real, which he doubtless receives from the consciousness of well-doing is anything but an equivalent for the sufferings he undergoes, or the wishes which he may have to renounce.'*

Here we encounter a view of Mill's that has occupied us once already, viz. that all willing and desiring are egotistical to begin with and that all disinterested desires grow out of these through association and habit. This view may or may not deserve our approval; that remains to be seen. In any case, we should note that Mill denies emphatically, as contradicting experience, the possibility of a smaller pleasure overcoming a greater in cases of disinterested love.

(*c*) Other determinists have interpreted matters differently. No,

*_Logic_, Book VI, chap. 2, sect. 4. As Brentano's German version is quite accurate, except where he has failed to indicate omissions, I have simply reinstated Mill's English.

they say, when we teach that experience shows the stronger motive always wins out over the weaker, we do not mean the one stronger with respect to pleasure or displeasure or anything of that sort. Rather, we mean with respect to the will, yet we do not in the least allow ourselves to become trapped in that embarrassing tautology of which Reid accuses us. It is easy to answer this accusation. Even indeterminists distinguish between stronger and weaker motives; how do they understand the distinction? By stronger motives, they mean those that are most suitable for moving the will and which therefore are more apt to move it and which move it more often and more easily, although they do not always necessarily do so. Very well then, we determinists also call stronger that motive that is better suited to determine the will —which statement need not be an empty tautology. When we say the stronger motive always determines the will, we only wish to give expression to the fact that whenever precisely these circumstances recur the aforesaid motive will always, and necessarily, be the one that determines the will. Thus J. S. Mill says, 'We say, without absurdity that, if two weights are placed in opposite scales, the heavier will lift the other up, yet we mean nothing by the heavier, except the weight which will lift up the other. The proposition, nevertheless, is not unmeaning, for it signifies that in many or most cases [one weight does lift the other up],* and that this is always the same one, not one or the other as it may happen. In like manner, even if the strongest motive meant only the motive which prevails, yet if there is a prevailing motive— if, all other antecedents being the same, the motive which prevails today will prevail tomorrow and every subsequent day . . .'†

This remark is, in fact, quite accurate. The proposition that the motive stronger with respect to the will—i.e. the one that is better suited to move it—always does move it makes good sense. But it is equally clear that this point cannot be established by experience in the way that has been attempted. We cannot tell from an isolated experience whether the stronger motive prevails, nor can we tell from several observations, if they are made under differing circumstances. In order to gain knowledge respecting

---

* Mill: . . . there *is* a heavier . . .

† Mill, *Examination of Sir William Hamilton's Philosophy*, chap. 26. I have reinstated the English, except for the phrase in square brackets.

even one single type of choice, we must repeat the experiment a sufficient number of times under the same conditions. Only then can we tell whether the motive in question prevails over the other not only often, but always. This holds not only for pleasure and displeasure, but also for other types of motives.

It is plain to see that the induction has become far more intricate and complicated. It is, in fact, questionable whether the motive which was previously proven to be the stronger will always be the one that determines the will under the same circumstances. The indeterminists are of the opposite opinion. They claim that we make opposing choices under the same circumstances, and they appear to say it with a certain degree of justice. Certainly they cannot prove it, for they can never prove that the circumstances are exactly the same—but then, neither can the determinists. All that can be said with certainty is that certain cases are similar. And experience shows that in these similar cases the same motives are not absolutely always decisive, but only frequently so, as even the indeterminists will concede.

We must conclude that the second argument in favour of determinism, viz. that the stronger motive prevails absolutely without exception, is not decisive.

ad 3. And so we come to the third argument with which the determinists plead their cause: the appeal to the regularity that is to be found among ourselves and our acquaintances and in statistics concerning criminals.

(a) These statistics are not irreconcilable with indeterminism, as Quételet noted some time ago.[35] Because the statistics rest upon a great mass of cases, it would be contrary to the law of probability, he said, if fortuitous factors that do not fit in failed to cancel each other out. But the influence exerted by freedom is also to be regarded as such a factor. The regularity that has been observed as established by statistical studies also appears to be comprehensible if, like the indeterminists, we take into account a greater

[35] L. A. Quételet (1796–1874), the founder of so-called social physics. His principal work is *Sur l'homme et le développement de ses facultés, un essay de physique sociale*, in 2 vols. (Paris, 1835). Concerning Quételet, see Oettingen, *Die Moralstatistik und ihre Bedeutung für die Sozialethik*, 3rd edition (Erlangen, 1882), and for greater thoroughness, G. F. Knapp, 'A. Quételet als Theoretiker', Hildebrands *Jahrbücher der Nationalökonomie,* vol. XVIII, Parts 2 and 3.

or lesser degree of freedom in our acts of will, rather than a factor determining them necessarily. However, Quételet does not express himself happily. A reasonable indeterminist would find it as impossible to approve of his views as would a determinist, for they make it appear that freedom is just a particular cause alongside the other motives that work necessarily. And this cannot be correct under any circumstances. The indeterminist would instead consider the entire mental condition preceding the act of will, or of a significant part thereof, as a free, i.e. an undetermined, cause of the act. But if we eliminate this error and simply draw, as do modified indeterminists, a distinction between stronger and weaker motives, i.e. between those that are more apt to move the will and can do so more easily and those that are less apt to, it remains none the less true that statistics offer the same results whether we assume that there is freedom or that the will is necessarily determined.[36]

Clearly, then, whether we follow the doctrine of freedom of the will or the doctrine of necessity, we can expect to find the same results when we observe similar relations within very large groups.

(*b*) It is the same with anticipating the acts of will of our intimates as with the results of statistics. No matter how well we know people, we occasionally find our expectations as to their future action disappointed. Only in certain cases do we make a judgment without any doubt whatsoever; in such cases we say that we are, though not mathematically certain, morally certain. And the indeterminists, too, concede the existence of this sort of certainty.

(*c*) The same applies to our knowledge of ourselves. We frequently note similar action in similar cases, but even here our foresight is not absolutely certain but merely probable, sometimes

[36] Cf. the third proposition in Jakob Bernoulli, *Ars Conjectandi* (1713). 'As the number of experiments increases, there is an increase in the probability that the relation between the number of occurrences of phenomenon A and the number of occurrences of phenomenon B will not vary more than a certain amount from the relation between their respective probabilities; and no matter how nearly these limits approach one another, we can bring the probability in question as near to one as we like, provided we can make the number of repeated experiments to be as large as we like.'

more so, sometimes less. It is only when we know certain motives to be extraordinarily strong that our foresight attains virtual certainty.

The determinists might object, 'If all our experience of regularity of events is not sufficient to prove necessity in the case of the will, then we must in all honesty assume indeterminism in the realm of physical nature as well, for the arguments for necessity are no stronger there than here.'

Answer: 'If this were so, we could indeed not claim that determinism has been proven in the realm of nature. But in fact matters stand quite differently in the sphere of physical events, for there we are able to isolate phenomena and to observe absolutely identical cases again and again—not just two or three times, but, by observing continuous action, an infinite number of times. If an exception to the law, e.g. of gravitation or of inertia were possible and nevertheless never came to be in so much as a single case, that would mean that it would not occur once in an infinite number of cases, which is tantamount to infinite probability, or so-called physical impossibility.'

To be sure, the necessity of events can only be proven in this manner in simple cases; in more complicated ones we are usually not in a position to make such a crucial experiment directly. But once we have proven that each single event taken by itself is necessary, we may conclude that an event resulting from the united action of all of them is necessary.

78. *The counter-attacks of the determinists upon indeterminism do not tell against modified indeterminism*

The proofs of experience that determinism presents as speaking in its favour and against indeterminism neither prove determinism nor strike a decisive blow against indeterminism, or at any rate not against its modified form. We have yet to refute the accusations made against the indeterminists, but after what has already been said this will not require many words.

1. Indeterminism has been accused of eliminating the distinction between moral and immoral acts of will, for this distinction is based upon differences between motives, and indeterminism does not acknowledge any motives for acts of will.

But modified indeterminism does recognize motives.

2. It has been asserted that from the standpoint of indeterminism punishment would not be a reasonable measure, for it aims at deterring us through motives of fear.

But this is false. Indeterminism also ascribes efficacy to these motives—if not of necessity, at least with a greater or lesser probability.

3. It has been said against indeterminism that, were it true, so-called opportunities for immoral action would be without influence and would consequently not need to be avoided and, furthermore, habits and dispositions would exercise no power and consequently would not be worth cultivating.

But this accusation also fails to affect modified indeterminism, for it only denies that these factors have a necessary effect, not that they have a probable effect. The accusation that indeterminism makes all human action incalculable is particularly unjustified. The calculation simply fails to offer absolute certainty, partly because of its great complexity and also because of a certain leeway due to our freedom of action.

PART FOUR: A DECISION IN FAVOUR OF DETERMINISM[37]

79. *A. The initial improbability of indeterminism*

1. We have watched determinists and indeterminists in their efforts to decide the question of freedom in their own favour on the grounds of experience. The battle has been waged with every weapon their ingenuity could muster. Yet once again it appears that no one side can claim the victory for its own. For a time the determinists charged ahead powerfully, but ultimately they were driven back to their original position by the indeterminists. The indeterminists suffered a similar fortune: happy, perhaps, in their defence, they, too, were unable to claim a victory.

It is nevertheless possible to say, simply on the grounds of the previous positions assumed in this battle, that the indeterminists occupy the weaker position.

2. The indeterminists have no argument in favour of their view. Even if the attacks made by determinism did not force us to a

---

[37] Cf. Brentano's *Versuch über die Erkenntnis*: *Vom Dasein Gottes*, pp. 126, 129; and *Kategorienlehre*, pp. 56, 185, 256.

decision, we would lack any reasonable grounds for allowing an exception such as indeterminism wishes to admit, for it is clearly an exception of a very peculiar sort. Contrary to every analogy with our experience in every other sphere, acts of will are supposed not to be necessarily determined.

(*a*) In every other realm, both physical and mental, we count upon necessary connections between all events. The more general a law, the less probable an exception appears to be: for instance, we can expect what is known to be true of all atoms to hold for one newly discovered as well.

(*b*) Furthermore, not only the analogy with other fields of experience but also our experience with willing itself speaks for determinism. To be sure, the induction cannot be carried out completely; it is impossible to measure the motives for some decisions. But in so far as its intensity is measurable, our choice is generally determined. Hence the existence of exceptions can only be assumed within spheres which do not admit of being measured, and surely there is something distinctly suspicious about this. The induction that led us to assume necessary connections everywhere else is not without a certain power.

(*c*) It is always simplicity that recommends an hypothesis. *Ceteris paribus* the simpler hypothesis is more probable than the more complicated one; the improbability grows in geometric proportion to the complexity. If we compare the assumptions of determinism with those of indeterminism from this standpoint, the latter appears at a great disadvantage, for it is full of complexities. Where determinism makes out with one simple exception, indeterminism makes many exceptions. Let me just recall the six laws we enumerated, according to which decisions were sometimes supposed to be made freely, sometimes not. This complication must be reckoned with, for none of these laws can be deduced from any of the others. Nor can all of them be deduced from some seventh law.

(*d*) All in all, indeterminism is to be viewed as an unjustifiably complicated and consequently improbable assumption, if only because the objective it assumes is arbitrarily invented. Indeterminists wish to explain the uncertainty involved in making predictions by the hypothesis that in certain cases there is no necessary connection between the various phenomena, and absolute chance is called into play. But the uncertainty of our predictions regarding human behaviour can be adequately explained simply by the imprecision of our knowledge—a fact not open to doubt. Would a meteorologist ever think of explaining the deficiencies in his prognoses by assuming the existence of absolute chance? He is content with indicating that the phenomena are very complicated and that not all the data upon which the weather depends are available to him. Why, then, the assumption of objective chance, which is to be observed neither here nor anywhere else in the universe? If Newton's hypothesis explaining the motion of the stars by the law of gravitation commended itself particularly because the principle had already been established elsewhere, the presence here of precisely the opposite circumstance should make us quite cautious. If the fundamental principle that entities are not to be multiplied beyond necessity has ever been violated, surely it is here.

Perhaps someone will say that it lies in the nature of the case that objective chances, that is, the coming into play of chance, cannot be observed, even if they do exist. But this is quite false. If so many objective chances and so many individual laws really exist, it is prima facie just as conceivable—even, indeed, to be expected as probable—that such phenomena will be observed in some of our experiences. We ought to be able to establish a law stating that, for example, a certain factor, whenever it is added to certain given circumstances, makes the occurrence and non-occurrence of its usual consequences equally probable, and so on. That we none the less can never find such a factor speaks strongly against the claim that it exists.

80. B. Defects in the explanatory value of indeterminism

We have seen that the hypothesis of indeterminism is highly improbable from the outset. Now someone might say that even initially improbable hypotheses can be established if they explain certain facts infinitely more simply than all other conceivable hypotheses. But there are no facts for which indeterminism offers a superior explanation. Everything to which it made appeal turned out to be illusory. Let me simply recall the essential point of the whole dispute. Indeterminism is supposed to explain what constitutes the freedom of human beings when they make choices; that is why it is called the doctrine of the freedom of the will.

But not only does the indeterministic hypothesis fail to explain human freedom; it positively denies such freedom. Under what circumstances do we say that a person is free? When he has a certain sort of power; the more power he has, the freer he is. We also speak of freedom where we can assume the person acting to be in such a state that he can be held responsible for his action, i.e. that it is reasonable to praise or blame him, to reward or punish him. If human power and responsibility appear to be increased from the standpoint of indeterminism, then it deserves to be called a doctrine of freedom; otherwise it does not. Let us pursue this line of thought. If extreme indeterminism were the correct doctrine, our acts of will would take place without any cause. The causes neither of immoral nor of moral decisions would lie within ourselves. We would simply be, as it were, the stage upon which they took place. Acts of will would take place within our soul, but they would have no causal connection with our character. A person could be animated by the very best dispositions, yet whether the right or a morally wrong act would result from them would be a matter of a fortunate or unfortunate coincidence, as the case may be. Even a person possessing a most noble character and most pure love of the good could commit a criminal act of will, and the poor unhappy man would have to attribute to this coincidence, of which he was quite innocent, the fact that he suddenly finds himself standing before a judge.

If, on the other hand, we consider matters from the standpoint of modified indeterminism, it becomes clear that it, too, does far less justice to freedom in this sense than does determinism. To precisely the extent that it eliminates necessity it allows chance a role in our acts of will, thus limiting our power. To be sure, it gives personality, the character of the person making the choice, the role of a contributory principle in acts of will, yet in a certain sense it means that I cannot help myself and cannot do anything about it if I make the one choice and not its opposite. The principle working within me is the same one in the case where I make the right choice as in the case where I make the wrong one. In neither case do I deserve any more praise or blame for having the principle within me. Only the act of will itself would deserve praise or blame; but again, I myself would not be the actor, but merely the stage upon which the act takes place.

Every sort of indeterminism proves to be entangled in a most peculiar kind of deception. It has the task of eliminating the influence of any foreign principle; no factor other than our own self is to play any decisive role in our acts of will, not even as an earlier cause. To this end it posits a theory that eliminates, or at least limits, our own influence. Indeterminism wishes to secure our freedom, yet it decreases and even destroys it in that it divests us of power. If, then, it is possible to speak of freedom and constraint here at all, we are bound to say that indeterminism is the doctrine that the will is not free, that it is constrained. It does not limit our power by means of another power, but it affixes to it natural limitations, of a kind quite foreign to determinism, by permitting the realm of chance to extend to the will.

81. C. The absurdity of indeterminism

Indeterminism possess neither adequate explanatory value nor sufficient initial probability. In order to finish it off altogether, we would only have to demonstrate that it is also positively absurd. And in fact, indeterminism cannot be spared this accusation, either in its extreme or in its modified form. For it includes both the thesis that the will is uncaused and also the thesis that the will has no *determining* causes but is ruled by absolute chance. These theses contradict each other, as we shall demonstrate.

1. Even the man who does not doubt the universality of causal connections between events occasionally uses the words 'by chance'. He means that something was not intended or that two temporally coinciding events have no direct causal connection with each other. The philosophical application of the word chance is to be distinguished from this popular usage. When the philosopher asks whether there can be things that exist by chance, he has in mind things that are neither directly necessary, like God, nor indirectly necessary, i.e. made necessary by causation.

However, we require some clarification of what it means to be caused, in preparation for the following investigation.

Our concepts are partially simple, partially composite. Our simple concepts, and therefore all the elements comprising our composite concepts, are culled by means of abstraction from perceptions, be they so-called external or sense perceptions, or inner perceptions. No concepts are innate. If a concept requires elucidation, it is supplied, in the case of a composite concept, by giving its elements, while in the case of a simple concept it is achieved by giving examples of perceptual images from which it is abstracted. If such a demonstration proves impossible, we can be sure that the word to be explained does not belong to those that denote a concept.

Now the question is, are there any perceptions from which we can cull directly the concept of causation, a cause, or an effect?

Some people believe themselves to have abstracted these concepts from sense perception. They think that under certain circumstances they have a direct perception of causation; for instance, when they view a tree falling at the blow of an axe or a billiard ball being set into motion by being pushed. But Hume pointed out that this is an illusion. What we immediately perceive in these cases is simply a temporal contiguity: a *post hoc*, but not a *propter hoc*. Consequently, if the concept of causation is an elementary one, we would have to search for its origin within the sphere of inner perception. Hume tried to do this, in fact, without finding it, and believed as a result of this failure that we had to sacrifice the idea of causation as a genuine concept. He does not dispute that we have something in mind when we call an event B the result of an event A, but thinks that we are stating a proposition not about A or about B, but about ourselves. We simply mean to state, Hume believes, that we have observed B to follow A time after time and now expect B whenever A occurs. He points out that there can be no logical justification for such expectations; they are not the result of rational considerations, but of habit. From this he deduced far-reaching sceptical consequences about all the sciences in which causal laws play a role. But let us not linger on this point. It is of far greater importance to consider whether Hume searched thoroughly enough in inner perception for the concept of causation.

For we must agree with him that this concept is not present in external perception, and even in inner perception some people have looked in the wrong place. They have thought of cases in which by an effort of will we recall to memory a forgotten name, or of the voluntary movements of our limbs, but here, too, it is only a *post hoc* that is given to us directly. This is particularly easy to see in the last case mentioned, for what the will sets directly into motion is not the visible member of our body, e.g. our hand. Rather, this effect occurs only after an entire chain of physiological antecedents, the first of which is an event in our brain that we do not perceive.

Yet this is not true of all connections that we perceive internally. When we draw a conclusion, we think of the premises at the same time. But not only are we aware of this temporal connection; we also perceive that we form the concluding judgment *because* we form the judgments that constitute the premises. We perceive the thinking of the conclusion as motivated by the thinking of the premises. Another example of an immediate perception of something's being caused occurs where we will something as a means for the sake of an end. Here one act of will is brought about by the other and appears as an effect in our immediate perception. It is not necessary for us to cull the concept of causation from some other source in order to apply it in this instance. Quite the contrary; we find ourselves here at one of the sources from which it springs. We could give more examples, but these suffice for our purpose. They demonstrate clearly enough that causes are not identical with temporal antecedents, as Hume held. If so, it would be proper to call the night the cause of the day and the glitter of gold the cause of the tinkling of gold which it leads us to believe we will perceive. We proceed to use the concept we have won in this manner in countless instances where we cannot directly perceive a thing's being caused but are none the less rationally convinced that the concept applies. These are the cases in which it is a question of conceiving of a certain regularity or complication, which would otherwise appear very improbable, as following a law. In designating a certain event A as the cause of an event B, we are regarding the latter as made necessary by A under the given circumstances: B *must* occur here and now because it is caused by A.

We can see that modified indeterminism contradicts itself when it says that motives are causes that can bring about acts of will, but need not necessarily do so. This motion only makes sense where several causes must act together to produce a certain effect, and one or more of them are missing. Then the effect can, and indeed must, fail to take place, unless some cause with the same efficacy is substituted. All this has nothing to do with indeterminism, which maintains that it is possible for all the conditions required for a certain act of will to be given without its occurring and, indeed, that the opposite act may take place, or at least could just as well have done, even if it does not. It is easy to demonstrate that these views make it impossible to speak of causes in any sensible way.

Take the first case. All the antecedents, all the motives and whatever else is required in the way of preconditions, are present, but the act of will fails to take place; how, then, can the motives be called its cause? Assume that under the given circumstances the act of will for which the motives are given does not take place, but its opposite does; then the act cannot be explained by reference to the antecedents, which would do far better at explaining the occurrence of the opposite act. The act which in fact takes place appears to be without any explanatory cause.

But if this is how things are in the first instance, then the same is true in the second instance, in which all the antecedents are present and the act of will does take place. With what justification can we say that the act is caused by the motives if we believe that the opposite event could equally well have taken place? We would still have to explain why it did not. The so-called causes of the event would not offer any explanation of it.

Thus it is self-contradictory to say that, on the one hand, motives are causes of willing but that, on the other, they are not necessarily efficacious. In one and the same breath we are declaring untenable as an explanation precisely what we are appealing to as an explanation.

Perhaps the indeterminists will say at this point that we have not represented their views accurately, or at any rate not completely; we have neglected an essential point in our presentation. They do not, they may say, maintain that the effect which is not necessarily determined by its causes could equally well come into being or fail to do so; rather, they claim a greater possibility for the former. This admission, in fact, characterizes modified indeterminism. The supposition is not that both cases are equally probable but that the first is more probable than the second, even though it cannot be accounted strictly necessary.

However, this excuse is completely unwarranted. What justification is there for speaking of unequal chances? That can be done only where the case in which the effect occurs represents a combination of a greater number of equally possible cases than the case in which it fails to occur. But what are the equally possible cases that we are to compare here? We cannot imagine. Once again we find ourselves faced with opinions that are either contradictory or lack any comprehensible meaning.

The following has been established beyond doubt: in so far as anyone holds that there are events that are not necessarily determined, he holds that there is such a thing as absolute chance. And it is demonstrable that this notion is intrinsically contradictory.

2. As the concept of a cause that does not determine is self-contradictory, the only alternative left to indeterminists is to adopt the extreme form of indeterminism, according to which decisions are made by the will without any cause. The modified form has been eliminated. Now the question is, is it directly self-contradictory to assume there are events without causes? In what would the contradiction consist? Does the very assumption that something exists contradict the denial that it is caused? This is not immediately evident; such important thinkers as Aristotle and Leibniz did not hesitate to teach the existence of a being, namely God, who has no cause and no need of one, as he is immediately necessary. Nevertheless they admit that everything which is not immediately necessary must be caused. Otherwise, they say, such things would come to be by absolute chance, which is an absurd assumption.

If these thinkers are right, then all we have to do to refute indeterminism altogether is to prove the absurdity of this assumption. For the indeterminists must admit the existence of absolute chance, since they acknowledge the existence of what is neither immediately necessary nor caused.

The proposition that everything which exists exists necessarily is among those least disputed in the whole of philosophy. Nevertheless, as the example of indeterminism shows, there is no lack of thinkers who do not wish to admit that this proposition is universally true. And some believe not only, as they do, that some things come into being by chance, but also that some things exist eternally by chance. Epicurus believed also in an existence by chance within inanimate nature, and J. S. Mill, whom we know to be a thoroughgoing determinist with respect to the will, did not exclude the possibility of accidental occurrences in remote times and places. Among those who believe that things have existed by chance throughout eternity are to be accounted Democritus in antiquity and a number of materialists in modern times, while

Kant and Schopenhauer restricted the principle that everything must have a sufficient reason to phenomena, while excepting things in themselves.

Leibniz made use of the aforementioned formulation, for his famous principle of sufficient reason reduces to nothing more than the proposition that everything existing exists necessarily and that there can be no objective chance. And as we have remarked, the great majority of philosophers agree with him.

Yet if we ask from whence they derive their faith in the universal validity of this proposition, the answers vary greatly.

Aristotle contented himself with saying that no one would be so foolish as to claim that opposite effects could occur under exactly the same circumstances. However, we have shown that this is historically inaccurate. Leibniz thought the principle of sufficient reason was evident, like all analytic judgments, since whoever denies it finds himself caught in a contradiction. However, he did not know how to make such contradictions clearly recognizable. Kant, indeed, rejects out of hand the possibility that we could ever prove the existence of such contradictions. A contradiction would occur, he says, if someone wanted to contest the existence of something which is necessarily, but the man who maintains that something exists, yet not necessarily, does not appear to be contradicting himself in any direct way. Kant held the principle of sufficient reason to be *a priori* but not analytic. Yet the cognitions which, according to him, form the basis of all experiential knowledge, and even the synthetic *a priori* cognitions underlying mathematics, ought properly to be called correct prejudices rather than cognitions, and if the principle that there can be no pure chance belongs among them, then it, too, is a blind prejudice.

In fact, however, this principle is an analytic judgment, i.e. one that is evident from the concepts. All that is necessary to make the contradiction quite apparent is to subject the concepts to a certain analysis—as, indeed, we must do with all mathematical principles.

This analysis starts out from the assumption that 'something is' means the same as 'something is present', just as everything that was, was present, and everything that will be, will be present.

Furthermore, everything that is is simultaneously with everything else that is. The only difference is temporal; among the things that are present, one is beginning while another is continuing and a third is ending. In other words, it is either the beginning or the end of a temporal episode, or else it is one of the internal boundaries of a temporal episode that connects what has already taken place with what will come out of it.

Precise observation discloses that we are dealing in every case with continuous temporal change, even in the cases where we speak of 'unchanging continuity'. Otherwise, the distinction between a longer and a shorter duration makes no sense. However, the continuous connection need not extend in both directions of time; the episode need not be such that its existence extends into the past as well as extending into the future. Yet it cannot lack both directions simultaneously; one connection or the other must be preserved. In other words, it is impossible for something to begin and end abruptly within the same moment, but what begins abruptly now may end abruptly at a later moment, and likewise, it is possible for what ends abruptly now to have begun abruptly at an earlier moment. Between the beginning and the end we always find an intervening time. We may imagine this to be as small as we wish, but it remains a continuum of finite size and as such allows elements to be distinguished *ad infinitum* that either have been or will be such infinitesimal changes.

Now, is it possible to unite these infinitesimal temporal changes, which every being must undergo, with existence by chance?

Let us get clear about this by means of a concrete example. Suppose that a white dot appears by pure chance upon a black slate. Is it more probable that it will remain for some time or that it will disappear again at some arbitrarily selected moment?

Because the dot comes into being by absolute chance, there is no necessity for its being or continuing to be. The opposite is to be expected with equal probability—indeed, with far greater probability. For the case is not as simple as it would be if there were just two possibilities: that at some arbitrarily selected moment either the white dot exists or nothing exists. For a dot of any other colour might take up this space. The other possibilities are numerous, and since all of them are equally accidental and none is the least bit more likely than any other, it is from the very outset highly unlikely that this white dot, which came into being by chance, would maintain its accidental existence for even the most minute finite time.

In other words, at every single moment during the existence of something arising by absolute chance, an abrupt alteration between existing and not existing is at least as probable as its enduring.

But this is the precise opposite of what we established earlier for each thing existing, without exception; namely that it must remain free from abrupt change for some time, be it ever so short, for one moment of abrupt change cannot directly follow another. They must be separated by a period during which no change occurs, and this can be subdivided into moments *ad infinitum*.

We can express this even more simply:

At any given time, it is more probable that whatever exists will not change abruptly, and at any given time, it is more probable that whatever exists by chance will change abruptly. In other words, the assumption that something can exist by absolute chance contains two contradictory conditions. The one is that at any given moment a thing is equally likely, indeed, even more likely, to change abruptly than to continue existing; the other is that an abrupt change must take place incomparably less often than a continuous chain of before and after.

The proof of the impossibility of absolute chance establishes directly the universal law of causation, which says that everything not immediately necessary must have a cause.

Now that we have demonstrated the logical impossibility of every sort of indeterminism we can end our discussion of this theory. Yet I do not wish to omit a parenthetical glance at the relations between the two parties in the determinism–indeterminism dispute with respect to philosophical theism.

APPENDIX

THE RELATION OF DETERMINISM AND INDETERMINISM
TO THEISM[38]

The champions of the two theories coincide in that they accuse their opponent of the same fault, viz. that his doctrine is incompatible with the theistic view of the world.

[38] The conception of the proof of a universal law of causation employed here was not contained in Brentano's course of lectures on ethics. Insight into the further development of his thought on this matter may be gained from *Versuch über die Erkenntnis*, Part IV, and *Vom Dasein Gottes*, particularly p. 446 ff.

82. I. Indeterminism's case against determinism: it is in contradiction with God's goodness

If all willing is necessary, then sinful willing must be, too. But how could the being of infinite perfection produce creatures who necessarily sin? This contradicts the idea of God, for the evil acts of will that follow necessary laws follow laws of nature, i.e. if there is a God, in accordance with divine laws. But a being of infinite perfection cannot lay down laws that further evil.

This is the form the objection sometimes takes, but when it does it fails quite visibly. It ignores the ambiguity of the term 'law'. It can mean a norm, a prescription, or a command: consider laws of logic and laws of ethics.

The term has another sense when we speak of mathematical or physical or physiological laws. In the former cases it means, 'It ought to be like this'; in the latter it means, 'It must be like this'.

If God has created beings, they will, of course, act according to laws of nature, i.e. whether they have knowledge or are in error, whether they make moral or immoral decisions, they are making their judgments and decisions out of necessity. But we cannot say that God assigned to them an incorrect system of logic or a false code of ethics, that he has commanded them to make errors and immoral choices as though they were logically or ethically correct, as the case may be. The fact that these creatures make wrong choices is no more in contradiction with God's sanctity than the fact that they make false judgments is in contradiction with his omniscience.

But is it not in contradiction with his perfection that he created beings in such a way that they must go so badly astray under certain circumstances?

If it were, indeterminism would find itself equally at variance with theism. Indeterminists do not hold that the will is totally uncaused; they admit that the will, too, follows laws of nature, as a consequence of which one decision is to be expected with far greater probability than its opposite in certain cases. Now, is it not just as much at variance with God's sanctity for him to have created beings who under certain circumstances are highly likely to fall into the ways of sin? Suppose that an event does take place in external nature that is not perfectly determined. Is the man who sets off an undetermined fire any the less a pyromaniac? He foresaw the harm he was about to do, at least with probability, if not with certainty.

Determinism and indeterminism, then, are faced with the same difficulty: either theism is compatible with determinism as well as with indeterminism, or it is compatible with neither.

But how do matters really stand? How can we reconcile with God's perfection the fact that he laid down laws for spiritual nature which lead us to expect, either with certainty or with probability, that morally evil acts of will will take place upon occasion? I believe it is not impossible to answer this question.

To begin with, it is not a question of ultimate, particular laws.

There is no more a fundamental law that human beings will make an immoral decision under certain circumstances than there is a fundamental law that they will make an erroneous judgment under certain circumstances. Rather, it is in both cases a question of a complicated interaction between forces that under different circumstances and in other connections bring about true knowledge and virtuous decisions. It is not as though there were devilish beings who willed evil upon every conceivable occasion. Certainly, anyone who thought there were such creatures would have a hard time attributing them to a perfect being.

But someone might make the following objection. If the evil that takes place is in accordance with laws of nature only to a certain generally conceded extent, it is nevertheless ultimately willed by God. But how can something morally perfect will evil?

Answer: 1. Indeterminism would be faced with the same problem.

2. Even if God wills that man have a sinful will, he does not will the same things as this will. The human will is his object, but he is not identical with it. Man has chosen what he knows to be worse; God has chosen what in its proper place will serve the perfect whole. For it is certain that everything that happens, and therefore also the evil in the world, is willed by God, yet it is not willed as an end, but because it contributes to that work which he in his wisdom recognizes as right. This is the view of all the great theists; if they are in error in this matter, then theism is in error. But if so it is untenable for both parties, for the indeterminists as well as for the determinists. But no finite mind will ever succeed in proving that the evil in the world cannot be justified by one who

is able to survey the happenings in the world over their entire course.

83. II. *Determinism's charge against indeterminism: it contradicts divine omniscience*

It is a necessary part of divine omniscience that God know everything, not only every truth that is evident from the concepts but also every mere fact, not only those concerning what is but also those concerning what was and what will be, and consequently also our acts of will, whether they be determined or not. But how can God know them if they are not determined?

They do not take place as a matter of course. Quite the contrary; because they are not necessarily determined, they are supposed to be free from both absolute and relative necessity. Thus there are only two possibilities: either God knows them because they are the grounds of his knowledge, or he knows himself as their ground. But both are untenable from the viewpoint of indeterminism.

1. Acts of will cannot be the ground of God's knowledge, particularly not future acts, which do not yet exist and cannot be efficacious. But if they could have any effect on anything, they nevertheless could not affect God, who, because he is immediately necessary, cannot be conditioned by anything and cannot be subject to any influence.

2. But God also could not know undetermined acts of will through knowing himself as the cause necessitating them, for they have no cause that makes them necessary.

Thus God would only be able to guess at our acts of will, and even this guessing would happen by chance, just like the acts of will themselves, and to just the same extent. But God's knowledge is a part of his being, which would then be tainted by elements of chance. In other words, God's knowledge of our acts of will could only be rescued at the cost of his immediate necessity, and at that it would not be real knowledge, but only belief which happened to be correct.

To our initial formula, 'Indeterminism is the doctrine that the will has no freedom', we can add a second: 'Indeterminism is atheism.'

III

Three Further Possible Meanings of Freedom of the Will

---

84. *Power over the determining factors in future acts of will*

The question concerning freedom divides into several questions, i.e. there are yet other senses in which the will might be free. However, some of these can be dealt with quickly, as they were already mentioned in connection with the dispute over indeterminism. The matter arose because the indeterminists confused some cases of genuine freedom with their imaginary ones. In order to refute their claims, we had to call attention to the distinctions they overlooked. None the less, let us deal explicitly with those three remaining meanings of free will that are most important.

The question is raised occasionally whether we cause our acts of will simply by means of our inclinations or whether we also have *power over the causes of our willing*. Clearly, this question concerns cases of freedom of the *actus a voluntate imperatus* and the power to realize what we will within the spiritual realm. The crux of the question is whether we can deliberately arrange our future acts of will; can we will to will, just as we can will to make a judgment? The question may sound paradoxical, but when the sense of it is whether we can influence our future acts of will under certain circumstances, it is a reasonable question and calls for an affirmative answer.

Of course, my power over my future acts of will is not direct. It is connected to certain preliminary conditions that can be realized at the present time. Under certain circumstances I can act today in such a way as to prevent my future decision from being

271

in conflict with my duty, either by 'burning my bridges behind me' or by practising and training myself each day in sundry small ways and thus arming myself for greater tests in the future. Every normal person is able to do this to a certain extent. Far from according with indeterminism, this ability is comprehensible only when we assume determinism.

85. *Freedom of choice*

We have established that some things are loved for themselves, while others are loved for their consequences, as means to an end. Occasionally it may happen that we immediately start thinking about the consequences as soon as we start thinking about the object, but this is not always the case, particularly when the consequences are remote and no strong associations have been established through repeated experience. But if we love some things for their own sake and have to choose among several of them, even this can become complicated in significant ways. On either hand we have a complex of various elements each of which is loved or hated in itself and accordingly is awarded either more or less attention. It consequently makes a great difference whether we act according to the impulse of the moment or first turn our attention to the details of what is immediately present as well as to the future consequences, whether we step in blindly right away or first make comparisons and give them our consideration.

We ascribe *freedom of choice* to the man who, under certain circumstances, has the power to postpone his decision at first, rather than giving in to his immediate impulse. It is this that Aristotle has most particularly in mind when he speaks of the freedom that distinguishes the adult person from the child and the animal. He sees a very close connection between deliberation and choice, and he is right; snatching more or less blindly at something is not really making a choice, even when it is selected from among other possibilities.

There is no doubt that we possess this freedom within certain limits. It, too, belongs to the *libertas actus imperati* and is a special case of particular importance. The power to deliberate before we decide is one of man's most valuable characteristics, and teachers consider one of their most important tasks to be training their pupils into the habit of choosing with deliberation. No one seems more ill-bred than the man who always gives in to his first impulse, whether in speaking and acting or in his expressions and gestures.

Yet we do not possess this freedom of choice under all circumstances. For instance, being in a state of passionate agitation can interfere with our deliberation. We then speak of decreased responsibility, meaning that the way a man acts when he is in such a condition should not necessarily lead us to conclude that he is morally inferior. In such cases even a good and rational man will behave badly, being overwhelmed by emotion and rendered incapable of thinking of some essential factors. A good part, indeed the best part, of his self is eliminated, as it were, during his action. The impassioned man can be held responsible only for the fact that he got into this state, in the same manner in which people can be held responsible for their ignorance.

Aristotle, we remarked, stressed the importance of this sort of freedom. However, he believed deliberation to apply only to the means, holding that there can be no choice between ultimate ends —a view related to the fact that Aristotle acknowledges only *one* ultimate end: happiness ($\epsilon\dot{\upsilon}\delta\alpha\iota\mu o\nu\acute{\iota}\alpha$). None the less, our own previous investigations have shown that there are a number of things intrinsically deserving of love which we may call into view and compare when deliberating our choice. (The situation is much the same with theoretical thinking. We investigate not only what is to be known indirectly but also inquire into immediate insights, particularly into the question of which are to serve as the correct starting-points for the special inquiry we have in view. For instance, we can retrace our steps back to immediate perceptions or to memories or to axioms.)

In the very act of comparing ultimate ends and weighing their relative worth, we are introducing considerations relating to freedom of choice. Such deliberations, then, need not always involve only causes and effects or means and ends, though we certainly have indirect knowledge of the preference involved.

Freedom of choice has also often been confused with the freedom connected with indeterminism. For that reason, we had occasion to mention it incidentally while discussing the dispute between determinism and indeterminism. But could it be that this is not a confusion and that freedom of choice really does have something to do with indeterminism? Aristotle said we cannot deliberate about what is necessary and hence not, for instance, about whether the square of the hypotenuse is equal to the sum of the squares of the other two sides, or about the past. However, this is quite a different matter from indeterministic freedom. In this context, to say that something happens necessarily means only that it lies outside our power, that it is independent of whether we will it to happen or not. It concerns the limits of our power, the boundaries of *libertas actus a voluntate imperati*.

Some have attempted to construe a connection between freedom of choice and indeterminism in a different fashion. They say that an interval comes between the present moment and the definitive decision, so that the decision cannot take place at once, even though the conditions required for it exist. This view, however, amounts to indeterminism. The freedom described here is known as *libertas exercitii*.

Answer: If a person finds himself in a position in which he is able to postpone his decision, then not all the conditions for its emergence have been realized. Rather, the situation is such that, instead of making, by necessity, the decision that constitutes the ultimate choice, the person has decided to continue deliberating— and this decision, too, is determined. But in so far as it is determined, it necessarily hinders the final decision from taking place immediately. The intervening period is not an interval in the sense of a causal vacuum.

86. *Moral freedom in the sense of moral eminence*

Does moral knowledge also belong to the powers that determine our will? Of all the questions concerning freedom, this is the one most important for ethics. Can our decision be influenced by the insight that one among the objects of choice is the best, or are we unable to take the value of the object into account in choosing? Kant formulated the question in this manner: Do we possess the ability to act out of regard for the categorical imperative, or are we attracted and driven solely by empirical motives (pleasure and pain)? (Kant confounded the former situation with indeterminism.)

The Socratic teaching is extremely optimistic, viz. that virtue is given along with moral knowledge. Indeed, he defines virtue as the knowledge of what is good, which is to say that no one ever brings about consciously and willingly what is recognized to be wrong. Socrates held knowledge of the good to be, not one of the motives determining the will, but the motive that always turns the scale. But it is just this consequence that displays his error. His optimism is contradicted by experience, which accords far better with the dictum, *scio meliora proboque, deteriora sequor.* Nevertheless, Socrates' exaggeration is based upon the correct notion that the good exercises a power of attraction over our emotions. As we established previously, it is not only worthy of love, but also lovable; otherwise, we would never perceive that it deserves love.

Preferring what is preferable is a part of the good. We take pleasure in acts of loving and preferring that are experienced as being correct, just as we do in knowledge. It is consequently quite comprehensible that the consciousness that one stance is preferable to another can be a motive for our moral decisions. To be sure, the motivating power of the knowledge of what is good and what is preferable varies from person to person. If this power affects a person so strongly that it overcomes all countermotives and he grows into the habit of making choices motivated by the knowledge of what is preferable, we say that he possesses moral freedom in an eminent degree, contrasting his state to the bondage of the morally weak and depraved. It was this sense of freedom that St Augustine had in mind when he said true freedom reigns where the love of what is known to be good, the *cupiditas boni*, is the determining ground of the will. Far from confounding all this with indeterminism, as Kant did, he speaks much more about the freedom of the divine will than about the *beata necessitas boni.*

It was in order to establish the existence of moral freedom in the sense of moral eminence that we took up the question of freedom, for if there were no such freedom, if the knowledge of what is morally right possessed no motivating power, there would be no sense in making an effort to acquire moral insight. And, on the other hand, the more important this conception of moral freedom shows itself to be, the more justifiable appears the careful investigation into the various meanings of the freedom of the will which has occupied us for so long a time.

PART FOUR

MORALITY IN GENERAL

I

Conditional and Absolute Aspects of
Moral Standards

---

87. *The absolute character of moral precepts*

1. Our investigations into the freedom of the will, while not leading us to accept indeterminism, have brought us to a recognition of the existence of freedom in several senses, particularly freedom of choice and the freedom to be influenced by a knowledge of what is preferable in making choices and forming preferences. Hence it is probably not without value to set up rules for forming preferences and choices.

These rules are related to our discussion of the good and the preferable. The man who is acquainted with the relative values of goods and evils, with the causes and effects connected with them, and also with the extent of his own powers possesses in their essence the rules for forming preferences. All he need do then is formulate them.

These rules are also called moral laws. They are not, however, psychological laws, but laws in the sense of precepts, like the norms of logic or the canons of an art or craft. Our whole spiritual life unfolds in accordance with psychological laws, whether we are acting rightly or wrongly. Even what logic rejects as erroneous conforms to psychological law. However, like the laws of logic, the laws of ethics tell us not what must be but what ought to be. In this respect they do not differ from the rules for various other arts.

2. But in one point they are unlike the rules of all other arts. While the latter are merely hypothetical precepts, the laws of

ethics are absolute. Its imperatives are categorical. The reason for the difference is that the other arts either merely give instructions for attaining something useful (medicine for attaining health, architecture for attaining a residence) without troubling themselves about intrinsically desirable ends, or else, if they are concerned directly with something good in itself, ignore the relation between its value and that of other goods. These rules can fall into conflict with one another and thus be rendered null. Even the rules of logic are hypothetical. In setting up rules for making correct judgments, logic pays no attention to whether they will lead to a violation of the precepts that we should love our neighbour, show gratitude, and be pious and thereby encroach upon a good more supreme than strict truth. Ethics, however, calls everything into consideration and consequently deviates somewhat from the rules that logic sets up for judging our fellow men. Ethics demands that we consider any person good until he is shown to be otherwise (although we need not have absolute proof of this), while logic considers us justified in entertaining a greater degree of suspicion and treats indifferently at the outset the hypothesis that someone is good and the hypothesis that he is bad, demanding that we prove the one or the other. As stated, ethics modifies this approach. It commands ultimately and absolutely.

88. *Exceptions to ethical rules*

However, there is an obvious objection to the claim that ethical norms are absolute: If they are, how can duties conflict, as they sometimes undeniably do?

Answer: A conflict of duties is possible only if the conflicting rules have been set up either on the basis of certain tacit presuppositions or by abstraction from certain circumstances. A more exact conception, taking into account these complications, would exclude any such conflicts. Even physical laws are formulated by abstracting from concrete circumstances; for instance, the law of inertia treats only of bodies in isolation. It is up to us to make a mental note of the provision that the law holds only if the body is not disturbed by some other body. Similarly, to make quite accurate the precept that a student ought to devote several hours a day to his studies, we must add: when illness does not prevent him or chance circumstances do not impose other more pressing demands on him.

Indeed, there are so many circumstantial complications that almost every moral law has to be qualified. The qualifications are so obvious that it is unnecessary to add them expressly. In a certain sense, then, most ethical norms, too, can be called hypothetical, but in a sense different from the rules of any other practical discipline. These are absolutely valid with respect to their goal, but their goal is conditional. The other rules of a given art do not render invalid the hypothetical rule, for the assumption is always that the goal is in fact desired: 'If you wish to build a sturdy house (stay healthy, educate yourself in such and such a discipline, etc.), do . . .'

In ethics it is other precepts that supply the means for establishing whether a universally held, and therefore hypothetical precept is valid or invalid in a particular case. Certainly if ethics were developed to an infinite degree, all the rules that under present circumstances apply to any single case would combine together into a single, quite concrete rule which would be valid without exception. But any such development is quite impracticable, for we can never set up so many rules that we exhaust the infinite number of possible complications of circumstances.

However, if we do discover the concrete rules for a completely analysed case, it is valid without exception, and any possibility of its conflicting with another rule is excluded.

89. The most general principle is universally valid

But how about the rules that are not completely individualized, or particular? Is there no universally valid ethical principle concerning preference? Kant believed himself to have discovered a principle of this kind in his categorical imperative, but we have shown it to be devoid of content and incapable of being applied. On the other hand, no one can doubt the validity of the precept, 'Give preference rightly.' It is evident, being analytic. Although right preferring is not itself the supreme good, it is nevertheless a universally valid principle that we ought to prefer what is preferable, and our previous investigations have taken care that this imperative should not remain devoid of content. What is preferable consists in what is best for the greatest sphere within which we can bring our influence to bear—which is simply to say that it consists in the greatest amount of spiritual good and the greatest possible freedom from spiritual evils within our sphere of influence.

Or is this precept, too, not always binding? Someone might object that it is quite impossible to be thinking of the supreme practical good at all times, let alone to take it into account at the moment of action. If this objection held, no single moral principle would be universally valid, with the exception of those that are quite concrete.

Answer: Long ago some light was shed on this problem by Scholastic moralists, who pointed out that precepts may be interpreted as positive or negative. No positive precept, they maintained, demands fulfilment at every moment; in that sense, no principle is universally valid, not even the command, 'Love God above all else, and love thy neighbour as thyself.' If it were, we would not be permitted even to sleep, for we cannot be actively thinking of God or our fellow men when we are asleep. On the other hand, these thinkers did hold to be valid without exception such precepts as, 'You ought never to make a decision that conflicts with God's demands' and 'You ought never to place some form of pleasure above the fulfilment of God's commandment and of your conscience.'

This is a legitimate distinction. We ought in fact, then, to give the principle, 'Choose the best of what is attainable', the negative interpretation, 'In choosing, never opt for something less good among what is attainable.' The same holds for the principle, 'Choose rightly'. We may not demand positively that people always will rightly, for we cannot even demand that they continuously perform acts of will.

According to what we have said, both the most general moral rule and the most concrete moral rules are valid unconditionally and without exception; it is only those in between that hold conditionally. And this is quite easy to explain: the most general rule sets forth the end, while all the rest are rules for what serves the end, and they formulate the means to the end either with a certain degree of indefiniteness or else quite specifically.

II

The Domain of Morality

---

90. *The limits of morality*

1. In measuring acts of will and choice by the standards of moral rules, we are declaring them to be moral or immoral. When and how is it permissible to apply these standards? We may not apply them to animals or to children, nor always to adults. Every act of loving or choosing is good or bad (right or not right), but not all are moral or immoral. Where are the boundaries of morality, and to what are they related? Many thinkers are unclear about this.

Some have insisted upon a distinction between *actiones hominis* and *actiones humanae*. The former are actions that people perform, while the latter are those performed in a specifically human manner, viz. as a result of reflection and rational consideration of the objects of choice and of the circumstances. *Actiones humanae* do not include what we do when carried away by the first impulse that happens along (*motus primo primi voluntatis*); what we do in our sleep or in a state of insanity; or pure reflexes, performed from instinct or habit without our rational judgment inclining us one way or the other.

These thinkers claim that only the *actiones humanae*—those acts that, according to our earlier definition (Pt. III, chap. 3, sect. 85) result from a free choice—are to be called moral.

2. It is certainly true that we are responsible only for acts of this kind, but the question is, are all such acts either moral or immoral? If I must choose between going to the theatre or to a concert, does my decision deserve this predicate? It is certainly an *actio humana*, but who would call it moral or immoral?

283

Someone might say that a choice is moral (or immoral) whenever the supreme practical good, that is, the best of the attainable ends, is taken into consideration and one act comes to be acknowledged as better.

But there remains the question of just how the supreme practical good is to be taken into account: is a merely negative regard sufficient, or are we also required to take it positively into account? That is, am I acting immorally only when I act in opposition to it even though I have considered it, but not when I have failed to think of it at all? Or am I obligated to think of it?

There are arguments on both sides.

How can constant positive consideration of the supreme practical good be demanded if it is impossible to be thinking about it all the time?

On the other hand, it would appear to be very dangerous for us not to be always thinking of it; hence, the demand that we do so ought not to be evaded.

The right answer is probably as follows: A person well schooled in moral ways will certainly not fail to think quite often of the supreme practical good or, alternatively, of what he has once and for all recognized to be a necessary condition for it, and even if he does not and cannot do it in making every decision, it is none the less a requisite of perfect moral behaviour that virtually all of our acts aim at what is best. I say 'virtually', for a single purpose may easily govern and animate, as it were, an entire chain of undertakings.[39] We need not be actually thinking of the supreme practical good at all times. Not only is that frequently impossible; even where it is possible, it would under certain circumstances be disturbing and consequently harmful. But we ought, and can, behave in the way that any rational man does when he wants to attain a goal; we make a plan, and then follow it. In order to serve a purpose that aims at the supreme practical good, we make a

[39] Here Brentano touches upon the problem of one's outlook, or basic stand, which plays an important role in present-day psychology but which has not yet been thoroughly clarified in all its aspects. An attitude is found where there is given the image or idea of an end which stands out against a background of associations standing in readiness. This idea of an end, even if it is not always present to our consciousness, stimulates the appearance of certain ideas, thus serving indirectly the goal in view.

life plan, and since our life consists of days, we make an orderly schedule for every day, to which we hold unflinchingly. Only in this way does our life take on a noble unity of purpose. Every hour is enhanced by the sublime end, every moment given moral significance through its relation to this end. And even though the demands of this plan are less severe, we actually attain better results through following it than by bearing in mind at all times the ultimate end. Constant contemplation of the goal would make it impossible for us to concentrate adequately on what is close at hand, and all our activities would suffer.

91. *Is only the will morally good or bad, or actions also?*

The following reasons are sometimes given for the claim that these predicates apply only to the will and not to action.

1. Any person will find that he is often not in a position to carry out his will, so that the action he willed to perform fails to take place. Nevertheless, his moral character is in no way diminished; his will is as deserving of praise as it would have been if he had acted.

2. On the other hand, the same act loses its moral character if it does not result from a moral act of will, as when something beneficial as such is performed with evil intent.

This is said to show that action is morally indifferent as such, a theory from which the medieval sects of Beghards and Béguins drew the most monstrous consequences. They argued that every outrage is permissible, since morality is purely internal; inside, we remain pure and are united with God. (*Homo potest libere corpori concedere quidquid placet. Se in actibus exercere virtutem est hominis imperfecti.*)

The sophistry of this argument is quite apparent. It rests upon two absurd fictions: on the one hand, upon the assumption that a mental act can remain the same even though its object changes, and on the other upon the treating of the soul and the body as though each were an individual possessing a will.

In support of the morality of actions it is said that we attribute to them a moral character even when the will is not concerned at all with the best end attainable, provided only that the undertaking in question results from moral intent.

How can we resolve the *aporia*? It is very simple: only the will possesses a (good or bad) moral character in the strict sense, while action is moral just in so far as it results from a moral will. Consequently, it is moral in a derivative sense, viz. with respect to the will. The predicate moral, then, is similar to the predicate true, which is used in various senses, all of which refer, if not directly, at least ultimately to a true judgment, and to the predicate healthy, which refers ultimately and strictly only to the healthy body. Of course, we cannot simply add what is moral in the derivative sense to what is moral in the strict sense in order to get a sum of morality, as it were. If the will is eliminated, we do not simply lose one factor which together with another, the morality of the act, could have enhanced the total moral character of the given mode of behaviour. Instead, we lost the condition required for the act to have a so-called moral character at all.

3. The first argument mentioned does not in the least prevent us from calling acts moral in this derivative sense, and the other arguments make no further stipulations. That the will is moral in the true sense is not refuted by the demonstration that some acts may be considered moral even though the will was not occupied with considerations of what would be best, for such acts have simply been guided by a past act of will which indeed aimed for the best.

Still less do there follow the consequences drawn by the sectarians. Certainly, the morality of willing is not determined by a previously given morality of the act; quite the opposite. It is, however, determined by the utility of the act—that is, its efficacy in promoting the supreme practical good—which is given independently of the will. Consequently it is impossible to indulge oneself in just any act while maintaining a morally pure will.

92. *Objective and subjective morality*

1. We have just touched upon this distinction, which is applied to willing as well as to acting. An act is subjectively moral if, and in so far as, it springs from a moral act of will. Its objective morality, on the other hand, consists in its usefulness in furthering the best, upon which the morality of an act of will largely depends. The subjective morality of the act depends, in turn, upon the morality of the act of will.

Thus a man makes a subjectively moral choice when he chooses something because he believes it to promote the supreme practical good. On the other hand, the will is objectively good in so far as it really *does* further this good. If the choice is made from other motives, it may be objectively moral, but it cannot be subjectively moral. There are a variety of reasons why a thing may be preferred, and it consequently happens that things are in fact preferred for reasons other than those for which they deserve to be preferred.

The opposite combination is also to be found: subjective morality without objective morality. This happens where errors occur. For instance, I may will what is best but err in holding that the means which I employ are conducive to it, or I may err in my evaluation of the relative merits of the goods in question.

2. The distinction between genuine and spurious acts of virtue rests upon the difference between objective and subjective morality. Truly virtuous acts are determined by subjective morality, while spurious ones are only objectively moral. This point dates back to Plato: only the virtue of the wise man is true; other men are abstemious only out of incontinence, brave only out of cowardice. Contrasting with the five kinds of false courage, which arise from a desire for honour, from fear of disgrace, from ignorance of the danger at hand, from habit, or from a passionate temperament, is only one true kind, courage διὰ τοῦ καλλοῦ (for the sake of the good).

III

Differences of Degree within the
Moral Sphere

---

93. *Are there such differences?*

1. The Stoics denied it. They considered all virtue, on the one hand, and all vice on the other to be one; they recognized no differences of value. The deed, they said, is not good as such, but only in so far as it proceeds from the correct sentiment, which consists in holding that the good, i.e. virtue, is valued over everything else. If we insist upon a multiplicity of virtues, for instance, the four so-called cardinal virtues, we divide what is in reality one. In every act of the wise man they are all present together, for they are merely an expression of the esteem that he assigns to virtue above all else. A truly virtuous man displays his perfection equally in each of his acts, while the man who in even so much as a single case does not act from esteem for virtue never does act from such esteem.

Similarly, vice displays itself equally in every immoral act. For a virtuous disposition is a characteristic like the straightness of a line, permitting neither of a greater nor of a lesser degree. No doubt there are differences in the extent to which a line approaches being straight, but even crooked lines that are almost straight belong entirely within the class of crooked lines and partake in no way of the characteristic of straightness.

However, the Stoics themselves were not always able to maintain this harsh view. Indeed, their qualms eventually became so great that they finally concluded there was no such thing as perfect virtue. Thereafter they separated human beings not into those who are bad and those who are good, but into those who are bad and those who are more advanced (*prokoptontes*).

2. How should we decide this question? To clarify matters, we will apply it separately to objective morality and to subjective morality. There are undoubtedly degrees of objective morality, varying with the extent to which an act promotes the supreme practical good, but it also cannot rationally be denied that there are degrees of subjective morality. A good act arising from a greater love of the supreme practical good is more moral; a bad act betraying a greater lack of such love, or even hatred of the good, is less moral. Hence we value more greatly:

(*a*) the act performed cheerfully, for it indicates a greater inclination towards the good (Aristotle);

(*b*) the right decision that is made without the slightest wavering or hesitation once it is recognized wherein the better lies (Aristotle emphasizes this factor in his discussion of courage); and

(*c*) the noble motive unadulterated by any other, the choosing of the good without any admixture of sensual, egotistical impulses. Think of the description Plato gave of the ideal just man: without having committed any injustice, he takes on the reputation of great injustice in order that the justness of his nature may be tested. But he does not allow himself to be shaken either by the infamy or by horrendous threats. Though tormented, racked, bound and branded with hot irons, and finally, after enduring all this, run through with a spear, he remains unswervingly true to what he acknowledges, having appeared to be unjust all his life while in truth he was just.

The same ideal was professed by the so-called prophets, who were among the Jewish people the bearers of an enlightened moral attitude, and above all by the founder of Christianity. Nietzsche was mistaken in his repeated attempts to play off the moral sensitivity of the Greeks against Judaeo-Christian morality, casting the latter as the morality of weakness because of its advocacy of loving one's neighbour and of compassion, the former as the embodiment of ruthless greed for power—the latter being the morality of the slave, the former of the master. He was overly preoccupied with certain of the Sophists; Socrates, Plato, and Aristotle held quite different views, and they doubtless have a greater right to be accounted the flowers of the Greek spirit.

(*d*) We deem an act more moral when what is preferable was

chosen in the face of greater opposition, when greater sacrifices have been made. (The circumstances can be combined; we speak of a readiness for sacrifice when someone makes a sacrifice without hesitation or wavering and of a willingness for sacrifice when someone sacrifices himself with gladness and good cheer.)

(*e*) We see greater value in an act when the strongest inclinations and temptations to do the opposite are outweighed by the fact that it is just slightly more likely to further the general good, and also

(*f*) when there is only a slight chance that it will further the supreme practical good, while it is certain that this good will not be furthered unless a great personal sacrifice is made.

On the other hand, we judge an act to be particularly bad:

(*a*) if it is committed without scruple, or even with positive delight;

(*b*) when the greater good is sacrificed frivolously and without hesitation to our own advantage, as soon as it is recognized as such;

(*c*) where impulses in favour of the good, such as a fear of scandal or natural distaste, are overcome;

(*d*) when the personal advantage involved is very small (Judas' reward); and

(*e*) and (*f*) when there is a great preponderance on the side of the general good, yet the small personal sacrifice called for is not made.

94. *Are there any morally indifferent actions?*

If there are degrees of morality, is there also a zero-point, or area of complete indifference? Here, too, opinions vary, yet it is easy to reach an agreement once the required distinctions have been made. We must divide the question in two parts, asking it first for objective morality and then for subjective morality.

Applied to objective morality, it divides into two further questions: whether there are acts that are indifferent *in specie*, and whether there are acts that are indifferent *in individuo*. It is possible for an act to be indifferent *in specie*, for an act can be beneficial in some circumstances and harmful in others, so that the cases of harm and benefit average out. But only when an act is considered in abstraction from the particular circumstances can it be called indifferent. The individual act, taken in itself, is always either more or less beneficial or harmful: as regards objective morality, it is not indifferent.

What about subjective morality? Here there can be acts that are indifferent *in specie*, for an act may be carried out sometimes for this reason, sometimes for that, so that it may on the average be done as often from moral as from immoral motives. But what of acts *in individuo*? Given a precise knowledge of the spiritual state of the actor, can we ever say that his choice is morally indifferent? There are two cases where this might happen: first, where the supreme practical good has not been thought of at all, not even virtually, and failure to think of it is not to be accounted a moral defect; second, where we are not in a position to recognize which of the possible decisions will promote the supreme practical good, either in the concrete case or on the average. Under any other circumstances, an act is always moral or immoral.

95. *Can an act be both moral and immoral?*

If the gist of this question were whether an act can be moral in some situations and immoral in others, we would of course have to answer it in the affirmative, but this is not its sense.

The answer would be yes if there were a multiplicity of independent and unconditionally valid moral precepts, for then collisions would be unavoidable. However, that is not the case. We have established that there is only one valid law, which is unlimited and applies under all circumstances, viz. to promote the best within the greatest possible sphere. Hence there can be no genuine conflict of duties; at most there can be a subjective doubt about what is preferable under a given set of circumstances.

Yet even from our standpoint there is a certain sense in which a concrete act can be at the same time both moral and immoral: it may be the one as a virtual performance, yet the other as an actual performance.

Suppose, for example, that by means of the wrong treatment a doctor causes the death of a sick person, or at least bears part of the responsibility for it. In this particular case he has made every possible effort, but when he was a student he was more concerned with his fraternity than with his studies, so that it was just by luck that he squeaked through his exams. In this case the virtual decision deserves censure, but not the actual decision. Take another example: the man who kills another in self-defence may not be immediately guilty, yet his fault may lie in the past; he may have provoked his victim deliberately.

On the other hand, there are situations in which the actual decision is to be censured and the virtual to be praised. Suppose a man knows that he has a role to play in a publicized political gathering, but also knows that on such occasions he is invariably aroused to making impassioned insults and unfeeling criticisms. Because it is a matter of some importance, he attends none the less and succumbs to his usual weakness.

96. The obligatory and the supererogatory [Pflicht und Rat]*

1. The common, conventional conception of the moral varies somewhat. Some people speak of immorality only in cases where the supreme practical good is blatantly and flagrantly ignored, of morality where the opposite occurs. We embraced the idea of those of the most advanced sentiment, according to which we ought to be guided by a regard for what is generally best virtually all the time. If one among the objects of choice serves this end better, it is our moral duty to apply ourselves to it. But is it not possible that

* There is no single correct way, applicable in every context, of translating these terms into English. 'Pflicht' I have translated as duty, obligation, or the obligatory (act). 'Rat' presents more difficulties. In ordinary German it simply means advice. However, Catholic theologians have distinguished between precepts, which are binding upon all, and counsels (Räte), to be carried out, voluntarily, by those who wish to lead a life of perfection. They speak of the evangelical counsels (die evangelischen Räte), which are recommended in the New Testament (see text below), but have also listed a large number of other counsels, which they also call merits—the term used by Mill—or supererogatory works. The term supererogatory, or supererogatory act, is commonly used by philosophers.

'Raten' in ordinary German means simply to give advice or counsel—which could, of course, be bad or wrong. Therefore I have translated such terms as 'ratsam' and 'zu raten sein' as, e.g., 'morally advisable as being meritorious', 'supererogatory and therefore merely advisable', etc., in order to make clear that, in the technical sense employed here, they are always positive terms: 'Rat' is always *good* advice, or advice to do what is good.

the ought does not have the same rigorous sense in every case? Do we not have to distinguish another, stricter sense of 'moral', and particularly of 'immoral'? Or should we condemn unconditionally as immoral every act of preference that is not the best under the given circumstances, thus admitting degrees only of immorality?

Some people have taught this view, for instance, the Calvinists. A harsh doctrine indeed! Who would not be accounted predominately immoral by such standards? Public opinion does not condone such severity, and some thinkers of undeniably refined moral sentiments are also inclined to the more moderate view. Alongside the demands of duty, many Catholic theologians also permit room for what is merely advisable. In this they anticipate the judgment of several philosophers. For instance, J. S. Mill points with approval to the Catholic doctrine of the Evangelical Counsels or Perfections (poverty, chastity, and obedience).

But what is the difference between the obligatory and the supererogatory, between duty and counsel, and where is the boundary between the two? Here, too, opinions differ. I cannot consider all of them, but here are the most important.

(a) Some have said that duty is what is necessary for bringing about the ultimate end, whereas counsel is what will bring it about more easily and more certainly. To be sure, eternal blessedness is everyone's goal, but we must distinguish degrees thereof. Whoever wishes to attain it in the highest degree, they say, must do more than what duty demands; he must also follow the Evangelical Counsels. But since we consider the best of what is attainable to be the ultimate goal, this attempt at a conceptual distinction between duty and counsel is not applicable.

(b) A more recent attempt runs as follows: a supererogatory act is one that no particular individual can be obliged to perform, but only the collective whole; for instance, getting married.

However, the collective whole is here treated as though it were a sort of fictitious person. To express the point clearly, we would have to say that the general good requires the majority of people to marry, but not everyone. But is it then merely supererogatory for every individual? That conclusion does not follow: rather, to enter into matrimony may well be the duty of a particular person, since his position is such that he will promote the general good more by marrying than by remaining single. If his position is otherwise, to marry would not even be morally advisable as being meritorious.

(c) J. S. Mill believes that our duty is nothing more than to abstain from injuring each other and to keep any promises to help people that we may have made. Any good over and above this is mere merit. (Cf. *Auguste Comte and Positivism*, London: Trübner, pp. 143–4.)

But this seems too little. Is it not our duty to leap to the aid of someone we can save from drowning without endangering ourselves? Does the talented man who fritters away his life deserve no moral condemnation? Does he do less that is detrimental to the supreme practical good than the man who steals an apple from his neighbour's tree?

(d) Mill himself modifies his remarks by adding that, as regards assisting and benefiting our fellow men, it is our duty to do only what is customary, what is generally done. Anything beyond this, he says, is simply meritorious; the man who does more is praised, to be sure, but no one is to be blamed if he does not take on this extra burden. The average man, then, is to be the standard.*

But even this appeal to what is common and customary seems dubious. What if the average man were morally evil (οἱ πλεῖστοι κακοί)? Would our duty then be only what corresponds to this low average? To be sure, Mill thinks that the realm of duty is forever being extended, thanks to moral progress, so that a previously rare virtue becomes common and what was formerly a matter of merit becomes a matter of duty.* There is some truth in this view—but is it really all right for a morally cultivated man to lower himself without self-reproach to the level of an inferior society in which he happens to find himself? May he with impunity bribe officials, help himself to public funds, and spend hours sitting in cafés? And does this view even allow us to speak of moral progress? Since the extent of moral demands also changes with the times, would not the number of cases in which duty is fulfilled and in which it is neglected remain forever constant? It appears that we would have no right at all to distinguish moral from immoral eras.

2. The problem seems to be resolved more satisfactorily by relating the distinction between the obligatory and the supererogatory

---

*Cf. the passage mentioned above in *Auguste Comte and Positivism*.

to the various degrees of morality of which we spoke earlier.

In that case, our duty would be simply to give preference to the best. This requirement appears to be fulfilled even if we choose the best hesitantly, without pleasure, and with the support of extraneous impulses. Our behaviour is morally correct and in accordance with duty even if we do not have to undergo any difficult tests. Where, in addition, we embrace our duty joyfully and readily and for its own sake, in the face of forces working against us, there obviously is a greater degree of morality present. But if these are absent, ought we to cast blame and point only to the defects? Should we not rather give credit for the fulfilment of duty wherever it occurs?

This is more than a mere question of moral judgment, of whether the act was right or not; it is a matter belonging under the heading 'moral guidance'. All of us receive such guidance from our fellow men even when we are grown up and we are able in turn to bestow it upon others. It includes the praise and blame that we express openly, and also the tasks we set ourselves and others, the demands we place upon both. It would be unwise to give once for all a strict formulation of these demands. An excessively rigorous order is followed not readily, but reluctantly, which is detrimental to the construction of a general moral disposition. The bow that is strung too tightly will break; severity will make the entire realm of duty odious. It is sensible, then, to distinguish between the moral ideal and the demands that a particular moral teacher will make upon individuals.

3. In this light, let us recall one by one the various gradations we discussed.

The situation is undoubtedly ideal when the morally correct decision is made without any admixture of alien impulses, and it can be said that it is a duty to do the good for its own sake. But is it a duty for everyone? Even this precept is relative; we must consider whether it would not bring about more harm than good in the particular case at hand. For a man not habituated in moral ways there can be little purpose in foregoing the use of non-moral motives that lend support. Even the more advanced person cannot fulfil every duty equally well without such assistance. We must view as a single whole the good that we are to achieve and permit, with an eye to this whole, what is less perfect for the sake of what is more perfect.

Much the same can be said of the duty to do the good without hesitation. If someone decides to do his duty only after a struggle, we do not reproach his action as being contrary to duty. It would be highly unwise to point out this defect, for it would only make the man feel ashamed, and perhaps bitter, and render the future fulfilment of his duty more difficult. Taking this into consideration, we formulate more carefully the precept that we ought to do our duty without hesitation, presenting it not as an out-and-out duty but 'as counsel', as being advisable. Indeed, under certain circumstances we will avoid even declaring it to be advisable and, instead of criticizing the wavering, praise all the more the victory that ultimately arrested it.

How about the cases in which powerful forces opposing the right act lead an otherwise morally good man to succumb to temptation? He has failed in his duty: so much is clear. We cannot say that the act he did not perform would have been merely supererogatory. No, it was the only right thing to do. However, it is advisable to avoid the danger of temptation in such cases in future. While we are in general obligated to seek out opportunities for doing good, it is best in this case to evade this duty. But where undergoing the temptation is not to be avoided, the moral guide will take care not to discourage the pupil by a harsh formulation of his duty. He will say, rather, that succumbing would be forgivable in this case, but that for that very reason the person who does not surrender even here is to be lauded all the more.

Yet one more distinction is appropriate here. Deviation from the moral ideal may reveal a weakness deserving reproach, but there are also cases in which conduct proves strength of character, while still falling short of the best conceivable. For instance, suppose a man does not take revenge on his enemy despite powerful impulses and favourable opportunities for repaying with evil the evil he has suffered, yet he has not brought himself to make use of the opportunity at hand to do his enemy a good turn. His abstention from revenge is quite praiseworthy enough, and it would be unwise to reproach him. Although we realize that he has left unused an opportunity to do good and has to that extent acted wrongly, it is excusable in this case not to lay down a duty but simply to give counsel as to what would be still more meritorious.

After all that has been said, how does our conception of the distinction between the obligatory and the supererogatory look?

We, too, can agree when it is said that duty consists of what is common in human behaviour, but unlike Mill we have in mind not the great mass of people, but the best among them. Duty is what the average among the best men will do; whatever goes beyond this is supererogatory, and hence merely advisable.

We will speak more clearly about this matter when we discuss the moulding of the moral dispositions.

IV

The Erring Conscience and the Doubting Conscience

---

97. *The concept and the divisions of the conscience*

The capacity to make a practical judgment as to whether something is to be chosen as morally good, or avoided as morally bad, is called our conscience. This term is also used in a narrower sense, viz. for the consciousness that an act we have ourselves performed was morally right or wrong, and thus for a concrete judgment that can be described graphically as the 'pronouncement of conscience' (in the first sense). We speak of a good or a bad conscience, depending upon whether the pronouncement expresses approval or disapproval (cf. Aquinas: *Applicatio legis naturalis ad facienda*).

There are various obvious distinctions to be made. Our conscience in the sense of a judgment concerning a particular action or failure to act is either right or wrong; furthermore, it is either firmly convinced or harbours doubts. In the latter instance we waver back and forth, uncertain as to whether we are to hold an act to be morally permissible or not.[40]

[40] Here Brentano unites, under the concept of the voice of conscience, two different things: the evident moral judgment and the blind moral judgment. By 'voice of conscience', we may mean acts of loving or hating that are characterized as being correct. But what is commonly known as conscience is undoubtedly also under the influence of associations, of concatenations of ideas that we have either constructed ourselves or taken over from others. Sometimes these influences are so strong that the genuine germ of evidence gets lost and is replaced by

98. *The erring conscience*

Needless to say, it is our duty to follow conscience when it is firmly convinced and is in the right, but what about when it is wrong and feels doubts? If we know that someone erred but was firmly convinced he was right, we must concede that he acted morally in following his conviction. His decision is beyond reproach, at any rate with respect to the immediate circumstances, and it would be appropriate to blame him only if he were responsible for his error because of a previous act of will. To act against the firm convictions of his conscience would only add yet a further fault to the error of which he was already guilty.

Perhaps someone will object that it is harmful to translate the pronouncements of an erring conscience into deeds; that it is a duty to avoid what is harmful; and, consequently, that to follow an erring conscience is contrary to duty. We ought rather, he will continue, to act against it.

Answer: This objection is similar to the advice to look for things only where they are. The difficulty is precisely that the agent does not know the pronouncement of his conscience is wrong.

Nevertheless, the proposition that an action which accords with a firmly convinced yet mistaken conscience is irreproachable requires an amendment. We must observe how the conviction came into being. There are cases in which the error could have

---

prejudices, which explains why individuals and peoples have held different things to be good or bad at various times—an objection frequently brought against the doctrine of evidence and the general validity of moral principles. Where this has happened, people have been guided no longer by evidence, but by blind impulses and desires and by 'hand-me-downs' in the broadest sense, that is, by what from their earliest childhood has been impressed upon them as being right or wrong. The 'inner voice' speaks directly only in certain very simple cases (cf. Pt. II, chap. 2, sect. 53, and chap. 4, sect. 61); in more complicated situations we must call in deductions and considerations of probability to our aid. Consequently there are advantages to a firmly established moral system such as is contained in the decalogue, which makes these deductions easier for people and relieves them of the burden of relatively complicated deliberations.

been recognized, and corrected, if some thought had been given to it. Not every error is incorrigible, and only those that are prevent the addition of further guilt. And we also have a duty to learn to form moral judgments—a duty, to be sure, of which those who are forever talking of liberal education appear to know very little. Many so-called highbrows are moral simpletons. The more easily our conscience is deluded by passion, the more effort we ought to put into forming and educating our moral judgment. The study of the sophistry of the passions is a fairly important part of logic. Anyone who is able to profit from the study of it will not neglect to review from time to time his moral convictions with an eye to possible prejudices.

99. *The doubting and the perplexed conscience*

Everything is clear enough up to this point, but what happens when our conscience harbours doubts?

Let us set aside the question whether a certain pronouncement of conscience is right or wrong and concentrate only upon the case where a person ought to act but is in genuine doubt as to whether a particular act is permissible or not. Is he permitted to make a choice at all in this situation?

Here, too, opinion is divided. Some people answer in the affirmative on the grounds that we would otherwise be extremely limited; complete certainty, they point out, is seldom allotted to a human judgment, and less often in moral matters than anywhere else. Consequently Aristotle held that a less exact form of proof was acceptable in ethics than in, say, mathematics. Conceptual precision is to be demanded, he said, only to the extent the material permits, and here we cannot aim at anything more than probability.

Others say, 'No!'; we cannot do good on the grounds of a bad conscience.

Once again the difficulty can, I believe, be resolved by drawing a distinction. The doubt cannot centre upon subjective morality, but only upon objective morality. Whether the act will result in more benefit than harm cannot be foreseen with anything more than probability, and at that it is often not overwhelming. However, if it is certain that no greater probability is to be sought or that we have no time for lengthy meditation but must act immediately, then the subjective morality of the presumably more beneficial act is assured. In spite of a lack of objective certainty, we can then act with full conviction of our morality.

Even when no one of the possible decisions is more likely to be beneficial than any of the others, and yet it is certain that one must be made in order to save the supreme practical good from harm, the subjective morality of any one of them is beyond doubt. Descartes made this point: 'Even where the probability is the same for several things, we must make a decision in favour of one, and then, for purposes of carrying it out, treat it no longer as dubious, but as true and certain; for the rule that we follow in so acting is right.'* Suppose I am expected at a certain time in connection with a matter of importance. I have just enough time to take the shortest of six routes, but I cannot discover which is the shortest. So I set out upon one of them with a probability of 5/6 that I have taken the wrong one. But since I must go, I possess the certainty of being subjectively beyond reproach.

The person who acts in this way will, incidentally, turn out on the average taking actions that are objectively moral as well.

None the less there are cases in which, for want of good sense, a person fails to attain to certainty concerning the subjective morality of his action. His conscience is in a state of perplexity. Everything seems wrong, no matter what possibility presents itself to him. Whether he does this or that or nothing at all, he thinks, there will be some wrong with which he must reproach himself. But any of these accusations will certainly be inappropriate, for the fact is that neither his action nor his inaction is determined by a morally relevant distinction, and therefore they are indifferent from the moral standpoint.

*Brentano appears to have the following passage in mind: 'And thus since often enough in the actions of life no delay is permissible, it is very certain that, when it is beyond our power to discern the opinions which carry most truth, we should follow the most probable; and even although we notice no greater probability in the one opinion than in the other, we at least should make up our minds to follow a particular one and afterwards consider it as no longer doubtful in its relationship to practice, but as very true and very certain, . . .' See *Discourse on the Method*, Part III, in *The Philosophical Works of Descartes* (trans. Haldane and Ross, Dover Publications), vol. I, p. 96.

100. *Defective theories concerning possible ways to reach an opinion in cases of doubt as to whether an action is permissible*

1. In the past moral philosophers, and particularly theologians, occupied themselves frequently with the following question. Suppose a man is in doubt as to whether a certain action is permissible or not. He does not know whether there is a precept forbidding it, yet the possibility that there is does not seem to him to be out of the question, which makes him uneasy. What ought he to do?

If we take a look at actual practice, we see that people take a variety of attitudes. Some hold themselves as strongly obligated as they would be had they clearly recognized a precept, on the grounds that we ought never to risk transgressing against our duty and ought, therefore, to refrain from action if we harbour even the slightest suspicion that it is forbidden. But others think, 'What I don't know won't hurt me! As long as I am not sure of a law, it does not exist for me. I shall do what suits me best and will continue to do so as long as I am not sure that it is morally forbidden.'

In the first case we speak of a scrupulous conscience, in the second of a lax conscience.

2. Theorists, too, have taken hold of this question and constructed various systems, according to the position taken.

(*a*) Rigorism, or absolute tutiorism: We ought always to decide in accordance with the suspected precept, even when there is only a very slight possibility that it exists and there are far more substantial, although not perfectly decisive considerations on the side of making a free choice.

(*b*) Modified tutiorism: We are permitted to make a decision to act freely if the probability that it is all right to do so is overwhelming and the probability that the precept exists is minute.

(*c*) Probabiliorism: We ought to decide in favour of the precept if the opposing probability is not significantly greater.

(*d*) Equiprobabilism: We are permitted to decide in favour of acting freely when there is just as much, or almost as much, to be said for doing so as against.

(*e*) Modified probabilism: We may opt for freedom even in cases where probability speaks far more strongly on the side of the law, provided only that the considerations on the other side are not so slight as to be insignificant. Defenders of this view cite instances in which a majority of lawyers or moralists speak in favour of the precept, yet an eminent authority speaks against it.

(*f*) Laxism: We have no obligation unless there is strong proof of it. (Representatives of this view are quite extreme. Even when it seems to me that the existence of a proscription has been proven, if a single authority disputes this view I may tell myself, 'I am as likely to be wrong as he is', and decide in favour of acting freely.)

3. The expressions used in this classification do not have sharp boundaries, with the exception of absolute tutiorism and laxism, so that there are in addition to these two not just four systems, but a vast variety of systems shading imperceptibly into one another. Now, which is the right system?

In my opinion they are all wrong. All? How is that possible? Is there room for still other solutions?

Answer: The question itself is wrongly formulated. It places law in opposition to freedom, but that is not how matters stand. We are always bound by a law, namely the most general precept that we ought to choose what is best; i.e. that one among the things attainable which seems likely to promote the supreme practical good the most. Thus any doubt we may harbour will always refer only to the circumstances, to the question whether this or that line of action is more likely to have the most beneficial results. If it were certain that one would be more beneficial, that one would be the law. We may say neither that it is permissible to give preference to the act less likely to be beneficial nor that the act more likely to be beneficial must always be chosen. We cannot say the first, because even when the same benefit would result from either action, the choice between them is like a choice between goods of unequal value whenever the prospects of attainment are not the same. And we cannot say the second, because the prospects of attaining the greater benefit may be uncertain.

No doubt the right thing to do is to act in such a way that the greater benefit would result if everyone always acted that way. Even if this seems no more than probable at the moment, that is enough to allow us to recognize with certainty that the action is moral and consequently determines the precept for the case at hand.

4. If, then, all these 'systems' are useless, we are justified in

asking how people strayed off into these blind alleys in the first place. Two errors have played a role:

(*a*) Most thinkers who laboured at the construction of these systems held the erroneous view that freedom from law is a good, whereas it is in fact quite the opposite. Moral action is a good, as is the knowledge that this action is the most beneficial. The same is true respecting judgment and its subjugation to the laws of logic. How could freedom be a good here, when it would only be freedom to indulge in nonsense!

(*b*) The second mistake was that of not setting out from the fundamental law of ethics, the law of the supreme practical good, but reckoning from the first with a multiplicity of precepts by treating positive laws of the state, the church, and religion as though they were ultimate precepts. Laws of this kind may be poorly formulated, so that under certain circumstances they lead to torment instead of good deeds. Then, of course, freedom from them is to be desired. But this is unthinkable with a genuine precept of ethics or logic.

Incidentally, it was truth itself that necessitated corrections in these systems and permitted the emergence of eclectic thinkers who ferreted out of each one what seemed useful to them, taking into account the range and importance of false decisions. Papal decisions, too, played a role here and were made wisely. Indeed, it has been the strength of the Roman church, over against the Eastern church, that its decisions have not been grounded upon speculative principles but have been limited to the repudiation of extravagant conclusions.

PART FIVE

INDIVIDUAL MORAL PRECEPTS

I

The Value of Moral Precepts of Intermediate Generality

---

101. *There cannot be individual precepts*

We have become acquainted with a universally valid precept, applicable over the entire realm of our activity: We are never to place an inferior value upon what is best for the greatest possible sphere that falls under our influence—indeed, we are always to be guided by a regard for this, the supreme practical good. And we have also remarked the existence of other precepts of a lesser generality, some quite particular, to be applied to the individual case.

These precepts result from the variety of circumstances in which we find ourselves. Here one act, there another, will bring about the best for the greatest sphere. But, as we have already noted, ethics cannot present such individual rules. A book that included all of them would have to be bigger than the biggest library. Ethics should avoid the treatment of individual cases, yet, on the other hand, it cannot content itself with just the one, most general rule, leaving the actor to undertake the entire task of deducing from it the individual precept in every single case.

102. *Casuistry*

This process of deduction is no doubt easier for some people than for others, and the extent of our training and practice is a highly significant factor in our success. That is why the various schools of morals thought it worthwhile to train their students in the art of making deductions by teaching them so-called casuistry. There is moral casuistry and legal casuistry; both are useful, although both have their pitfalls. Some people imagine that casuistry can exhaust the whole of reality and, relying upon their judgment to this effect, are inclined to force any new case that bears a certain resemblance to past cases into the same mould. To cope with this inconvenience, some thinkers have drawn up rules of intermediate generality, deducing them from the most general rules and taking into account the circumstances that are most frequently influential.

103. *Rules of intermediate generality*

Some of the rules of intermediate generality are formulated as precepts for everyone, others as precepts for particular classes, as duties pertaining to a certain station. But even those that are addressed to everyone do not apply universally, without exception, for it is possible for them to conflict—in which case inspection of the most general rule of all must be decisive. The Bible offers us some nice illustrations of this principle. Take the confrontation between Jesus and the Pharisees, who were thoroughgoing casuists. Jesus had no interest in all their petty rules, and when they asked him whether it was permissible to do such and such a thing on the Sabbath, he countered, 'Does man exist for the sake of the Sabbath, or the Sabbath for the sake of man?' But when he was asked directly about the supreme commandment, he replied, 'Love God above all things, and your neighbour as yourself. On these two commandments hangs all the law.'

104. *The value of these rules*

Attention to what is generally best diminishes the value of the individual rule, yet does not annihilate it. Since such a rule is correct for the majority of cases, I will, in following it, act correctly most of the time, even when I do not have time to investigate the best attainable under the circumstances. But where there are conflicts, and when I have the time to undertake deliberations, my work is simplified by the possession of rules of intermediate generality. My obligation to review and compare the few considerations is frequently still greater as a consequence.

II

The Traditional Classifications of Moral Precepts

To every precept of intermediate generality corresponds a class of duties, which includes in turn classes of graduated generality. Hence the task emerges of constructing these in a suitable manner. Moralists and moral philosophers are not in agreement as to how this task is to be carried out. For example:

The oldest scheme for classifying duties is that of the four cardinal virtues: prudence (*prudentia*), courage (*fortitudo*), temperance (*temperantia*), and justice (*justitia*). This division dates back as far as Plato and is the basis for his practical ethics and his political theory. Later on the Church adopted the Platonic division, as did some philosophers: e.g., Alexander Bain. More recent Christian moralists maintain the division into duties towards God, duties towards others, and duties towards oneself. Some, particularly theological moralists, lay down the Ten Commandments, the Mosaic decalogue, as the basis for classifying duties.

The first scheme mentioned is based on *virtues*, which tacitly assumes that the classification of duties must correspond to that of virtues, i.e. of good dispositions. However, this is not initially certain; indeed, more precise consideration will show it to be false. Virtues are moral dispositions that are preserved in the face of strong counter-motives (temptations). But duties need not always be confronted with counter-motives. Kant was probably assuming that they are when he stated that action in accordance

309

with duties is always bound up with difficulties. However, action in accordance with duty can undoubtedly be cheerfully undertaken from the first.[41]

The second division is a different matter, yet objections have also been raised against it—that is, against the first part of it—and not without good reason. For do we really have duties to God in the same sense that we have duties to ourselves and to others, a duty, say, not to hurt God, or to promote God? Either of these is unthinkable. Neither good nor evil can befall God. Evidently the members within the divisions are not properly coordinated.

Someone might maintain that it is a duty to love and honour God. But this is not a duty towards him in the sense intended, but rather a duty towards ourselves, since love and preference experienced as being correct, and consequently also the love of God as the highest good, are goods that are realized within our own soul. God is not a practical good for us, but the love of God is, and it is one that overrides all others. It is a duty, but not a duty towards God. We could also say that showing respect towards God, praising his perfection, avoiding disrespectful discussion concerning him, and disseminating the knowledge of him are not only duties towards ourselves, but also towards our neighbour, inasmuch as our acting in accordance with them will lead our neighbour to cherish noble feelings towards the supreme and most lovable being.

Jeremy Bentham retained the last two members of this division in his classification of duties, distinguishing:

(*a*) duties towards ourselves, which correspond to the virtue of prudence (*prudentia*) and which we possess to the extent that our happiness depends upon our own behaviour, from

(*b*) duties towards others, which arise inasmuch as the interests of others are promoted, damaged, or otherwise affected by our action.

We can show regard for the happiness of our neighbour in two ways: negatively, by avoiding any infringement upon it (honesty), and positively, by endeavouring to promote it (charity in the broadest sense of the word). Taken together, these can be described as the virtue of justice (*justitia*).

We find that in Bentham, too, duties and virtues are co-

[41] This section has been expanded in accordance with F. Hillebrand's lectures on ethics.

ordinated, but since the duties are here made the standard of the virtues the effect upon our question is not so great.

We have duties towards animals, too. Bentham subsumes them under his second class, whereas some thinkers have distinguished them as a special class of duties. Hence it is that, e.g. Pierre Janet, who also retains the concept of duties towards God, comes to have a division consisting of four members.

Obviously, Bentham's subsidiary division is into precepts and prohibitions. This distinction is made by other thinkers as well, and some make it the primary distinction.

A number of other attempts have been made to classify duties, but no scientific moral philosopher has made such serious efforts as Bentham did to establish a truly rational division. He had in mind the aims of jurisprudence. Pure philosophers have usually avoided the problem, as though investigating it were a task unworthy of philosophy. In modern times, Locke, Leibniz, and Mill have been exceptions, but all of them were politicians as well, as were their forerunners in ancient times, Plato and Aristotle.

Bentham points out the correlation between prescriptions and offences, presenting positive rules within the classification of offences.[42]

He, too, held the best within the greatest possible sphere to be the ultimate principle. Yet his peculiar formulation of the best—the greatest possible amount of pleasure combined with the least possible degree of pain—has a detrimental effect upon his classification.

In the place where he goes into the matter most thoroughly, he thinks of the greatest sphere as being the state, the good of which legislation is supposed to serve. This does not quite correspond to the aim of a classification based upon our fundamental principle, yet it is not seriously disturbing, since Bentham requires that the state be dedicated to the welfare of everyone. Nothing can benefit or harm the community which could not benefit or harm one or

[42] Cf. Bentham's *Deontology, or the Science of Morality*, ed. Bowring (1843), and *Traité de la Législation Civile et Pénale*, ed. Dumont [and trans. into English as *Theory of Legislation* by Hildreth (London: Trübner, 1864). The German editor has given the pages in the French editions—221 ff. for the *Deontology* and vol. II, pp. 62 ff. for the *Theory*—but I was unable to locate either of these.]

more individuals within this community. This thought may appear banal, but it is necessary to express it again today, for there is no lack of thinkers who wish to separate the state and the individual by viewing the state as an organism unto itself, as a higher level object possessing its own particular good and evil, apart from the happiness of the individual.

The persons injured by an offence are either assignable or not assignable, according to Bentham.

When they are assignable, the injured individual is either the offender himself, or someone else.

When they are not assignable, either they are to be found within a certain sphere within the state in that they, say, occupy a certain position, belong to a certain occupation, or live in a certain district, or they are distributed quite indefinitely among the individuals of which the state is comprised, without belonging to any more specific group.

This disjunction is exhaustive and produces four classes of offences:

1. Private offences; i.e., those that, in the first instance, affect assignable individuals other than the offender.

2. Personal (self-regarding) offences, or offences against one-self. These are acts that in the first instance are detrimental to the offender and no one else, unless as a consequence of the evil that he inflicts upon himself. (For instance, the father of a family who ruins his own health by excesses may ruin the health of his family as well.)

3. Semi-public offences, which can be detrimental to persons who are not assignable but comprise a smaller group than the state; e.g., a trade union or a religious sect. The offence is directed against a portion of the community.

4. Offences which are detrimental to an indefinite number of individuals who are not assignable, or which threaten them with a greater or lesser danger, although no one person appears initially to run a greater risk of the danger than another. These are public offences, or offences against the state.

Subdivisions:

This four-part division intersects with another four-part (or six-part, as the case may be) division in which Bentham distinguishes offences according to the respects in which people suffer injury. The happiness of man is conditioned by a number of things. It depends upon the condition of the person himself and upon the external objects surrounding him. Thus two kinds of injury are possible. A person may suffer from an offence by being injured in his own person or in something which stands in a certain relation to him, either things or other persons: things of which he makes use, as being his own property, and persons from whom he derives advantage because they are prepared to render him certain services.

This readiness to render service may have various grounds. It may be based simply upon the general bonds that tie men to one another, or it may be based upon *special* relations that bring certain individuals close together.

These closer ties constitute a species of fictitious, incorporeal property that is called our condition. (Conditions consist of the relation to our spouse, child, servant, professional colleague, fellow member of a political party, and so forth.)

Benevolence is the name given to the readiness to render one another service that is based upon the universal bond among men. To be the object of this willingness is most auspicious, and our chances of becoming such an object also constitute a sort of fictitious property, our so-called honour, or reputation. It is a store of funds, as it were, that constitute a guarantee that we will receive free and gratuitous services upon the basis of benevolence.

A person can only be injured by means of acts that affect him in one of the four afore-mentioned respects. From this fact we can derive the existence of four species of private offences—or six, if we include certain complex cases: (1) offences against the person; (2) offences against his property; (3) offences against his condition; (4) offences against his reputation; (5) offences against a person and his property together; and (6) offences against a person and his reputation together. (A simple offence is one that is detrimental to the individual in only one of the respects mentioned here.)

These six classes combine with the preceding four-member division in such a way that each of the first four has six subdivisions included under it. For instance, a crime by means of which the offender inflicts evil upon himself can injure him in his person, his property, his good reputation, or his position in life.

I shall not further pursue Bentham's classification, in all its carefully worked-out detail. For no matter how well it may answer the needs of lawyers, it leaves something to be desired for the moral philosopher. Aside from the aspects already touched upon, I am hindered from using it as the standard for a system of duties because its divisions are not based upon the principle I regard as fundamental. Consequently I am forced to attempt the construction of a classification from a new standpoint.

III

Variations in the Precept According to the Situation of the Actor

---

106. *The principle of the classification of precepts*

1. In the construction of a classification, the most important question concerns the principle of division. It all depends upon the end being pursued: zoologists place whales among the mammals, while legislators in charge of hunting and fishing consider them fish.

When speaking of the purpose of classifying duties, we may have either a remote or an immediate end in mind. The former will be the promotion of the supreme practical good, the latter the derivation of the action suitable in a particular case from the idea of the supreme practical good and from the supreme law that it ought to be promoted. With the help of the classification, this derivation should be abbreviated and secured.

How would we go about forming a judgment if our only clue were that supreme universal rule? We would have to endeavour to gain an overall view of just what lies either directly or indirectly within our power and then make a comparative evaluation of the results, in so far as it is possible to survey them. The mode of behaviour from which the best results can be expected is the supreme practical good, the best end in the case at hand, and the means that lead to it are the right means. (Needless to say, the degree of certainty with which the results can actually be expected to follow is to be accounted a factor.)

2. The task of shortening the derivation is identical with the task of identifying the precepts which always, or usually, protect

us against making gross errors of judgment. The best way to approach the task seems to be to figure out the main differences between the various situations in which we are called upon to make a decision, i.e. to distinguish from one another the cases in which our sphere of influence, and consequently the supreme practical good, is essentially different.

I have spoken of essential differences. That is, I am speaking not of cases in which the same sphere, which is to be reckoned with in a certain manner, comes into consideration, here to a lesser extent, there to a greater, but rather of those which involve different spheres, which in every case are to be dealt with in a different manner and which require, indirectly, that the other spheres be treated differently. (Compare, for instance, the life of a Robinson Crusoe with life in a society.)

3. From this viewpoint, there are five conceivable classes of cases.

I. The sphere in which the actor is able to bring about good and evil does not extend beyond himself and also not beyond the present time; i.e., it is limited to his present welfare.

II. The sphere remains isolated in the same way, but the actor's own future also comes under consideration.

III. The future of others is also to be taken into account.

IV. The present welfare of others is to be taken into account, but they include only beings who lack reason or are at least not fully responsible, such as animals and children.

V. Finally, there is the case in which the actor's sphere of influence is a society of rational beings. This is the only kind of case that actually occurs, but it is so complicated that it requires analysis before we can place ourselves in a situation from which we can survey all the aspects and evaluate their significance. The best way to make this analysis is by means of the fiction that the actual case is composed of these sorts of simple cases. In pursuing this course, we make use of a method very similar to that which physicists, physiologists, and political economists employ in order to master the complications of reality.

4. Let us consider each case in itself.

I. Our method demands beginning with this case. It offers no difficulties, for we do not have to consider a multiplicity of spheres of influence, but simply the present welfare of the actor. The goods that can be realized in this case affect only his inner being. Obviously, the thing to do in this situation is to carry out for the moment some noble activity, and, as Aristotle remarked, the most sublime activity is to become elevated to divine height in knowledge and love. The idea that the world owes its existence not to accident and to blind material forces but to infinite wisdom and love, which lead it to loftier and loftier goals, fills the soul with a kind of bliss that is most closely related to the blessedness of God.

II. Even the second case is significantly more complicated. Along with his own present welfare, the actor is now to combine a regard for his own future. The present is to be understood as extending up to the next occasion upon which he decides what to do with regard to the supreme practical good, which is composed out of partial present and future goods. The actor must take care of both, but in different ways. With respect to the future, a certain restraint is called for, though often not carried out. But of course positive care and attention is needed, too, and this in turn partially relates to one's own person and partially to the surrounding circumstances.

1. Care of one's own person is of two kinds:

(*a*) Care of our inner selves; i.e. of our spiritual dispositions and accomplishments, be they of a higher order—aesthetic, scientific, or ethical—or of a lower order—memory, emotions, and acuity of perception.

(*b*) Care of our exterior; i.e. of our physical health, strength, and skilfulness.

2. Care with regard to the circumstances surrounding us pertains to our possessions: food, tools, and whatever assists us in simplifying and beautifying life and in carrying on cheerfully noble activities.

To some extent this care can be concentrated upon doing away with dangers and obstacles. Yet we must be cautious here, in order not to violate the duty of exercising restraint. If it burdens his spirit too heavily with homesickness, it is permissible for a person in a foreign land to destroy the image he has of his homeland in order to steel himself against such emotions, yet it would be wrong for him to cut off his retreat before being sure he could make a success of remaining. And if he does free himself of the image, there will remain open to him other, less enervating means of preserving his impressions of his native land from total obliteration.

No restraint is called for regarding the present. The goods of the present, however, are only to be promoted in so far as they do not clash with regard for the future, which takes precedence over it. For that very reason we are sometimes more concerned with what is useful than with what is intrinsically good, but to some extent these two factors can easily be reconciled, for moral care and attention is itself a good, as are other well-ordered mental activities, while on the other hand noble activity itself is in turn a means of cultivating good dispositions for the future.

III. The third case introduces yet another complication. A new sphere is to be considered, in addition to our own future and present: the future of other living beings. But it is easy to accommodate this factor. The future of others is to be regarded in the same manner as our own, except that we have at our disposal more means for attending to the latter than to the former; e.g. exer-- cising, inherent dispositions, etc. Consequently it is my duty first and foremost to take care of myself and, within this sphere, to pay particular regard to my own future.

But if restraint is demanded even within the personal sphere, it is called for all the more with respect to others. We must guard with the greatest care against indiscreet interference, even on benevolent grounds. Parents trespass against this precept whenever they autocratically and without being asked subject the happiness of their children to their own plans, particularly in matters of choosing an occupation and a spouse. They should restrict themselves to playing the role of a natural adviser.

IV. The fourth case adds to the complexity by bringing in the present welfare of other beings, even if they are only such as possess no reason or but a small amount: animals, small children, and others without the capacity for moral responsibility.

Animals are to be regarded as much with an eye to my own advantage as to theirs. In the former respect, they are to be treated in the same way as inanimate objects: I avoid any danger with which they threaten me and use them as a means to my own well-being, thus placing myself in the position of a master over them. However, they are living beings who possess feelings and, consequently, interests of their own, so that I am at the same time their guardian—and here again I am called upon to exercise restraint. Despite my superior intelligence, I am not able to be a perfect judge of what will cause them pleasure and pain.

Cases involving children are of greater significance. As regards my own advantage I have nothing to fear from them; on the contrary, they are in danger of being exploited, for instance, by being sent out to work prematurely. In the past, the want of parents and the greed of employers brought about in some countries conditions in which even five-year-olds were burdened with heavy labour. They were employed in factories, and even in mines, yoked together like animals, and yet their exploiters were people who edified themselves on Sundays by reading the Bible. The further removed they are from the full use of their reason, the more children require the attentive guidance of grown-ups. For even if they are more or less incapable of bearing responsibility now, they will later attain the same status as we have at present, and it is possible to start forming already some dispositions that will eventually be advantageous. Our aim, then, should be to keep them from everything that will restrict and interfere with their development.

Similarly, it is best to leave to each person the responsibility for his own nourishment. And it has proven to be most beneficial to the general good to allow any person to retain as his own a plot of unowned land that he discovers.

A simple regard for the supreme practical good makes the limiting of spheres of influence appear justified, even without positive law or external compulsion. Where no boundaries are set, society descends into a chaos incomparably worse than the isolation of Robinson Crusoe's existence. But where this regard holds sway it leads inevitably to the insight that everyone must in a special way hold something as a possession in the most extended sense, which embraces more than merely external goods.

IV

Duties of Justice and Duties of Love

---

107. *Natural law and positive law*

1. In a society made up of rational beings, everyone could attain the insight disclosed at the end of the previous chapter simply by his own reflections. This process would not even require understanding among the individuals, although it in fact never happens that communication is impossible. Even without a mutual agreement each person can be led by reflection to the insight that things will work out better if this person administers this sphere, that person another. We would then have a state in which natural law existed without positive law, an arrangement concerning property which, in the strictest possible sense, would not be created by positive legislation. It is not at all necessary to have recourse to inherent concepts of principles in order to establish the validity of a natural law, for this is properly defined as that mode of dividing spheres of influence that shows itself to be suitable upon the grounds of purely moral considerations. (The definition given by Roman lawyers—*jus, quod natura omnia animalia docuit* [The law that nature has taught to all creatures]—lacked the advantage of clarity.)

2. But this is a situation we have dreamed up, not one that actually occurs. In administering various affairs, not everyone is guided by a regard for the supreme practical good. And even if every person wished to be, not all would have sufficient insight to demarcate the various spheres of influence in the way most profitable to what is universally best. Thus dissension would be un-

avoidable even if good will reigned on all hands. (Consider, for instance, the various possible rights of inheritance.) Disputes can only be avoided by positive determination brought about through some sort of understanding and agreement, along with an obligation to hold to it.

In this manner the disadvantages arising from living with other people are not only resolved but transformed into an overwhelming advantage. Not only does the determination reached through mutual agreement sharpen the formerly hazy boundary; the communication of each party's aims makes possible a mutual retreat from spheres that would otherwise fall on the other side of the boundary. The various individuals promise to render each other services and unite in undertakings that would be too much for any single person. Joining forces and working harmoniously together is a tremendous source of additional power.

What we have described here is a state under positive law (which we can think of, for the moment, as having a purely moral sanction and not being secured by force). Natural law requires positive law and demands that such of its stipulations as accord with nature be held sacred. A lack of positive legal stipulations determining the natural law more precisely would violate natural law itself.

3. But our action is not guided exclusively by morality. A variety of motives lead us astray, and consequently it is necessary to have not only more definite laws concerning property but also stronger guarantees that they will be obeyed. The more important portions of positive law must be supported by certain powers compelling compliance. Natural law demands not only positive determination but also a force that punishes transgressions. And this is the actual situation; it is not the internal sanction of our natural inclinations, but rather the external sanctions that secure positive law.

In the nature of the case, then, there are three levels of law:

(1) the pure natural law,
(2) positive law with a purely moral sanction, and
(3) positive law with an external sanction.

4. But I must warn the reader against a possible misunderstanding: this is not the historical sequence. Quite the contrary: we have assumed moral maturity and insight in our construction and set forth the factors out of which and the standpoint from

which the man of moral insight would construct the idea of positive law as we actually find it. The actual historical development does not start from moral insight but from egoism. Egoism creates arrangements that are in some ways similar to those promoted by morality, but the guiding spirit is different. Egoism, too, leads to a separation of territories, frequently puzzling them out with great legal acuity. Logic is generally accorded a lofty position in these proceedings; the resulting positive ordinances, however, often conflict with ethics, which asserts itself only gradually. From the standpoint of the *beati possidentes*, the holders of wealth and power, Roman law is a masterpiece of logic, but it does rather less justice to morality. And practice is frequently far worse than the law.

The moralization of law proceeds only gradually, and it is far from being completed. Much that is found in positive law is a leftover from premoral arrangements. In the domain of international relations, particularly, we are only beginning to have a legal order that is moral, and even these weak beginnings are still encountering strong resistance. Men who advocate morality within this sphere have difficulty gaining a hearing and are often treated with hostility and disdain.

5. I should not neglect to mention that it is of great advantage to a system of law to be backed up by force, even if it is not in accord with natural law. For then we can say that, where they conflict, natural law demands that we follow the positive law. Socrates was so thoroughly imbued with this notion that he scornfully refused to flee, although he was aware that he had been unjustly sentenced. To be sure, there is a limit to the extent to which natural law is to be subordinated to positive law. It is possible to go too far, and the question is whether Socrates did not do so. Certainly, it is better to have bad laws than none at all, to have an unjust order than anarchy. Indeed, that is why morality bids us obey even bad laws, endowing them with a temporary sanction, as it were. On the other hand, resistance becomes a moral duty where the evil involved is too great. At those times, we should bow to the precept that we are to obey God more than man; i.e. we are to give heed to our natural knowledge of what is morally right and to shun injustice, even when the positive powers stand behind it. Under such circumstances the man of good moral counsel withdraws his obedience from the laws until they are replaced by laws

that deserve it. However, I do not mean to plead for the violent resistance of the revolutionary so much as for the passive inflexibility of the martyr.

108. *Duties of justice and duties of love*

1. We have culled from our various reflections the basis for the essential division of duties. We must distinguish:

(*a*) duties of justice; i.e. duties relating to mine and thine. These are the duties which consist in observing the boundaries of the spheres in which other people's wills have dominion. To be more specific, they are duties of restraint towards what it is someone else's business to administer and of fulfilling actions that he has a right to demand of me at the time he requests them.

(*b*) simple duties of love (towards the supreme practical good). They bid me always to order in accordance with the supreme practical good those affairs that fall within my own legal domain, which I may administer without outside interference.

Several simple consequences can be deduced.

(α) No one can inflict an injustice upon himself. We can speak only of something analogous to this, for instance, when, by hesitating where he should not, a person damages his own future in much the same way that he might infringe upon someone else's legal sphere.

(β) *Volenti non fit injuria* [Injustice is not brought about through willing]. An act of will may be uncharitable, but it cannot be unjust. None the less we can speak of something analogous to injustice with respect to someone else's future, particularly when the person in question is still in a state in which he cannot be held fully responsible.

(γ) We cannot, in the strict sense, do any injustice to the dead, though, again, we can regard them uncharitably. It may be immoral to take an unkind attitude towards the dead, but it cannot be called unjust. It is despicable to malign the dead, but it can only be an injustice to those he left behind, whom it affects. He himself no longer possesses a private domain or property.

(δ) It is also impossible to do God an injustice, for it is impossible to alter the domain of his power.

2. The distinction between duties of justice and duties of love

dates from ancient times, and its significance is generally recognized. However, the concepts have not always been determined as I have attempted to determine them here. Some have been of the opinion that duties of justice were those formulated in positive law. But this is too narrow on the one hand, since some duties of justice have not been formulated, and too broad on the other, for some positive laws are positively unjust—so unjust, in fact, that they are not morally binding, in spite of having the force of law (cf. Antigone).

Others say that duties of justice are what positive law ought to be, endowed with the sanction of punishment against transgressors. It is correct to say that anything the positive law ought to contain is a duty of justice, but the reverse is not true. There are several good reasons for not including every duty of justice in the positive legal code and for not threatening every infringement thereof with punishment. It is not a good thing for the law to have extremely extensive powers. Furthermore, the resulting situation would lead to an inconceivable quantity of legal cases and ultimately to a weakening of respect for the law, for many of the violations could not be dealt with effectively.[43]

Still others think that duties of justice consist of whatever is found in positive law and ought to be sanctioned by punishment, except in the presence of the afore-mentioned factors. Here too, then, the desire for punishment becomes an essential criterion of duties of justice, as opposed to mere duties of love. This concept may well be equivalent to that of the duties of justice; it is really true that no duties of love are objects of the law, since it is not the law, but the owner, who has jurisdiction over his property. It must also be conceded that respect for the boundaries of other people's property ought to be supported by effective threats of punishment, in so far as this is possible. Nevertheless, these concepts are not identical after all. That the wish to inflict punishment is justified does not constitute the nature of duties of justice but is, rather, a consequence of their particular character. This determination of the concept also fails to indicate that there must always be some person whose rights are infringed upon

---

[43] Concerning the concept of positive law, see O. Kraus, 'Rechtsphilosophie und Jurisprudenz', *Zeitschrift für die gesamte Strafwissenschaft*, vol. XXIII (1902).

by an offence against the law. For this reason some thinkers have added the stipulation that a duty of justice is one, transgressions against which injure specific persons. Yet the determination is still defective. The factors in this complicated concept have been arbitrarily strung together, whereas in our concept—if I am not mistaken—full justice is done, with fewer intricacies, to the connection between the essence of duties of justice and their peculiarities.

3. That the boundaries of justice have basically to do with the sphere of influence for the individual will has also been pointed out by noted lawyers, such as Windscheid and Arndts. Arndts defines justice as 'the dominion of the will with respect to an object', Windscheid, as 'a certain act of will which the law declares shall be realized in preference to any other.' Ihering tried to reduce this definition to absurdity, but in a simple-minded way. The aforementioned lawyers are only dealing with duties of justice and not embarking upon the moral question of how, and to what end, the individual ought to employ his sphere of influence. But Ihering presents their view as though they held that the ultimate end and supreme good at which the legal system aims were the act of will as such and the pleasure we take in it, the joy of exercising our own will. In his *Geist des römischen Rechtes* (vol. III, chap. 1, p. 320), he writes: 'According to this conception of matters, the whole of civil law is nothing more than an arena within which the will may be exercised. The will is the organ through which men enjoy justice, which pleasure consists in experiencing the glory of power, the satisfaction of carrying out an act of will; e.g. arranging a mortgage or bringing a suit, and thus getting oneself inscribed as a legal personage. What a miserable little thing the will would be if its proper realm of activity were simply the inferior and more prosaic regions of the law.' This would indeed be a foolish view, but whoever maintained any such thing? The lawyers coming under attack had only the immediate aims of legislation in mind when they formulated their concepts and described its task as being the limiting of spheres of influence; they were not concerned with its ultimate and supreme end, which is nothing other than what is generally best. They may not have felt it necessary to point this out explicitly, but they did not deny it in any way. Ihering is fighting with a mere chimera.

Furthermore, the definition he suggests is a poor substitute:

'Justice is the legal guarantee of pleasure'. Certainly not! It is, rather, that arrangement of matters that allows the individual to promote the supreme practical good, the general best, freely and without interference. It is a grave error to believe that whatever falls within the boundaries of my rights is thereby simply left at the disposal of my egoism. Even within this sphere, I am merely the manager of the realm of power that has been entrusted to me, and I have no business exploiting the treasure placed in my hands for the purposes of my own pleasure; I ought, rather, to employ it in the service of the supreme practical good. The whole of my personal and material property is merely held in trust for this, the crowning good. Clearly it is the critic who has committed the gravest error here: what Arndts and Windscheid say is merely incomplete, but Ihering's assertions are altogether false.

109. *The priority of duties of justice over duties of love*

1. As a first step, the person about to act ought always to establish whether there is a duty of justice requiring him to perform some specific act at that time. Such services may become the property of someone else, as I already remarked. Where this has not happened, he turns to his own property, and there he finds the spheres we distinguished: the sphere of his own present welfare, and the sphere of his own future. The former demands that we carry out some worthy activity, except when we have a supervening need for respite; the latter requires internal as well as external preparation. However, I have already discussed all this and wish only to add that, living in the society of other rational beings, we must not only take care for the future but also for our present property —as, indeed, we must in a life of solitude.

Alongside the duty of taking precautions there are duties of restraint with respect to our own future. We must exercise special care when placing restrictions upon our personal freedom that will hold for the rest of our lives, but there are cases where this is necessary; e.g. when we undertake a marriage or choose our occupation. As the saying goes, 'Let him who binds himself forever take care, for folly is brief, but repentance long.'

2. After all this, we must give thought to duties of love towards other people, whether towards individuals or towards a greater collective whole. Occasionally they require the transfer of pro-

perty, whether by contract or promise, or simply as a present. Self-interest may have a voice here, too, not only when we relinquish property by contract but also when we give it away, for love is returned by love and good deeds by grateful reward.

3. On the other hand, we must consider other people's future as well as our own when cultivating our dispositions. When we are in training for an occupation, regard for our own dispositions becomes a duty of justice towards other people. We are future officials, doctors, teachers, technicians, and so forth, and as such we step outside the private sphere in which duties of self-love take precedence, for duties of justice also come into play.

4. Even in cases involving only duties of love, care for the welfare of others may take precedence; i.e. when disregarding it would be unduly detrimental to the supreme practical good. Under these conditions, self-sacrifice may become a duty.

110. *Subdivisions of the duties of justice*

1. Duties of justice are of two kinds, being either determined by positive stipulations or simply set forth by nature. The former can be separated again into those duties that are directly determined and those that are intertwined with such. (Shylock had the right to spill the blood that would inevitably have poured forth had he exacted his pound of flesh—but it is also true that the contract itself rested upon a *conditio turpis* [evil terms] that made it inherently invalid.)

2. For a practical survey of the duties of justice, it is most useful to divide them according to the object of our obligations. Following out Bentham's line of thought, we must say that a duty of justice binds us either to a physical or to a legal personage.

(*a*) Into the first category fall not only the cases concerning the property of a single individual but also those in which a violation is injurious to the property of several persons. In the latter case, we are faced with a complex duty of justice. We have the same kind of case when the persons injured can be grouped together as a class under a single concept, as long as they do not constitute a class that can only manage the object in question as a body. An orator who tells lies is infringing upon a duty of justice towards individuals, even though, taken together, they constitute an audience. Indeed, the class can be as big as an entire nation, or can even consist of the whole of mankind. Veracity with regard to scientific questions is a duty of justice towards everyone, as is also the duty not to propagate immoral principles.

(b) The second category is made up of duties of justice concerning respect for the property of a collective whole. Here lawyers posit a so-called legal person. Indeed, believing these fictitious entities to be useful, they go so far as to allow things to count as legal persons; they speak, e.g. of the property of St Stephan's. Strictly speaking, the owners of such property are the persons whose interests are involved, as members of the collective whole in question.

It sometimes happens that neither the individual nor the group is permitted to make decisions about the manner in which a piece of collective property is to be managed. In extreme cases, the objection of a single person can prevent action from being taken.

A legal personage is either one to whom the person acting belongs or one to whom this person stands in opposition, as not being a member of the collective whole.

The first of these two possible cases is particularly important and requires a number of considerations. A legal personage of which I am a member can be either a private group or the state or the church. It could be the whole of mankind only if there were an organization embracing this whole, in which case the management would lie solely in the hands of an international administration or government.

It would be a great blessing for mankind if there were such an organization, capable of preparing an end to the rule of might that holds sway among nations at the present time. It is quite wrong to be suspicious of efforts in this direction, even if it is not clear what they can accomplish, and by what means. In the history of mankind, great steps forward have not been taken overnight, and in any case an excessively rapid transition would cause too much turmoil. Developments up to this point would seem to indicate that some such organization will sooner or later come into being. There are already some conventions upon which the representatives of all nations have agreed and which can only be placed outside the realm of force by common consent, although as yet there is no power securing these, for lack of public spirit among the nations. Nevertheless, trying to break such a convention unilaterally would constitute a breach of justice, for the concept of justice does not involve merely power.[44]

3. Further distinctions can be made within each class, both that of duties of justice towards individuals and that of duties of justice towards legal personages.

Within the first class—and here we follow Bentham again—we can distinguish duties concerning an individual's property, duties concerning his reputation, and duties concerning his condition.

Similarly with the second class. The most extreme affliction a society, as such, can undergo is dissolution, which is analogous to the individual being robbed of his life. In the same way, the good organization of a legal personage can be compared to the good health of a physical person.

4. Duties of justice towards the state are, of course, of particular significance.

From our point of view, a foreign state is not essentially different from a private society.

Within our own state we must distinguish:

The merits of its existence and its internal organization. (The life of the state is its constitution, says Aristotle.)

Its possessions in the way of natural riches and the value of its works.

Its reputation.

Its condition.

With respect to the first, consideration is due to the external security of the state and the merits of the most essential of its internal institutions: the military, the judiciary, public instruction, etc. An offence against the state is, of course, also an offence against its sovereignty, but an offence against religion is not an offence against the state, for religions are included among private societies, at least in the advanced nations.

Among the riches of the state is included the size of its productive population. From this standpoint, emigration is a violation of the state's property. To be sure, however, Bentham was right in saying that every law forbidding emigration should commence

---

[44] Cf. the writings of O. Kraus concerning legal philosophy: *Das Recht zu strafen* (Stuttgart, 1911), and 'Rechtsphilosophie und Jurisprudenz', *Zeitschrift für die gesamte Strafwissenschaft*, vol. XXIII (1902).

as follows: 'We, who fail to understand the art of making our citizens happy, recognizing that if we permitted them to flee they would all emigrate to foreign lands with better governments, hereby forbid . . .'

As for the reputation of the state, it is possible to transgress against it in much the same way that we can injure the reputation of a private society. But not everyone who openly admits the harm his own state has inflicted upon other states is guilty of such a transgression. Quite the contrary, it may sometimes be our duty to declare our opposition to the whole world. For nothing does more injury to a guilty state in the eyes of the world than having all of its citizens identify with its guilt by trying to disguise it or by approving of it.

The person who, e.g. fails to fulfil his duty as an official or undermines national alliances, offends against the condition of the state.

All this has been merely a brief sketch.

5. One and the same act can infringe simultaneously upon several duties, in which case it is a complex offence. We may safely say that all offences are of this sort in real life.

I wish to select just one question from the theory of complex offences; viz. the question of private property, which ought to be examined critically from the standpoint of socialist and communist principles.

V

Complex Offenses

---

111. *Offenses against property; is private property morally justified?*

1. I have already declared that I consider property a moral necessity. It is in the interests of the supreme practical good for each being, particularly each being who can be held accountable, to have exclusive management of one certain sphere. Only in this way can communal life be a blessing. But which things ought to be individual property?

Certainly our own person, body and soul. But opinion is divided on the question of material property.

Some people defend an inflexible and unlimited right to property. According to Malthus, a person born into a world that is already occupied has not the slightest right to any portion of the available means of nourishment. He is superfluous in the world; no place has been set for him at the great feast of nature, and nature bids him depart. And some people actually carry out what Malthus expressed as a theory. Is it any wonder that the harshness of this theory and the cruelty of its practice have caused some to react and go to the other extreme? Beccaria calls property a terrible and by no means necessary right, and Proudhon says, 'Property is theft.'

The theory opposing property has found a large circle of followers. We are not, however, interested in the historical question concerning the extent to which this theory has been absorbed into the programme or the practice of so-called socialist or communist parties. We wish to confine ourselves to considering the advantages and disadvantages of private property without going into side issues.

It can be deduced simply from my mention of the distinction between duties of justice and duties of love that I hold material possessions to be necessary in the interests of the supreme practical good. It seems to me that the personal freedom and division of labour that promotes morality cannot be carried out unless the individual has the exclusive management of certain material property. This is a prerequisite even simply for the maintenance of the life of the body, but it is also necessary for the acquisition of spiritual goods.

This is not to say that my personal property is something absolute. Whatever is included in the sphere over which I have jurisdiction is entrusted to me for the purpose of serving the good. The moral order stands supreme over all arbitrary and positive orders, and they derive sanctions from it. From the moral point of view—which may never be set aside—I am an administrator rather than an absolute master, and as such I am bound, not by duties of justice, but by duties of love towards the supreme practical good.

2. Yet these duties of love are often neglected and infringed upon in a most inflammatory manner, particularly during eras in which the spirit of mankind has alienated itself from religious ideals and is intent only upon gain and pleasure. At such times loud voices are to be heard urging guarantees against the resultant uncertainty. They feel the mere existence of duties of love, unsupported by any power to enforce them, is not enough, and consequently they work to transform these duties into duties of justice, and to make them compulsory. They regard force as more effective than love and goodness against self-seeking and the greed for profit; the historical development of individual ownership has led everywhere, they say, to the exploitation of the small by the mighty and eventually to the exact opposite of what was supposed to be the aim of the institution of private property. The purpose, presumably, was the division of the available goods among everyone, but unlimited competition and exploitation have subsequently led all property to be concentrated in the hands of a few. Then away with the sovereignty of private property, they cry! Replace it with collective property! The state alone shall be the supreme owner; the individuals shall receive the means of

subsistence and of production from the state and shall be held accountable for them to the state.

The faction in question wishes, then, to change duties of love into duties of justice over as broad a sphere as possible.

They promise, also, that economic advantages will result from the elimination, or at any rate the fundamental limitation, of the sovereignty of private property. In union is found strength; if large private operations have shown themselves economically superior to small, then think how much more can be accomplished by operations run by the state. The transition to state ownership need not be brought about by force; it can be accomplished without a bloody revolution and without reducing the former owners to misery. This is particularly easy where the operations are in any case already very concentrated, for then the only really essential change is the conversion of the produce from the profit of a private capitalist into the revenue of all.

3. Unmistakable as are the good intentions of such proposals, and earnest as are those idealistic men and women who stand up for the realization of this idea in their enthusiasm and in their willingness to make a sacrifice, it nevertheless contains grounds for grave misgivings.

If the state were the sole possessor of property, it would also be the sole master, and its subjects would be slaves. This order can scarcely be reconciled with any form of government permitting freedom. It would promote a patriarchal administration—or, to be more honest about it, despotism. Life in such a state has notable similarities to life in a barracks. The optimist would perhaps rather hear it compared to life in a convent, but there is considerably more justification for comparing it with life in prison.

Such an order poses a threat to the germ of cultivated society, the family. It is no coincidence that the family is eliminated in Plato's state. Bonds of friendship also appear to be threatened: have they not suffered in monasteries? When freedom is withdrawn, the most noble delights and virtues find no nourishment and wither. What place is there for the bliss of doing good or the fulfilment of the duties of love if everything is done under compulsion? In such a society, fear becomes the motive for doing good, but fear is torment; in an order based upon freedom of ownership it is hope, and hope is joy.

Furthermore, all high-minded enterprise is thwarted when

private initiative disappears. Arts and sciences fall under regulations that cripple their life at its source and steadily lower their standards. The process of levelling leads to mediocrity on all sides, in pleasures as well as in work. Work becomes a mere common commodity, joy becomes mere vulgar revelry. Hence it is precisely the most gifted and ambitious people who oppose the process of levelling; they do not wish to live like animals in a herd.

This and many other considerations will arouse the impulse to retain private ownership when, presently, an inquisition for the purpose of suppressing it becomes active. Either life will be made into a tribulation for the citizenry by means of endless law-suits, or, if no amount of terrorizing proves sufficient, the authority of the state and the legal order will be reduced to objects of ridicule.

The less latitude is permitted the acquisitive drive, the more enflamed become the political passions. A boundless urge to get the powers of state into one's own hands takes over. Woe to such a state when it falls into bad hands—as the hands of the power-grabbers usually are—for, in it, the power of the man in control is incomparably greater than elsewhere.

Those who believe that such a state would exclude every sort of exploitation are deceiving themselves, for it will simply take other forms, particularly the form of indolence, in which the lazy survive at the cost of the industrious. To be sure, total inactivity can be prevented by force, but it would be difficult to bring a worker to exceed the prescribed minimum and achieve superior results in this manner. Why should anyone exert himself more than the laziest people, if they will in any case gain as much as he does? The output of increased labour would expand the total output very little and the portion allotted the individual not at all. Contrary to the expectations of optimists, an economic order based upon collective ownership would result in a very great decrease in total achievement, the impoverishment of society, and a marked depreciation of its cultural wants.

Furthermore, it must be remembered that there are different kinds of work. Is it possible to discern a common standard for them? Should we consider them equivalent if they require equal amounts of time, without giving consideration to the expenditure of spiritual and physical powers? If not, how ought we to take due account of these? We cannot even make a satisfactory estimate of the expenditure of health, yet this differs for miners, spinners, glass-grinders, and farm-hands. Some people have tried to escape this dilemma by suggesting that each person undertake every sort of work in turn. A marvellous suggestion from the armchair philosophers! It would destroy all the advantages of the division of labour; no one would attain to special skills and knowledge in a given sphere. Indeed, species of work that of necessity take a long time could not be carried out at all. Bellamy thinks we would have to compensate for particularly unpleasant work by shortening the work-time accordingly, thus giving people an incentive to undertake it voluntarily. However, if this arrangement were to make anyone decide to spend one-half hour cleaning out a canal instead of eight hours weaving, sixteen times as many people would be required to carry out the former, unpleasant task; i.e. in many places it would have to remain undone altogether.

4. It appears, then, that whoever wishes to flee from the undeniable evils of a capitalist economy to a form of economy owned and run by the state can only succeed in escaping Scylla for Charybdis.

But this flight is by no means required. A solution lies between the two, and this middle road is being followed everywhere, although it is often trodden hesitatingly and in the face of resistance. Have we not taken significant steps in the direction of state control of property in the form of taxes, including graduated taxes, tariffs, embargoes, laws controlling interest, compulsory health and old-age insurance, child and woman labour laws, laws prohibiting cruelty to animals, and in the management and regulation of goods (e.g. laws restricting hunting and the use of forests)? These institutions do not eliminate private property; its essential advantages are preserved. We still have duties of love alongside duties of justice, and it is possible to change the boundaries between these two spheres without impairing freedom more than we promote the supreme practical good. Like all moral rules—with the exception of the supreme standard—the rules concerning property are merely secondary, and consequently any state that has as its goal the correct moral end also has the right to limit private property.

Certainly, the division existing at present is unjust; it is highly detrimental to moral progress to have overabundance and the unlimited amassing of goods on the one hand and bitter poverty on the other. Privation leads to crime, luxury to arrogance and presumption.

In order to bring about equality, the state can interfere not only by means of just tax programmes, but also by means of partial expropriations. As it is, spendthrifts are occasionally placed privately under trusteeship; why should not the same be done at the initiative of the state in certain situations, the existence of which has been tolerated up to the present?

Perhaps we will gradually reach the point of requiring the wealthy to give some sort of public account of the administration of their possessions. This would not have to be done under the sanction of punishment by the state; a wholesome influence can be exercised simply by the verdict of public opinion, as expressed by the voice of the people and in an independent press. How often wealth is purchased with the misery and tears of others, and how often it is wrongly used! Men often make light of the corrupting influence of luxury with foolish pronouncements; they will say, for instance, that it does, after all, bring money among the people—as though the wealth of a nation lay in the mere symbols of value, rather than in the gifts of nature and in the power of human labours. Where these are squandered on the one hand, deprivation must appear on the other; where the masses live in want, the few revel in outrageous pleasure.

PART SIX

REALIZING MORAL PRECEPTS

I

Moral Dispositions

---

112. *The nature of virtue*

Like presenting and judging, choosing and deciding are subject to necessary laws. None the less, given the choice between the same two objects, one person will give preference to the first, while another will give preference to the second. This difference results from the difference in their dispositions, which is also revealed in their moral decisions. Dispositions favourable to a morally correct choice are called virtues, those fostering a morally wrong choice, vices or sins.

What is virtue? Some have defined it as some kind of knowledge. This is correct inasmuch as the knowledge of good and evil does influence the right choice; if it did not, moral rules would be useless. None the less the knowledge of virtue is not identical with virtue, for people in possession of the same knowledge can differ in the strength of their inclination towards the good.

In rejecting this Socratic doctrine concerning virtue, we also reject the consequence drawn from it: that virtue is teachable. The acquisition of virtue is no simple process of learning; not only our judgment must be trained but also our faculties of loving and choosing. This training is required for the construction and maintenance of a virtuous disposition. Our character is developed gradually, and our inclinations are capable of undergoing many changes. Hence we also reject the opinion of the older Stoics, who denied that there could be degrees of virtue. Virtue is thoroughly capable not only of increasing, but also of diminishing; it can even vanish altogether. The proverbial claim that virtue cannot be forfeited is only half true: that is, it *is* the case that virtue is quite durable once it has been developed to a certain degree, for the opportunity to exercise it arises again and again.

Virtue endures and grows in the same way in which it comes into being; viz. by habituation, which not only gives us practice but also offers us the repeated experience of a good example.

A virtuous disposition diminishes, on the other hand, through lack of exercise, and still more when acts contrary to it are performed. In this manner it can disappear altogether.

The person who performs virtuous acts swiftly, easily, cheerfully and frequently displays the signs of a highly developed disposition to virtue.

Yet all of this is imprecise and incomplete until we dispose of the following question.

113. *Is there only one virtue, or are there many virtues?*

The Stoics preached the unity of virtue, but anyone who goes by his experience cannot reject the assumption that there is a multiplicity. Who can deny that one man chooses the good in the same situation in which another man rejects it, and yet fails to do so in another case, in which the second man upholds the good? If there are many virtues, what is the most suitable standpoint from which to group them?

Some wish to group the virtues according to the most important categories of moral action—that is, in accordance with duties, so that every particular virtue corresponds to some particular duty. But this proposal is worthless, if only because it would require us to say everything in ethics twice, under two different headings. It appears far more useful to group the virtues according to the ways in which people can be led to disregard what is preferable. The man who cannot be corrupted is completely virtuous. In setting up our categories, then, we give regard to the various factors that can thwart the coming into being of a morally correct choice and lead to a wrong choice.

I. Factors that prevent the formation of a correct judgment. Cases in which we must make a moral decision often require a certain degree of analysis before we can establish which side is preferable. If a person capable of performing it refrains from doing this mental work, he displays *moral indifference* or moral frivolity, a particularly dangerous disposition. (We must set aside the case of the man who is too stupid to undertake moral considerations, since an imbecile cannot really be accused of subjective immorality.) The kind of mistake I have in mind is not exactly intellectual, but it is clear that the person possessing such a disposition cannot make a reliable decision about morally correct and morally incorrect behaviour.

The virtue corresponding to this adverse disposition is *moral conscientiousness*, which is possessed by the man who has made a habit of undertaking the regular exercising of morality. This is the most important of all the virtues.

When moral reflection is undertaken with particular care and prudence, we speak of good moral counsel, or *moral acuity*. This does not denote something purely intellectual, for it is not simply a matter of succeeding in moral analysis whenever it is undertaken, but also of undertaking it regularly.

In so far as moral reflection pays particular attention to moral risks, we speak of moral prudence.

Even when a person has formed a correct judgment about the moral preferability of a certain line of action, obstructions can still stand in the way of the correct choice. Overcoming these requires special virtues.

II. We must consider, on the one hand, the greater inclination to what is less valuable and the greater aversion to the lesser evil and, on the other, the lack of control over our emotions.

Disharmony in our inclinations is related sometimes to differences between persons or classes of persons and sometimes to differences between objects.

The virtue standing in opposition to the first of these is *moral objectivity*. However, I prefer to use the expression 'justice', since this brings duties of love and duties of justice equally into consideration. Partiality can express itself:

(*a*) as egoism,
(*b*) as so-called ipsissimism,
(*c*) as *acceptio personarum*.

(*a*) A choice is egoistic when its realization tips the scale in favour of the actualization of a certain good within my own mental sphere. The objective person regards the differences between goods as though he were an outsider and favours the greater good, no matter where it lies.

There are degrees of egoism, depending upon the amount of damage a person is ready to do to the general good for the sake of his own good.

(*b*) Ipsissimism might be called a milder form of egoism. It consists of giving an undue amount of regard, not to our own person, but to a limited circle of people who are for one reason or another close to us: friends, professional colleagues, co-religionists, fellow citizens. The name was invented by the Jesuit Mariana (died 1624). Comradeship, nepotism, and favouritism are to be included here. One particularly dangerous vice of our times is national ipsissimism. I do not fail to recognize that it represents progress over brutal egoism, for the advocate of ipsissimism knows what it is to make a sacrifice for a greater whole. Yet there are grave dangers attaching to it. In pursuing ipsissimism, a person believes himself to be doing something noble, when he is, in fact, often committing a cruel injustice. The man who has got into the habit of thinking everything permissible that is in the supposed interests of his nation lacks an enlightened conscience, and the more powerful his voice and his example, the more he does to cloud the world's conscience. Anyone who has lived for a long time in a country where there are passionate national battles knows how easy it is even for gifted persons to lose their sense of justice and equity. It is no advantage to belong to a people whose spirit is held in the clutches of national excesses, and it is a misfortune to be opposed to such a people in a national battle, for it is difficult to remain chivalrous when faced with an unchivalrous opponent. Oppression is followed by rebellion, rebellion is followed by retaliation, and the hatred on both sides increases constantly, until finally both are visited with a catastrophe that teaches them a lesson—often too late, unfortunately.

Party spirit is also a fertile source of ipsissimistic vices. The reverse side of the irrational preference for one's fellows in the party is intolerance towards others. At one time intolerance of persons of different religious beliefs was the very worst kind, whereas today sectarian ipsissimism lags further and further behind the other two forms.

(*c*) Even where we are not bound to persons or classes by common membership in a party, an undue preference for them may arise, posing a danger to our moral judgments and decisions. In these cases, Scholastic moralists speak of *acceptio personalis*. Who is not acquainted with examples of bias towards people distinguished by riches, beauty, or social status, not only causing us to act partially in carrying out our duties of love, but also leading us to infringements of our duties of justice? Seduced by the pretty face of one of the defendants, jurors sometimes will make a harsh judgment in one case and a mild judgment in a very similar case. Even in examinations, chivalry towards the female sex may occasionally be overdone. And some people reveal these weaknesses when confronted with those in certain positions.

So much for undue regard to differences between persons. As for the inequitable evaluation of objects, it varies immensely. The Scholastic moralists emphasized, as being of particular practical significance, the over-estimation of the value of pleasure and the vice of the greed for pleasure. This sort of irrational preference for a class of objects, if habitual, can grow into a mania. The passion of the miser or the greedy person, the connoisseur's propensity for collecting, ends up shunning not even the most absurd and immoral sacrifice.

Ideally everything ought to be loved according to its true value. This is what Aristotle had in mind when he described virtue as the correct mean between two extremes. But both innate blind drives and the constantly fluctuating forces of habit obstruct the way leading to this ideal.

III. *A lack of mastery over our emotions*—pain and pleasure, hope and fear, anger and vanity, and whatever others there may be— frequently wins out over rational judgment. A clear conviction and a correct evaluation fail to come to the fore in the face of the power of the emotions. Since no man is free from these drives and their enticements, no one unable to control his sensual impulses is to be called truly virtuous. Such control is not direct; rather, the will initially acquires power over the emotions by regulating the flow of our ideas. It is a matter of driving certain thoughts out of our mind when we are in a state of temptation, while at the same time stirring up and retaining others that foster the good.

Mastery of the will over the life of instinct is acquired by practice. The possession of a certain degree of physical hygiene is also important, for the better the functioning of our nervous system the more reliable our self-control. Excessive asceticism is injurious to the nerves, but prudent practice in bearing hardships and pain is quite another matter from refusing even pleasure that is permitted. A sensible degree of asceticism is undoubtedly advantageous to the virtue of mastering the emotions.

114. *The origin and decline of moral dispositions*

After this survey of the main classes of virtues, it is easier to answer the question of how virtues originate, grow, and decline. Some education is required in order to attain the virtues of the first class, whether through some popular means of moral training, such as religious instruction, or through some more scientific form, such as a course of lectures on ethics at a university.

The second class of virtues arises by means of practice and example, the third by means of practice and physical hygiene.

Practice, by the way, plays an essential role in all three classes. In addition, they are related to one another inasmuch as; e.g. ill-will depraves our judgment.

Regarding training, we have still to remark that a practice carried out for some time for the sake of some other thing can grow into an inclination detached from its original purpose. This is a law of great practical import, capable of being employed in the service of virtue as well as in the service of vice.

115. *Can a virtue also be a vice?*

Odd as it may sound, this question, taken in one sense, requires an affirmative answer. A person may harbour a stronger inclination towards a certain good than it deserves as such, but so long as it is competing with something less valuable this preference will secure the making of the right choice. It is only where this preferred and unduly loved good is engaged in a contest with a higher good that the inclination has a detrimental effect. Under such conditions, even so noble a disposition as a love of knowledge may become a temptation; Faust sold his soul to the devil. To give another example, the virtues pertaining to one position may become vices if practised when we come to occupy another position.

Are all virtues such that they can become a temptation upon occasion? This question, too, calls for an affirmative answer. Only one preference constitutes an exception. There is one good that ought to be loved above all and can be loved above all without the strength of our inclination towards it becoming morally harzardous, and this is the love of God, the infinite good. But this is not a practical love, not a choice. St Augustine's definition applies to all other virtues: *Virtus bona qualitas, quae nunquam nocet* [Virtue is a good quality that never does injury].

116. *The value of virtue and misery of vice*

Aristotle, nicknamed the sober, raised a eulogy to virtue and said that justice in the general sense, in which it denotes fulfilment of the moral law, is more beautiful than the morning star and the evening star. The great poets, too, bear witness to this beauty. Virtue is indeed more sublime than intellectual and aesthetic advantages, not only in its intrinsic value but also in its power to bring about happiness. Fully developed virtue is related to our joy in exercising it. Anyone who doubts the sweetness of virtue should make a try at devoting himself to its service. He will enjoy the most sublime happiness that can be imparted to any man here on earth.

Along with the joy of exercising it, virtue offers the additional advantage that there are many occasions for exercising it and that, as a result, it has great endurance. Anyone who makes use of each opportunity for being virtuous cannot possibly get out of practice. Hence Aristotle pronounced virtue more durable than knowledge. To be sure, our own era, which has great reverence for the arts and sciences, does not hold virtue in equally high esteem; it is more awed by victorious crimes. All the purer, then, will be the hearts of those who have sworn loyalty to virtue, and in their happiness they will find it easy to forego external honours. *Beatitudo non est virtutis praemium sed ipsa virtus* [The reward of virtue is not happiness but virtue itself].

Vice is as ugly and wretched as virtue is sublime and blessed. Aristotle distinguished two levels of vice. The first is ἀκρατὴ, or moral weakness. Men who suffer from this have not closed their hearts to the yearning for purity and moral perfection; they always pay for their weakness with the pain of remorse, yet they have another relapse whenever the temptation recurs. The second level of vice is κακία, or wickedness, which consists, as it were, of the fundamental decision not to pay the slightest regard to the moral law. This is the highest degree of depravity and hardness of heart, which is insensitive to the prickings of conscience. Has the man in this state also attained the highest degree of misery? Some might wish to deny this, since he feels no thorn. Yet it cannot but be acknowledged that the man who is depraved is barred from the greatest, most genuine happiness. Furthermore, no matter how indifferent a person is, hastily piling up crimes will ultimately lead even him to experience a breaking through of conscience and cast him into the infernal torment of self-contempt. Simply recall the gruesome description of the destiny of the wicked given in Schiller's *The Robbers* and in Shakespeare's *Richard III.*

II

Moral Guidance

---

117. *The importance of moral guidance*

Moral guidance has no less an effect upon our moral behaviour than does virtue. Without it, even an already virtuous character will deteriorate, whereas with it a weak character can be fortified and a poor disposition can even be transformed into a good one. For our dispositions are partially innate and partially acquired, and this includes our disposition to make correct or incorrect preferences. We cannot be held responsible for innate, bad dispositions, yet our parents and ancestors may bear some of the responsibility, for there is no doubt that heredity, in general, plays a role. Yet even if we have no responsibility for our innate dispositions, we none the less need not accept them as an unalterable fact. It is the task of moral guidance to construct the best that is possible out of the materials given by nature.

Through practice we acquire new dispositions which may have the effect of transforming our character, at least to a certain extent. If even people who lack several senses from birth, such as Laura Bridgeman and Helen Keller*—both of them blind and deaf—can attain by practice a considerable degree of intellectual education, a skilfully exercised influence should be able to bring about amazing cases of regeneration in the moral sphere as well.

A methodically and consistently carried out influencing of the

---

* These two women were not, in fact, born deaf and blind but became so around the age of two as a result of illness.

construction of moral dispositions is called moral training. Essentially, it consists in getting accustomed to making the correct preference. But how can such influence be brought to bear at all? Habit, after all, arises through repeatedly carrying out one kind of act while avoiding its opposite. If a person already has a good disposition, he will find it easy to carry out the one and restrain himself from carrying out the other, but if he does not, he will not find it easy. It appears, then, that the habit we wish to enlist as a means to the development of virtue presupposes its own existence. We are threatened with a vicious circle.

But this circle turns out to be illusory, for there is no lack of means for bringing even a character that as yet possesses only weak moral powers to perform good acts of preference, and it is precisely these means that the doctrine of moral guidance wishes to place in our hands. The influence of education is well known. We praise a good mentor as we would a second father; indeed, he may be our spiritual father. It is reported that Alexander the Great, in writing to Aristotle, said that he had his father to thank for his life but his teacher, Aristotle, to thank for what gave his life value. And the ruinous influence of the seducer is just as notorious, which is why parents and teachers endeavour to keep him away.

Yet it is also possible to train ourselves, keep ourselves from temptation, and counteract evil tendencies—just as it is possible for us to inculcate in ourselves inclinations to evil. When speaking of freedom, I had in mind the power that we have over our dispositions and over external circumstances that, acting in consort, produce a morally correct choice. The man who guides himself wisely is like the skilful general who has but a few troops at his disposal and yet operates so cleverly that he manages to have the superior force whenever there is a battle. In making moral decisions, we ought also to avoid those battles we may lose and to face the enemy, temptation, only when we are certain of success. By such a clever moral strategy we not only avoid losses, but we also gain small victories and, in so doing, increase our power. Every victory strengthens us, until finally we are able to face the enemy in the open battlefield.

The importance of moral guidance has been acknowledged since ancient times. Just think of the prominent role it played among the Pythagoreans, whose entire school took on the character of a religious community by means of it. For it is precisely popular religions that tend to take a prudent account of the means of moral guidance, and much that they decide upon is chosen with wisdom. In contrast, moral guidance is usually lamentably limited among those who do not profess any positive religion. That is why a number of noble men—J. S. Mill in England, Payot in France, and Fechner in Germany—have dedicated themselves to moral missions for pagans, as it were. The mention of popular education usually conjures up an image of just about anything that could be presented to the understanding—except a genuine training of the heart and the will. The error of supposing that systematic moral guidance is unnecessary on the grounds that whatever is called for in that sphere will make itself known, as it were, will be bitterly avenged. For our feeble attempts in that direction in daily life—saying to ourselves, as we all have at one time or another, 'I shall not go there, or do that, or I will be lost,' etc.—are not nearly sufficient, as can be seen in the case of individuals and of whole peoples. Political seducers, rebels, and apostles of revolution have an easy time of it where the masses lack moral training and are ultimately able not only to deaden their sensitivity to the gravest injustices and most terrible atrocities towards their opponents, but also to exploit them as tools to these ends.

Hence moralists who have remained aware of the practical character of their discipline have greatly emphasized moral guidance and self-education in accordance with a carefully constructed and consistently observed plan. Unfortunately, German philosophers of the present day usually fail to comprehend that ethics is, after all, a practical discipline. That is why we find, in the various compendia of ethics, all sorts of abstract, and sometimes abstruse, psychological and metaphysical theories, but little or nothing that could assist the men in need of moral guidance. Consequently, some practical men of healthy judgment have become so puzzled by scientific ethics that they reject it as a discipline into which intellectuals stumbled by mistake. Yet this error is almost as serious as the others, for modern man starts out with a sceptical attitude and is particularly susceptible to destructive forms of scepticism regarding ethics. Our task is, above all, to convince him that the moral realm is capable of being known naturally. And still it is true that the thinker must not be content with examining fundamental questions but should place greater and greater weight upon the theory of moral education and self-training as the authority of the popular moral teachers of our time is more and more severely shaken. Here, ethics is like logic. If logic is to fulfil its task as a practical discipline, it cannot rest content with presenting the rules for drawing conclusions and, perhaps, complementing it with an index of the normal fallacies; it must also investigate the psychological presuppositions that cause people to stray out of the path of logic and show how they can be avoided. Here, too, the English are superior to us. J. S. Mill's *Logic* compares favourably to our logic texts in this respect, and, as already noted, the same author took account of our practical needs in ethics as well. Comte also made great efforts in this direction, and some scientists and practical politicians who have not accounted themselves philosophers have known how to serve this important cause. Benjamin Franklin took it so seriously that he considered writing a work on moral guidance. Because he was occupied with so many other tasks, he never got around to carrying out this plan, but he left behind him sketches indicating his intention.

We also wish to mention some of the viewpoints most essential for moral guidance. The most prominent are moral vigilance, care in avoiding and removing danger, and concern for the general promotion of moral dispositions.

118. *The first and most important aspect of moral guidance: moral vigilance*

The admonishment, '*Toujours en vedette* [Be always on guard!]', applies to moral behaviour as well as military. Moralists speak of moral vigilance, of changes in our course of conduct made in the light of truth. The following are the most prominent rules.

1. We ought always to keep sight of the moral goal and to maintain for ourselves a vivid feeling for the overwhelming value of virtue. These ends are fostered by:

(*a*) being alone from time to time;

(*b*) reading ethical works, such as: Epictetus' handbook of morals (*Encheiridion*), Marcus Aurelius' *Meditations*, Aristotle's *Nicomachean Ethics*, parts of Holy Scripture, the works of Chrysostomus, Hutcheson, etc.;

(c) reading poetical works of lofty moral content; and

(d) leading an orderly life, which itself offers the guidance of moral associations.

2. But we ought also always to remain conscious of the particular situation in which we find ourselves with respect to:

(a) the means that stand at our disposal or that would stand at our disposal in the various situations among which we have to choose;

(b) the temptations that may confront us. They are different under different circumstances, and also vary within the same circumstances, according to our internal dispositions. For whether or not something can become a temptation depends upon these dispositions—hence the importance of self-knowledge for moral vigilance. It is wise to procure for ourselves an image of the typical character of our acts of will by means of a sort of historical survey. This is the real significance of searching our conscience; it is not merely a matter of recalling the past to our memory. It is vital to become acquainted with our character through this survey and to gain a more precise knowledge of the details of our dispositions. We must recall not only the acts that we really carried out, but also our wishes and desires, so that we are clear about all the mental factors from which we may draw conclusions about the habitual structure of our will.

Once we have recognized by these means what constitutes a danger for our moral behaviour, it is our task to avoid or eliminate these elements.

119. *Avoiding and eliminating danger*

When a knowledge of our dispositions causes us to feel that a situation poses dangers for us, our best move is to avoid getting into it. But if it is unavoidable, we must prepare ourselves for it in good time.

The following preventive measures come into consideration. First of all, we should seek out useful occupations, never remaining idle. Idleness is the morass that creates an unhealthy moral climate.

But it is also possible to remove the danger by doing something immediately to anticipate our decision. In so doing, we destroy what would be a danger later on, even if it does not actually exist now.

If it is impossible to forestall the danger in this manner, we must simply prepare ourselves for it, by:

(*a*) forming immediately a firm resolution, while producing every conceivable motive for doing the good;

(*b*) practicing in simpler cases for the more difficult cases;

(*c*) adding on supporting motives. Think of the connection between evil and misery, of the later regret, the internal rupture that would remain with us if we acted wrongly, of the displeasure of others, especially of those we love. Remember that each act adds a new link to the fetters with which passion and bad habit bind us. We must subject ourselves to rewards and punishment; a punishment administered to ourselves by our own authority can work in much the same way as an external punitive law.

(*d*) seeking out situations that promise to serve as a good inspiration.

120. *Caring for the general promotion of moral disposition*

In the preceding section we have discussed the best means for preparing ourselves for particular situations which threaten to pose a moral danger for us. But we also take precautions against individual dangers by arming ourselves in indirect and more remote ways against *all* dangers; that is, by attending to our good moral dispositions in general. Here we must consider both the maintenance and the improvement of our moral dispositions.

A. 1. Concerning the first, we must above all prevent a good disposition from being destroyed by physical influences. *Mens sana in corpore sano*. It is also in the interests of morality to care for our physical health.

2. A moral disposition can also disappear through lack of exercise. If no opportunities have arisen for a long time for exercising certain virtues, we should create them artificially. For instance, we can subject ourselves to certain difficulties under conditions in which it is of no great significance whether we succeed or not. The importance lies in the exercise itself, in the fact that it upholds the good disposition. Every now and then we should reject permissible pleasures in order to remain moderate. This measure is also advisable in the raising of children. In general, the value of asceticism is that it instils moderation; as an end in itself it is to be repudiated. Good manners can also be regarded as a practice ground; we ought to maintain them even

where neglecting them would give no offence—even, indeed, when we are alone. Bear in mind the story of the Englishman who always changed for dinner, even though he was the only white man living among the natives. We ought to take care about our clothing even at home, for such matters should become second nature.

3. The effect of good examples is related to our own practice and training. This effect rests upon the fulfilment of the act, if not in actual fact, at least in our imagination. Consequently we ought to seek out good examples, and if they are not easy to find in real life, we should gather our incentives for doing good from history or from works of art. History is superior for this purpose because an example that we believe to have actually occurred is more efficacious; the fact that it really took place often gives moral heroism a significance far exceeding the immediate value of the sacrificial acts involved. Entire centuries may be held in its sway. Here we can see, too, the elevated pedagogical significance of the monastic life. For it is shortsighted to judge whether or not the existence of a religious order is justified merely in terms of its direct social utility. It is not simply a matter of what the order achieves, let us say, in the way of charity, but also, and more importantly, what it achieves as an example, as a proof that such sacrifices do not exceed human strength. We say to ourselves, 'If these heroic people have taken this upon themselves, voluntarily and for life, we would certainly show ourselves unworthy if, where duty demands that we do something similar for a brief period of time, we failed to bring about this lesser achievement.' I cannot understand how philosophers of religion who deny that Jesus was an historical person can believe that this has no detrimental effect upon the value of his personality as a moral example.

4. A good disposition can also decay through the practice of inconsistent acts—that is, by the fostering of the opposite disposition. Therefore we should avoid acts conflicting with the good disposition even where they appear to be harmless. We ought most particularly to avoid seductive literature, groups whose members habitually display bad examples—everything, in short, that is apt to promote a vicious disposition.

5. We ought also to take care—and this requires more subtlety— that our general good disposition does not suffer from disproportionate exercise. No one disposition should be built up at the

cost of others that are more valuable. Rather, we ought to preserve a certain equality among the moral faculties; sympathy ought not to be nourished at the cost of justice, nor the love of peace at the cost of the other, more sublime goods, such as truth. The danger of overemphasizing the care of ourselves is universal. We have a duty to take care of ourselves, but because this duty occupies us continually it tends to nurture self-love excessively. This, in turn, has caused some moralists to overrate the value of self-mortification, which errs in the opposite direction.

6. It is an interesting fact, of practical significance, that moral dispositions can also be strengthened through the carrying out of acts that lie outside the moral realm. For there are perfect activities within other spheres, too: beauty and artistic activity within the sphere of judgment. Experience demonstrates that the practice of a worthy undertaking within one realm also fosters perfection in the others, just as the exercising of one member is beneficial to homologous members. A lively sensitivity to aesthetic values can increase our feeling for moral values. This fact has not remained unnoticed, but it usually has not been explained very well.

What I am thinking of is not the same phenomenon that some people, e.g. Plato, who like to speak of the morally uplifting character of music appear to have in mind. There is no use asking musicians themselves about this, for they begin straightway to go into ecstasies; furthermore, they do not have any real idea of just what happens. Above all, it is an error to attribute the expression of thoughts to music. Musicians themselves appear not to believe that it has this function, for whenever they wish their audience to think of something quite definite in connection with the music they take the precaution of having it printed in the programme. Nevertheless, music is able to create moods, to stimulate sequences of emotion, and to strengthen feelings we already have. And it can do these things very effectively and powerfully. Noble acts are also frequently associated with certain moods, and that is why music has the power to strengthen our inclination to perform certain moral acts. Military music encourages bravery, while the works of Palestrina and Bach promote piety. In considering the morally uplifting effect of music in his meditations on education, Plato does not close his mind to the dangers that may threaten from this direction. Some music is distinctly sensual and enervating, tending to rouse our erotic instincts. As an example, he compares the Phrygian mode of music to the serious Doric mode, and expresses a desire to have Phrygian music banned from public performances. Tolstoy passed a similar judgment on Wagnerian music.

Yet, as I said, it was not this subsidiary effect of music that I had in mind when I remarked that the pleasures of art can strengthen our dispositions for moral emotions and desires. I was thinking, rather, that the love of the true and the good can be refined and purified along with the love of the beautiful, which tends to elevate the human niveau. In an aesthetically refined environment we are less likely to submit to the coarser pleasures. By analogy, we can establish a law concerning the structuring of habits. Those who disagree may point to the moral degeneration that has set in precisely at times when art was at its height, such as the Renaissance. Yet without the cult of beauty, matters would probably have been still worse in Italy at that time, when the temptation to overstep the limits in the war of all against all was very strong. Moreover, we must not overlook the fact that the same men whose manner of life we condemn also showed themselves capable of great heroic deeds.

The church, too, has shown great appreciation of the moral efficacy of art. She did not decorate her cathedrals in the most heavenly manner possible for the purpose of serving God—who can only be served by the internal trappings of the soul—but the vision of what is beautiful purifies and elevates souls. Hence we ought to maintain, in the interests of morality, our capacity for aesthetic pleasure, preserving it from being extinguished.

B. In the preceding remarks, I had in mind primarily the maintenance of such good dispositions as we already possess, but we must also give thought to the improvement of our moral state. Just by making work on our moral progress into a conscious basic principle we promote our good dispositions. But we are also required to proceed systematically according to a thoroughly considered plan, the object being to lead virtue step by step to greater and greater perfection. We proceed from inferior pleasures to spiritual joys, and from them to even loftier spiritual joys. We destroy the power of egoism by extending love and care to our families, to our friends, to our homeland, and to the whole of mankind.

Our success will depend greatly upon suppressing any trace of self-satisfaction, for to remain at a standstill is to take a regressive step. It is said that Maximillian II of Bavaria, a lord who understood how to lead his people well, made a note of a particular virtue each day so that he could practice it.

From time to time we ought to reconsider our environment, giving thought to whether or not it has come to hinder our moral progress. It can become an impediment not only by setting forth bad examples but also by lacking ideals and the power to motivate. That is why it greatly assists our own moral progress when we have an opportunity to extend our horizons by making acquaintance with important personalities. Where we cannot do this, we ought at least to substitute reading literature of a kind that stimulates our worthier powers. Auguste Comte drew up a calendar of secular saints, along with examples calculated to inspire moral enthusiasm.

Flattery, on the other hand, is a dangerous poison. There is danger in every zealous attempt at mollification, in every effort to avoid hurting each other by seeking to make excuses for everything. People will say, 'Oh, but everyone lies,' 'No one who has never been drunk is a real man,' or 'If you don't do it, then someone else will.' This attitude of *laissez-faire, laissez-aller* is the deadly foe of moral progress. The man who is seriously concerned with his higher development will avoid the flatterer and bid the honest critic welcome. We have little esteem for the scholar who, content with what he has already learned, concerns himself solely with remembering it, closing his mind to all new ideas and to progress in knowledge, yet we are quite tolerant of people of average morality who forego moral progress. But it is precisely in this most worthy of all spheres that we should know how to prize properly new stimuli; just as we are happy to consult with professional colleagues, we ought habitually to seek counsel with morally superior persons, so as not to remain at a standstill in this respect, either.

III

Social Relations Based upon Virtue

---

121. *Friendship*

Social relations based upon virtue are one of the most profitable means of strengthening an individual's moral powers and of permitting him to attain to achievements that no person could bring about in isolation. Friendship is an example of such an alliance. It is found where two people are bound together by a conscious and mutual love and by a desire for future association. The motives determining this desire may be of a superior or of an inferior nature. The doctor and the pharmacist seek each other out for business purposes and become what are known as business friends. So-called companionship or fellowship is based upon enjoyment. True friendship, however, is based upon great merits, and particularly virtue. Whoever holds the name of friendship in honour will reserve it for true friendship, which is based upon unselfish love and receives its inspiration from common moral endeavour. Other kinds of friendship are merely a mockery or a caricature of the genuine variety.

The motives for continuous association need not be the same for both parties; one may seek pleasure, the other services. Needless to say, such mixed forms bear even less resemblance to true friendship than do the other lesser varieties.

True friendship is of a great moral value. Merits and esteem for them seal the bond between the parties and are increased by its endurance. Every happiness which one of the friends experiences through the friendship becomes a source of happiness for the other, just as the consciousness of having a friend who, in his love, rejoices in our success as though it were his own increases our own happiness.

The ancients held the goods of friendship in high esteem in their moral code. All the Socratic schools undertook to investigate it. Aristotle devoted two of the ten books of his *Nicomachean Ethics* to friendship, and Epicurus went into it thoroughly and at length. Aristotle expresses the opinion that no one would wish to live without friends. But a good man who has found no friends will soon fall into evil company, since the human heart requires expression and company, and evil company is the ruin of the idealistic endeavourings of youth. Faggots bound together remain ablaze: when they are separated, the fire becomes extinguished.

In the investigations instigated by the ancient moralists, one of the questions we encounter is whether friendship is possible only among equals or also between persons occupying quite different stations. The former case is the more auspicious. In order for a friendship to be formed under the latter circumstances, the more highly placed person must regard the merits of his position as inferior to those upon which the friendship is based. *Amicitia pares aut invenit aut facit* [Friendship either seeks out or creates equals]. In any case it is a good thing to seek those who are noble and who are roughly our equals as friends.

Aristotle also studies how friendship is maintained and how it comes to be dissolved, and whether it is more desirable when we are happy or when we fall into misfortune. The noble person, he feels, will have more need of it when he is happy; he would rather bear unhappiness and misfortune alone, for no matter how comforting he would find a friend's love, the knowledge that he was causing others suffering would be painful to him himself. His happiness and good fortune, however, he wishes to share, for the reason he is to be accounted good is precisely that he does good to others and allows them to share his enjoyment, which in turn causes him to be twice as happy.

122. Marriage

1. Marriage is a special form of the bond of friendship. It is grounded upon virtue and is also a means to virtue. Bentham

sees in it the basis of civilization, and he praises it for the freedom it has brought to women. Marriage orders society in a natural and purposeful manner and has created a domestic magistracy that is often far more effective than the magistracy of nations; it turns the attention of everyone who has children towards the future and serves to multiply the social sympathies. What would man be without marriage!

2. Like friendships, marriages are formed for many reasons, some for the sake of material welfare or because they are otherwise useful, others out of passion, and still others upon the basis of merits that inspire true love. Once again, the participants can be moved by the same or by different grounds. The only true marriages are those based upon worthy motives; only such marriages can be a guarantee of enduring happiness. Marriages formed from inferior motives are far removed from the ideal, and furthest from the ideal are those into which the partners have entered from different motives.

3. I am in substantial agreement with Bentham's view of the position of the two partners in relation to one another. He demands:

(*a*) the subordination of the woman. The man should be the guardian, not the wife. Affairs are in a bad way when the legislature and the executive are working at odds with each other. It may be said that, in general, the spiritual strength of the man is greater; it is not that women are less clever, but that most of them have less endurance for mental work. If this should happen to be untrue in some individual cases, there is still no harm to be feared from this arrangement, for experience has shown how much women are able to accomplish by their kindness and amiability. If womenly advantages should ever come to be combined with a superiority in matters where the man usually has the advantage, the woman will *via facti* become master. Incidentally, the stipulation that the wife should be subordinate to the husband does not mean that she should be subject to his favour or disfavour. Like others, the domestic regime should be constitutional, not despotic.

(*b*) On the other hand, it is a consequence of what I have said that the administration of the domestic realm should be placed solely in the hands of the husband.

(*c*) But this is not true of wordly possessions, which ought to lie equally in the hands of both parties. The man takes leadership in acquiring them, but should have no greater right to the enjoyment of them.

(*d*) Marital fidelity is a duty for both husband and wife. The man who violates it commits an injustice just as much as the woman and does an equal amount of harm in that he violates the tender duties of love towards the woman's feelings. The injustice that lies in infidelity was recognized as far back as Aristotle. A woman comes to a man's hearth as one begging for shelter, he says; she stands under the protection of the gods. It is not permissible to do her a wrong, and whoever breaks the marriage bond does just that.

4. Marriage should not be undertaken when the parties are too young—and here youth does not include merely physical immaturity. To be spiritually mature, the partners must attach great weight to those merits upon which lasting happiness can be based. Whoever enters a marriage thoughtlessly offends greatly against his own future, especially in places where marriages cannot be dissolved. Aristotle thought that 37 was the age at which a man should marry, while 17 was the right age for a woman, but it is in fact not possible to give any precise limits. However, the very early marriages practiced in the Orient are quite wrong. The girl is dragged into marriage not because she has matured at an earlier age but from lack of insight, and the women are destroyed prematurely, both in soul and in body.

5. Who is to decide upon the marriage? The partners themselves; who would allow even a mere friendship to be formed for him? Children and parents do not see eye to eye. Children wish to *be* happy because of love, while the parents wish them to *appear* happy because of comfort. In some countries it has become an established custom for the parents to choose the spouse. Frigidity and infidelity frequently result, as can be seen from the French example. '*En France on ne s'aime pas, on se convient*' [In France, people do not love each other; they suit themselves to each other]. None the less, it seems to me to be desirable for parents to have some influence upon the choice of their children. More specifically, they should influence the choice of their young daughters by determining the company they keep. It is possible to set some appropriate age limit up to which parents may hinder a marriage by their veto. Yet even after the child has passed this age, it may

be proper for the parents to delay a match in order to prevent excessive haste.

6. There are both physical and moral reasons for the avoidance of marriage between close relatives. We increase the bonds of sympathy by preserving their particular character. Forbidding such marriages prevents dangerous disorders. Moreover, experience with the descendants of such marriages speaks against them; degeneration frequently results.

7. How many parties should be involved in the contract? Two. Polyandry is absurd and frequently ruinous. And because polyandry is inadmissable, polygamy is unfair to women. Under certain circumstances it may suit men, but it will never suit women— leaving aside certain deeply ingrained conditions in some cultures. For it is a matter of sacrificing the interests of a number of women to each favourably situated man. Polygamy reduces the woman to a slave and a mistress, and it also poses severe disadvantages in the bringing up of children. In order for mankind to continue, it is not only important that children be born, but also that they be raised and educated. Yet how can this succeed in a polygamous family, where the bond between father and child is necessarily weakened? The man will inevitably favour some of his many wives over others, and the result will be partiality towards certain children, and hence rivalry and intrigues. The institution of the harem in oriental dynasties entailed that a man who came to power regarded it as the first duty of his government to rid the world of his brothers. The familial atrocities to which polygamy led in the houses of David and Solomon demonstrate what serious damage is done to morality by this system, even among peoples who are morally superior. To the wrong against the position of the woman is added a still greater wrong against the siblings. Evil conditions result even under idyllic circumstances, as for instance among the patriarchs: just think of the rejection of Hagar or the jealousy of the brothers of Joseph, who was sold into slavery.

Furthermore, polygamy is an injustice to the poor. How is the poor man to procure a single wife if the rich man can take as many wives as he likes?

Among other follies, our age has not been spared subjection to propaganda for polygamy. It has been based partially upon a concern for the biological progress of man; monogamy has been

N

accused of offending against the constitutional powers of the race by not exploiting sufficiently the procreative abilities of the healthy man, thus hindering human breeding according to Darwinian principles. Others base their pleas for polygamy or polyandry, as the case may be, upon the demand for the development of personality, claiming that monogamy is excessively limiting. Consequently they demand full freedom for both men and women.

But, as I have said, all this offends against the duties of love and of justice. In particular, we can counter the propaganda based upon Darwinism by pointing out that human progress does not depend primarily upon the production of bodies; it is human *souls* that we ought to be breeding. Now, the advocates of polygamy can themselves see its disadvantages with respect to upbringing and education, and consequently they usually leap at the suggestion that this task be left to the state. But this suggestion shows short-sighted thinking and ill-considered speech. Who is the state, and is everything it does *eo ipso* excellent and reliable? Is it true that paid officials will do a better job of bringing up children than parents? How is the state to adapt its method of child-rearing to individuals? Clearly it cannot, and a regrettable process of levelling will set in. The arguments for polygamy, then, come to this: on the one hand, monogamy is to be abolished, that the parents may freely pursue their everchanging inclinations, and this freedom is demanded in the name of the cultivation of personality; on the other hand, the children—in whom, more than in anyone else, personality is to be nurtured and cultivated—are from their earliest youth to be forced into a uniform mould and turned into stereotypes. These two proposals are in absurd contradiction to each other and reflect the most superficial thought. History shows that it is precisely the family that offers the soil which nurtures valuable personalities. The more solid its structure, the better the results we can expect.

8. Should marriage be undertaken for a period of time or for an entire lifetime? Certainly, the object should be a life-long union, and the contract should run in accordance with this aim. After all, when we form a friendship we do not make stipulations about giving notice. Only upon a permanent basis can definite limits be drawn excluding those loose alliances that are unfair to the female sex and are consequently immoral.

9. Is it permissible to dissolve the bonds of marriage? It is no doubt clear enough from what has already been said that a marriage may not usually be dissolved because of the wishes of only one partner; as with other sorts of contracts, this is only allowable where the other party is guilty of a grievous wrong. But may we approve of divorce where there has been no wrong, yet there is mutual agreement? That is to say, ought the state to permit it? There are weighty arguments on both sides.

One particularly strong reason against divorce is regard for the children, the rearing of whom is one of the most important duties of married couples. The separation of the parents is often no lesser a sorrow than the death of one of them; it may be even sadder.

Moreover, to allow separation to depend upon the wife's consent does not seem to offer her sufficient protection, for there is a danger that she may be forced to consent. In contrast, the consciousness that the bonds are indissoluble has a most salutary power, bringing calm to our moods and desires and holding us in check.

None the less, there are good reasons for not making marriage absolutely indissoluble. Where passionate aversion exists on both sides, a marriage can become hell on earth. In such cases, certainly, separation ought to be permitted; whether divorce, too, should be allowed remains an open question. Not all liberal thinkers have answered it in the affirmative. I do not wish to decide upon the answer here, for it requires more thorough investigation. Without question, the Author of Christianity assigned the woman to a superior position in marriage than the one she had had under Mosaic law. In the law of Moses, the proscription against adultery protects only the rights of the husband, whereas the wife has no safeguards against her husband choosing any other woman as the object of his love, even her neighbours. But Jesus gives both the right to fidelity; according to his teaching, it is not only wrong for the woman to commit adultery, but also for the man.

123. The state

1. What is the state, and how does it come into being? What end does it serve, and how can it serve it best?

In textbooks of political law and related disciplines, we

frequently find definitions characterizing the state as an organism. Some conceive of it as a copy of the human body, others as a copy of the human being as a whole. In endeavouring to establish the basic divisions of the activities of the human soul, Plato felt it to be methodologically advantageous to begin by taking a look at the various occupations within the state, for he believed the state to be the individual writ large, as it were. Hobbes sketches his theory of the state under the title *De Corpore Politico*. Now as long as people remain conscious of the figurative character of this manner of speaking, we may let it pass, but it has frequently been taken too seriously. The state has been exalted to a kind of superman, a god, indeed: a being of a superior and of so elevated a kind that the individual dwindles to nothing but a mere means to this superior existence. The brain, or rather the rational faculty, of this superman is, of course, the government, and so we ought not to be surprised when the theory of the organic nature of the state leads in practice to despotism.

2. We can only acquire a sensible determination of the concept by constructing it inductively, i.e. by seeking to establish its characteristics from our experience of existing states and also from our experience of the needs and wants that guide human beings when they are forming a state.

Experience shows us that the state is a society more extensive than the family in its circumference, and it is easy to understand how men came to form these more extensive societies. Common sympathies, as well as the obvious advantages of cooperation, led them to do so, particularly the great benefits arising from the division of labour, whereby our accomplishments are not only increased, but multiplied manyfold. If everyone had to care for all of his needs himself, precious little would come to pass in the course of a human era. Thus the state is seen to be a community that extends beyond the family and thereby serves the end of a complete life sufficient unto itself.

3. Nevertheless, history tells us that this great community grew out of the family. The family is the starting point of the tribe, and from there more and more members are added, and increasingly extensive societies are formed.

4. Yet no matter how considerable the number of members in such a community is, it is not in itself sufficient to constitute a state. For this, the community must also have a certain purposive

formation, or organization. In addition, it must possess a certain power, sufficient to protect this order against disturbances from within and also to preserve it in the face of attacks from without.

The purpose of all this is clear. Life in society requires order if it is really to yield all the expected advantages. Yet, for this order to come about, it is not sufficient for rational people to recognize what should be allotted to each individual as his own property. Rather, positive determinations are required, and, in order that these should be maintained, a force guaranteeing obedience in general, so that the individual can count upon enjoying the fruits of his labours in such a society. It is necessary that there be a unified, regulative form of leadership, fitted out with power and authority, whether it be a single person or a body of people, and this is what we call a government.

The organization of regulative power and authority is very ancient, both in practice and in theory. When Montesquieu distinguished three varieties of such power, the legislative, the executive, and the judicial, he was only repeating what was already a commonplace when Aristotle wrote his *Politics*.

5. The question has been posed whether the state comes into existence by nature, whether it is an invention, or whether it is to be attributed to a contract. There has been, and still is, much dispute on this point, and this is quite comprehensible, for each of the opinions expressed is true in one sense and false in another.

We may view the state as a natural product in so far as it originates in man's natural need for socialization. Man is a political animal; whoever is sufficient unto himself is either a beast or a god. The state is not, however, to be considered natural in the sense that it would be had it always existed or had men brought it into the world with them along with their heads and limbs. Quite the contrary: the state was first realized as a product of mental activity. If that is all that is meant by calling it a human invention, the description is perfectly acceptable. Of course, it would be foolish to think that somebody sat down one day and thought up the idea of the state in order subsequently to teach it to other people. None the less, Schlöger says, in his *Staatsrecht* (*Political Law*), that people invented the state for the sake of their well-being, just as they invented fire insurance. The same is true of the theory of the social contract. In the *Contrat social*, Rousseau has sovereign people form a contract and then arrange for a government in order to guarantee its maintenance. Such a sequence of events might ultimately be possible, but not in the beginning. Rather, we must imagine the process leading up to the coming into being of the state as very gradual. To be sure, each step towards it required mental activity, but none of the innumerable participants had an image of the eventual result. Perhaps an analogy will clarify the process: the analogy with the gradual evolution of speech. As with the state, there have been disputes as to whether speech was given us by nature, was invented by a single individual, or came about by mutual agreement. Now, speech is not 'by nature' in the sense that human beings brought it with them from the first, yet it certainly is 'natural' in the sense that it corresponds to man's natural need to express himself. Neither is it an invention; no one thought it up, and it is not a result of a calculated combination. Speech evolved gradually, and innumerable people contributed to its construction, yet here again they did not do it as workers work on a building for which there has all along been a plan. No one had the final product in mind. Each person involved was thinking only of the next step; viz. how he and another man could attain an understanding in a concrete case. However, since so many people were trying to attain the same end under similar circumstances and were, in the process, gaining increasing experience as to the best means of serving this need for understanding and—as in all other spheres of human activity—permitting themselves to be guided by the laws of habit, there eventually arose a form of speech that was not only better adapted to its purpose but that also revealed in its individual parts characteristic regularities and analogies suggesting intentional composition. Yet human speech was constructed without any special reflection aimed at harmony; when the edifice was finished, no one knew anything about its structure and the harmony of its parts until the grammarians came along and sketched out a plan of the whole that no one had, in fact, set up ahead of time.[45] The state, then, is also

[45] This theory concerning the origin of human speech, which avoids two opposing errors, lies at the basis of A. Marty's unfortunately much-neglected book, *Über den Ursprung der Sprache* (*The Origin of Speech*, Würzburg, 1875). In later works, he laid yet more emphasis upon the theory and defended it against both the theory that speech was invented and against that condemnation of every teleological view of human speech which rests on the grounds that it overshoots the mark. Cf.,

not a work resulting from reflection; if it were, it would have to be the work of a single man. It grew gradually into the organization that it is, and initially no one knew how to explain it; no one could oversee the whole, and no one could interpret the uses of the individual parts or the nature of the whole. Only afterwards did the lawyers and the philosophers of law come along to view the completed work. Had the state been an invention or the result of a formal contract, the process would have had to go in the opposite direction.

6. Yet this is not to say that the process of reflection, aroused *ex post facto*, has a purely descriptive and explanatory task; i.e. that it must be purely theoretical. Rather, it will attend most particularly to what the structure that has arisen in the manner described is able to accomplish and whether it cannot be systematically improved and worked out. Indeed, people will come to wonder whether the state is not intended for loftier purposes than those it would have served in its initial stages had the forces working upon it had any conscious purpose. Thus ethics comes to face the state with its demands—just as it does every other human institution. The end that it sets for the state is the supreme practical good. As Aristotle puts it, the state arose in order to make life possible, but it now exists to make a good and complete life possible.

This does not mean that the state ought to participate in everything. It will serve the general good far better if it pursues its end with a certain restraint. Positive law leaves many spheres untouched that the natural moral law cannot refrain from regulating.

7. Within which realm should the state legislate, in order that it may fulfil its high purpose?

(*a*) To begin with, it must give security to property taken in the broadest sense, which does not include only material goods. In fulfilling even just this task, the state has not failed in its aim; indeed, it dispenses bountiful blessings.

(*b*) Yet I do not necessarily wish to concur with those people

---

in particular, his *Untersuchungen zur Grundlegung der allgemeinen Grammatik und Sprachphilosophie* (Halle, 1908), paying especial attention to his disagreement with Wundt's theory concerning regular and singular semantic changes, which is presented in the appendix.

who want to see the state confined to this single task. Contrary to the beliefs of that excessively dry and sober thinker, Hobbes, the state is not merely an institution for insurance into which the individual pays obedience, in exchange for which he receives security. The individual must care more for himself than for others; the state owes equal care to all. It stands in the same position with respect to each citizen, and its aim must be the best for the collective whole. In the light of this end, the manner in which goods are distributed is of great moment. The same quantity of goods brings a greater amount of happiness when it is justly distributed than when it is not. A dollar is more valuable to the poor man than to the millionaire. Unjust distribution is a curse both to those who are too poor and to those who are too rich; in both cases, it is a source of immorality. However, the state must undertake the task of insuring a just balance with great discretion. Socialism is not in possession of the correct formula, for there are severe disadvantages to brutal interference in the existing, historically grounded relations involving property. A process of levelling would be no less disastrous, as Aristotle has warned us.

(*c*) None the less, the state should not concern itself solely with justice, any more than it should be a mere police state. It must also care for the welfare of its citizens. Bentham, to be sure, thought it should not interfere in this matter at all, believing that it would bring about more harm than good. A prudent egoism, in his view, will yield far better results. However, experience would seem to show that, at times, legislators who are well advised in matters of political economy can have a beneficial influence and may, moreover, be the only ones in a position to avert great evils.[46]

---

[46] On Bentham's theory of the state, see 'A Plan for a Universal and Perpetual Peace', in *Principles of International Law: Works*, ed. Bowring (1843), vol. II (trans. into German as 'Grundsätze für ein künftiges Völkerrecht und einen dauerden Frieden' by Camill Klatscher, with an introduction by Kraus about Bentham, Kant, and Wundt (Halle, 1915)).

In order to complete Brentano's sketchy presentation, and also to honour Oskar Kraus, 'the scientific colleague and friend of Kastil who deserves more credit than anyone else for working untiringly and effectively to bring about the publication of Brentano's literary remains', Kastil included in this place a portion of Kraus's lectures on ethics concerning the care the state is obligated to take to uphold not only protective but also distributive justice.

'From the point of view of the end, distributive justice takes precedence; from that of realization, protective justice. What is meant by
distributive justice? The usual reply is "equality" and, true enough,
under certain circumstances a division into equal parts is also the most
just division, as, for instance, when a stock of provisions is to be
divided among a number of adults. It is not that equality is a good
in itself, but that it is the best means to the best utilization. But this is not
so in other cases—not even, for instance, where we have essentially the
same situation, but children are included. Furthermore, we are frequently concerned with a stock of goods of a variety of very different
kinds. In that case, the just division is the one whereby each person
receives what he can best put to use. For instance, if scientific books are
to be divided among students, it would be absurd to distribute them
in a way that does not correspond to their leanings and previous
knowledge. Distributive justice demands something analogous concerning the relation between economic goods and the people having
jurisdiction over them. People who are intellectually, artistically, and
morally superior have claims to different, and more valuable, instruments than those who are inferior. Insofar as excellence is a quantitative
function, the superior person deserves more than others. The value of
the goods to be distributed to A ought to bear the same proportion to
the value of the goods to be distributed to B that A's ability bears to
B's. That is why the ancients said the geometric ratio should be the
standard for distributive justice.

'Now for the concept of protective justice. It is difficult to realize
the ideal aim of distributive justice: that everyone be granted what is
owed to him in the light of his abilities. Every reorganization that is
brought about through force is particularly dangerous. To bring about
a just distribution at one stroke is a utopian dream. We ought rather to
try to bring about a gradual improvement, while sparing as much as
possible the powers that be; in other words, precedence is taken by
legal security, whereby everyone is permitted to keep what in fact
belongs to him and is protected in the possession of the sphere over
which he has jurisdiction, as though it were his legal due. Nevertheless,
the present *de facto* order is of merely temporary significance. It bears the
same relation to an ideal order, in which everyone would have his due,
as does occupancy to possession within our present legal order. Hence
the politician must make unceasing efforts towards the achievement of
distributive justice that is truly just, i.e that preserves legal security as
much as possible. This to be done most particularly by gradually evening out gross inequalities of possession. One man ought not to be permitted excessive luxury while many are suffering from want and
starvation. Distributive justice is most easily brought about where
spheres of influence and jurisdiction are as yet unowned, by the taking

on of positions and the bestowing of honors: the right man should be in the right place. Nepotism and ipsissism—in short, corruption—are the very opposite of this. Distributive justice can also be upheld with respect to material possession, as in instances of exchange and the various forms of transferring belongings. This can be achieved partly by proportional taxation of income, taking over of property, and transfer of property, and partly through protection and promotion of those who have less economic power in the face of exploitation and imposition in economic intercourse.

'So much for the duty of the state to preserve justice within its own boundaries. To repeat: internal politics is obligated to take a moral stance, while giving precedence to legal security. A provisional order will temporally precede the just order. However, international politics is also subject to moral demands; it, too, must preserve justice. Yet many heads of governments have not even reached the stage of taking into account the maintenance of protective justice. Conquest by force is still held in high esteem, and success is practically the only measure of value. The duties of protective justice are largely disregarded in dealings between nations. But even here, there are signs that some thought will be given to justice in the future. This is not to say that we can count upon national egoism in international relations giving way in one fell swoop to an unselfish devotion to the precepts of ethics. It is more likely that the progression will be like that in private business, where an astute grasp of where our own real interests lie leads gradually to a regard for the interests of others. During this process people will come to perceive with increasing clarity that the greatest and most constant threat of war lies where the power structure fails to answer the demands of distributive justice. For instance, peoples possessing everything necessary for a blossoming industry may not be allowed to remain cut off from essential raw materials and important transport routes. Furthermore, their excess population must have the possibility of emigrating to the colonies. Even prudent egoism on the part of the nations will lead gradually to the construction of forces extending beyond each of them, regulating a just distribution within world commerce and averting the outbreak of wars.

'Yet this cannot be the moralist's last word. What we have outlined here is, rather, a regard for the duties of justice towards other states which has become detached from the initial regard for our own interests. As with individuals, it is not permissible for one state to infringe upon the *suum cuique* of another [what belongs to another]. So long as they are intended merely as technical remedies for egoism, international organizations represent, to be sure, relative progress, but their full and enduring benefits will only be revealed when they are upheld and fulfilled for the sake of justice. And even in international relations, distrib-

124. *The religious society, or church*

1. A religious society is a special organization that sets up moral precepts which are not upheld by any temporal—that is, physical —power. The power of the society over our conscience is purely spiritual. Is the existence of such religious societies desirable? The question has been decisively answered in the mind of anyone holding beliefs. But what should be the position of the man who professes no positive religious creed and rejects the claims of religion to a supernatural origin?

A number of significant thinkers who take this latter attitude have spoken out in favour of religious societies, for instance, Theodor Fechner in his *Drei Motive des Glaubens.*[47] Trendelenburg, too, tends to take this view, and Lotze is of the opinion that the state cannot tolerate an absence of religion; he positively demands that the state be Protestant. The liberal thinker Dahlmann, one of the so-called Göttingen Seven, believes that it is not only undesirable for the state to ignore religion, but also that it is downright impossible. He declares himself to be in favour of

---

[47] Apparently Brentano learned of these views of these philosophers from personal conversations. The opinion attributed here to Fechner is not expressed directly in his *Die drei Motive und Gründe des Glaubens,* but there is a place in the final chapter of his *Der orthodoxe und freie Standpunkt* (Leipzig, 1863), pp. 242 ff., where he expresses scepticism as to the possibility of survival of certain dissenting sects. 'Independent as is the position I have taken in this work, I have nevertheless been more pleased by the orthodox believer when I have encountered him elsewhere than by the free thinker—if not in every instance, at least on the average. And I have found more agreeable the firm and unshakeable belief in the words of the Bible, even if it does include accepting Noah's ark along with the entire present world of animals and the sun standing still on the day Jericho fell, than the most rational of destructive critiques. The new Catholic and dissenting congregations have always seemed to me like herds who are glad to be free of the dog protecting them, and even of their shepherd, and who hence fall prey to the wolf, or at any rate only remain a single herd as long as there is enough grass in one meadow to hold them together.'

---

utive justice takes precedence over protective justice—if not in its actual fulfilment, at least in its aim.'

religious marriage and education and has no wish to see the church tower disappear from the landscape. Auguste Comte[48] lists three criteria for qualifying as a religion: a conviction concerning man's destination that claims to give shape to his whole life; a feeling that lends this conviction an internal sanction; and an ideal that serves as an object of veneration for those who believe. He takes this all so seriously that he himself tried to found a religion fulfilling these criteria, going into great detail. His completed plan provides a substitute not only for prayer, but also for the sign of the cross. The question as to whether these thinkers are in the right is certainly an object worthy of philosophical investigation.

2. Supposing they are right, the first question that arises is what relation religious societies ought to bear to temporal power. History offers examples of the subordination of temporal power and examples of the subordination of spiritual power. Both kinds are instances of union, for the subordinate power always becomes the servant of the predominate. But there is also no lack of historical examples of a separation of powers; the Catholic church, in particular, has realized completely such a separation. Which sort of relationship is preferable?

I do not doubt that a separation of powers is to the advantage of both sides. To be sure, this separation came later in history than the union, but the initial arrangement is by no means always the correct one. The disadvantages of having the spiritual powers hold the superior position have been clearly revealed again and again during the course of history. However, disadvantages are also to be found where temporal power is superior to spiritual, for here the spiritual sanction loses its dignity and sanctity, and this loss is of all-embracing significance. Furthermore, there has often been a lamentable lack of tolerance on the side of the temporal powers. A separation of powers is most advantageous to progress. To verify this, we need only glance at the Mohammedan world, on the one hand, and the Christian Occident on the other, and compare the fate of the sciences in the one world and the other. In Syria, as in Spain, the power of the state succeeded in eradicating philosophy altogether. Even if there have been attempts to do this in the Christian West, they have failed to succeed

---

[48] Auguste Comte, *Catechisme positiviste* (Paris, 1852); trans. as *Catechism of Positive Religion* by Congreve (London, 1858).

as a result of the separation of the two swords, which have confined each other within certain limits. No one recognized this more clearly than Comte, and it is precisely what brought about his admiration for the Catholic church.

3. But now we come to the central question: are such societies necessary at all? Do they offer advantages?

The need for a moral authority exists without any doubt, for in this sphere, as in the realm of the sciences, no single individual can have adequate experience. But do we require an organization specifically for this purpose? Why could it not be the same here as in other fields of knowledge? Only a few understand the proofs of the astronomers or are able to follow the research of the physicists, chemists, and biologists, yet the layman believes the scientist, and his belief is not entirely blind. He acknowledges quite rationally that the scientist knows these things, or has at any rate a better chance of knowing them than he does. To be sure, this does not hold for every science in just the same way, nor does it hold for each stage in the development of a science, for the layman can only look to the representatives of a science as his authority when he knows them to be basically in agreement. Such unity has been lacking in philosophy right up to the present time, but let us hope that it will some day be achieved. If it is, the authority of the professionals will command the belief of the laity, as in the other sciences. If such trust were gained within the moral sphere, it would not be without practical consequences. The belief in moral doctrines and in the theoretical doctrines that serve to support them; e.g. the doctrine that God exists, would necessarily have an influence upon our practical behaviour, just as a belief in scientific results does elsewhere. An organization, an association the purpose of which is to inculcate in the individual what is morally good and to lead him in moral matters would seem to be no more necessary here than in connection with other sciences.

But here Comte[49] disagrees. Ethical theory is not enough, for the strength of the conflicting inclinations makes this case different

[49] This is probably a reference to *Cours de philosophie positive* (Paris, 1864), vol. V, lecture 54. It is recommended that the reader consult instead Harriet Martineau's translation, *The Positive Philosophy of Auguste Comte* (London, 1853), vol. II, Book VI, chap. IX, which is far more precise and omits none of the substance of the original.

from the others; an association, a church, is absolutely indispensable for the attainment of the moral perfection of human society, in his view. But the experiment has not yet been tried, and that unity which could exercise authoritative influence has not been achieved. Moreover, while the organization of the church has special advantages, not only because of the beneficial effects arising from its sublime doctrines but also because of the leadership it offers the faithful through its various organs, we must not forget what we have said about moral guidance in general, and about friendship in particular: every person is able to form moral associations by his own free choice and to seek his own counsellors and leaders for matters involving his conscience. It does not appear absolutely necessary that everything be ordered from above. Comte's pronouncement, which was ventured before any experiment was made, appears overly rash. With Fechner, discussion would perhaps be possible. He would probably consider sufficient the advantage arising from the unified conviction and the leadership and counsel which every person seriously concerned with his own moral progress could provide for himself quite easily in a society of such firm beliefs. But to convince Comte— were he still living—would be a desperate undertaking, for his enthusiasm for his ideas, which undoubtedly arose from a nobility of purpose, made him little inclined to take objections sufficiently into account. Lotze, in presenting the basic features of his philosophy of religion, also shows himself a firm advocate of religious societies. He says that to stand alone would be in intrinsic contradiction with his religious conviction, which binds man to the whole universe. What we acknowledge to be the supreme being would not be supreme were it not acknowledged by everyone. Here, too, we have a need to be united to all other men, and universally valid dogmas and symbols are indispensable. It is an evil of the present era that the state must exist without a religious foundation, and believes itself to have no need of one.—Thus Lotze.[50] But we indicated earlier that no authority is needed for the founding of morality: what is good is revealed by the experience of acts of loving and preferring that are experienced as being correct.

[50] Hermann Lotze, *Grundzüge der Religionsphilosophie*, 3rd edition, (Leipzig, 1894), p. 98.

Meanwhile, even if, for the reasons given, a church is not absolutely required for the moral progress of the individual, there is perhaps yet one more idea to which we ought to give consideration, an idea expressed by Benjamin Franklin. Every great upheaval, he says, has been set into motion by some party, and he relates to this the idea of a party representing humanity and the supreme practical good. It, too, would be a party of reform, but it would support a programme of moral reform, just as the Pythagoreans strove not only for self-perfection but also for the moral regeneration of society. Conceived in this manner, the idea of a moral organization has significance and should not be cast aside. It is regrettable that Franklin himself never attempted to set one up. He would certainly have proceeded with discretion, as can be seen from the fact that entrance into this party, as he envisaged it, was not supposed to have as a prerequisite relinquishing one's membership in a positive religious society.[51]

The ethical culture movements have a certain relation to Franklin's idea. They undeniably rest on noble inclinations, yet they reject not only dogmas but also any unified world view, and unlike Franklin they disregard the notion that each person should work on improving himself above all. They also fail to test in any serious way potential members, for they reject the idea of being selective. Their motive for this rejection is that they must have a large and powerful party in order to be effective, and they never will if they are too strict in their choices. In contrast, the great moral reformers to whom history has granted success have selected their disciples and have not set out upon the basis of a large party to propagate their teachings: think, above all others, of Jesus and his successor, St Francis.

Just as impracticable, or even more so, is the ethical culturalists' renunciation of all common principles with the exception of the principle of promoting the general good. They say that the movement will fall apart if the members are required to hold other principles—but how can they be unified without them? Think, for example, of the contrast between the theistic and consequently optimistic world view and the atheistic and consequently pessimistic world view. Existence or nonexistence is the question

---

[51] *Benjamin Franklin, Doer of Good: a Biography* (Edinburgh, 1865), chap. 10, p. 127.

here, and unless it is answered an ethical society, like Hamlet, cannot reach any practical decisions. Does the 'Ethical Society' wish to content itself with having its members united merely in the desire to serve the good of mankind; e.g. through the practice of tolerance or the improvement of the situation of the lower classes? If so, it ought instead to call itself the 'Society for the Promotion of Tolerance' or the 'Society for Fighting Poverty'.

These so-called ethical societies can probably only be regarded as symbols of the yearning for moral perfection. They, and similar endeavours, will never be able to replace the religious society with its well-founded moral principles, both precepts and prohibitions.

All this we can only sketch out, not execute in any detail. The intention is only to indicate the directions that must be followed in order to bring moral precepts to realization.

Yet, as we have demonstrated, secondary moral rules possess only relative validity. Unconditional and universal validity is only to be attributed to the principle of all morality: that nothing may take precedence over the supreme practical good, which requires that we select under all circumstances the best that is attainable.[52]

Here, once again, my views harmonize not only with the teachings of the advanced sciences but also with those of that religion which cultivated peoples have professed for centuries and which is undoubtedly morally superior to every other religion known to history. For Christianity acknowledges only *one* direct and supreme law, believing it to be the standard for the validity of every other precept in individual cases. 'From it hangs the law and all the prophets.'[53]

[52] Actually, the precept is negative: in choosing, never select a lesser good among the objects attainable. Cf. part IV, chap. 1, sect. 89.

[53] The conclusion has been expanded by the editor in accordance with Brentano's treatise, 'Zur Lehre von der Relativität der abgeleiteten Sittengesetze', Appendix III in *Ursprung sittlicher Erkenntnis*, 3rd edition (1934) ('The Relativity of Secondary Moral Principles', in *The Origin of our Knowledge of Right and Wrong*, trans. Chisholm and Schneewind, London Routledge & Kegan Paul, 1969, pp. 116–18).

Editor's Foreword
to the German Edition

Franz Brentano took up a position regarding the foundations of ethics in his treatise, *Ursprung sittlicher Erkenntnis*,* which appeared in 1889. He had originally presented it as a lecture before the Vienna Law Society on January 23 of the same year. After his death, this little work was published by F. Meiner (Leipzig) as a part of the complete edition of Brentano's works which was undertaken by Oskar Kraus and Alfred Kastil, the second edition appearing in 1921, the third in 1934. Both these editions appeared with an introduction by Kraus, together with several briefer essays by Brentano concerning ethics.

As Kraus says, this short treatise, comprising scarcely forty pages, exerted an enormous influence upon modern value theory. Most of the works on ethics that have appeared since can be traced back to it, either directly or indirectly. It represents, Kraus notes, the most significant step forward in the history of ethics and theory of value since Greek antiquity.

In reviewing the English translation which appeared in 1902, G. E. Moore said that it handled the foundations of ethics far better than any other work known to him: 'It would be difficult to exaggerate the importance of this work.'†

Nonetheless, the booklet remained relatively unknown to wider circles, and its basic importance was largely overlooked. Even those who appreciated its importance felt an urgent need

* Trans. into English as *The Origin of our Knowledge of Right and Wrong* by Chisholm and Schneewind (London: Routledge & Kegan Paul, 1969). There is also an earlier translation by Cecil Hague (Constable, 1902), referred to below.

† G. E. Moore, 'Review of *The Origin of our Knowledge of Right and Wrong*', *International Journal of Ethics* (October 1903).

for a more detailed account of the theory that we possess an immediate standard of good and bad, the features of which were outlined only very briefly.

However, as Kraus points out, it was not Brentano's intention to present a system of ethics in the *Ursprung*. That he had done already in his course of lectures on practical philosophy, which comprises the contents of this volume. Instead, he wished to trace 'the psychological analysis of the moral consciousness that lives in each of us to the ultimate experiences from which we derive the concepts of inherently justified emotions (evaluations and preferences) and the a priori axioms of value and preference related to them.'

The publication of these lectures on ethics has long been delayed, partially as a result of the dissolution of the Brentano Society in Prague in 1938 and Kraus' flight to England in the face of the reign of terror then setting in, and partially because of the events during the war and the postwar period. During this time, living in seclusion in Brentano's house in Schönbühel an der Donau, which had been placed at his disposal, Kastil organized and prepared for future publication Brentano's as yet unpublished works. The greater the dedication with which he devoted himself to his life's work of preserving, interpreting, and enlarging upon Brentano's teachings, the greater the difficulties he encountered. Left alone by the death, in 1942, of his comrade in scholarship, Kraus, and the loss of a number of promising students, he none the less did not allow himself to be discouraged in his endeavours by unfavourable circumstances.

It is thanks to Kastil's untiring preparatory work, grounded upon a most thorough knowledge of every detail of Brentano's theories, along with the understanding approach of the Francke publishing house in Bern, which undertook to continue the publication of Brentano's complete works during a difficult period, that I am in a position today to present Brentano's ethics to the philosophical world.

The present volume, the first in the continuation of the series, presents ideas that Brentano wrote down during the winter term, 1876 (as can be seen from the letters he wrote to Anton Marty between October and December of that year) and which were presented several times as a course during his tenure at the University of Vienna, which lasted until 1894. The original manuscript is now in the U.S.A., at Northwestern University in Evanston, where Prof. J. C. M. Brentano, the only son of the philosopher, is teaching. It was brought there a short time ago from Oxford, where Brentano's writings, rescued from Prague, had been given shelter in the Bodleian Library.

In the summer months of 1941 and 1942, and again in 1943 and 1946, Kastil reviewed and edited the copies of the lectures on ethics which had been put together in Prague many years earlier. He expanded some passages in accordance with his own lectures, which derived from Brentano's, and added sections from the works of Kraus. He also put in some parts from other works by Brentano. However, he explained in a note to the manuscript that it was in need of being worked over yet one more time. Kastil himself was unable to undertake the final revision. And so, after his death on July 20, 1950, when the scholarly writings left behind by Brentano were entrusted to my care, I attempted to carry out this task, submerging myself as much as possible in the spirit of the great master and accommodating myself to the intentions of my honoured teacher, Kastil.

The manuscript was altered so as to be in the form of a book, rather than in the form of lectures; more notes were added; and some sections were expanded by passages from the course on ethics given by Franz Hillebrand, who had been a student of Brentano's in Vienna for a number of years and who maintained contact with him until his death. All these additions are indicated in the notes.

A good introduction not only to Brentano's ethics but also to his other basic theories is to be found in Kastil's recently published comprehensive work, *Die Philosophie Franz Brentanos* (Verlag 'Das Bergland Buch', Salzburg, 1951). Hence I will make my introductory remarks brief.

When we survey the development of value theory, we are presented with the most extreme contrasts between those who affirm and those who deny the existence of universally valid principles. Plato and Protagoras: thesis and antithesis! However, if we take a closer look, it turns out that we cannot align ourselves on either of the two sides without reservation. Even the radical sceptic, Protagoras, was right in that we must begin with the subject and, consequently, cannot speak of right and wrong at all in the absence of an evaluator. But in Protagoras' view value is not universally valid; man is the measure of all things, and hence what he considers valuable will depend upon his experience. For waging a fierce battle against this form of relativism, Plato deserves an amount of credit that cannot be overestimated. Yet he constructed in the process a fictitious realm of ideas that proves to be untenable and full of contradictions. This battle has raged throughout the history of philosophy and value theory; the names change, but the ideas remain essentially the same.

It appears to be possible to construct a synthesis of the two points of view; viz. by maintaining the universal validity of moral principles while at the same time appealing to a being who forms an evaluation and who experiences an act of knowledge in which he recognizes his emotion concerning the value of an object or act to be correct. Seen this way, man as such is not the 'measure of all things', but rather the man who judges with insight, with discernment, i.e. the man who knows.

These are the facts of the case. They had been noticed and hinted at by some of his predecessors, but it was Brentano who analyzed them clearly. The theory of evidence and its analogues in the sphere of the emotions are probably among Brentano's most significant accomplishments. Even if we had nothing else for which to thank him, this theory would place him among the greatest teachers of wisdom humanity has produced. In pointing out the existence of acts in which love and preferences are immediately experienced as being correct, he grounded ethics upon a new and firm foundation, just as he had done already with the theory of knowledge when he indicated the evident character of certain judgments.

Some have attempted to refute Brentano's theory of evidence by charging it with psychologism; that is, they have accused him of transferring, in an unjustified manner, certain psychological phenomena—specifically, the experience of an urge to concur— over to epistemology and ethics, and of setting up as norms certain facts that are unique and unrepeatable. However, this accusation confuses the phenomenon of the evident with a 'feeling of conviction'.

Once the criterion of evidence has been established, it is possible to construct a table of goods and values and to derive precepts and prohibitions. But there is only *one* precept that is valid in all circumstances: choose the best that is attainable. Or, to put it in the more correct, negative form: In making your choice, never opt for a lesser good among those attainable. All other precepts and prohibitions are derivative or secondary rules.

The present volume also contains a comprehensive discussion of the problem of the freedom of the will. Brentano comes ultimately to the conclusion that determinism alone is able to guarantee freedom in willing and in action.

Thus Brentano's system of ethics emerges as a complete and harmonious whole. It is not heteronomous, for it does not recognize to be binding as such the precepts issued by a foreign will; nor is it autonomous, for it also does not acknowledge the precepts of the will of the individual to be the ultimate authority as such. Instead, his system is orthonomous; i.e., the individual possesses a secure consciousness of the correctness of his love and hatred. The present work fills in the lacunae left open in the *Ursprung*. Furthermore, in the first section Brentano offers a survey and outline of earlier attempts to supply ethics with a foundation and gives a very astute critique of these attempts.

Yet even if, as Brentano demonstrates, a system of ethics can be founded without metaphysics, it none the less cannot be completed without metaphysics. It is only the consciousness of the existence of a creator and ruler of the universe, which is constantly striving for greater and greater perfection, that makes possible an optimistic conception of life lending meaning to the struggle for self-perfection.

Innsbruck, March 1951   FRANZISKA MAYER-HILLEBRAND

Index